ish jurist and a Roman Catholic, Dr. St. John-Stevas disagrees with many of his co-religionists on how doctrine should be applied to law. He criticizes the political pressure tactics so often employed by Catholics against members of the community who do not share their views. On the other hand he opposes those who would completely divorce law from morality, for the law, he believes, is "the collective conscience of the community on those issues which cannot be left to individual choice" and "to that extent has moral authority."

After examining the positions of Protestants, Catholics and non-believers on the relationship of law and morals, the author considers each of the major controversies in turn, giving the historical background of each and subjecting the laws now on the books to critical analysis. Proposed changes in the law are then considered and some thoughtful recommendations are made.

"In democratic pluralist societies, social policies with moral implications are not laid down by *fiat* from above, but are evolved gradually through the rational reflections of free men." The author's purpose, therefore, is "to clarify the basic issues underlying existing controversies, and to assist their resolution through the medium of rational discussion."

Life, Death and the Law

'I find that people disagree with me either
because they hold that Liberalism is not
true, or that Catholicism is not true, or that
both cannot be true together. If I could
discover anyone who is not included in these
categories, I fancy we should get on very
well together.'

Lord Acton in a letter to Mandell Creighton

by the same author

WALTER BAGEHOT

Life, Death and the Law

LAW AND CHRISTIAN MORALS
IN ENGLAND AND THE UNITED STATES

NORMAN ST. JOHN-STEVAS

INDIANA UNIVERSITY PRESS / BLOOMINGTON

SECOND PRINTING 1961
COPYRIGHT © 1961 BY NORMAN ST. JOHN-STEVAS
MANUFACTURED IN THE UNITED STATES OF AMERICA
LIBRARY OF CONGRESS CATALOG CARD NUMBER: 61-8086

For Kitty

Contents

Introduction

Contemporary liberal society presents the Christian with many perplexing problems, for although Christianity and the liberalism of the Anglo-American – as opposed to the continental – tradition have much in common, being rooted in a tradition of respect for the human person and concern for human rights, they are also in conflict over issues which are far from being marginal and directly affect the general welfare. Tolerance of a wide variety of moral viewpoints is a feature of cardinal importance to the liberal society. This diversity is seen by many liberals as a good in itself, while Christians are more likely to regard it as a necessary evil. While uncommitted to any one social form every Christian looks to the transformation of society; to the day when it will approach nearer to the Christian ideal of a community in which Christian values are generally recognized. In the past Christians have expected the State to further their aims, especially through the agency of law, and while the attempt to impose theological doctrines directly by legal sanction is no longer made, many Christians still look to the law to enforce Christian standards of morality and social behaviour.

Such efforts are not in themselves unreasonable, although they are easily carried to excess, and they are certainly doomed to failure in liberal societies unless supported by the general moral consensus of the community. Many moral matters formerly governed by public law must today be left to be determined in the private sphere, either permanently or until society re-formed by persuasion is prepared to re-admit them to the public order. From the Christian point of view this move from public to private need not be unconditionally deplored, since there is gain as well as loss in separating moral standards from the application of physical sanctions.

The Christian citizen, like any other, has also continually to re-examine the relationship between law and morals in particular matters, not identifying conservatism with morality, and taking into account the new knowledge and insights offered by the non-theological sciences. The question whether a moral rule should continue to be backed by a legal sanction is distinct from one concerning its intrinsic validity. Knowledge gained from the social sciences may indicate – even in a Christian society – that legal sanctions should be withdrawn from moral rules.

In this book, however, I have been concerned only with liberal society, and in particular with that of the Anglo-American tradition. In the first chapter an attempt is made to formulate some general principles governing the relationship between Christian morality and the law in England and the United States, and subsequent chapters consider particular controverted legal-moral problems of the present time. The method used has been inductive rather than deductive, and I have preferred to approach the problems initially on the basis of how the law actually deals with them, rather than on that of laying down *fiats* from above. Wherever relevant, the influence of Christian ideas in shaping the law has been described. The satisfactoriness of the present laws is then considered in the light of the new scientific, sociological and psychological data available; proposed changes in the law are outlined; and their acceptability to the Christian conscience discussed.

In a work covering such a wide field I have naturally been indebted to many specialists in subjects other than my own. A number of theological references will be found in the book, but I have refrained from speculations of my own, and have limited myself to setting down the opinions of theologians, whether Catholic or Protestant. I have done this, I hope, with sympathetic insight, an approach essential to any serious assessment of theology's role, without which theological opinions can be – and have been – distorted or made to look ridiculous. Yet theology has not been presented in this book as an absolute sovereign, nor even as a constitutional monarch, but rather allotted a place as one amongst other advisers, on social matters affecting the commonweal.

For Christians there must always be a tension between religion and society which can never be finally resolved. This tension is especially marked where the forces of traditional Catholicism and English liberalism meet and join. The tension can be paralysing but it can also be creative. This book is intended as a modest attempt at its resolution in a limited sphere.

This work was begun under the auspices of the Yale Law School where I at one time held a fellowship. It was completed thanks to the munificence of the Fund for the Republic who in turn elected me to a fellowship. To both these institutions I tender my grateful thanks. My indebtedness to numerous scholars is evident from the text, but I should like to express my thanks in particular to Dr D. Sherwin Bailey of whose researches I have made much use in Chapter 5. I would also like to thank the Reverend Maurice Ryan for his services in connection with the book. Lastly I am grateful to Mr Adrian Stanford, the Reverend Anthony Hamson, and Mrs Thomas Main, for their kindness in helping with the reading of the proofs.

Norman St John-Stevas

1 Hampstead Square
Christmas 1960

CHAPTER ONE

Law and Morals

The relationship between law and morals is a cardinal and perennial problem of jurisprudence. In recent years the need of society to formulate legal policy on a number of controverted moral issues has extended the discussion and lent it a new urgency. Should the sale and distribution of contraceptives be restricted by law? Ought the State to foster sterilization policies? What should be the attitude of the law to artificial insemination? Should homosexual acts taking place in private between consenting adults be subject to the criminal law? Should euthanasia be countenanced by the law? Ought suicide and attempted suicide to be treated as criminal offences? These and other questions can only be answered after an exhaustive investigation of relevant moral, medical, psychological, and sociological data, but before these can be correlated, the attempt must be made to formulate some general principles of the relationship between law and morality, within the framework of which practical judgments may be made.

To attempt to formulate principles applicable to all societies would be an impossible task given the present diversity of social and legal systems, and an investigation can only be rendered fruitful by limiting the field of enquiry. On the other hand to confine it to a single country would exclude the valuable insights afforded by a comparative approach. A way out of this dilemma has been sought by limiting the discussion in the main to England and the United States, with only incidental references to the legal systems of other countries. Judaeo-Christian moral values, liberal democracy, and a shared tradition of the common law, provide the necessary common ground, while differences of history, temperament, and ethnic and religious composition, with their consequent variations in approach to moral and legal problems, make comparison possible and enlightening. Emphasis has been laid on Christian moral ideas because these are the values still generally adhered to within both societies and are those to which the author subscribes. This approach has the practical merit of enabling the tensions between conflicting Christian and liberal values to be included within the scope of the enquiry, so that it becomes an existential as well as an academic study.

That law is not co-extensive with morals is generally, although not universally, agreed within the Western tradition. This is true of morality in the limited sense of behaviour accepted as right or wrong within a given society, and much more so if morality is considered as ethical science, the theory of the nature of moral judgment, and the formulation of criteria as to what conduct ought to be. That there is some relationship between law and morals, that their spheres, although distinct, overlap, would also secure wide assent in contemporary society. The relationship between morals and the criminal law has been especially close. The common law's assumption that the criminal is responsible for his acts derives directly from the Christian view of man, as a being endowed with free will. Its most honoured maxim, *"actus non facit reum nisi mens sit rea"*, was a principle of moral theology before it was adopted by the law. Personal responsibility is still the basis of Western moral and legal systems, although it can be excluded in particular instances. For society to inflict pain, either by corporal punishment, fine or deprivation of life or liberty, on a human person, requires some moral justification. In theory this is provided by the notion of responsibility and in practice all serious crimes are also moral offences.

The distinction between law and morals is best indicated not by the erection of a general theory, but by pointing to certain features possessed by the one but not by the other. The most obvious point of difference is found in the sanctions respectively imposed. In law, the sanction is essentially physical, deprivation of property or liberty, and in the last resort, life itself. The sanction is imposed collectively in the name of society, after a formal judicial process which assesses responsibility and fixes the penalty within limits laid down in advance. The moral sanction is primarily interior and imposed by conscience, although in certain instances there may be secondary penalties, such as social ostracism. These, however, are imposed by individuals and not by the State acting as such.

The law is not normally concerned with interior attitudes but with external conduct. The standard of judgment in civil cases is not that of the individuals concerned but of the reasonable man. In criminal cases, certainly, responsibility, unless excluded by statute, must be established. Acts to be imputable must be voluntary and there must be a criminal intention in the sense of foresight of consequences, but this is established not by interior inquisition but by external evidence. Motives, it has been constantly reiterated, are not the concern of the law.[1] Morality has conduct for its subject matter, but the moral value of actions is ultimately determined by the motive of the actor. This is especially true of Christian ethics.

The third point of differentiation is one of scope. Law, in the Western tradition, is essentially limited, although the limits have varied in different epochs. Law is concerned with the general good of the community, and while this is also the concern of morality, it goes beyond this to consider the individual good. Law enforces only those standards of moral behaviour indispensable for community existence, morality has no such pragmatic limitation, but calls for conformity with the ideal. The man who limits himself to legal observance may be a tolerable citizen, but has no claim to be considered the good man of Western tradition, much less the good neighbour of Christian thought. English and American law, especially the criminal law, lacks the comprehensiveness of a moral code. Offences have been created in a haphazard fashion to meet particular social exigencies and not to accord with preconceived doctrine.

None of these distinctions are absolute, but this is hardly surprising since the connection between law and morals is in fact close. This factual connection makes the rigid distinction between law and morals elaborated by positivist jurists such as Austin, as unreal as the identification put forward by metaphysicians such as Petrazycki.[2] Austin and Bentham's rigid distinction between "is" and

[1] There are of course exceptional cases such as the tort of malicious prosecution where motive is of the essence of the offence. The law sometimes considers motives when imposing penalties as in the case of "mercy killings" where they are normally reduced, but again this is exceptional.

[2] See John Austin, *The Province of Jurisprudence Determined, and the Uses of the Study of Jurisprudence*, London 1954, and L. Petrazycki, *Law and Morality*, Cambridge 1955. Kelsen, although not strictly a positivist, also favours the non-ethical approach to law. See H. Kelsen, "The Pure Theory of Law", *Law Quarterly Review*, 50:474 (1934) and 51:517 (1935).

"ought" has been defended by the distinguished Oxford jurist, Professor Herbert Hart.[1] He points out that there is no necessary connection between the positivist approach and that of the supporters of non-cognitive theories of morals. Philosophers such as Hägerström dispose of the whole problem of the relationship between law and morals by denying objectivity to moral judgments which become mere emotive statements of approval and disapproval.[2] Austin, on the other hand, thought moral principles were the commands of God, and Bentham posited verifiable propositions about utility.

Professor Hart commends the Austinian approach because it makes for clarity. It avoids the twin confusions that a rule violating standards of morality is not law, and that a morally desirable rule should be sanctioned by law. Philosophic disputes about the nature and binding force of law are excluded.

A major objection to this view is that it leaves the individual helpless before the law. If law is constituted purely by form on what basis can the citizen resist an unjust law? The point is far from academic as the history of Nazi Germany has shown, and there is no doubt that the dominant positivist school of pre-war German jurisprudence aided Hitler in establishing his régime. Hitler came to power by legal means and continued to use the legal order to destroy the liberal basis of German society. Radbruch, the German positivist jurist, was so convinced by this experience that he renounced positivism in favour of a moral theory of the nature of law.

Professor Hart, himself a liberal, is aware of the problem, but denies that it can be solved by saying that an unjust law is not a law at all. Law in his view remains law if the due forms have been observed, but it may be too evil to be obeyed.[3] As Professor Fuller has pointed out, this leaves the question "What is the obligation of

---

[1] H. L. A. Hart, "Positivism and the Separation of Law and Morals," *Harvard Law Review*, 71:593–629 (February 1958).

[2] See Karl Olivecrona (ed.), *Inquiries into the Nature of Law and Morals*, Stockholm 1953. (Translated by C. D. Broad.) Hägerström, Olivecrona, and Lundstedt are the principal exponents of Swedish "realism".

[3] *Op. cit.*, p. 620. Cf. p. 618: "Surely the truly liberal answer to any sinister use of the slogan 'law is law' or of the distinction between law and morals is 'Very well, but that does not conclude the question. Law is not morality; do not let it supplant morality'."

fidelity to law?", unanswered.[1] It cannot be a moral duty since morality has been excluded from the law. It must therefore be a duty in an order of its own. Professor Hart indicates that it is not an absolute duty since he concedes that a tyrannical law should not be obeyed. The individual is thus faced with a conflict of duties which is truly irreconcilable since he is given no principle by which he can judge between them. If it is said that a moral "ought" is superior to a legal "ought", and should be followed, the legal system is once more made subject to morality. In practice an intuitive decision may be arrived at, but this does nothing to answer the theoretical question. There indeed appears to be no way out of the dilemma. The clarity which is said to be the merit of positivism vanishes as soon as an obligation to disobey law is admitted. It can only be retained by denying any obligation or right to disobey law once it has been passed in the form proper to the legal system.

Stated in this way the positivist position is certainly clear, but is clarity to be attained at any price? If it can only be achieved by a distortion of the facts the answer must be negative. Professor Fuller maintains that law is intrinsically moral because it is a principle of order, and this "internal morality" is ignored by positivism.[2] It is true that any legal system must mitigate the application of brute force by to some degree channelling or ordering it, but there seems nothing intrinsically moral about order in itself divorced altogether from ends. A more potent objection to positivism is that it is unrealistic: it does not accord with the social facts. In Western society the connection between law and the moral sense of the community is as real as its connection with a sanction. Law is obeyed by the majority as much because it is felt to be morally binding as because of the knowledge that breach will lead to punishment.[3] It is not an isolated phenomenon, but essentially a social

[1] Lon L. Fuller, "Positivism and Fidelity to Law—A Reply to Professor Hart", *Harvard Law Review*, 71:630–672 (February 1958). Cf. W. F. Cahill, "One Phase of the New Debate on the Iniquitous Law", *The Catholic Lawyer*, 5:119 (Spring 1959).   [2] Op. cit., p. 645.

[3] For a discussion of this see A. L. Goodhart, *English Law and the Moral Law*, London 1953. Cf. Frederick Pollock's definition of a rule of law as "a rule conceived as binding". *A First Book of Jurisprudence*, 5th ed., London 1923, p. 26. There are exceptions to the rule, such as customs laws, which are probably observed by the majority because of the sanctions rather than from any sense of moral obligation.

institution reflecting the life and views of society. Positive law ultimately loses its efficacy if it ceases to correspond with what Ehrlich
has called "the living law" of society, the underlying beliefs and
habits of a people.[1] The regulating principle ordering competing
social interests is ultimately to be found not in Pound's abstract and
static concept of "social engineering", but in the basic moral ideas
accepted by the community. A good illustration of the effect of the
living law of society is provided by the English law governing dissemination of contraceptive information. Books imparting such information were considered obscene in the nineteenth century, but
legal sanctions have been unobtrusively dropped now that contraception has secured general moral acceptance in the community.[2]
Again, in countries which have formally abolished capital punishment, the death penalty has generally been abandoned in practice
for some time before actual legislative abolition.

Certain theorists apart, then, the Western tradition regards law
and morality as inter-connected, although disagreement flourishes
as to the nature and degree of the connection. These disputes spring
from an underlying disagreement about the character and function
of the State. On the one hand there is the Greek tradition of Plato
and Aristotle, that the State is a natural and good institution, essential for the full development of man, who is by nature a social
animal, and which is consequently charged with the duty to promote
virtue. On the other is found the Augustinian view of the State, as
an institution permeated by evil, its necessity being dependent
on the fall of man, essential to check vice, but competent to do little
else.[3] Catholic Christianity has built its conception of the State on
Aristotelian foundations, while, broadly speaking, the Protestant and
Liberal State theories are within the Augustinian tradition. Given
a society which wholeheartedly espoused one of these two opposed

[1] F. S. C. Northrop refers to the living law as the inner order or pattern of
society which is not an objective phenomenon. "It is instead a common state of
mind expressing itself in the majority behaviour of the people of a given society."
"What should be the relation of Morals to Law? A Round Table", *Journal of
Public Law*, I:259–322 (1952), p. 261.

[2] See pp. 53–4.

[3] "There is not any justice in any commonwealth whatsoever but in that
whereof Christ is the founder and ruler," *De Civitate Dei*, II:21. See Ernest
Barker, "St. Augustine's Theory of Society", in *Essays on Government*, Oxford
1951.

views, the problem of the relationship between law and morals
would be easily soluble. It becomes immeasurably more difficult to
resolve in a pluralist society where powerful bodies of opinion
stemming from these rival traditions compete for dominance.

The Traditional Theory of Catholic Christianity

St Thomas Aquinas by baptizing Aristotelian theory was the first to
develop a comprehensive Catholic philosophy of the State. Its subsequent influence has been profound and is still operative today,
despite its manifest drawback that it was thought out in the context
of a unitary religious society. For St Thomas, as for Aristotle, the
State was a good and natural institution, designed to lead the citizens
towards virtue. He conceived the State as a perfect society in its own
right, deriving its authority from God, mediated not through ecclesi-
astics but through the structure of human nature itself. Hence the
State, although guided by the higher norms afforded by revelation,
was autonomous in relation to the Church.[1] All law came from God,
but was known in two ways, through direct revelation, the divine
law, or through human reason, the natural law. The two could never
be in conflict, since they were alternative modes of apprehending
the eternal law of God.[2] Positive law derived from natural law, and
if in conflict with it possessed no validity. An unjust law was no law
at all.[3]

The Thomist system is a magnificent statement of faith in human
reason and its ability to reach objective truth. As a synthesis of law
and morals it is unrivalled and may fairly lay claim to be the only

[1] See Thomas Gilby, *Principality and Polity*, London 1958, pp. xxi–xxiv.

[2] *Summa Theologica. Treatise on Law*, I.-II. questions XC to CVIII. "Now
among all others, the rational creature is subject to Divine Providence in the
most excellent way, in so far as it partakes of a share of providence, by being
provident for itself and others. Wherefore it has a share of the Eternal Reason,
whereby it has a natural inclination to its proper act and end: and this participation of the eternal law in the rational creature is called the natural law." Q. XCI,
art. 2.

[3] "As Augustine says, 'that which is not just seems to be no law at all';
wherefore the force of a law depends on the extent of its justice. Now in human
affairs a thing is said to be just, from being right, according to the rule of reason.
But the first rule of reason is the law of nature. . . . Consequently every human
law has just so much of the nature of law, as it is derived from the law of nature.
But if in any point it deflects from the law of nature, it is no longer a law but a
perversion of law." I.-II. Q. XCV, art. 2.

fully comprehensive philosophy of law. Its merit is that it places
law in the realm of value and excludes the equation of law with
force. But if law is a value and an instrument to promote virtue is
there not a danger that it will lead to a tyrannical supervision of the
life of the individual? May not personal liberty be seriously reduced?[1] This objection to the Thomist synthesis will only be advanced
by those unfamiliar with the actual texts of St Thomas's treatise on
law and the spirit informing his whole philosophy. For him, both
law and the State were essentially limited agencies: rulers were
"guardians of the peace not spiritual directors".[2]

The limited character of law is enshrined in his definition of law as
"an ordinance of reason for the common good, made by him who has
care of the community and has promulgated (it)".[3] The common
good was not an abstract concept, not the greatest good of the greatest
number, but a common good of persons.[4] The idea of personality
signified what was most perfect in all nature,[5] and the integrity and
inviolability of the human person placed an automatic limit on the
function of law. St Thomas was thus able to avoid the extreme conclusions of Plato of a system of laws forcing citizens to be good and
subordinating them to the common good of the State. The Greeks
had no conception of the absolute autonomy of the human person.

Hence although St Thomas expected law to respect the spiritual
good of the citizen and to operate within a framework of theological
values, it was not to promote every virtue nor to suppress every
vice.[6] Human law therefore forbade only the more grievous vices

[1] The ethical objection of positivism to a purposive interpretation of law,
according to Professor Fuller, "is not that it may lead to anarchy but that it may
push us too far in the opposite direction. It sees in a purposive interpretation,
carried too far, a threat to human freedom and human dignity", op. cit., pp. 670-1.

[2] Thomas Gilby, op. cit., p. 130.

[3] *Summa Theologica*, I.-II. Q. XC, art. 4. Cf. ibid. arts. 1, 2 & 3, and Q. XCVI,
art. 1. Cf. St. Thomas, *Ethics*, I:2.

[4] *Summa Theologica*, I.-II. Q. XCVI, art. 1. See also Jacques Maritain, *The
Person and the Common Good*, New York 1947.

[5] *Summa Theologica*, I. Q. XXIX, art. 3.

[6] *Summa Theologica*, I.-II. Q. XVI. arts. 2 and 3. "Nevertheless human law
does not prescribe concerning all the acts of every virtue: but only in regard to
those that are ordainable to the common good—either immediately, as when
certain things are done directly for the common good—or mediately, as when a
lawgiver prescribes certain things pertaining to good order, whereby the
citizens are directed in the upholding of the common good of justice and peace"

from which it was possible for the majority of imperfect human beings to abstain, "and chiefly those that are to the hurt of others, without the prohibition of which society could not be maintained: thus human law prohibits murder, theft, and suchlike".[1] Furthermore, law was to lead men to virtue not suddenly but gradually, and the legislator was always to bear in mind the danger that imposing too many precepts would lead the imperfect to break out into greater evils. In support he quoted the homely proverb: "he that violently bloweth his nose, bringeth out blood."[2] He showed the same caution in avoiding the opposite danger of anarchy, and while citizens might never obey a positive precept contrary to divine law, they were not to conclude lightly that a law was unjust and therefore to be resisted.[3]

St Thomas never forgot that law was not a science but an art, to be practised in the realm of the contingent, the relative, and the practical, amongst human beings who were not angels but fallen men. Certain conclusions could be derived directly from the natural law by way of deduction, but many political decisions and positive laws would not be immediately deducible. They were reached by a method he called "determination", the application of abstractions to social data.[4] The legislator was accordingly left with considerable scope provided he did not directly contravene moral rules. Thus, for example, the law of nature laid down that evil doers should be punished, but the method of punishment was not prescribed. The natural law system was accordingly as much dynamic as static, shaping the law to meet changing social conditions. The principles of natural law were immutable, but their effect varied with the subject matter.[5]

The flexibility of the Thomist system has not always been under-

(art. 3). A distinction is to be made between the ultimate end of man, supernatural happiness, the primary concern of the Church, and natural happiness in which the State is primarily interested. The two ends are distinct although they come together in man. The State promotes natural happiness in the perspective of man's final end but is not charged with the duty of seeing that he achieves it.

[1] Ibid., Q. XVI, art. 2.
[2] Ibid., *Proverbs*, xxx, 33.
[3] Ibid., Q . XVI, art. 4.
[4] *Summa Theologica*, I.-II. Q . XCV, art. 2.
[5] For a description of the process of change see *Summa Theologica*, I.-II. Q . XCIV, art. 5.

stood and it has sometimes been assigned a spurious rigidity.[1] Another misconception has been to confuse "natural" with "normal" and to seek to disprove natural law by empirical evidence of behaviour at variance with the alleged norm. "Normality" is a statistical concept but "Natural" is essentially an abstraction of reason considering man as he ought to be. As a free as well as a rational being, he may not always follow his proper ends, but this does not demonstrate that the ends do not exist. Indeed, given the Christian doctrine of original sin, one would not expect man always to act in perfect conformity with his nature. A further objection to natural law is that it denies man his essential freedom. "To assert the existence of a Natural law is one thing," writes Joseph Fletcher, "but to derive its content from the incidence of physical nature, rather than from the moral insights of men is to twist the classical Christian idea into a mechanistic strait-jacket, and to deny true morality by submitting to fatality, to helpless determinism."[2] This somewhat misstates the issue, since natural law thought is the reverse of mechanistic. Physical nature is not the basis of natural law, but merely provides the data which the reason uses as subject matter in reaching conclusions. The basis of natural law is the free operation of the reason and this can hardly be equated with "helpless determinism". The terms "unnatural" and "artificial" are sometimes equated in polemics against the natural law, and it is asked for example how Catholic natural lawyers can be so inconsistent as to allow the employment of false teeth while claiming that artificial contraception is contrary to natural law. There is nothing "unnatural" in the Thomist sense in an artifact as such, since the term "unnatural" is only meaningful when considered in relation to human ends. Hence contraceptives are rejected because they frustrate the purpose

---

[1] For a discussion of the problem, see George W. Goble, "The Dilemma of the Natural Law", *The Catholic Lawyer*, 2:226 (July 1956) and Edward T. Fagan, "Natural Law", ibid., 2:324 (October 1956). Referring to Suarez, Professor Fagan writes: "Change may be recognized as either intrinsic (formal), such as when a father ceases to be a father if he himself dies, or extrinsic (material), as when a father ceases to be such due to the death of a son. All principles and precepts of the natural law are immutable, according to Suarez, because they can suffer no formal change. They are liable to change only in the second manner, that is to change through changing subject matter."

[2] *Morals and Medicine*, Princeton 1954, p. 93.

of human sexuality while false teeth are accepted because they further the process of human nourishment by assisting mastication.

Traditional Protestant Theories

Within the Protestant tradition no one theory of the State has established a primacy comparable with that accorded to Thomism by the Roman Catholic Church. Luther's and Calvin's views of the function of State power are in one sense starkly opposed and this opposition has hindered the emergence of an exclusive theory, but in another sense they are linked because they both fall within the Augustinian tradition, each emphasizing the different poles of St Augustine's thought. Luther stressed even more than Augustine the utter corruption of man and the penetration of every form of human activity by sin. State and law far from being natural to man were the direct consequences of original sin. The role of the State was accordingly not to promote virtue, which its corruption did not allow it to undertake, but to keep sinful man in check, and so avoid a collapse into anarchy.[1] This view of the State, taken in conjunction with Luther's emphasis on a purely personal spiritual life, in theory should have limited the role of the State, but in practice it left the individual helpless before State power. As Troeltsch has put it: "The yielding spirit of its wholly interior sprituality adapted itself to the dominant theory of the day."[2] This adaptation was acceptable because no ultimate harm could be imposed by the State on the individual secure within his own private citadel of the spiritual life.[3] It was only when the liberal concept of the State as a mere mechanism to keep peace and order gained the ascendancy that these consequences of Lutheran political thought were avoided. Although widely separated on doctrinal grounds, Liberalism, Lutheranism, and Protestant sectarianism in general, have in common a conception of the minimum State. The liberal doctrine has been abandoned in economics, but its retreat has been matched by its wider application in the sphere of personal life, the phenomena

[1] See John C. Bennett, *Christians and the State*, New York 1958, p. 37.
[2] E. Troeltsch, *Social Teaching of the Christian Churches*, New York 1949, II, p. 574.
[3] See Sheldon S. Wolin, "Politics and Religion: Luther's Simplistic Imperative", *The American Political Science Review*, 56:24-42 (1950).

possibly being linked together, regimentation in one direction being compensated by emancipation in the other. Lutheran condemnation of the State might have been relegated to the history books, but the contemporary turning back by Protestant theologians to Reformation insights has made it relevant once again. "Every State represents human sin on the large scale," writes Emil Brunner, "in history, in the growth of every State, the most brutal, anti-divine forces have taken a share, to an extent unheard of in the individual life, save in that of prominent criminals. In the State we human beings see our own sin magnified a thousand times."[1] It is a curious paradox that this radical pessimism should have combined with liberal optimism in a working alliance to defend the minimal state.

Calvin rejected Luther's negative view of the State. ". . . the authority possessed by kings and other governments over all things upon earth," he wrote, "is not a consequence of the perverseness of men, but of the providence and holy ordinance of God, who has been pleased to regulate human affairs in this manner; forasmuch as he is present, and also presides among them, in making laws and executing equitable judgments."[2] He agreed with Luther in denying that natural law formed a bridge between God and man, but civil law was to be obeyed since it was based directly on the word of God. Unlike Zwingli, who abolished the distinction between Church and State, and charged the civil rulers with ecclesiastical functions, Calvin maintained a theoretical distinction between them, but in practice subjected the State entirely to the Church. He would have nothing of the distinctions of function elaborated by St Thomas on the basis of the different concepts of nature and revelation, and expected the State to maintain both religious doctrine and good morals.[3] Calvinist theory in a secularized form played an important part in developing the notion of absolute State sovereignty, but in its original religious manifestation is of little influence today.

In contemporary pluralist society many of the tensions and misunderstandings between Catholics, Protestants, and Liberals, may be traced back to radically conflicting views of the functions of the

---

[1] *The Divine Imperative*, Maryland 1943, p. 445.

[2] *Institutes of the Christian Religion*, London 1935, IV, XX, 4.

[3] Lord Acton, "The Protestant Theory of Persecution", in *Essays on Freedom and Power*, New York 1955, p. 134.

State. [In the United States the positive function of the State in moral affairs has tended to become identified with the Roman Catholic body, a development which has heightened conflict. In England, the existence of a State Church, within the Catholic tradition but with certain Protestant features, established under the law but accepting and exercising an independent responsibility of influencing society through institutional activity, has moderated the struggle, and blurred the lines of controversy.] The sense of outrage, to give one small but relevant example, expressed by Paul Blanshard, at Roman Catholic theologians' excursions into the field of practical medicine, would be foreign to the Anglican mind.[1] [Protestantism, it should be remembered, has generally not set out or been able to influence culture to the same degree as Catholicism.]

The contemporary problem is the establishment of common ground on which practical co-operation can be based. As the human race moves towards a greater degree of social and governmental unity it is likely to increase in urgency.

Contemporary Catholic Approaches

Many Catholic writers discussing the relationship between Church and State, make use of a dubious nineteenth century theological terminology of which the principal tools of thought are the concepts "thesis" and "hypothesis". According to these writers, who make some claim to be expressing the official view of the Church, the "thesis" or ideal solution to Church-State problems, is the establishment and full recognition by the State of the Roman Catholic Church. Other Churches are said to have no juridical claim to existence, "error has no rights", and while discreet private worship should be tolerated, any public manifestation of religious rites or propaganda opposed to Catholic truth should be prohibited. [The State should accordingly act as an instrument of the Church and enforce her dogmatic and moral teaching by means of civil law.[2]] The political and social situation, however, in many countries, prevents the implementing of the "thesis" and the Church in these countries has to act on a hypothesis, i.e. she avails herself of the

[1] Paul Blanshard, *American Freedom and Catholic Power*, Boston 1949, p. 107.
[2] See for example Ryan and Millar, *The State and the Church*, New York 1922, p. 38.

freedom conferred by the liberal State, and accepts on a temporary basis the rights afforded to other Churches. When Catholics have gained a majority, these latter spurious rights will be abolished and the one true Church will be recognized by the State.[1] The crude impudence of this view is enough to render it suspect, and its chief practical significance today is its utility as a weapon in the armoury of contemporary Protestant polemic.

Within the Catholic Church it has been subjected to a twofold attack. Some thinkers have modified its rigours, a process culminating in the late Pope Pius XII's address to the fifth national convention of the Union of Italian Catholic Jurists in 1953.[2] Others, notably Jacques Maritain and Father John Courtney Murray, the eminent American Jesuit theologian, have rejected it altogether.[3] Two principles were enunciated in the papal address, first that error has no theoretical right to exist, and second, that failure to impede it with civil laws and coercive measures can nevertheless be justified in the interests of a higher and more general good. The essence of the Pope's views is contained in the following extract: "Reality shows that error and sin are in the world in great measure. God reprobates them, but He permits them to exist. Hence the affirmation: religious and moral error must always be impeded when it is possible, because tolerance of them is in itself immoral, is not valid *absolutely and unconditionally*. Moreover, God has not given even to human authority such an absolute and universal command in matters of faith and morality. Such a command is unknown to the

---

[1] The thesis, it was said in connection with Mgre Chigi, a nineteenth-century papal nuncio in Paris, was that Jews should be burnt, the hypothesis-dinner with M. de Rothschild.

[2] December 9, 1953. *The Pope Speaks* (Maryland). I:64. Cf. "The Church and the Democratic State", by G. Weigel, S.J. *Theology Digest*, I:169–75 (Autumn 1953).

[3] For a symposium of "liberal" Catholic views of a group of French and Belgian theologians, see *Tolerance and the Catholic*, trans. George Lamb, New York 1955. See also Jacques Maritain, "Church and State", Chapter VI in *Man and the State*, London 1954. J. Courtney Murray, "Governmental Repression of Heresy", *Proceedings of the Catholic Theological Society of America* (3rd annual meeting 1948), Washington D.C. 1949, pp. 26–98. For a compact survey of the work being done in this area by Roman Catholic theologians in Europe and the United States, see *Roman Catholicism and Religious Liberty* by A. F. Carrillo de Albornoz, the World Council of Churches, Geneva 1959. References to Fr Murray's articles will be found in the bibliography.

common convictions of mankind, to Christian conscience, to the
sources of revelation and to the practice of the Church. To omit
here other Scriptural texts which are adduced in support of the
argument, Christ in the parable of the cockle gives the following
advice: let the cockle grow in the field of the world together with the
good seed in view of the harvest (cf. *Matthew* 13: 24-30). The duty
of repressing moral and religious error cannot therefore be an
ultimate norm of action. It must be subordinate to *higher and more
general* norms, which in *some circumstances*, permit and even perhaps seems to indicate as the better policy toleration of error in
order to promote *a greater good*."[1] Pius XII made it plain that this
reasoning would apply even were the Church in a position to
impose her will, so shifting the argument from considerations of
expediency to those of principle.[2]

Pius XII's statement gives a change of emphasis to official
Catholic teaching on the Church-State problem, but its severely
practical approach, together with its lack of definition of what
constitute "higher and more general norms", or "the greater good",
leave a number of questions open.[3] Must toleration for the Catholic
always remains a matter entirely within the sphere of the practical
judgment or are there discoverable principles which set permanent
bounds to the coercive power of the State? If God has not given an
absolute and unconditional command to suppress infidelity and
immorality what kind of command has he given? This is the
question to which Father Murray and others have addressed themselves. They have considered it primarily in relation to the State's
alleged duty to suppress heresy, but it is equally relevant to the
extent of the State's duty to impose standards of moral conduct and
to repress deviations from the norm.

As Fr Murray insists, the relationship between Church and State
cannot be treated as though it were a problem in deductive logic.[4]
To argue that men can only be saved by following the law of Christ,
therefore the State must enforce the law, therefore every heretic

---

[1] *The Pope Speaks*, I:68.
[2] Ibid., 70.
[3] It is not an entirely new departure, cf. Leo XIII's encyclical *Immortale Dei*
(1885). *The Pope and the People*, London 1932, pp. 62-3.
[4] "Governmental Repression of Heresy", op. cit., p. 29.

must be exterminated and every vice suppressed, is illegitimate, because it constructs a syllogism which takes no account of political philosophy or historical fact. Yet it is only within these categories that the relationship of Church and State can be meaningfully discussed. The starting point for discussion must be historical. The historical basis from which medieval discussion of the problem proceeded was that the Catholic faith provided the unity and foundations of civil society, and its preservation was therefore part of the political common good. Today this condition has vanished, since civil society has, as it were, come of age, and stands on its own feet.[1] The discussion now starts from the liberty of the human person, who creates the existential problem by his free adherence to Church or State. The Church cannot command an act of faith, much less can the State order one on her behalf. Equally the foundation of the State is the free consent of the individual person, through whom the authority of God is mediated. To live in society is natural and inescapable, but the form in which society is governed, the State, depends on the aggregate choice of individual persons.

Fr Murray follows St Thomas in treating civil society, and hence the State, as a natural institution, with its own temporal end, distinct from that of the Church. Individuals are bound by the natural law, and therefore the State is bound, but the State as such is not bound by the divine positive law of which it knows nothing. Even if, through its citizens, it comes to know of the nature of the Church and its laws, its duties are discharged by allowing the Church to pursue her mission freely. It may not usurp the mission of the Church by discharging a function it is not competent to perform, nor may it impose the definition of the Church on those of its citizens who do not freely by act of faith accept the definition.[2]

---

[1] This applies equally to Catholic and non-Catholic countries.

[2] I am fully aware that this summary does less than justice to the richness and complexity of Fr Murray's thought, as well as to the considerable difficulties which it raises. My purpose has been the limited one of indicating the existence of divergent theories of the relationship between Church and State within the Catholic tradition, and the different consequences these may have in endeavouring to define the derivative but subsidiary relationship between law and morals. A major difficulty facing Fr Murray has been to reconcile his theory with the concepts underlying the papal encyclicals on Church and State issued during the nineteenth century, especially Gregory XVI's *Mirari Vos* (1832), Pius IX's *Quanta Cura* and *Syllabus Errorum* (1864), and Leo XIII's *Immortale Dei* (1885)

If this view of the relationship of Church and State is accepted, it follows that in moral as in doctrinal matters, the State is only competent to enforce the dictates of the natural law. Moral obligations imposed by the Church, such as the requirement of Sunday worship, are not within its sphere of jurisdiction. Neither are moral obligations imposed by divine positive law. It does not follow however that the State must impose every obligation of the natural law; which precepts are to be the subject of positive legislation is a political decision to be taken after full consideration of contingent social conditions.

At this point, a practical difficulty must be noted. The distinction between natural law and divine law is sharp in theory, but tends to become blurred in practice. The nub of the difficulty is the interpretation of natural law. In theory, reason is the guide, but individuals employing their reason reach diametrically opposed conclusions about natural law rules. Who is to decide between them? The reason of individuals, maintain the natural law apologists, does not determine the issue, but "right reason".[1] In theory, this may be a satisfactory answer, claiming as it does that absolute values are not invalidated by individual error in apprehending them, but practically it merely adds another word to the question which now becomes "Who decides what constitutes 'right reason'?" The difficulty was recognized by the Vatican Council, which laid down that although supernatural revelation was not an absolute requisite for knowing the natural truths of religion, yet it was a moral or practical necessity for knowing them with certainty, and without any admixture of error.[2] In this the Council was following St Thomas Aquinas who had pointed out that lack of leisure, lack of interest, and lack of mental capacity, made Revelation a moral necessity for acquisition

and *Libertas Praestantissimum* (1888). Provided, however, they are strictly interpreted in accordance with their historical and ideological background, they do not present insuperable obstacles. For a full discussion of this point see Roger Aubert "Liberalism and the Church in the Nineteenth Century" in *Toleration and the Catholic*, New York 1955.

[1] See L. I. Bredvold, "The Meaning of the Concept of Right Reason in the Natural Law Tradition", *University of Detroit Law Journal*, 36:117 (December 1958).

[2] John Ford and Gerald Kelly, *Contemporary Moral Theology*, Westminster Maryland 1958, p. 4.

of truth.[1] Pius XII in his encyclical *Humani Generis* stressed that
man's senses, imagination, and evil passions, hinder him from
grasping truths that transcend the sensible order, and added: "It is
for this reason that divine revelation must be called morally necessary, so that those religious and moral truths, which are not of their
nature beyond the reach of reason may, also in the present condition
of the human race be known by all with ease, with unwavering
certitude, and without any admixture of error."[2]

In many controverted moral problems, then, the natural law does
not provide a certain guide. The perception of the evil of birth
control, from the standpoint of reason uninformed by faith, concedes Fr Bertke, requires the ability to make fine distinctions. "It is
certainly not among the immediate and evident deductions from
first principles," he writes, "and it has been seen that even acute
minds are capable of erring concerning remote conclusions."[3] This
admission is relevant since Catholics meet the charge that in supporting legislation restricting birth control or other immoral
practices, they are imposing Catholic views on those who are not
Church members and do not subscribe to Church doctrines, by
denying that it is Church law which is being imposed, but natural
law, binding on all men, whether members of the Catholic Church
or not.

Such an answer, while consonant with theory, carries little conviction in practice. Faced with such a situation Catholics would
be acting more reasonably if, for purposes of jurisprudence, they
treated the morality of birth control as within the sphere of moral
theology, a science based on revelation and the teaching authority
of the Church, rather than of natural ethics. Catholic jurists do not
suggest that the conclusions of moral theology should be backed
up by the civil law and made binding on all, and agitation for

[1] *Summa Contra Gentiles*, chapter VI.
[2] *Humani Generis*, August 12, 1950. A.A.S. 42:561–78 (1950).
[3] S. Bertke, *The Possibility of Invincible Ignorance of the Natural Law*,
Washington D.C. 1941, p. 99. Cf. "The Philosophical Concept of Morality",
by Dom. Illtyd Trethowan: in *The Springs of Morality*. Ed. John M. Todd,
New York 1956, ". . . we can *recommend* the Christian prescriptions about sexual
morality on grounds of pure reason, but that we cannot *demonstrate their
necessity* . . . we cannot prove that they are required absolutely by the facts,
unless we include the fact of Revelation", p. 20.

passage or maintenance of birth control statutes would accordingly be reduced.

Contemporary Protestant Approaches

Protestant theologians and political theorists are profoundly suspicious of the natural law approach, an attitude which Catholics find difficult to comprehend, since they are largely ignorant of the Reformation insights and ethical postulates which it reflects. To understand Protestant ethical theory, the Catholic must first clear from his mind the whole apparatus of Aristotelian and Thomist categories with which he has been familiar from the early days of his education and within which all his thinking has been carried out. Only through such an act of intellectual abnegation can he come to see that the Protestant rejection of natural law is not mere perversity, but like the Catholic acceptance, an ineluctable consequence of certain premisses of thought. The Catholic starts with the conception of the good but damaged natural man: the Protestant with an idea of man utterly corrupted by the Fall. For the Catholic the State would have been necessary for man had he remained a perfect being; for the Protestant it is the direct result of original sin. For Luther the world was an inn, and the devil its landlord. The employment of power to further social and religious ends seems reasonable to Catholics, but Protestants, at least in theory, are distrustful of all worldly power, as contaminated by sin.[1]

The Protestant attitude, at its most extreme, is exemplified in the thought of Karl Barth, for whom the Bible is the sole source of ethics.[2] Without Revelation, maintains Barth, man would be without any form of moral guidance. Natural ethics is a human vanity, the only standard of moral evaluation being the word of God in Christ. A more representative Protestant thinker is Reinhold Niebuhr, who

[1] For a good example of the Protestant approach see "A Symposium on Law and Christianity", *Oklahoma Law Review*, 12:45–146 (February 1959), especially Albert Mollegen, "Christ and Law" and a similarly entitled symposium, *Vanderbilt Law Review*, 10:879–968 (August 1957), especially S. E. Stumpf, "Theology and Jurisprudence", p. 885. Cf. Jacob Burckhardt's statement that "power is of its very nature evil", *Force and Freedom*, New York 1943, p. 234. Yet Protestants have often used power to further moral aims, e.g. the Volstead Act, establishing prohibition in the U.S.A.

[2] Karl Barth, "The Christian Community and the Civil Community", in *Against the Stream*, London 1954. Cf. *Church and State*, London 1939.

answers the question: "Does the State and Nation belong to God or the Devil?", with the reply of both.[1] For Niebuhr all man's "natural" or "rational" standards are involved in sin. The idea of natural law itself is sinful, a pretentious construction of human pride. "Undue confidence in human reason," he writes, "as the seat and source of natural law, makes this very concept of law into a vehicle of human sin. It gives to the peculiar conditions and unique circumstances in which reason operates in a particular historical moment the sanction of universality."[2] Exemption of reason from both finiteness and sin is the common fault of all rationalists, whether Stoic, Catholic, or modern. Like the individual, the national community and the State are ethically ambiguous. "The nation may be the incarnation of the principle of order within the community, but it is also the incarnation of the principle of anarchy between communities."[3] Yet Niebuhr does not adopt the extreme position of Barth. If the nation belongs to the devil when it claims to be God, it is also the bearer of genuine values. Natural law may be an illusion, but man cannot escape the natural conditions in which he has been placed by God. He replaces the complicated structure of natural law with the simpler Lutheran notion of the order of creation. This "limits the law to a natural fact, such as natural bisexuality for instance and does not introduce some specious universality of reason. It is not possible to escape the natural fact that the primary purpose of bisexuality in nature is that of procreation. But it is not easy to establish a universally valid 'law of reason' which will eternally set the bounds for the function of sex in the historic development of human personality."[4] Joseph Fletcher, expresses the same duality, in two negative *oughts*. Man should not submit absolutely to physical and physiological facts, for by doing so he denies his freedom, but he ought not to flout everything which is unchosen, for this would be to deny both human finitude and creaturehood.[5] This duality between the natural conditions in which man finds himself, and the liberty which enables him to transcend them, determine the Protestant approach

[1] *Does the State and Nation Belong to God or the Devil?* London 1937.
[2] *The Nature and Destiny of Man*, London 1941, I:298.
[3] *Does the State and Nation Belong to God or the Devil?* London 1937, p. 10.
[4] *The Nature and Destiny of Man*, New York 1949, I:282.
[5] Joseph Fletcher, *Morals and Medicine*, Princeton 1954, p. 213.

to many contemporary controverted moral problems. It stems from
the Reformation view that God's grace gives the individual a new
power to change nature and so escape from it, creating new conditions and relationships by the exercise of his will.[1] In the Catholic
tradition the emphasis is shifted, being placed on man's power to
interpret rather than alter nature. In his book, *Morals and Medicine*,
Joseph Fletcher at times seems to exalt this ability to choose into an
ultimate moral principle, without reference to the actual character
of the choice, so failing to distinguish clearly between moral and
physical freedom.[2]

The Protestant approach to morality is characterized not only by
a rejection of natural law, but by an emphasis on the role of ethics as
a critical inquiry into concrete problems of the moral life, rather
than the formulation of abstract rules of conduct.[3] This tendency
to abandon the task of establishing moral imperatives in favour of a
study of the reactions of the Christian to particular situations and
relationships drives Catholics and Protestants farther apart. It is
found in most contemporary Protestant ethicists, but most fully
developed perhaps, in the thought of Richard Niebuhr.[4] For him
ethics are analytic rather than prescriptive, charged with the task
of comprehending the Christian moral life by study of the data of
the moral experiences of the Christian community. No sharp line
of distinction can be drawn between sociological data and abstract
moral principles. Accordingly, Christian social ethics "becomes
principally the analysis of policy and social decisions by students
who have internalized the meanings of Christian revelation in

[1] Cf. Paul Ramsey, "Freedom and Responsibility in Medical and Sex Ethics",
New York University Law Review, 31:1157 (1956), p. 1194. "Protestant moral
theology (confessedly a small literature) simply points out that there is also
inscribed in nature, by nature's God, a transcendence and freedom of the
rational and the personal over the biological (which is still part of the reality to
be taken into account)."

[2] E.g. op. cit., pp. 26–7 and p. 35.

[3] Thus Joseph Fletcher writes: "Deliberately we have relied upon a cumulative support for our central thesis, choosing to bring out what it means in a
clinical style by examining concrete problems rather than by presenting a con-
trived and systematic construction of ethical doctrine", p. 214, op. cit.

[4] See *Faith and Ethics. The Theology of H. Richard Niebuhr*. Ed. Paul Ramsey,
New York 1955. Paul Tillich's approach is less concrete, see Paul Tillich,
Love, Power and Justice, Oxford 1954.

faith".[1] But does not this approach lead to a total moral relativism? What is left to distinguish the Christian from the individualist view of ethics? The answer is faith in God, whose total transcendence prevents any relativizing of values. God is love, and His law is the law of love mediated through the New Testament. The law of love is the dyke against relativism, not the alleged fixities of the law of nature.[2] The law of love is superior to all laws and is comprehended by the individual who leads the Christian life. It extricates him from the dilemma of denying all objective moral law, or admitting an absolute binding power which would destroy his God given liberty.

Protestant moral theory is thus an "ethic of inspiration" rather than an "ethic of ends".[3] Unlike the morality based on natural law which is a fully developed system resulting from rational reflection on man's nature, his relationship to society, and the role of the State, Protestant morality is an attitude towards life. It is based on a confrontation of persons, the meeting of the individual and his Lord, an experience rather than a rational working out of abstractions of justice. Here one finds the explanation for the comparative poverty and paucity of Protestant moral theology, and its stress on the importance of the personal in solving moral problems.

Common Ground in the Common Good

Whatever the differences between Catholics and Protestants on the relationship between Church and State, or law and morals, they have a common interest that the exercise of power should be regulated by the moral order. Can some principle be found acceptable to both, and possibly also to secular liberals, which will mark out the frontier between law and morals, and in particular draw a line between morality and the criminal law?

---

[1] Paul Ramsey, op. cit., p. 126. Paradoxically, this concrete approach has much in common with Aristotle's, who treated ethics as a branch of social science, and set more store by the judgments of the good man than *a priori* conclusions. See *Eud. Ethics*, 1216, b.32ff.

[2] Reinhold Niebuhr, *Love and Law in Protestantism and Catholicism*, London 1954, especially chapter 10. Cf. Paul Ramsey "Love and Law" in *Reinhold Niebuhr. His Religious, Social and Political Thought*. Ed. C. W. Kegley and R. W. Bretall, New York 1956. Chap. IV.

[3] See *The Church and its Function in Society*. Ed. W. A. Visser 't Hooft, and J. H. Oldham, London 1937, pp. 234ff. See also Edward Duff, *The Social Thought of the World Council of Churches*, New York 1956.

Such an attempt is made by the Wolfenden Committee in its Report on Homosexual Offences and Prostitution, published in 1957. The Committee concludes that the function of the criminal law in that field "is to preserve order and decency, to protect the citizen from what is offensive or injurious, and to provide sufficient safeguards against exploitation and corruption of others, particularly those who are specially vulnerable because they are young, weak in body or mind, inexperienced, or in a state of special physical, official or economic dependence".[1] It goes on to draw a sharp distinction between crime which comes within the sphere of the law, and sin, which is confined to the realm of private morality.[2] The Committee's statement of principle is made in relation to a limited subject matter, but it can be applied to the criminal law in general.

The Committee's principle is open to criticism on a number of grounds. First of all it is too rigid. As was pointed out earlier in this chapter, the spheres of morality and law are not in practice absolutely separated, but rather intersecting. Most criminal offences are also moral offences and moral responsibility is an essential element of criminal law. Furthermore the distinction between crime and sin is not the appropriate one to draw. Sin, as such, is a theological concept, concern with or jurisdiction over which is within the exclusive competence of the Church. The State as such knows nothing of sin *qua* sin, but it may well be concerned with conduct contrary to the moral standards accepted by the community, which may incidentally be sinful. By stating the issue as a dichotomy between crime and sin, and then classifying homosexual conduct between adults in private as sin, the Report obscures this point. The State, then, may well punish conduct which happens to be sinful without being committed as the Report suggests to a deliberate attempt through the agency of the law "to equate the sphere of crime with that of sin".[3]

If the Wolfenden approach is too exclusive, the alternative suggested by Sir Patrick Devlin in a lecture given before the British Academy in 1959 is too comprehensive.[4] There can be, he states, no

[1] Report of the Committee on Homosexual Offences and Prostitution, London, H.M.S.O. Cmd. 247. September 1957, para. 13.
[2] Ibid., para. 62.
[3] Report, para. 62.
[4] *The Enforcement of Morals* by the Hon. Sir Patrick Devlin. Maccabaean Lecture in Jurisprudence of the British Academy 1959, London 1959.

theoretical limits set to the State's power to legislate against immorality.[1] He reaches this conclusion by answering two questions.
First, has society the right to pass judgment on matters of morals?
Second, if society has the right to pass judgment, has it also the
right to use the weapon of the law to enforce it? He answers the first
question in the affirmative, on the basis that a recognized morality
is as necessary to society as a recognized government. The answer
to the first question, he maintains, may "very well dictate" the answer
to the second, and he concludes accordingly. Here, I think, is a gap
in the argument. The conclusion that society has the right to enforce
moral judgments by law does not flow from the premisses that it has
the right to pass them. The law operates within a framework of
moral concepts which directs and determines its dynamism, but it
has no right to enforce them all. Like other social agencies within
the Western tradition it is "charged with purpose beyond its ability
to establish", the achievement of the good life by the citizen.[2] Sir
Patrick's principle erects a Leviathan, in practice possibly a gentle
beast, tamed by the moderations of the common law, but a beast
none the less. In the latter part of his lecture, he does put forward
certain other factors limiting the application of his earlier principle,
such as the value to the individual of freedom, and the respect which
should be afforded to his privacy, but he fails to supply a principle
to mediate between these and his earlier categorical declaration of
the impossibility of setting theoretical limits to the power of the
State to legislate against immorality. Sir Patrick leaves no basis of
right for Church, conscience, or individual liberty, they are denied all
save practical status, and their relationship with the law can only be
established by juggling with a number of social contingencies.[3]

---

[1] *The Enforcement of Morals*, p. 14.

[2] Thomas Gilby, "The Crimination of Sin", *Blackfriars*, XLI:53, March 1960,
p. 57.

[3] Richard Wollheim in an article, "Crime, Sin, and Mr Justice Devlin", in
Encounter, III:34–40 (November 1959), has accused Sir Patrick Devlin of
logical inconsistency in postulating first a right in society to enforce morality,
in extent unlimited, and then at a later stage various social conditions under
which society should not exercise it. While a right to do something does not
mean one "ought" to exercise it, one cannot say one has a right and add later that
one "ought not" to exercise it. Mr Wollheim is of course correct in this latter
statement, but he is wrong in accusing Sir Patrick of inconsistency. What Sir
Patrick is saying is that the right exists, but that certain contingencies may make

Inherent in the common law tradition is the idea of the limited nature of law, its purpose being to make men good members of the earthly not the heavenly city, and its method being to establish probabilities by balancing evidence, not to set up absolutes by way of inquisition. In Curl's case, in 1727, when the common law courts were considering the assumption of jurisdiction over obscene literature, the Attorney General when urging the point was careful to limit his argument. "What I insist upon," he said, "is, that this is an offence at common law, as it tends to corrupt the morals of the King's subjects and is against the peace of the King. Peace includes good order and government, and that peace may be broken in many instances without actual force. 1, if it be an act against the constitution or civil government; 2, if it be against religion; and 3, if against morality. . . . I do not insist that every immoral act is indictable such as telling a lie or the like; but if it is destructive of morality in general, it if does, or may, affect all the King's subjects, it is then an offence of a publick nature. And upon this distinction it is, that particular acts of fornication are not punishable in the Temporal Courts and bawdy-houses are."[1] One may say then, disagreeing in theory with Sir Patrick Devlin and in practice with Sir John Wolfenden, that a theoretical principle limiting enforcement of morals by the law can be erected, a principle derived deductively from considering the nature of both, and inductively from the experience of the common law, namely that those moral offences which affect the common good are fit subjects for legislation. This is not to say that every moral offence affecting the common good should in practice be made a crime, but only that it may be so treated. Moral

it practically advisable, not *obligatory*, not to exercise it. He does not posit "oughts" in the order of obligation in the second part of his lecture, but only "some general statements of principle which it may be thought the legislature should bear in mind when it is considering the enactment of laws enforcing morals" (p. 17). This is precisely the point of my objection above that Church and individual are left helpless before the law. If Sir Patrick had used the words "practical considerations" instead of "general statements of principle" his meaning would have been clearer. This interpretation of Sir Patrick's meaning seems more likely than Mr Wollheim's rather technical point that Sir Patrick holds an erroneous doctrine of distinctions, namely that there is a fundamental difference between distinctions based upon a single criterion and those based on more than one criterion, the former being theoretical and superior, the latter practical and inferior.

[1] *R. v. Curl*, 2 Stra. 788 (1727), pp. 789–90.

offences not affecting the common welfare should be excluded from the scope of the law.[1]

The discussion then shifts to what constitutes the common good of society. Public order and civil peace; the security of the young, the weak, and inexperienced; the maintenance of the civilized decencies of public behaviour, all are included within the concept of the common good, but their enumeration does not exhaust it. Every community holds certain moral ideas and ideals of behaviour in common, concepts so fundamental that without them society would disintegrate, and which accordingly form part of the common good. This consensus may be reflected in legislation or constitutional documents, but much of it being "the wisdom of a great society" transmitted over the generations will not be reduced to written form.[2] It is, writes John Courtney Murray, "the intuitional *a priori* of all the rationalities and technicalities of constitutional and statutory law. It furnishes the premises of the people's action in history and defines the larger aims which that action seeks in internal affairs and public relations."[3] The extent and scope of this consensus will vary in different societies: it is not something given for all time. In religious authoritarian communities it is likely to be more defined and comprehensive than in liberal religious or agnostic societies. But it is found everywhere even in States constructed on the principle of the most doctrinaire liberalism whose pride is to tolerate different moralities, since some agreement is the prerequisite of community. It also affords a necessary protection against the tyranny, so feared by Mill, of the majority will. This consensus is more likely to be affected by public than private acts, but one cannot say arbitrarily that no private act can ever affect the common good.[4] Artificial

---

[1] Cf. J. S. Mill's famous maxims: "The maxims are first, that the individual is not accountable to society for his actions, in so far as these concern the interests of no person but himself. . . . Secondly, that for such actions as are prejudicial to the interests of others, the individual is accountable, and may be subjected either to social or legal punishment, if society is of opinion that the one or the other is requisite for its protection." *On Liberty*, Chapter V.

[2] Walter Lippmann, *Essays in the Public Philosophy*, Boston 1955, p. 99.

[3] "America's Four Conspiracies" in *Religion in America*. Ed. John Cogley, New York 1958, p. 19.

[4] There seems to be no clear logical distinction between "private" and "public" acts. Whether A takes B's life in B's house or on the public highway is irrelevant when considering whether this amounts to the crime of murder. This difficulty

insemination by a donor, for example, is a private act, but in a society
built on the concept of monogamous marriage and family unity, it
may well have public effects. Again, euthanasia of a sick person, is
an act which in one sense is private, but tolerated euthanasia might
well modify a principle of the sanctity of life, held in common by
society.

Whether behaviour, private or public, strikes at the common good
so gravely that it endangers the fabric of society and so should be
suppressed by law, is a question of fact, which can only be answered
after full consideration of the conditions prevailing in a given society,
including the rights enjoyed by the individual, and the division of
jurisdiction between Church and State. Even when conduct has
been so classified, it does not follow that the law should necessarily
be invoked. It may not be enforceable, or not enforceable equitably
or may give rise to greater evils than those it is intended to eradicate.
Political prudence, not jurisprudential theory, must, at this stage,
be the guide.

This conception of the common good tells us nothing of its ultimate validity. That must be left to the natural law theorists, or the
Church, or to ethical philosophers. I have used the term common
good, not in the sense of the Thomist, *bonum universale*, a theological value shared by all who live with God, nor in the ideal sense
of what is in accordance with right reason, but rather in Newman's
sense, of the "common possession" of society.[1] It is through this
medium, that natural law concepts operate, not by the rhapsodizings
of natural law enthusiasts, much of which appears to be nothing
more than rhetoric about reason, with neither social nor legal effect.
The end of law, as Newman stressed, is not mere raw justice as

is avoided if one defines a "private act" as one that does not affect the common
good. Cf. Mill's distinction cited at p. 38 n. 1. "Common good" is a broader
concept than "public order", the disturbance of which is a more usual criterion
employed to distinguish between "private" and "public" acts.

[1] "Next I lay down, that, whereas a State is in its very idea a society, and a
society is a collection of many individuals made one by their participation in
some common possession, and to the extent of that common possession, the
presence of that possession held in common constitutes the life, and the loss of
it constitutes the dissolution, of a State." J. H. Newman, *Historical Sketches*,
London 1872–3. I:161. For a discussion of Newman's idea of "common possession", see Terence Kenny, *The Political Thought of John Henry Newman*,
London 1957, pp. 77–8, 87–8 and 132–3.

such, but satisfaction of needs, peace, liberty and conservative interests.[1] The pursuit of the common good is not the chase of the absolute, but more often than not the selection of one amongst a number of warring expedients, none of which can be welcomed unconditionally. On some issues society must take a stand, solipsism is a doctrine of metaphysics not jurisprudence, but the law cannot provide infallible rules of moral guidance. The natural lawyers would like it to, but in fact it does not. The law is nothing else than the collective conscience of the community on those issues which cannot be left to individual choice. In so far as the community is faithful to the Western and Christian tradition it may reflect higher norms, but the State is not competent to create a moral order through the medium of law, as the eighteenth century encyclopaedists believed. Its true function is to define, make effective, and possibly preserve society's pre-existent moral views. The law systematizes consciences, and to that extent has moral authority, but consciences can err, and the law accordingly cannot guarantee rightness.

Assessing the Moral Consensus of a Community

How can the moral consensus of the community be ascertained? By employment of scientific techniques of social research? Some sociologists and lawyers have advocated developing this approach,[2] and possibly at some time in the future such methods will be perfected, but at present the methods themselves are the subject of acrimonious professional dispute. Even given reliable tools for sociological investigation, they would be of limited utility in establishing a society's moral consensus, since moral behaviour cannot be identified with moral opinion. The late Dr Kinsey, for example, may have established that the variations from the norm of sexual behaviour in American society were very much more widespread than had previously been supposed, but one can no more conclude from his findings that people believed such aberrations to be right even if they practised them, than one can conclude that because aberrations exist they are therefore right. The Christian will find the

---

[1] See J. H. Newman, *Discussions and Arguments*, London 1873, pp. 349–51.
[2] See J. Cohen, R. A. H. Robson and A. Bates, "Ascertaining the Moral Sense of the Community", *Journal of Legal Education*, 8:137 (1955). For a discussion see ibid., 8:319 and 469.

Kinsey reports no more than somewhat distressing glosses on the doctrine of original sin. Whatever problems sociological research may set for the absolute ethical systems of some modern philosophers, they do not arise for Christian ethics which is able to accommodate itself through its essential dualism. Polls of public opinion, with their loaded questions, limited scope, and snap responses, are even less reliable as guides to ethical opinion. They cannot, as Walter Lippmann has pointed out, deliver final verdicts, although they may well form the beginning of an argument.[1]

The law itself, as has already been suggested, provides more reliable insights into generally accepted moral views. The common law with its concepts of responsibility and fairness, its replacement of the moral standard of acting at one's peril by the ethical standard of reasonable conduct, its requirements of observance of the rules of natural justice, its punishment of certain modes of conduct as crimes, reflects the values accepted and developed by society over a period of many centuries. Christianity, as was stated in *Bowman v The Secular Society*, may no longer be part of the law of England, but Christian concepts, divorced from their doctrinal origin, are still active in it.[2] Furthermore, the law recognizes moral values not only in what it commands and punishes, but in what it refuses to countenance. Contracts made for an immoral purpose are not enforceable at law. Agreements which prejudice public safety, the administration of justice, or the status of marriage, are treated as being contrary to public policy and held void. Adultery, prostitution, homosexual relationships, are not recognized as sources of rights by the law.

Legal rules as such are not always reliable guides to community moral opinion, since they may with the passing of time have become dead letters. One must look beyond the letter of the law in the

[1] Op. cit., p. 42.
[2] A.C. 406, at p. 457 (1917). Richard O'Sullivan has published a number of monographs on the relationship between Christianity and the common law. See: *Natural Law and the Common Law*, Transactions of the Grotius Society, 31:117–38 (1945), *Christian Philosophy in the Common Law*, Aquinas Papers, No. 6, Oxford 1947, *The Inheritance of the Common Law*, London 1950, *What is a Christian Country?* London 1945. See also Brendan F. Brown, "The Natural Law Basis of Juridical Institutions in the Anglo-American Legal System", *Catholic University of America Law Review*, 4:81–94 (1954). Cf. J. B. Ames, "Law and Morals", *Harvard Law Review*, 22:97 (1908).

statutes and ancient law reports to the contemporary practice of
the courts and legal administration. Sir Patrick Devlin accordingly
directs attention to the man in the jury box, and finds the moral
judgment of society contained in his decisions. It is "something about
which any twelve men or women drawn at random might after discussion be expected to be unanimous".[1] Immorality, for legal
purposes, is "what every right-minded person is presumed to consider to be immoral".[2] Even within the narrow compass of morality
"for legal purposes", this conclusion is open to criticism. Jury decisions are one indication of society's moral opinions, but they are not
its sole source as he suggests. Lawmakers can look to other institutions, groups, and individuals, to help them reach conclusions.
Furthermore, in practice, juries may not afford explicit guidance
where it is most needed. Controversial moral issues are precisely
those on which society, and therefore the jury, has ceased to have a
unanimous opinion.

With these reservations, had Sir Patrick confined himself to the
role of juries as indicators of moral opinion, and maintained silence
on the nature of their decisions, he would not be open to criticism.
But he goes beyond the practical question of ascertaining the community's moral sense, to define its basic character. The juryman, he
tells us, is not the rational, but the reasonable man. "He is not
expected to reason about anything and his judgment may be largely
a matter of feeling."[3] At a later stage in his lecture he extends
this proposition as a basis for a general ethical theory: "Every moral
judgment," he says, "unless it claims a divine source, is simply a
feeling that no right-minded man could behave in any other way
without admitting that he was doing wrong."[4] He specifies three
forces behind the moral law, "intolerance, indignation, and disgust", and suggests that if these are not present, the "feelings of
society cannot be weighty enough to deprive the individual of freedom of choice".[5] These passages have caused their author to be
charged with resting morality on everything most arbitrary and unreliable in human nature and grounding it in total subjectivity.[6] The

[1] Op. cit., p. 16.   [2] Ibid.   [3] Op. cit., p. 15.
[4] Op. cit., p. 18.   [5] Op. cit., pp. 17-18.
[6] See Richard Wollheim, op. cit., p. 39. Cf. H. L. A. Hart, "Immorality and
Treason", *The Listener*, LXII:162-3, July 30, 1959.

charge certainly seems justified. Sir Patrick has excluded thought and rational processes altogether, yet surely there must be rational reflection before outraged feelings of popular indignation are translated into law? And are all moral judgments intrinsically emotional? Moral judgments based on reason are as possible, if not as common, as those based on emotion. Natural lawyers for centuries have built their systems on reason, and by no means all have posited an ultimate divine source. Furthermore, moral judgments resulting from ethical imperatives are not emotional. Expressions of disgust, as Sir Patrick states, may be helpful in indicating that the limit of some people's toleration is being reached, and lawmakers would be well advised to note them, but they cannot be a basis for legislative policy in a society which lays any claims to rationality. The law should be in touch with popular feeling, but not determined by it. It should strive to embody rational judgments and so modify public opinion, not blindly follow in the wake of emotional prejudice.

Some conclusions

A pluralist society in which divergent views on religion and morality are held by different groups may or may not be a higher state of being or social achievement than a unitary society where agreement on such matters is unanimous, but it is the society which we find in England and the United States today, and is likely to be the pattern for the future in the free world. In democratic pluralist societies, social policies with moral implications are not laid down by *fiat* from above, but are evolved gradually through the rational reflections of free men. Government, to use a phrase of Walter Bagehot, is government by discussion.[1] Controversial issues are resolved not by plebiscite, but by the gradual crystallization of society's views through the medium of rational discourse. In a democracy, participation in the dialogue is not confined to the intelligent or the virtuous, but is open to every citizen, who makes his contribution either individually or through one of a number of institutions, Congress, Parliament, the Churches, the Universities, the Press, using the medium of the spoken or written word. This continuous dialogue, like any other meaningful conversation is subject to self-

[1] See Walter Bagehot, *Physics and Politics* in *Walter Bagehot* by Norman St John-Stevas, London 1959, pp 445–55.

imposed limits, and rests on certain postulates. Where there is total disagreement, there can be no communication, and hence no argument. Justice and truth are accepted as both good and knowable; peace and order as desirable and attainable; trust is placed in the ability to resolve disputes by employment of reason and logic. Law is not equated with force or with the majority will, but is a limited agency, whether the limitations be imposed by natural law, the rights of the human person, the rights of non-governmental institutions, or a consensus of moral ideas.[1] Magna Carta, the Declaration of Independence, the Constitution of the United States are documentary embodiments of the doctrine of the Middle Ages, of which England and the United States are the joint heirs, that all political authority is intrinsically limited.

As the dialogue proceeds, differences do not disappear, indeed they may become more sharply defined, but mutual misunderstanding is reduced as the points at issue are clarified. Clarification, the role of the intellectual, is an essential preliminary before practical decisions and compromises, which fall to the politician and the lawyer, can be taken. Discussion reveals the gulfs between Christian and non-Christian, and between the Christian denominations themselves, and while it shows that some of them are unbridgeable, it indicates how others may be crossed. The difficulties facing the Christian moralist are formidable, for he has to communicate his views to a public which has lost any sense of the absolute and nearly all sense of sin, and is unwilling to accept precepts which restrict private interests and desires. In a society where an unconscious utilitarianism is widely diffused, and actions are judged by their consequences rather than by any inherent properties of good or evil, Christian morals are often derided as mere taboos.[2] The Christian will share the misgiving of Lord Radcliffe at the spectacle of a society "which combines a low level of thinking and feeling with a wide diffusion of general benevolence and good will".[3] Behind the

---

[1] See Edward S. Corwin, The "Higher Law" Background of American Constitutional Law, Cornell University Press, 1957. 'The attribution of supremacy to the Constitution on the ground solely of its rootage in popular will represents, however, a comparatively late outgrowth of American constitutional theory,' p. 4.

[2] See Bertrand Russell, Stanford Law Review, 10:382 (March 1958).

[3] Lord Radcliffe, The Problem of Power, London, 1958, pp. 123–4.

disputes as to the role of the law in certain moral issues, is revealed a
divergence of view over the essential nature of man. The Christian
view that man is not absolute master of his own fate, but holds his life
and body on trust for other purposes, evokes no response in an era
which places a supreme value on personal emancipation, and has provided man with the means of its achievement. But the technology
which promised a paradise now shows signs of delivering a hell.
Against the tyranny of scientific techniques, the emancipated man
finds himself defenceless, having rejected the Christian view of
human nature, which if it places limits on man's independence, by
stressing that he is the user not the proprietor of life, also preserves
his humanity, by erecting barriers beyond which technology cannot
pass. The scientific humanist may be as much repelled by the prospect of the replacement of the family by the stud farms of artificial
insemination as the Christian, but unlike the latter he has no final
argument against it. If the power is there why should it not be
used?

In his desire to preserve the fabric of society from agnostic cor-
rosion, the Christian, conscious of his minority position, seeks an
ally in the law. The law may well preserve moral ideas long after the
theology which gave rise to them has ceased to hold a general sway.
The law's view, for example, that the contract of marriage creates a
permanent status and is not dissoluble by mutual consent, is founded
on Christian principles. "It has got there," as Sir Patrick Devlin
points out, "because it is Christian, but it remains there because it is
built into the house in which we live and could not be removed
without bringing it down."[1] The Christian attempt to preserve
moral values by supporting existing institutions is thus not only
understandable—they could hardly be expected to facilitate the
complete secularization of society—but up to a point reasonable. It
ceases to be reasonable when the moral judgment expressed by the
law no longer has any correspondence with the general view of
society. The standards of conduct which the Christian can claim to
have imposed by law are limited to those held by the community in
general. Public enforcement of religious standards cannot extend
beyond the area of community agreement. As Newman has written,
it is imperative that "Public Opionion Should give the Law to Law,

[1] Op. cit., p. 11.

and should rule those questions which directly bear upon any matter of national concern. . . ."[1]

The Christian has also to be wary that in avoiding the shoals of relativism, he does not fall into the opposite error of treating legal and political science as if they were studies of the absolute. As Aristotle warned there is always a certain relativity involved in discussion of the practical.[2] One cannot, for example, without an examination of relevant social factors, conclude that because an action is forbidden by natural law, it should also be forbidden by positive law. The Christian lawmaker must constantly scrutinize the data provided by the social sciences, by history, economics, and psychology, to see how theological principles are to be modified into law. This is not to subscribe to the view put forward by Dr Glanville Williams, that "theological speculations and controversies should have no place in the formation of the rules of law",[3] but to deny them a determining role. Other disciplines must be allowed to speak for themselves.[4] Good theology is no guarantee of good government; if it were, Catholics would be placed in a nice dilemma by the history of the papal states.

The achievement of unanimity on all moral issues in a pluralist society is clearly impossible, but more modest objectives may be attained. We could, in John Courtney Murray's phrase, limit the warfare and enlarge the dialogue. "We could lay down our arms (at least the more barbarous kind of arms!) and take up argument."[5] We could recognize that both liberty and equality pre-suppose fraternity. "All, too," said Jefferson in his first inaugural address, "will bear in mind this sacred principle, that though the will of the majority is in all cases to prevail, that will to be rightful must be reasonable; that the minority possess equal rights which equal law

---

[1] See *Discussions and Arguments*, London 1873, pp. 349–51.

[2] *Nic. Ethics*, 1:3.

[3] Op. cit., p. 229.

[4] They may even, suggests James Gustafson, afford some particular insight into human life precisely because they are not occupied with theological problems. See *Faith and Ethics. The Theology of H. Richard Niebuhr*. Ed. Paul Ramsey, New York 1955, p. 121. Cf. H. R. Niebuhr, "Theology, Not Queen, but Servant", *Journal of Religion*, XXXV:1–5 (1955).

[5] "America's Four Conspiracies" in *Religion in America*. Ed. John Cogley, New York 1958, p. 40.

must protect, and to violate would be oppression."[1] Fraternity requires that the majority should not impose its will whenever it enjoys numerical superiority, but should respect conscientious convictions of minorities.

The limits of tolerance will not be easy to define. The United States Supreme Court itself, having upheld the expulsion of Jehovah's witnesses from a public school because they declined to salute the flag as required by State law, on the grounds that it violated their religious beliefs, later reversed itself and allowed their abstention.[2] Judge Frankfurter who wrote the opinion in the first case, delivered a dissent in the second, which states the issue succinctly. "That which to the majority may seem essential for the welfare of the State may offend the consciences of a minority. But, so long as no inroads are made upon the actual exercise of religion by the minority, to deny the political power of the majority to erect laws concerned with civil matters, simply because they may offend the consciences of a minority really means that the consciences of a minority are more sacred and more enshrined in the Constitution than the consciences of a majority." The crux of the issue is to decide whether conformity with the majority will is "essential for the welfare of the State". Judge Jackson in Barnette's case reached the conclusion that abstention from saluting the flag by Jehovah's witnesses was so harmless to others and to the State, that it should be allowed in the interests of freedom.

A working rule might be that the majority should abstain from obliging the minority to follow any practice which they condemn as immoral, provided abstention does not injure the common good.

---

[1] Quoted by Henry Steele Commager in *Majority Rule and Minority Rights*, London 1943, p. 8.

[2] *Minersville School District v. Gobitis.* 310 U.S. 586, 84 L.Ed. 1375, 60 S.Ct. 1010 (1940). Expulsion upheld. But this decision was overruled in *West Virginia State Board of Education v. Barnette.* 319 U.S. 624, 87 L.Ed. 1628, 63 S.Ct. 1178 (1943). The Court has also held that conditions of vaccination imposed by public schools for admission may not be resisted on grounds of religious belief, see *Jacobson v. Mass.* 197 U.S. 11, 49 L.Ed. 643, 25 S.Ct. 358 (1905), and *Zucht v. King.* 260 U.S. 174, 67 L.Ed. 194, 43 S.Ct. 24 (1922). Fluoridation of water has also been upheld against contentions that the programme violates religious beliefs. *Kraus v. City of Cleveland.* 121 N.E. 2d. 311 (Ohio Ct.App. 1954) affirmed 163 Ohio St. 559, 127 N.E. 2d. 609 (1955). Appeal dismissed, 351 U.S. 935 (1956).

Saluting the flag has been held to come within this rule, the practice
of polygamy and bigamy to fall without it.[1] Protestants should
recognize that Catholics take their natural law views seriously even
if they cannot accept them themselves. The State, which represents
citizens of different faiths, should not commit itself to policies which
outrage the views of adherents of any of them without grave reason.
This is not to recommend a surrender to secularism, or to subscribe to the concept of an amoral State, but to recognize that civil
peace is itself a moral value, which is placed in jeopardy by ignoring
the conscientious convictions of a substantial minority of citizens.
Catholics also, should exercise a self-denying ordinance, and recognize that religious pluralism implies to some degree a moral pluralism. Under these conditions, some past public moral judgments, such
as the condemnation of contraception, may have to be treated as
private judgments. The Church may be assured of her own right-
eousness and claims, but cannot act as though these were recognized
in full by civil society. Her minimum requirement, which may
possibly be enough, is that on issues where agreement is impossible,
her members should not be bound by the State to act in violation of
their consciences.[2]

Society, of course, is not a simple construction of conscience or of
reason, but the arena of a power struggle. A conception of society as
merely a higher form of genteel debating society, in which all the
members are capable of forming their own judgments with false

[1] *Church of Latter Day Saints v. U.S.*, 136 U.S. 1, 34 L.Ed. 478, 10 S.Ct. 792
(1890) ". . . the Thugs of India imagined that their belief in the right of assassina-
tion was a religious belief; but their thinking so did not make it so. . . . The
offering of human sacrifices by our own ancestors in Britain was no doubt
sanctioned by an equally conscientious impulse. But no one, on that account,
would hesitate to brand these practices, now, as crimes against society. . . .".
136 U.S. at 49–50.
[2] See address of Pius XII to Fifth National Convention of the Union of
Italian Catholic Jurists. December 9, 1953. "Above all it must be clearly stated
that no human authority, no State, no community of States, whatever be their
religious character, can give a positive command or positive authorization to
teach or to do that which would be contrary to religious truth or moral good.
Such a command or such an authorization would have no obligatory power and
would remain without effect." *The Pope Speaks* I:67–8. For an application of this
principle to medical law, see Pius XII, "Address to Seventh International Congress of Catholic Doctors", September 11, 1956. *The Catholic Lawyer*, 3:242
(July 1957).

emphases corrected by discussion, does violence to the facts. In Connecticut and Massachusetts for example, Catholics and Protestants are not debating the jurisprudential merits of birth control statutes, but clashing over them as symbols of power and prestige. The purpose of the dialogue is not to ignore the power struggle, but to keep it in check. It strives to modify excesses and asperities, and to subject the strife to the ultimate ordering of morality and rationality. Tensions between Church and State can never be totally eradicated as long as there is not one power but two. Perpetual peace can only be ensured by the Church swallowing the State, or by Christians executing a mass abdication, content that religion should be treated as a private affair with no contribution to make to the commonweal. The struggle will continue, but the clash of arms or the stridencies of debate should not be allowed to obscure the deeper reality, that in a mature democracy, the basic problem is not the relation of Church and State, but the relation of Church and Society. Society cannot be redeemed by the coercive will, imposed through the instrumentality of the State, but by the individual citizen spurred to action by persuasion. In this connection, the words of Pius XII to his new cardinals in an address of February 20, 1946, are worth pondering. "It is not the office of the Church to include and in a manner embrace, like a gigantic world empire, all human society. This concept of the Church as earthly empire and worldly domination is fundamentally false. She follows in her progress and her expansion an opposite path to that of modern imperialism. She progresses before all else in depth, then in extension. She seeks primarily man himself. . . . Her work is completed in the depths of each man's heart, but it has its own repercussions on all the duration of life, on all the fields of activity of each one. With men so formed the Church prepares for human society a base on which it can rest with security."[1]

---

[1] A.A.S. XXXVIII:143 (1946).

CHAPTER TWO

The Control of Conception

HISTORY

From the earliest times, man has attempted to control conception. Anthropologists have established that both magical and rational methods were employed by primitive tribes.[1] Amongst the civilized nations of antiquity, the Egyptians, the Jews, the Greeks, and the Romans, all possessed knowledge of contraception.[2] Plato wished to restrict all procreation by law, confining it to men between the ages of thirty and thirty-five, and women aged twenty to forty. Aristotle also recommended the legal regulation of conception, and approved both abortion and infanticide. By scientific research, Greek physicians and medical writers greatly improved existing contraceptive techniques.[3] Their discoveries were utilized by the Romans, but contrary to popular belief, contraceptive knowledge was not widely diffused in the Roman world, being confined in the main to medical writers, physicians, and scholars.[4] Islamic contraceptive medicine, which owed much to the Greeks, was developed during the middle ages, but little progress was made in Europe during the same period, the attitude of the Church being unfavourable to such researches. It was not until the sixteenth century that a new advance was made with the publication in 1564, two years after his death, of Gabriele Fallopio's "De Morbo Gallico", a treatise on venereal disease. His treatise contained the first published account of the condom or sheath, which Fallopio claimed to have invented. The condom was employed during the eighteenth century, both in England and on the Continent, being mainly used in brothels,

[1] See Norman E. Himes, *Medical History of Contraception*, Baltimore 1936. Chapter I. For the early history of family limitation see also Marie Stopes, *Contraception: Its Theory, History and Practice*, London 1934. Chapter IX.

[2] "Contraception" is used in this chapter in the sense of artificial methods of birth control.

[3] Himes, op. cit., Chapter IV. Soranos of Ephesus (98–138) made the greatest single contribution.

[4] Himes, op. cit., p. 100.

but also sold in shops in London and elsewhere.[1] At the end of the century, contraceptives were still associated exclusively with immorality and vice, but by the close of the nineteenth century, this position had been deeply undermined and the way prepared for the general acceptance of contraceptives which has been so marked a feature of our own time.

Thomas Malthus, an Anglican curate, was the unwitting founder of the modern birth control movement, by means of his famous *Essay on the Principle of Population*, published in 1798. His thesis was simple. Both population and food supplies tend to increase, but since population increases faster than means of subsistence, the majority of the human race is doomed to perpetual poverty and malnutrition. Disease and war act as natural checks and so prevent a universal cataclysm. In the first edition of his book, Malthus offered no way of escape from this dreadful treadmill, but in 1803 the second edition of his *Essay* included recommendations for "moral restraint". By this Malthus did not mean that sexual intercourse should be restrained in marriage, but that marriages should be postponed to a late age or complete celibacy embraced. Far from advocating any means of contraception, he expressly condemned recourse to "improper arts".

Radical reaction to Malthus' pessimistic and conservative doctrine was sharp. Generally accepted, it would put an end to all efforts at social reform, for by his hypothesis these were automatically condemned to failure.[2] Godwin wrote two ineffective replies to refute Malthus, but it was left to Francis Place in his *Illustrations and Proofs of the Principle of Population*, published in 1822, to suggest that in the use of artificial contraception lay the answer to population problems.[3] If, he wrote, "it were once clearly understood, that it was not disreputable for married persons to avail themselves of such

[1] Francis Grose, *A Guide to Health, Beauty, Riches and Honour*, 2nd ed., London 1796, p. iii. Mme de Sévigné, in the previous century, had referred to the condom in a letter written to her daughter in 1671, as "a bulwark against enjoyment, and a cobweb against danger".

[2] It is interesting to note a similar reaction of the radical *New Statesman and Nation* to the suggestion that aid to underdeveloped countries was not an unmixed benefit since it exacerbated population problems. (44:253 September 6, 1952.) For subsequent discussion of this editorial, see 44:319, 349–50, 378.

[3] Jeremy Bentham had advocated the use of birth control to reduce the poor rates in 1797. Himes, op. cit., p. 211, n. 4.

precautionary means as would, without being injurious to health, or destructive of female delicacy, prevent conception, a sufficient check might at once be given to the increase of population beyond the means of subsistence; vice and misery, to a prodigious extent, might be removed from society, and the object of Mr Malthus, Mr Godwin, and of every philanthropic person, be promoted, by the increase of comfort, of intelligence, and of moral conduct, in the mass of the population".[1] Place supplemented his argument by distributing amongst the working classes, a series of "diabolical handbills", recommending contraception. Despite their outlining a particular method of contraception—the use of a sponge and attached ribbon—they were not legally suppressed. Similar immunity was enjoyed by the publications of Place's disciples, Richard Carlile, Richard Hassell, and William Campion. Place's influence spread to the United States, where Robert Dale Owen was emboldened in 1830 to publish the first American booklet on birth control, *Moral Physiology*.[2] Two years later, Dr Charles Knowlton, a Massachusetts physician, published anonymously a further treatise on contraceptive methods, curiously entitled, *Fruits of Philosophy*. Knowlton eventually served a term of imprisonment for his part in publishing this book, and later it was the subject of a celebrated English trial. Malthusian contentions were revived by George Drysdale in his *Elements of Social Science*, published in England in 1854, in which he advocated "preventive sexual intercourse".

By mid-century, Malthusian prophecies and their suggested remedies were generally discussed in educated circles, but the general public was still ignorant of contraception and the arguments for its use. In 1877, however, the trial of Charles Bradlaugh and Annie Besant for publishing an English edition of *Fruits of Philosophy*, made contraception a hotly debated subject throughout the country and amongst all classes.[3] Mrs Besant utilized a golden opportunity

[1] *Illustrations and Proofs of the Principle of Population.* Ed. Norman Himes, London 1930, p. 165.

[2] This went through several editions within a year and had achieved an Anglo-American circulation of 75,000 by 1877, the year of Owen's death.

[3] See *The Times*, June 18, et seq. 1877, for an account of the trial. For a reconstruction of the trial see Norman St John-Stevas, *Obscenity and the Law*, London 1956, pp. 70–4. For the appeal decision, see *Bradlaugh v. R.* (1878), 3 Q.B.D. 607. See also vol. II of Hypatia Bonner's *Charles Bradlaugh*, London 1894.

to spread the good news, speaking at inordinate length, and spending much of her time addressing the public on the laws of Malthus and the necessity for birth control, rather than defending herself against the charge of publishing an obscene libel. Both defendants were found guilty, but the following year the conviction was set aside for a defect of the indictment. The effects of the prosecution were startling. Before 1876 the circulation of *Fruits of Philosophy* had had been only 1,000 per year, but by August 1881 no less than 185,000 copies had been sold, bearing out the words of Sir Alexander Cockburn at the trial that "a more ill advised and more injudicious prosecution never was instituted".[1] Knowledge of contraceptive methods became widespread, and the work was carried forward by the Malthusian League, founded in 1878, with Annie Besant as its first secretary.[2]

Of itself the Bradlaugh-Besant trial would not have resulted in a popularization of contraception, but it came at a moment peculiarly favourable to the cause. Industrialisation and the fall in the death rate had resulted in a vastly increased population, the great depression of 1873–96 led to widespread dislocation in agriculture and industry, women were becoming more emancipated and unwilling to bear the burden of unrestricted families, while legislation forbidding child employment had reduced the value of children as income earning assets.[3] Shortly after the trial, in 1880, education for the first time was made compulsory, and this further increased the financial burden of large families. Contraception had still to win general social acceptance, but after 1878 few attempts were made

---

[1] Himes, *Medical History of Contraception*, p. 243. Edward Truelove, a Freethought publisher was summonsed in 1877 for publishing Owen's *Moral Physiology*. Hearing of the case was postponed until 1878 to enable the Bradlaugh-Besant case to be disposed of. In February 1878 the first jury failed to agree, and a second trial was instituted. Truelove was sentenced to prison, and efforts to secure his release failed. Truelove's case is an important landmark in the history of birth control in England, but at the time was overshadowed by the more spectacular trial of Bradlaugh and Besant.

[2] Annie Besant renounced contraception in 1891, after becoming a theosophist.

[3] Not unimportant was the discovery of the vulcanization of rubber by Goodyear and Hancock in 1843–4 which made possible the production of a cheap, reliable, condom.

to suppress *bona fide* birth control propaganda by law.[1] The way was thus opened for a flow of publications advocating birth control. In 1879 Annie Besant published her own treatise, "The Law of Population".[2] By 1891 it had sold 175,000 copies in England alone, at the low price of sixpence each. English law had become quiescent but private opposition to birth control was still strong. Thus in 1887, Dr Henry Allbutt's name was erased from the medical register by the General Medical Council for publishing a popular work on birth control, *The Wife's Handbook*.[3] In 1913 the Malthusian League for the first time published a practical handbook on birth control, *Hygienic Methods of Family Limitation*, and put it in general circulation without legal incident. After the First World War, the social restrictions on dissemination of birth control information dissolved. Marie Stopes founded the *Society for Constructive Birth Control*, and in 1921 opened the first birth control clinic in London. Her work was carried on by Harold Cox, Julian Huxley, Norman Haire, Dean Inge, Lord Dawson of Penn and others. In 1930 the Lambeth Conference gave a grudging approval to family planning by contraceptives, a concession which led to a more whole-hearted approval by the Lambeth Conference of 1958. The official visits paid by the Minister of Health to the headquarters of the Family Planning Association in London, in 1955 and 1958, symbolized the nearly complete triumph of the birth control movement in Great Britain.[4]

In the United States, the movement has not met with such unqualified success. Dr Knowlton was succeeded by other medical writers advancing the cause of birth control, including A. M. Mauriceau, J. Soule, Edward Bliss Foote, and his son Edward Bond Foote. John Humphrey Noyes founded the Oneida colony in New

---

[1] Truelove's publications, as a result of an appeal, were not finally destroyed until 1879. However, this destruction order was intrinsically part of the original proceedings initiated in 1878.

[2] This was never prosecuted in England but was prosecuted in Australia and condemned at first instance. The conviction for publishing was later set aside on appeal, the judge holding that the test of obscenity was not whether it promoted immoral ideas but whether the language itself was obscene. *Ex parte Collins* (1888), 9 L.R. (N.S.W.) 497; 5.W.N. 85.

[3] See H. A. Allbutt, *Artificial Checks to Population*, London 1889, p. 7.

[4] Advice on contraception is still to some extent restricted when sought as part of the National Health Service, see pp. 58-9 of this work.

York and advocated his own particular method of birth control.[1]
Birth control suffered a severe setback in 1873 when, thanks to the
efforts of Anthony Comstock, Congress enacted a statute excluding
contraceptives and contraceptive information from the mails,
declaring them obscene.[2] Many States followed suit and passed
statutes banning the sale and distribution of contraceptives. These
laws were enforced with a varying degree of efficiency in different
parts of the country but undoubtedly hindered the acceptance of
birth control by the community. In 1912, Margaret Sanger, a New
York nurse, started her life's work as a zealot for birth control. She
began studying the subject and gave her first public lectures. In
1914 she began publication of a new monthly magazine, *The Woman
Rebel*, and was arrested and indicted under the Comstock law. She
fled to Europe and the following year her husband was imprisoned
for a short term for handing out a copy of her pamphlet, *Family
Limitation*. Mrs Sanger returned to the United States and on
October 16, 1916, opened the first Birth Control Clinic in the United
States in Brooklyn. The clinic was raided and closed by the police,
Mrs Sanger and her sister both being sentenced to thirty days
imprisonment in 1917. Nevertheless she continued her work and
propaganda, basing her appeal on the suffering caused to women by
unlimited child bearing rather than on Malthusian arguments. In
1917 the National Birth Control League was founded and Mrs
Sanger began publication of the *Birth Control Review*. National
and international conferences were held and in 1921 the New York
Birth Control Clinical Research Bureau was opened. Repeated
efforts by Mrs Sanger and Mary Ware Dennett were made to repeal
or amend the federal laws restricting birth control, but were not
successful.[3] In 1929 the New York clinic was raided and its director

---

[1] *Coitus Reservatus:* intercourse which stops short of ejaculation.

[2] S. 211 of the Penal Code.

[3] See *Birth Control Laws* by Mary Ware Dennett, New York 1926, and *My
Fight for Birth Control* by Margaret Sanger, New York 1931. In 1929 the
National Committee on Federal Legislation for Birth Control was organized
with Mrs Sanger as President to secure alteration of federal statutes. In 1930
a Bill was introduced into Congress by Senator Gillett (Mass.) to exempt the
medical profession from their operation. The Bill failed. Earlier in 1923 a
straight repeal of the federal statutes in so far as they affected birth control had
also failed (the Cummins-Vaile Bill). Attacks were also made on State legislation.

and assistant arrested. They were later discharged and the clinic continued its work. Public opinion gradually began to favour birth control. The gynaecological section of the American Medical Association had passed a motion in 1925 recommending the altering of the law to allow physicians to give contraceptive advice: in 1931 the Federal Council of the Churches of Christ published a report favouring birth control: support also came from the American Neurological Association, the Eugenics Society and the Central Conference of Rabbis. In 1936 the Court of Appeals upheld a ruling of the District Court that contraceptives imported for a lawful purpose did not come within the restrictions of federal law.[1] In 1937 the American Medical Association unanimously agreed to accept birth control "as an integral part of medical practice and education".

Today birth control, the Roman Catholic and Orthodox Churches excepted, is generally approved in the United States. The courts have modified the operation of federal statutes and most State statutes have been liberally interpreted. Hundreds of different types of contraceptives are in use and contraception has become big business. In April 1958, Robert Sheehan estimated that the contraceptive trade in the United States grossed two hundred million dollars a year, no less than one hundred and fifty million being spent on condoms.[2] Despite this activity and considerable medical research, the ideal method of contraception still does not and probably cannot exist. Such a method should display five features: it should be wholly effective and reliable: harmless to users and to subsequent children: aesthetically acceptable: moderate in price: and unobjectionable on religious and moral grounds.

ENGLISH LAW

Traditionally, the law of England has followed the Prayer Book in recognizing the procreation of children as the primary purpose of marriage. Thus in an early nineteenth century case, Sir John Nicholl referred to the procreation of children as "the primary and most

---

[1] *United States v. One Package*, 86 F. 2d. 737 (2d. Cir., 1936).

[2] "The Birth Control Pill", *Fortune Magazine*, April 1958. Cf. *Fortune*, February 1938, for estimation of pre-war industry.

legitimate object of wedlock".[1] The continued operation of the doctrine was illustrated by a Court of Appeal case of 1946, where it was held that a man who had consistently refused to have intercourse without employing a contraceptive, against the wishes of his wife, had wilfully refused to consummate the marriage, thus entitling her to a decree of nullity.[2] "We are of opinion," said Lord Justice du Parcq, "that sexual intercourse cannot be said to be complete where a husband deliberately discontinues the act of intercourse before it has reached its natural termination or when he artificially prevents the natural termination, which is the passage of the male seed into the body of the woman. To hold otherwise would be to affirm that a marriage is consummated by an act so performed that one of the principle ends, if not the principal end, of marriage is intentionally frustrated."[3] Two years later, the House of Lords abandoned the principle.[4] "It is indisputable," said Lord Jowitt, with remarkable confidence, "that the institution of marriage generally is not necessary for the procreation of children; nor does it appear to be a principal end of marriage as understood in Christendom, which, as Lord Penzance said in *Hyde v. Hyde* (1866), L. R. 1 P. & D. 130, 133, 'may for this purpose be defined as the voluntary union of one man and one woman to the exclusion of all others'."[5] Accordingly a spouse has no right to a nullity decree at English law if the other spouse insists that intercourse shall only take place with the employment of a contraceptive.[6]

[1] *Brown v. Brown* (1828), 1 Hagg. Ecc. 523, p. 524. Cf. *G. v. M.* (1885), 10 A.C. 171, p. 204, per Lord Fitzgerald: "The procreation of children being the main object of marriage, the contract contains by implication, as an essential term, the capacity for consummation." See also *D. v. A.* (1845), 1 Rob. Ecc. 279, p. 298, per Dr Lushington.

[2] *Cowen v. Cowen* (1946), p. 36.

[3] Ibid. (1945), 2 All. E.R. 197, p. 199.

[4] *Baxter v. Baxter* (1948), A.C. 274. Refusal of a nullity decree to husband whose wife declined intercourse unless the husband took contraceptive precautions. He agreed under protest.

[5] N.B. Lord Penzance when defining marriage for *this purpose*, was referring not to procreation but to the effect of polygamous marriages.

[6] The effect of *Baxter v. Baxter* will largely depend on whether it is confined strictly to the category of "wilful refusal to consummate" as a ground for a nullity suit, or whether this type of consummation is accepted as valid in all matrimonial causes. Lord Jowitt's dictum on the purpose of Christian marriage has been much criticized. See *The Report of the Commission appointed by the*

As has been noted, contraceptive information was in the nine-teenth century classified as obscenity, and sale of contraceptives doubtless came within the common law offence of publishing obscene matter, but this is no longer the case. Books are no longer considered obscene if they advocate or describe methods of birth control. "It cannot be assumed," said the Home Secretary in answer to a question in the House of Commons in 1922, "that a court would hold a book to be obscene merely because it deals with the subject referred to."[1] Sale of contraceptives is not subject to common law or statutory restriction save for certain by-laws which restrict the sale of contra-ceptives from slot machines in public places.[2] Advertisements for contraceptives are not *per se* considered obscene. This lack of legal restraint is not surprising since it accords with prevailing English opinion on the subject, summed up by the Royal Commission on Population when it stated: "Control by men and women over the numbers of their children is one of the first conditions of their own and the community's welfare, and in our view mechanical and chemical methods of contraception have to be accepted as part of the modern means, however imperfect, by which it can be exercised."[3]

Under the National Health Service, however, advice on birth control can only be given in certain circumstances. The Ministry of Health allows contraceptive advice to be given in maternal and child welfare clinics to those married women for whom a pregnancy would be detrimental to health.[4] Many medical officers refer patients out-

---

Archbishops of Canterbury and York in 1949 to consider the Church and the Law of Nullity of Marriage (London, S.P.C.K. 1955). Insistence on the use of a contraceptive can be held to be cruelty so giving grounds for a divorce, see e.g. *Ward v. Ward* (1958) 2 All E.R. 17. Cf. *Rayden*, 7th edition, p. 121.

[1] St John-Stevas, op. cit., p. 70.

[2] The by-laws were suggested by the Home Secretary in a circular of October 22, 1949, after public controversy over sale of contraceptives from slot machines. He circulated a model by-law, suggesting this was the appropriate remedy since the practice was an evil only in some public places. For a discussion of what constitutes a *public place* see *The Justice of the Peace and Local Government Review* (January 7, 1950), 114:4.

[3] Cmd. 7695 (1949), para. 427. The Commission hoped that voluntary parent-hood would become universal (p. 430).

[4] Ministry of Health Memorandum 153, Birth Control, of 1930. Circular 1208 of 1931. Circular 1408 of 1934. Circular 1622 of 1937. Contraceptive advice is to be given only to (a) married women who, being expectant or nursing mothers, are attending welfare centres and for whom further pregnancy would

side this category to the voluntary birth control clinics which are found in many areas. Local authorities may themselves, with the approval of the Minister open contraceptive clinics and give advice to nursing mothers requiring it on medical grounds. They may also contribute to voluntary organizations providing such advice.[1] Many clinics of the Family Planning Association are conducted on the premises of the local authority or regional hospital boards.[2] General practitioners in the Service are not forbidden to provide contraceptive advice for their patients. They may not charge for advice given on medical grounds, but may do so when no medical reason exists for limitation of pregnancies.[3] Contraceptive appliances are not obtainable on National Health Service prescriptions, but if a patient needs them on medical grounds and cannot afford to pay for them, payment may be authorized by a local authority medical officer or hospital consultant. The Royal Commission on Population recommended that all restrictions on giving contraceptive advice to married women under public health services should be removed.[4] Public authorities, held the Commission, should not view the furnishing of advice as a concession, but as a positive duty. This accords with its expressed view that "public policy should assume and seek to encourage, the spread of voluntary parenthood".[5]

be detrimental to health: and (b) married women attending clinics for women suffering from gynaecological conditions for whom pregnancy would be detrimental to health, either because of some gynaecological condition or because of some other form of sickness, physical or mental, such as tuberculosis, heart disease, diabetes, chronic nephritis, etc.

[1] S. 22 of National Health Service Act, 9 & 10 Geo. 6, c. 81 (1945–6). Under s. 136 of the Local Government Act, 11 & 12 Geo. 6, c. 26, grants may be made by Local Authorities with the consent of the Minister to bodies giving services to residents in the area. These grants are not confined to medical cases. In the case of the Family Planning Association a special consent is necessary for each grant. In 1954, 76 Local Health Authorities made direct payments to the Family Planning Association, 122 referred cases to the Association, and 62 had their own clinics.

[2] In 1954 three-quarters of the F.P.A. clinics were held on Local Health Authority or Regional Hospital Board premises.

[3] See supplement to the *British Medical Journal*, November 6, 1954, p. 166.

[4] Paras. 536 and 667. The Report did not suggest giving advice to unmarried women but this recommendation was made in the P.E.P. study "Population Policy in Great Britain" (London 1948), p. 152. As early as April 28, 1926, the House of Lords had passed a motion introduced by Lord Buckmaster calling for the removal of restrictions on advice to married women.

[5] Paras. 434 and 657.

UNITED STATES LAW

A. FEDERAL LAW. Federal law restricts the distribution of contraceptives in several ways. Knowingly to deposit any contraceptive in the mails or to take such articles from the mails for the purpose of distribution is a felony under federal law.[1] The ban extends to any information as to where contraceptives may be obtained, and any written or printed matter telling "how or by what means conception may be prevented". A further federal felony is constituted by depositing contraceptives or information where they may be obtained with an express company or other common carrier. Books on contraception are not specifically mentioned, but obscene books are included in the ban. To import contraceptive articles or obscene books is also a felony and prohibited by federal statute.[2]

Read literally, these statutes impose an absolute and universal ban, and many attempts have been made to modify their scope by legislation. All have failed.[3] They have, however, been modified by judicial interpretation. A first step was taken in 1930, when Judge Swan stated that: "The intention to prevent a proper medical use of drugs or other articles merely because they are capable of illegal uses is not lightly to be ascribed to Congress."[4] Without deciding the point, he suggested that the Criminal Code should be interpreted as requiring an intent on the part of the sender that "the articles mailed or sent by common carrier be used for illegal contraception or abortion or for indecent or immoral uses". This reasoning was

[1] 18 U.S.C.A. 1461.
[2] 18 U.S.C.A. 1462 (transport and import). 19 U.S.C.A. 1305 (import). The penalties are fines of not more than $5,000 or not more than five years imprisonment or both, for a first offence; and fines of not more than $10,000 or ten years imprisonment, or both, for a second offence. The higher penalties also apply to customs officers who aid or abet such offences. (18 U.S.C.A. 552.)
[3] For full list see Alvah H. Sulloway, *Birth Control and Catholic Doctrine*, Boston 1959, p. 190 n. 20.
[4] *Young Rubber Corporation v. Lee*, 45 F. 2d. 103 (2d. Cir. 1930) p. 108. The case arose from an action for trade-mark infringement by a manufacturer of prophylactics, the defence being that redress was contrary to public policy since the federal statutes were being violated in carrying out the business. "We conclude," said Judge Swan, "therefore, that a manufacturer of drugs or instruments for medical use may in good faith sell them to druggists or other reputable dealers in medical supplies, or to jobbers for distribution to such trade", at p. 109.

applied in *Davis v. United States* (1933), when an intent to use the articles for illegal purposes was held necessary for a conviction under the postal and transport statutes.[1] The decision permitted manufacturers of contraceptives and others in the trade to dispatch their wares to druggists, jobbers, and physicians. These decisions led logically to that of *United States v. One Package* in 1936, when Dr Hannah Stone was allowed to import a package of vaginal pessaries into the United States.[2] Judge Augustus Hand conceded that the Tariff Act of 1930 exempted only those articles excepted by the Comstock Act of 1873, but went on to say that the court was satisfied "that this statute as well as all the Acts we have referred to, embraced only such articles as Congress would have denounced as immoral it if had understood all the conditions under which they were to be used. Its design, in our opinion, was not to prevent the importation, sale, or carriage by mail of things which might intelligently be employed by conscientious and competent physicians for the purpose of saving life or promoting the well being of their patients".[3] Judge Learned Hand was clearly uneasy about these verbal gymnastics, but contented himself with observing that people had changed their minds about such matters in recent years, and concurred in the judgment.

Books on contraception are specifically banned from the mails by the postal statute, but the section restricting imports mentions only "obscene" books. It is now established that a book on contraception is not *per se* considered obscene by the federal courts.[4] Dismissing a charge against "Contraception" by Marie Stopes in 1931, Judge Woolsey stated: "It is a scientific book written with obvious seriousness and with great decency, and it gives information to the medical profession regarding the operation of birth control clinics and the

---

[1] 62 F. 2d. 473 (6th Cir. 1933). Two charges were involved: (*a*) mailing circulars on contraception contrary to 18 U.S.C.A. 334, and (*b*) transporting articles for preventing conception contrary to 18 U.S.C.A. 396.

[2] 86 F. 2d. 737 (2d Cir. 1936).

[3] P. 739. Judge Augustus Hand stressed that all the federal statutes should be interpreted by a common standard since they were intended to constitute a single moral code.

[4] For a first suggestion of this see *United States v. Dennett* (2d. Cir. 39 F. 2d. 564 1930). See also *United States v. One Obscene Book Entitled, Married Love*, 48 F. 2d. 821 (S.D.N.Y. 1931), where the book, by Marie Stopes, was declared admissible at any port in the United States.

instruction necessary to be given at such clinics to women who resort thereto." Such a book, he held, was not obscene, "for the reading of it would not stir the sex impulses of any person with a normal mind".[1]

The federal statutes are accordingly by no means dead letters, but contraceptives intended for *bona fide* medical use, for the treatment or prevention of disease, and contraceptive books and pamphlets which are not written in obscene language, may be freely imported, transported and mailed. In practice this means that contraceptives must be going to or coming from doctors or other professional persons, or anyone acting at their direction or under their supervision. Druggists, jobbers and dealers, provided they are legitimate traders, thus enjoy immunity. This rule applies to contraceptive books and pamphlets going through the mails, but not to the importation of such books, or to their transport in inter-state commerce.[2] Under the customs law, only obscene books are excluded, and, as has been noted, *bona fide* contraceptive manuals are not any longer within this category. To secure a conviction under the statutes an intention to use the materials illegally must be established by the prosecution. However, for administrative purposes, consignments may be stopped by the authorities temporarily, pending the production of *prima facie* evidence by the addressee that he is a privileged recipient. The Family Planning Association makes it a practice to consign contra-

---

[1] *United States v. One Book Entitled "Contraception"*, 51 F. 2d. 525 (S.D.N.Y. 1931), pp. 527–8. See also *United States v. Nicholas*, 97 F. 2d. 510 (2d. cir. 1938). A book for Nicholas and some magazines for Himes coming from abroad through the mails were seized under the Tariff Act. "We have twice decided," said Judge Learned Hand, "that contraceptive articles may have lawful uses and that statutes prohibiting them should be read as forbidding them only when unlawfully employed. . . . Contraceptive books and articles are of the same class and those at bar were therefore lawful in the hands of those who would not abuse the information they contained", p. 512. The magazines were sent on to Himes as editor and therefore an appropriate person to receive them. The book was detained in the post office pending an application by the addressee. "Only the addressee can prove whether he is among the privileged classes: he ought at least to go forward with the evidence, even if the burden of proof is not eventually on him." Judge Learned Hand, p. 512.

[2] U.S.C.A. 18, 1462, the section dealing with inter-state transportation, and import, does not ban books on contraception as such, but only those "giving information directly or indirectly where or how they [contraceptives] may be obtained or made".

ceptives and information under a doctor's signature, and thus obviate vexatious delays. Private persons, importing, mailing or transporting contraceptives, purely for the purpose of preventing conception, with no medical indication for their employment, would still, at least theoretically, be caught by the statutes.[1]

B. THE LAW OF THE STATES. Of the fifty American States, twenty and the District of Columbia have no legislation on the subject of contraception.[2] Seventeen States prohibit traffic in contraceptives, but exempt doctors, pharmacists, or others operating under special licence, from the statutory prohibition. Five States, Connecticut, Kansas, Massachusetts, Mississippi and Nebraska, prohibit the sale of contraceptives and advertising. The statutes make no exceptions.[3] Eight States have no law against contraceptives but restrict or prohibit their advertisement. In all, thirty States prohibit such advertising, fifteen making an exception for medical journals and textbooks, etc. Sixteen States regulate the trade by requiring contraceptive information to be accurate and prohibiting the sale of articles which do not comply with certain defined standards.[4] In some States, sale of contraceptives from slot machines is forbidden.[5]

In New York, Connecticut, and Massachusetts, considerable litigation has taken place to interpret the birth control statutes.

New York. New York law prohibits distribution of contraceptives and birth control information, but contains the following proviso: "An article or instrument, used or applied by physicians lawfully practising, or by their direction or prescription, for the cure or prevention of disease is not an article of indecent or immoral nature or use, within this article. The supplying of such articles to such physicians or by their direction or prescription, is not an offence under this article."[6] In 1917, Margaret Sanger was sentenced to thirty days imprisonment for violating the statute. Her appeal was

---

[1] Such persons could import or transport contraceptive books, provided they did not violate the provision in footnote 1, p. 62, but presumably could not mail them except subject to the restrictions on mailing contraceptives.

[2] For a table of laws in the various States, see Appendix I.

[3] These prohibitions, although absolute in form and theory are not absolute in practice, see pp. 67–9.

[4] E.g. Oregon (*Revised Statutes*, 1957) 435.090: Idaho (*Laws* 1948) 39.806.

[5] E.g. Wisconsin (*Statutes*, 1955) 115.15.

[6] (*Consolidated Laws*, 1944) 106.1145.

dismissed, but the judge gave a liberal interpretation of the section. It protected, said the court, the physician who "in good faith gives such help or advice to a married person to cure or prevent disease". "Disease" was not limited to venereal disease, but defined as "an alteration in the state of the body, or some of its organs, interrupting or disturbing the performance of the vital functions, and causing or threatening pain and sickness; illness; sickness; disorder".[1]

Connecticut. The Connecticut law forbidding birth control dates from 1879, when it was dealt with as part of the obscenity statute, but since 1887 it has been a separate enactment. "Any person who shall use any drug, medicinal article or instrument for the purpose of preventing conception, shall be fined not less than fifty dollars or imprisoned not less than sixty days nor more than one year or be both fined and imprisoned."[2] The statute is unique in that it prohibits not merely the sale but the use of a contraceptive. In 1940, two physicians and a nurse, indicted for counselling a married woman to use a contraceptive, contended that the statute was unconstitutional, unless it was interpreted to except the medical profession. The Supreme Court of Errors rejected this argument, which had been accepted by the lower court, and upheld the statute.[3] The court confined its decision to situations where the "general health" of the woman would be endangered by lack of contraception, and left open the question whether an exception existed where "pregnancy would jeopardize life". This loophole was closed in 1942. In that year, a doctor sought a ruling whether the statute would apply where pregnancy would entail specific dangers to health because of high blood pressure, tuberculosis, or three pregnancies within twenty-seven months. The court held (3–2) that it did apply, and that abstention in such predicaments must have been considered

---

[1] *People v. Sanger*, 222 N.Y. 192: 194–5, 118 N.E. (1918) 637. In *People v. Byrne*, 163 N.Y.S. 680 (1916), the statute had been held constitutional. "Nor is it to be doubted, in my opinion that the legislature has the power to declare that articles should not be used to prevent conception by married women, except in cases where attending physicians believe that pregnancy would be dangerous to the health of the woman." Judge Crosprey.

[2] (*Statutes*, 1958) 53–32. Also 54–196: "Any person who shall assist, abet, counsel, cause, hire or command another to commit any offence may be prosecuted and punished as if he were the principal offender."

[3] *State v. Nelson*, 126 Conn. 412, 11 A. 2d. 856 (1940). Decision taken 3–2.

by the legislature as an alternative to the use of contraceptives, when passing the statute.[1] Various attempts have been made to modify the law, but all have failed.[2]

Massachusetts. Publication of any printed matter containing birth control information and distribution of instruments and articles for preventing conception are prohibited by a statute dating from 1879.[3] The statute was upheld as constitutional and applied in 1917, when certain pamphlets containing birth control information were held to be obscene.[4] In 1938 the courts rejected a plea that physicians were exempt from the operation of the statute when prescribing for health reasons.[5] In 1940, however, it was held that the distribution of prophylactics, which could also be used for contraception, did not come within the statute, unless it could be proved that the distributor intended to prevent conception rather than venereal disease, or knew that such unlawful use was intended by the buyer.[6] As in Connecticut, unsuccessful attempts have been made to modify the law. In 1930 a Bill was introduced to give licensed physicians the right to provide information to married couples, but was later withdrawn. The following year a petition for change was signed by 7,000 laymen, 1,300 doctors, and 400 ministers of religion, but failed to be implemented. An amendment to the same effect was defeated in the House of Representatives in 1941 by

[1] *Tileston v. Ullman*, 129 Conn. 84, 26 A. 2d. 582 (1942). An appeal was taken to the Supreme Court of the U.S. and dismissed, the physician being held to lack standing to raise a constitutional issue. *Tileston v. Ullman*, 318 U.S. 44 (1943).

[2] E.g. 1923, 1925, 1927, 1929, 1935, 1954–7. The Bills either repealed the law or inserted an exception for doctors when counselling married women for health reasons. Although sometimes passed in the House, all were defeated in the Senate.

[3] *Annotated Laws*, 1956, 272: 20 & 21. Whether information on the *safe period* would be construed as "contraceptive advice" is dubious. In 1934 the Customs allowed Mrs Hazel Moore to import a book on rhythm but seized others on artificial contraception. Sulloway, op. cit., p. 29.

[4] *Cw. v. Allison*, 227 Mass. 57, 116 N.E. 265 (1917).

[5] *Cw. v. Gardner*, 300 Mass. 372, 15 N.E. 2d. 222 (1938). An appeal to the U.S. Supreme Court was dismissed *per curiam* "for want of a substantial federal question". *Gardner v. Mass.* 305 U.S. 559 (1938).

[6] *Cw. v. Corbett*, 307 Mass. 7, 29 N.E. 2d. 151 (1940). *Cw. v. Werlinsky*, 307 Mass. 608, 29 N.E. 2d. 150 (1940).

133 votes to seventy-seven, and in the Senate by eighteen votes to sixteen. Referendums in 1942 and 1948 also failed to alter the law.[1]

The Constitutional Question

It has been suggested that the federal and State statutes regulating birth control are unconstitutional, in that they deny the individual his personal right to pursuit of happiness and also take away the rights protected by the due process clause of the fourteenth amendment.[2] Physicians, when the laws are strictly interpreted, are also denied a fundamental right to advise patients on professional matters involving life and health. The courts have taken an opposite view. The federal courts have upheld the federal statutes as constitutional, with an exemption for physicians and others professionally qualified.[3] Prohibition of the sale or advertising of contraceptives or the dissemination of information on birth control has consistently been held to be within the police power of individual States.[4] Until 1938, none of the cases had included a qualified physician as party to the proceedings, or else the statute under review contained a clause exempting physicians from its operation. In that year, however, in

---

[1] Both referendums concerned an act "to allow physicians to provide medical contraceptive care to married persons for the protection of life or health". 1,179,023 votes were cast in 1942, the proposal being defeated by 683,059 votes to 495,964. 247,697 blanks were cast. In 1948, the proposal was defeated by 1,085,350 votes to 806,829, with 263,168 blanks.

[2] See Dudley D. Miles, "The Constitutionality of Anti-Birth Control Legislation", *Wyoming Law Journal*: 138–42 (1952–3). Also H. Kalven, "A Special Corner of Civil Liberties", *New York University Law Review*, 31:1223–1229 (1956), "Despite the lack of judicial success to date it would seem that the freedom of sex relations within marriage and the freedom to have children when wanted rank high among the basic personal liberties in our society and their curtailment presents a serious civil liberties issue", pp. 1228–9.

[3] See pp. 62–4.

[4] That the police power may be exercised to protect public morals, health and safety is firmly established. See e.g. *Peterson v. Widule*, 157 Wis. 641, 147 N.W. 966 (1914) (physical examination required for issue of marriage licence): *Zucht v. King*, 260 U.S. 174, 43 Sup. Crt. 24, 67 L.ed. 194 (1922) (vaccination case). For cases on birth control, see *Byrne, Allison, Sanger, Nelson, Tileston, Corbett*, discussed olim. See also *McConnell v. Knoxville*, 110 S.W. (2d.) 478 (Tenn. 1937): *State v. Arnold*, 217 Wis. 340, 258 N.W. 843 (1935); *Barretta v. Barretta*, 182 Misc. 852, 46 N.Y.S. 2d. 261 (1944). See also L.F.Jr., "Constitutional Law, Police Power, Birth Control and Contraceptives", *George Washington Law Review*, 7:255–7 (December 1938).

Gardner's case, a statute imposing an unconditional ban was upheld by the Massachusetts courts, and an appeal to the United States Supreme Court dismissed. In June 1958 five suits were filed in the Connecticut Superior Court challenging the constitutionality of the birth control legislation.[1]

An attack on the birth control statutes may develop in the future on rather different grounds. While the police power may be exercised to protect public morals, it must be reasonable.[2] With the general acceptance of birth control as a normal part of married life, the statutes might be held unreasonable at some point in the future. The statutes could also be challenged for violating the separation of Church and State guaranteed by the first amendment. Recent theological developments have left the Roman Catholic and Orthodox Churches practically isolated amongst Christian denominations in condemning artificial birth control. It could, then, be contended, that the birth control statutes enforce the doctrine of particular denominations at the expense of that of other religious communions. Alternatively, it might be argued that the statutes limit religious freedom.[3]

Effectiveness of Laws

The effect in practice of the federal laws has already been described.[4] The effect of the State laws varies in different areas. In the seventeen States which exempt doctors and other qualified persons from the operation of the laws, their effect is negligible. Birth control clinics are free to operate, provided they are in charge of someone medically

---

[1] In May 1959 a county judge declared New Jersey's statute, banning the sale and distribution of contraceptives "without just cause", unconstitutional. He maintained that it was so vague and indefinite that it would not fairly inform a defendant "of the elements constituting a quasi-criminal infraction". See *New York Times*, May 13, 1959, p. 27.

[2] See *Plessy v. Ferguson*, 163 U.S. 537; 16 Sup. Crt. 1138; 41 L.ed. 256 (1896).

[3] This point has been raised in Connecticut. On May 4, 1959, three Protestant ministers, an Episcopalian, a Lutheran, and a Methodist, asked the Superior Court for a ruling on the Connecticut statute. The ministers claimed that the law prohibiting dissemination of birth control advice deprived them of their "liberty, freedom of speech and right to freely practice their religions". They stated they were "bound by the teachings of the church and their own religious beliefs to counsel married parishioners on the use of contraceptive devices and to advise them and to counsel to use same and to give such advice in pre-marital counselling". *The New York Times*, May 6, 1959.

[4] See pp. 62–3.

qualified, and contraceptives are freely purchasable at drugstores and elsewhere. In the five States that theoretically ban all sale of contraceptives, the law has practical effects only in Connecticut and Massachusetts.[1] There are no birth control clinics in Connecticut, although the Planned Parenthood League of Connecticut has an office in New Haven. A number of medically supervised clinics were opened in 1935, but in 1939 these were raided and after the decision of the Supreme Court in 1940 (*State v. Nelson*), all were closed and have not been re-opened since. Doctors are officially barred from prescribing birth control appliances for patients, but, as has been noted: "It is common knowledge that this statute is being violated daily, except perhaps by a few high-minded doctors."[2] Certain contraceptives may even be legitimately prescribed if they have other than contraceptive uses.[3] Contraceptives, creams and jellies are sold everywhere, and condoms may be obtained at drugstores and even from slot machines. Supplies are sent to doctors and patients by mail and literature on contraception is sold openly on bookstalls.[4]

Like Connecticut, Massachusetts has no birth control clinics. From 1932–7 clinics were opened in various cities, but as a result of the Gardner case in 1938, they were closed and have not been re-opened. Thousands of doctors, in the privacy of their offices, fit and prescribe diaphragms.[5] Condoms may legally be sold when marked "for prevention of disease" and diaphragms are sold by drugstores using devious methods of prescription. Vaginal creams and jellies are also sold, marked "for feminine hygiene". The Planned Parent-

---

[1] In Mississippi, despite the law, contraceptive advice is offered as part of the public maternal health services. In Nebraska, the law while forbidding the trade, also regulates it by laying down minimum standards for prophylactics. See *Statutes*, 1943: 71–1106.

[2] *Boston University Law Review* 23:117 (1943).

[3] See letter from the Connecticut Commissioner for Food and Drugs to the Secretary of the Bridgeport Pharmaceutical Association, dated September 15, 1954: "Since diaphragms have such therapeutic and other uses there is no reason why vaginal diaphragms may not be prescribed or ordered by a physician and such order filled by a pharmacist. We have always taken the stand that a pharmacist is entirely within his rights to fill any prescription or order from a physician. Such order may be given orally or in writing."

[4] The prohibition of the "use" of contraceptives has of course never been enforceable.

[5] Letter of October 29, 1958, from the Executive Secretary of the Planned Parenthood League of Massachusetts to Norman St John-Stevas.

hood League refers women to out-of-State clinics, and is able to tell
them orally of certain new and simple contraceptives. "I am not too
concerned," concludes Judge Ploscowe, "about this failure of Massachusetts and Connecticut to permit the dissemination of contraceptive information. The corner drugstore is always available for
the purchase of prophylactic devices which are used mainly for
contraceptive purposes. If more is desired, then the doctors in
neighbouring States are available for consultation."[1] This judgment
is not shared by the Planned Parenthood Leagues, who point out that
whereas women who can afford a private consultation with a doctor,
may obtain contraceptive care, poorer women cannot; that the law
makes the less efficient types of contraceptive available but outlaws
the more effective; and that the poor who depend on public clinics
for medical advice are kept ignorant of the subject, many of them
being unaware that contraceptives can be obtained at drugstores,
provided they are purchased as prophylactics.

CONTRACEPTION: EXTENT IN ENGLAND
AND THE UNITED STATES

Birth control is widely practised in England amongst all classes. In
June 1956, the Family Planning Association had 181 branches,
operating 215 clinics, all offering advice on contraceptive techniques.
In the previous year, 250,000 people had visited the clinics. The
Royal Commission on Population estimated that whereas only 15
per cent of couples married before 1910 used birth control, for those
married between 1940 and 1947, the proportion had risen to 55 per
cent. The commission estimated that in this group the proportion
would ultimately exceed 70 per cent.[2] The result has been a heavy fall

---

[1] "Contraception" by Morris Ploscowe, Symposium on Morals, Medicine and
the Law, *New York University Law Review*, 31: at 1241 (1956). Cf. the conclusion of the American Medical Association. "The Committee has been unable to
find evidence that existing laws, federal or State, have interfered with any
medical advice which a physician has been called on to furnish to his patients.
Clarification of such laws, however, is desirable." Report of the Committee to
Study Contraceptive Practices and Related Problems, appointed by the Board of
Trustees of the American Medical Association, *Journal of the A.M.A.*, 108:2217
(1937). This judgment might now be revised.

[2] *Papers of Royal Commission on Population*. Vol. I. Family Limitation and
its influence on human fertility during the past fifty years, pp. 7–8.

in the number of births. In the period 1931–41 there were three million fewer births than in that from 1871–81, the marriage rate remaining stable. The Commission found no evidence of a decline in reproductive capacity and attributed the change to "the spread of deliberate family limitation".[1]

In the United States, birth control is equally widespread.[2] Planned Parenthood Centres are found in twenty-eight States and the District of Columbia, and throughout the country, save in Connecticut and Massachusetts, medical birth control care is provided by 594 maternal health clinics and other child-spacing information centres. In 1942, 60 per cent of the approved medical colleges provided some instruction in contraceptive techniques.[3] The American Medical Association has recommended that medical students should be "taught the clinical considerations and therapeutic application of contraceptive methods".[4] In 1955 a national survey on family planning was carried out by a group of social scientists.[5] 2,713 white wives, in all their childbearing years (18–39), were interviewed, as a sample of the 17,000,000 women of this group in the United States. Asked whether they approved of family limitation in any form, including the safe period, only 5 per cent gave a negative answer. 73 per cent of those questioned gave family planning approval, whatever the method employed. 83 per cent of the fecund couples interviewed had adopted some means of birth control, and 7 per cent planned to

---

[1] Paras. 617 and 619. *The Report of the Royal Commission on Population.* Cmd. 7695 (London 1949).

[2] Dr Rock estimates that 90 per cent of the married population in the United States uses some method of birth control, including the safe period and *coitus interruptus*. John Rock, "The Scientific Case against Rigid Legal Restrictions on Medical Birth Control Advice", *Clinics*, 1:1598 (April 1943).

[3] A. Stone. "The Teaching of Contraception in Medical Schools", *Human Fertility*, 7:108 (August 1942).

[4] See Report of Committee, 108, *Journal of the American Medical Association* 2217 (1937). At its annual meeting (1959) the American Public Health Association issued a policy resolution on family planning stating that public and private programmes concerned with population growth and family size should be integral parts of the health programme and should include medical advice and services "which are acceptable to the individuals concerned".

[5] Conducted by the Scripps Foundation and Survey Research Centre of the University of Michigan. Results published in *Family Planning, Sterility and Population Growth* (New York 1959), and also in an article "Family Planning in the United States", by Ronald F. Freedman, Pascal K. Whelpton and Arthur A. Campbell, *Scientific American*, 200:50 (April 1959).

do so after they had had the one or more children they wanted. The general consensus on the ideal size of family was not less than two children and not more than four. In seven States, birth control services are made available through State or county maternal health clinics.[1] North Carolina was the first State to take this step in 1937. South Carolina followed suit in 1939, and Alabama in 1940.

CHRISTIAN OPINION—OTHER THAN ROMAN CATHOLIC

Outside the Roman Catholic and Orthodox Churches, Christian opinion on contraception has undergone a profound change. Until the end of the nineteenth century, contraception was condemned by all Christian denominations as immoral or unnatural and contrary to divine law. Today the Roman Catholic and Orthodox Churches are practically alone in adhering to this position.[2] By contraception, is meant artificial methods of birth control, since the Catholic Church is in agreement with other Churches that families should be planned, but limits the methods employed to abstention[3] or use of the safe period. "To produce children without regard to consequences," states an authoritative Anglican Committee, "is to use procreative power irresponsibly, the more so when there is involved the imposition of one partner's will upon the other."[4] Similar judgments

[1] North Carolina, South Carolina, Alabama, Florida, Georgia, Mississippi and Virginia. All are Southern States where the Roman Catholic population is small and uninfluential. In 1942 a memorandum was sent out over the Surgeon General's signature from the Federal Security Agency to officers and employees of the United States Public Health Service. This stated that State proposals for child-spacing programmes should be given "the same consideration" as any other health programme proposal and added: "Federal Funds allotted to the States under the provisions of Title VI of the Social Security Act, and the Venereal Disease Act may be used for the purpose of carrying on planned parenthood programmes by State and local health departments."

[2] See letter of the hierarchy of the Church of Greece of October 1937 signed by Archbishop Chrysostom and 55 metropolitans condemning both abortion and contraception. See *The Problem of Child Birth*, Athens 1947. Cf. a statement of the late Archbishop Michael (of America) condemning contraception (1956). See R. M. Fagley, *The Population Explosion and Christian Responsibility*, p. 166.

[3] Abstinence is used for spacing children in a number of African societies where a taboo operates against sexual intercourse while a woman is nursing a child.

[4] The Family in Contemporary Society, London 1958, p. 15.

have been passed by Protestant leaders. Thus, Dr Gustafson, President of the New York Conference of the Augustana Lutheran Church, recently declared: "An unrestrained production of children without realistic regard to God-given responsibilities involved in bringing them up in the discipline and instruction of the Lord may be as sinful and as selfish an indulgence of the lusts of the flesh as is the complete avoidance of parenthood."[1]

The changes in the Church of England attitude to contraception are interesting to trace. The first Anglican position was a clearcut condemnation of contraception as a threat to both Church and State. The Lambeth Conference of 1920 issued a solemn warning against "the use of unnatural means for the avoidance of conception", and stressed that the primary purpose of marriage was the procreation of children.[2] This judgment was echoed by the House of Bishops of the Protestant Episcopal Church, meeting at Portland, Oregon, on September 15, 1922.[3] The Lambeth Conference of 1930 again declared that the primary purpose of marriage was the procreation of children, but conceded that in certain limited circumstances, contraception might be morally legitimate.[4] In a resolution, passed by 193 votes to 67, the Conference declared: "Where there is a clearly

---

[1] *The New York Times*, Friday, July 25, 1958.

[2] The first Lambeth Conference met in 1867. Its resolutions are not theologically binding but are taken to express the mind of the Anglican Church. The 1908 Conference, like its successor of 1920, condemned contraception. The resolution of 1920, No. 68, reads: "The Conference, while declining to lay down rules which will meet the needs of every abnormal case, regards with grave concern the spread in modern society of theories and practices hostile to the family. We utter an emphatic warning against the use of unnatural means for the avoidance of conception, together with the grave dangers—physical, moral, and religious— thereby incurred, and against the evils with which the extension of such use threatens the race. In opposition to the teaching which, under the name of science and religion encourages married people in the deliberate cultivation of sexual union as an end in itself, we steadfastly uphold what must always be regarded as the governing considerations of Christian marriage. One is the primary purpose for which marriage exists, namely the continuance of the race through the gift and heritage of children; the other is the paramount importance in married life of deliberate and thoughtful self-control." Resolution 70 called for a campaign against the open or secret sale of contraceptives. See *The Lambeth Conferences 1867–1930*, London 1948.

[3] See Margaret Sanger, *My Fight for Birth Control*, New York 1931, p. 202.

[4] Resolution 13 on purpose of marriage; resolution 15 on contraception. *The Lambeth Conferences 1867–1930*.

felt moral obligation to limit or avoid parenthood, the method must be decided on Christian principles. The primary and obvious method is complete abstinence from intercourse (as far as may be necessary) in a life of discipline and self-control lived in the power of the Holy Spirit. Nevertheless, in those cases where there is such a clearly-felt moral obligation to limit or avoid parenthood, and where there is a morally sound reason for avoiding complete abstinence, the Conference agrees that other methods may be used, provided that this is done in the light of the same Christian principles. The Conference records its strong condemnation of the use of any methods of conception-control from motives of selfishness, luxury, or mere convenience."[1] In 1958, the Lambeth Conference gave unanimous approval to contraception, passing a resolution in the following terms: "The Conference believes that the responsibility for deciding upon the number and frequency of children has been laid by God upon the consciences of parents everywhere: that this planning, in such ways as are mutually acceptable to husband and wife in Christian conscience, is a right and important factor in Christian family life and should be the result of positive choice before God. Such responsible parenthood, built on obedience to all the duties of marriage, requires a wise stewardship of the resources and abilities of the family as well as a thoughtful consideration of the varying population needs and problems of society and the claims of future generations."[2]

[1] In the Report accompanying the resolutions, "The Life and Witness of the Christian Community", it is pointed out that contraception is not condemned in the New Testament, nor by any ecumenical council of the Church. The Protestant Episcopal Church again followed the lead of Lambeth. On October 9, 1934, the Bishops passed a resolution 44–38 approving "the efforts now being made to secure for licensed physicians, hospitals and medical clinics, freedom to convey such information [on birth control] as is in accord with the highest principles of eugenics and a more wholesome family life wherein parenthood may be undertaken with due respect for the health of the mother and the welfare of the child". See *Journal of Social Psychology*, 8:229 (May 1936).

[2] *The Lambeth Conference* 1958, London 1958. Resolution 115. Cf. The Report on "Responsible Parenthood and the Population Problem", the conclusions of a study group appointed by the World Council of Churches which met at Mansfield College Oxford, April 12–15, 1959. The twenty-one members were drawn from the main confessions represented on the World Council. With the exception of the Orthodox members, they reached similar conclusions to the Lambeth Conference on the use of contraceptives. *The Ecumenical Review*, 12:85–92 (October 1959).

The change in attitude from 1920 to 1958 was brought about partly by social changes. In 1920 there was widespread fear of under-population, while in 1958 prospects of overpopulation aroused anxiety, especially in India, Africa and the West Indies, all strongly represented at the Conference. A second factor affecting the decision was the modern development of knowledge of the safe period, showing that nature provided her own method of birth control. A third influence was the theological development of the doctrine of Christian marriage which had taken place since 1920. The Confer-ence of that year had been unequivocal in stressing procreation as the primary purpose of marriage, and this had been repeated in 1930. The 1958 Conference, on the other hand, did not stress the re-productive end of marriage in this way. Biblical revelation, it was agreed, did not limit the function of sexuality and the family to the reproductive process, but stressed equally the companionate purpose of marriage. These two ends are not separable in importance, "are not subordinated one to the other; they are not directly related to one another; their relationship, in the developing experience of Israel, is to be found in yet a third area—that of the place of the family in giving responsible security to the children born of the love of husband and wife."[1] Procreation of children and the promotion of the mutual love of the spouses are thus accepted as co-equal ends. A parallel development in Anglican theology has been the increasing stress on "henosis", the union of man and wife in one flesh, that takes place within the marriage relationship.[2] Christ himself stressed this aspect of marriage, and St Paul developed the doctrine.[3] The act of *coitus*, far from being a merely physiological device to perpetuate the race, has a quasi-sacramental character, of the highest importance in developing the personal and spiritual life of the married couple. Traditional theology is inadequate in stressing the procreative purpose of marriage and underestimating the intrinsic importance of the sexual act. Some writers have gone so far as to suggest it is *henosis* that is primary in marriage and not procreation. Thus Canon Warner writes: "The unitive achievement of sexual intercourse pre-

---

[1] *The Lambeth Conference* 1958, 2:143.

[2] See for example, D. S. Bailey, *The Mystery of Love and Marriage*, London 1952.

[3] *Matthew* xix, 6. St. Paul. *Ephesians* v, 23–33.

cedes procreation and is primary in time sequence as well as in its inner constitutive nature as *object*."[1] He adds that the traditional doctrine is right in the sense that procreation must not be totally excluded from marriage, but it is not the primary end of every act of *coitus*, nor is it its object.[2]

Given that the ends of marriage are co-equal, may the parties separate them at will or are they restricted for separation to the periods of natural infertility? Anglican theologians have given different answers to the question, but the consensus of opinion appears to be that at least in certain circumstances the use of contraceptives is legitimate. Contraception may be a positive good. It extends man's rational control over his own nature, the children born are desired and welcomed, and sexual intercourse can be regulated according to the needs of a personal relationship and not controlled by decisions about the desirability of conception. But may the couple manipulate natural processes at their own will? If one regards the biological pattern as something "given", which a couple are required by God to submit themselves to in order to receive the blessings of matrimonial union, the answer will be negative. Man may use his reason to fulfill the biological pattern more completely but not to supersede it. *Coitus* accompanied by the use of a contraceptive is ontologically and morally distinct from *coitus* without such a device. If, on the other hand, one regards *coitus* as a purely spatio-temporal event without metaphysical implications, then contraceptives may be freely employed.

With these considerations in mind, the anonymous contributor of the first of three articles on contraception in the authoritative

[1] "Theological Issues of Contraception", *Theology*, 57:8–14, p. 11 (January 1954). Canon Warner means by *object*, "that at which the action aims and in which it naturally results, and with the attainment, of which it is completed". R. C. Mortimer, *Elements of Moral Theology*, p. 63. Procreation is thus the possible result of *coitus* but is not its object. "We are left, then, with the act of *coitus*, which in its natural functioning has one 'object' in uniting (or deepening the union of) man and woman, and an *occasional* end (among others) of fertilizing the ovum."

[2] The reason for this is that the act of procreation is necessarily associated with the act of union in the natural order. The writer seeks to save himself from inconsistency by invoking the natural order at this point by stressing that the use of contraceptives must not be judged in relation to isolated acts of intercourse, but in the context of actual or prospective family life,

Anglican publication, *The Family in Contemporary Society*, concludes that the Church should not give its approval to contraception
as a positive good. "It is, to say the least," he observes, "suspicious
that the age in which contraception has won its way is not one which
has been conspicuously successful in managing its sexual life. Is it
possible that, by claiming the right to manipulate his physical processes in this matter, man may, without knowing or intending it,
be stepping over the boundary between the world of Christian
marriage and what one may call the world of Aphrodite—the world
of sterile eroticism against which the Church reacted so strongly
(perhaps too strongly) in its early days? For one of the characteristics of the latter world was (and is) the exercise of unlimited self-
determination in sexual activity."[1] Despite this condemnation in
general, the writer points out that it is possible to conclude that
contraceptives may be used in particular circumstances, for although
the act will be ontologically distinct, it may be morally equivalent,
as the best symbol of love and union available in the circumstances.
The justifying circumstances are not specified.

The second contributor concludes that contraception may be used
legitimately as a normal part of married life.[2] It represents a responsible use of human freedom in the interests of personal relationship or
the needs of the community as a whole. The conclusion is identical
with that in Canon Warner's article, where he writes: "In general it
is morally legitimate to use a material agent in order to forward the
well-being of man in his personal relations in society, e.g. wearing
glasses or deaf aid. If on moral grounds the unitive object of an act
of *coitus* must be achieved without involving the procreative end,
then there is nothing in principle wrong in using a material agent,
for that agent is forwarding the personal relational factor essential for
marriage, and good marriages are essential for society and the welfare
of children."[3] Both these latter theologians reject the view that the

---

[1] (London S.P.C.K. 1958) p. 135. The first contribution is found at pp. 132–7.
[2] Ibid., pp. 137–47.
[3] Op. cit., p. 12. Canon Warner concludes that complete abstention is morally
wrong, as is the exclusive use of the safe period. *Coitus interruptus* and *reservatus*
are neither procreative nor unitive in the full sense and must therefore be condemned. The use of a condom is illegitimate as it impairs "unitive orgasm".
Diaphragms and suppositories are legitimate. On oral contraceptives he writes:
"We have here an interference with the actual function of an organ (the ovary),

spiritual effects of *coitus* are dependant on its conforming to certain empirical physiological features. But what then is the criterion by which the morality of physical sexual acts between man and woman is to be judged? The conclusion is ineluctable that there is no objective criterion, but that the rightness or wrongness of using contraceptives will depend on the integrity of the parties' assessment of the circumstances and the purity of their motives. How, then, one may legitimately ask, is one to distinguish between use of a contraceptive and other sexual actions, such as sodomy, which have a relational value but which are condemned by Christian moralists? Perhaps it might be answered that whereas the use of a contraceptive preserves the physical structure of the act, a perversion such as sodomy destroys it altogether, but this is not wholly convincing. At any rate, neither of the writers disposes of the difficulty.

The theologians, whose views have just been described, criticize the terms of traditional moral theology, and question their applicability at the present time, but they adopt them in modified form for their own use. They are writing within the Catholic tradition. Other contemporary theologians have considered the problem from the Protestant viewpoint. Reinhold Niebuhr has not dealt with the subject at great length, but he indicated his views briefly in the course of the first series of Gifford lectures for 1939.[1] "The prohibition of birth control," he said, "assumes that the sexual function in human life must be limited to its function in nature, that of procreation. But it is the very character of human life that all animal functions are touched by freedom and released into more complex relationships. This freedom is the basis of both creativity and sin." Dr Niebuhr, while drawing no immediate concrete conclusions, asserts the transcendence of the personal and rational over the purely biological, while taking the latter into account. It would thus seem that given certain circumstances man may morally use contraceptives in sexual intercourse.[2] What those circumstances are,

by which the biological processes are prevented from achieving their 'object', " p. 14. Their use is not justified if a contraceptive is available which does not radically inhibit a physiological function.

[1] *The Nature and Destiny of Man*, New York 1949, pp. 281–2.

[2] Cf. Joseph Fletcher: "With the medical technology of contraception, parenthood and birth control become matters of moral responsibility, of intelligent choice. We are able to control our fertility. No longer do we have to choose

must be left to the Christian insight of the individual, an approach commended in the third of the articles appearing in the Anglican publication already referred to.[1]

This approach is at first sight identical with that of utilitarians and libertarians who assert that conception of children should be the full voluntary choice of the parents.[2] The difference lies in the motivation determining the choice, for utilitarians would lay no claim to Christian insight. Karl Barth is another contemporary theologian who has discussed contraception at rather greater length.[3] Having conceded that family planning is generally accepted by theologians as desirable, he goes on to discuss the legitimacy of the means that may be employed. Abstinence he characterizes as an "heroic" course, which is not wrong in itself but may be psychologically dangerous. The safe period might seem the ideal expedient, but the anxiety caused by its unreliability as well as its check on the spontaneous nature of sexual expression are grave objections to its use. *Coitus interruptus* is fraught with psychological dangers and its practice may well imperil marital union. There remains the last alternative of contraception, the use of mechanical devices, which are not evil in themselves. If, says Dr Barth, human interference with the natural act of *coitus* is regarded as wrong in itself, then all

between reproduction and continence. Sex is no longer a helpless submission to biological consequences. Nor is the only alternative a denial of sexual love, either *in toto*, or according to lunar calculations in a sophisticated and doubtful rhythm mathematics. When such calculations enter in, the spontaneity of love goes out. Rhythm is a denial of freedom; it offers only an alternation of necessities, not a method of true control." *Morals and Medicine*, Princeton 1954, p. 96. Also Paul Ramsey: "Freedom and Responsibility in Medical and Sex Ethics: A Protestant View." *New York University Law Review*, 31, p. 1194 (1956).

   [1] *The Family in Contemporary Society*, pp. 149–54. Cf. The second article: "The fact that man in his freedom stands above nature and is therefore at liberty to interpret sex in terms of personality and relation and to use it for personal and relational ends, leads to the conclusion that contraception is morally right in certain circumstances", p. 145.

   [2] See Horace M. Kallen: "I similarly appraise the right of men and women to full knowledge of all that the sciences of nature and man have established regarding sex and reproduction, and to decide for themselves upon the number of children they want and the intervals at which they want them." "An Ethic of Freedom: A Philosopher's View", *N.Y.U.L.R* 31:1167 (November 1956). Cf. Glanville Williams, "The Control of Conception", in *The Sanctity of Life and the Criminal Law*, New York 1957, pp. 34–74.

   [3] *Die Kirchliche Dogmatik*, III:300–11.

four methods must be rejected without distinction. If, on the other hand, family limitation is recognized as desirable, then it should be recognized that all the methods are open to some objection, and this is the price to be paid for an extension of freedom. In making the choice between the various methods certain considerations apply. The choice must be made in faith and with a free conscience, and it must be a joint decision of husband and wife taking into account the significance of their joint life together and the whole purpose of the matrimonial union. These Protestant approaches are similar in that they offer no binding principle which can be universally applied, but rather state that in certain circumstances the informed Christian conscience can conclude that contraception is lawful without the incurring of sin.

Official acceptance of birth control by Protestant Churches has kept pace with theological developments. In March 1931, the Federal Council of Churches of Christ in America approved of artificial methods of birth control by a vote of 24 to 4.[1] Since then, numerous other Protestant Churches and Sects have followed suit.[2] In 1954 the Synod of the Augustana Church at its meeting in Los Angeles endorsed birth control.[3] The Methodist Church in America

[1] See Margaret Sanger: *My Fight for Birth Control*, p. 344.

[2] These include the Connecticut Council of Churches; the American Unitarian Association; the General Council of Congregational and Christian Churches; the Protestant Episcopal Church (House of Bishops and House of Deputies); the Quakers. Outside the U.S. the General Synod of the Nederlandse Hervormde Kerk (1952), the International Convention of the Disciples of Christ (1958), and the Baptist Union of Denmark (1959) have approved contraception. Baptists, Disciples, and Jehovah's Witnesses leave the matter to be decided by the individual. For various statements of Christian views see *The Churches Speak Up on Birth Control*, published by the Planned Parenthood Federation of America, New York. The pamphlet quotes a statement of the Federal Council of Churches: "The public has a right to expect guidance from the Church on the moral aspects of birth control. As to the necessity for some form of effective control of the size of the family and spacing of children, and consequently of control of conception, there can be no question. It is recognized by all churches and physicians. There is general agreement that sex union between husbands and wives as an expression of mutual affection without relation to procreation is right. This is recognized by the Scriptures, by all branches of the Christian Church, by social and medical science, and by the good sense and idealism of mankind."

[3] But not all Lutherans accept this, e.g. the Missouri Synod of the Lutheran Church has condemned it as sinful. The United Lutheran Church in the U.S.A., however, gave its approval to contraception in 1956.

took unanimous similar action at its General Conference in 1956.[1] In England, Methodists have expressed similar views.[2] In May 1959, the United Presbyterian Church in the U.S.A. at its General Assembly reversed its former condemnation of birth control. Typical of numerous Protestant statements is the following by the Reverend James L. Novarro: "We Baptists definitely consider fertility and conception as providential and a power given to man to be properly utilized. Fertility and conception should not be left up to accident, but should be well planned, thereby contributing to the moral, spiritual, and physical health of all concerned."[3] Baptists, however, like many Protestant sects have not officially supported birth control but leave it to the consciences of individual members of their congregation to decide for themselves. It seems beyond question that the overwhelming weight of Protestant opinion favours artificial birth control at least to some degree.

Judaism has no agreed opinion on birth control. The Central Conference of American Rabbis, as well as individuals have supported contraception, but Orthodox Judaism has taken a different stand. The Rabbinical Alliance has stated that: "Orthodox Judaism does not condone any artificial birth control measures by the male spouse, under any circumstances. Only in cases where the health of the female is jeopardized are certain birth control measures allowed and then only through direct consultation between the medical and rabbinic authorities."[4]

[1] *New York Times*, May 4, 1956: 19.1. Ibid., October 17, 1956, for acceptance by United Lutheran Church Convention. 39.4.

[2] See Norman H. Snaith's, President of Methodist Conference, welcome to the Lambeth Report. *The Times*, August 27, 1958. In May 1960, the General Assembly of the Church of Scotland was advised by its Committee on Temperance and Morals to approve the practice of birth control, provided it is not employed for selfish purposes. *The Times*, May 5, 1960. The advice, with some dissentients, was accepted during the Assembly Session, May 24–June 1, 1960.

[3] See *Simple Methods of Contraception*, New York 1958, p. 43.

[4] See *Planned Parenthood News* (Fall 1958) No. 22, p. 4 (New York). See also "Morality in Medico-Legal Problems: A Jewish View", by Rabbi Emanuel Rackman, *N.Y.U.L.R.* 31:1207 (November 1956). Amongst lay Jews the practice of contraception is said to be widespread.

ANGLICAN AND PROTESTANT OPINION
AND THE LAW

Although Protestant opinion was responsible for the passing of the Comstock law and its State derivatives, the profound changes which have taken place in its assessment of birth control now render it hostile to such legislation. Those who accept contraception as a positive good could hardly favour its theoretical outlawing. The same is true of those who favour its use in exceptional circumstances only, and those who leave the whole matter to be decided by the individual conscience. To legislate on the matter would be to substitute the collective moral assessment of the community for that of the individual. In Connecticut and Massachusetts, the Protestant Churches have taken a leading part in seeking to repeal or amend the legislation passed by their predecessors. This zeal may not have been totally disinterested since the laws in question are now by an historical paradox enthusiastically supported by the Roman Catholic community, and the movement for repeal is certainly influenced by dislike of Catholic power, as well as by a less reasonable anti-Catholicism. Protestants and others might well be satisfied by the lifting of the ban on contraceptive advice given for medical reasons, and although this limitation has become illogical with the theological acceptance of contraception as part of married life, it might well be acceptable since in practice it means that married couples who wish to obtain contraceptives may do so. In England, of recent years the Anglican Church has made no effort to secure legal restriction on the distribution of contraceptives, save for an intervention to ban the sale of such articles by slot machines.

Protestant opinion would not, however, favour the complete withdrawal of the law from this field. Rather, it would limit its role to preserving public order and public decency. It would be generally agreed that advertisement of contraception should be restricted, both for aesthetic reasons, and as a means of keeping contraceptives from the unmarried and from the teenager. The same motivation would restrict sales from slot machines, and might well favour a ban on the sale to unmarried persons under a certain age. The argument that unrestricted sales would lead to an increase in promiscuity is a powerful one and appeals to many who do not object to the use of contraceptives by married couples. The difficulty is that such laws are difficult to enforce, although they are not totally ineffective, as is shown by the restrictions imposed on sale of liquor to minors. The law could also be usefully employed in setting minimum standards to which manufacturers and distributors of contraceptives should adhere.

CONTRACEPTION AND THE ROMAN CATHOLIC CHURCH

The Catholic Church has always condemned contraception and, despite the changed attitude of other Churches, maintains its traditional position.[1] The Church Fathers, and later St Thomas Aquinas, held contraception to be sinful and contrary to scriptural teaching.[2] Thus St Augustine declares that "intercourse even with one's legitimate wife is unlawful and wicked where the conception of the offspring is prevented. Onan, the son of Juda, did this and the Lord killed him for it."[3] This interpretation of the sin of Onan is not universally accepted. Some scholars have maintained that Onan was punished not so much for indulging in *coitus interruptus*, as for breaking the levirate law which required a man to raise children to his brother's widow, so that she should not be left without a child and the tribe would continue. The punishment for breach of the levirate marriage law, however, is laid down elsewhere in the Old Testament.[4] Apart from the Onan text, the Old Testament also contains the general injunction to "increase and multiply", but this

[1] See the various condemnations of the Holy Office, e.g. May 20, 1851, April 19, 1853, March 26, 1897, November 23, 1922.

[2] St Augustine *De Nupt-et Con.* i, 15: Lombard, *Sent.* iv, d.31: St Thomas, *Summa Theol.* II.II, 154, a.1. St Paul, in a passage possibly referring to contraception, denounces women who "exchanged natural for unnatural intercourse", *Romans* 1, 26.

[3] *De adulterinis conjugiis*, II, XII.

[4] *Deuteronomy* 25:7-10: "The woman shall come to him before the ancients, and shall take off his shoe from his foot, and spit in his face, and say: 'So shall it be done to the man that will not build up his brother's house': and his name shall be called in Israel, the house of the unshod."

passage is also open to varying interpretations.[1] It has also been suggested that the slaying of Sarah's seven husbands by the devil was a punishment for their employment of contraception, but this seems unlikely since the angel, when overcoming the reasonable reluctance of Tobias to marrying her, and so risking the same fate, refers to her as a virgin.[2]

Scriptural texts apart, the Church has based its condemnation of contraception on the natural law. The nub of the Catholic position is contained in canon law where it is stated that the primary end of marriage is the procreation and education of children.[3] Pius XI, in his encyclical on Christian Marriage stressed the "unnatural" character of contraception: "since therefore the conjugal act is destined primarily by nature for the begetting of children, those who in exercising it deliberately frustrate its natural effect and purpose, sin against nature and commit a deed which is shameful and intrinsically vicious."[4] The Pope thus re-stated the traditional teaching of the Church, basing himself on the doctrine elaborated by St Thomas Aquinas.[5]

The Catholic natural law tradition accepts as self evident that the primary purpose of sexual intercourse is procreation, and relegates as secondary such ends as fostering the mutual love of the spouses and allaying concupiscence. This conclusion is based on two propositions, that man by the use of his reason can discover God's purpose in the Universe, and that God makes known his purpose by certain "given" physical arrangements. Thus, man can deduce that the purpose of sexual activity is procreation, the continuation of the human race; and the physical arrangements God has provided

---

[1] *Genesis* 1: 28, repeated to Noe, *Genesis* ix: 1, and to Jacob, *Genesis* 35:11. The Bible has numerous references to the blessing of fruitfulness and the curse of sterility.

[2] *Tobias* 3: 8; 6: 22. The reason given for the death of the husbands is that they were among those "who in such manner receive matrimony, as to shut out God from themselves, and from their mind, and to give themselves to their lust, as the horse and mule, which have not understanding, over them the devil hath power". (6. 17.) For a discussion of the text see Michael J. Gruenthaner, *Catholic Biblical Quarterly*, 8:98 (1946), who concludes that the text does not refer to contraception.

[3] Canon. 1013. 1.

[4] *Casti Connubii*, New York 1931, p. 26.

[5] See *Summa Theologica* II-II. Q. 154, art. 1.

may not be supplanted at man's will. We now know that not every act of *coitus* is conceptual and Catholic theology recognizes that some coital acts are conceptual and relational, and others relational only. But to recognize this fact is not to conclude that acts may be rendered conceptual or non-conceptual at man's will. Man is free to act only within the pattern imposed by nature.

It is frequently objected that this argument from "nature" is inconclusive, since in other matters nature is not allowed to run its course. Beards are shaved, fingernails are cut, rivers dammed. Catholics do not suggest that such activites are immoral, why therefore should they in the case of sexual relations equate unnatural with immoral? To this objection Catholics answer that there is no purpose perceived by reason in allowing hair or nails to grow to inordinate length, or rivers to flow always in the same channels. The chief purpose of sexuality, on the other hand, is undeniably reproduction. Some Catholic writers, however, have accepted this objection to the condemnation of contraception, pointing out that the argument is not universally applicable.[1] They still condemn contraception as contrary to natural law, but rather on the grounds of its eventual harmful effects on the race than on its perversion of a faculty. However beneficial a contraceptive act may be in the individual case, it must be condemned, for, if raised to a general line of conduct, evil results would inevitably follow.

The somewhat stark Augustinian-Thomist approach to marriage, with its emphasis on its social and procreative purpose and underestimation of the personal factors of friendship and love between the partners has been challenged by a number of Catholic writers, and rejected as inadequate.[2] They would like to see stress laid on the personal aspects of marriage, its role in increasing mutual love

[1] See W. Breen, "Neo-Malthusianism: A Critique of its Critics", *Irish Ecclesiastical Record*, November 1931, p. 467. E. J. Mahoney: "The Perverted Faculty Argument against Birth Prevention", *The Ecclesiastical Review*, 79: 133–45 (1928). Cf. *The Ecclesiastical Review*, 79:408 (1928) and 79:527 (1928). One example might be "chewing gum" which employs the natural faculties of the salivary glands and frustrates their purpose, yet is not considered immoral.

[2] See Dietrich von Hilderbrand: *Die Metaphysik der Gemeinschaft*, Munich 1930, Herbert Doms: *Vom Sinn und Zweck der Ehe*, Breslau 1935, Bernardine Krempel: *Die Zweckfrage der Ehe in Neuer Beleuchtung*, Zurich 1941, Benoit Lavaud: "Sens et fin du mariage. La thèse de Doms et sa critique", *Revue Thomiste*, 44:737 (1938).

and perfecting the personalities of the spouses. To further this aim the traditional terminology of "primary" and "secondary" ends should be abandoned. Dr Doms denies that the constitution of marriage consists in a subservience to a purpose outside the spouses themselves, for which they marry. "It consists in the constant vital ordination of husband and wife to each other until they become one. If this is so, there can no longer be sufficient reason, from this standpoint, for speaking of procreation as the primary purpose (in the sense in which St Thomas used the phrase) and for dividing off the other purposes as secondary."[1] The meaning of marriage is the community of life between the spouses, of which the child is the fruit and visible embodiment. This approach, claim its supporters, does not diminish the importance of the child in marriage, but stresses it in a different way. It is peculiarly apposite at a time when many seek to explain man in purely physiological terms, and brings theology up to date by taking into account a whole range of biological and psychological data of which scholastic theologians were unaware. It is helpful in disposing of the problems raised by sterile unions, virgin marriage, and the practice of periodic continence.

Pius XI seems to have foreshadowed this view to some extent in his encyclical on marriage. "This mutual, interior moulding of husband and wife," wrote the Pope, "this determined effort to perfect one another, can in a very real sense, as the Roman Catechism teaches, be said to be the chief reason and purpose of matrimony, provided matrimony be looked at not in the restricted sense as instituted for the proper conception and education of children, but more widely as a blending of life as a whole, and the mutual interchange and sharing thereof."[2] While retaining the traditional doctrine of the ends of marriage, the Pope is taking into account the motives of the parties, which in most cases will be based on mutual love rather than on a desire to have children. Dr Doms and his followers have had a profound influence on contemporary Catholic writing on marriage, and have concentrated the attention of religious writers on the hitherto neglected "secondary" ends of marriage, of the complexity of which theologians are now much more aware. They

[1] *The Meaning of Marriage*, New York 1939, p. 87.
[2] Casti Connubii. Francis W. Carney. *The Purposes of Christian Marriage.* Washington D.C. 1950, p. 260.

have not, however, secured the abandonment of the traditional terminology. Had they done so, the way might possibly have been opened for the acceptance by the Catholic Church of contraception in certain limited circumstances, and it was perhaps this fear which lead to an ecclesiastical censure for Dr Doms' book, and a categorical reassertion of the primary and secondary ends of marriage in a Vatican decree of 1944.[1] Dr Doms' views do not, however, lead inevitably to this result. Even if relational and conceptual ends of marriage are placed on an equal basis, the condemnation of contraceptives is not excluded, for *coitus* can still be treated as a given act, the intrinsic nature of which is the giving and receiving of seed. Unless it is this, then neither its conceptual nor relational ends are achieved, and it becomes an onanistic act of self love, ontologically distinct from true *coitus*.[2]

Catholics employ a number of subsidiary arguments in their condemnation of contraception. It has, they maintain, certain harmful effects on personal and social health, which are the inevitable result of disregarding natural law. First, the health of the woman suffers for she needs certain vital substances contained in male semen, and absorption of these is greatest from the womb.[3] Contraception may be a contributory factor in causing cancerous growths, and cancer of the breast is more common amongst sterile married women than in those who have born children.[4] It is said that the use of contraceptives induces sterility and one physician, not a Catholic, has maintained that it causes lunacy.[5] By interfering

---

[1] The following question was addressed to the Holy Office: "Can the opinion of certain recent writers be admitted who either deny that the procreation and education of offspring is the primary end of marriage, or teach that secondary ends are not essentially subordinated, but equally principal and independent?" Reply: Negative. *A.A.S.* 36:103 (April 1, 1944).

[2] This presumably would be the Catholic reply to the Anglican arguments discussed earlier. Furthermore, if any variation is admitted in *coitus* of a fundamental nature, unlimited variations must be allowed.

[3] See Dr Halliday Sutherland: *Laws of Life*, London 1935, p. 41.

[4] Ibid., p. 47.

[5] For the lunacy statement by Sir Robert Armstrong-Jones see Edward Moore, *The Case Against Birth Control*, New York 1931, p. 28. For a full discussion of the harmful medical effects of birth control, see R. de Guchteneere, *Judgment on Birth Control*, New York 1931, pp. 135–64; E. Podvin, *A Doctor Speaks out on Birth Control*, Int. Catholic Truth Society, Brooklyn 1937, and Moore, op. cit., pp. 21–31.

with the consequences of pregnancy it may cause neurasthenia and an unsatisfied sex craving which leads to over indulgence and destroys matrimonial harmony. These views are supported by some medical opinion, but there is weighty authority which rejects them. Thus the Biological and Medical Committee of the Royal Commission on Population concluded that the methods generally in use in England for preventing conception cause no injury to the genital passages, if employed in accordance with instructions, and added that there was no evidence that birth control methods approved by the medical profession impaired fecundity.[1] Other doctors point to the beneficial effect on a mother's health when she is relieved from the prospect of endless pregnancies, and the dangers of pregnancy to women suffering from tuberculosis, diabetes, nephritis or heart disease. Birth control has the negative virtue that it prevents recourse to abortion which is considerably more dangerous.[2]

Catholics further stress that the use of contraception leads to population decline, and the truth of this is now firmly established. The Royal Commission on Population concluded that the decline in the birth-rate was not due to a fall in reproductive capacity, but to the spread of deliberate family limitation.[3] Similar conclusions were reached by the French authorities, and in 1920 a law was passed outlawing sale of contraceptives in order to arrest population decline.

Whether population decline is an absolute evil is open to question. The high standard of living in Western Europe and the United States could never have been obtained without a massive growth in population, but it seems equally evident that increasing population is holding back living standards in many undeveloped parts of the world, especially in the Far East.[4] A nation that fails to increase its population may have valid economic reasons for not doing so, but a

[1] *Papers of the Royal Commission on Population*, Vol. IV, paras 46 and 52. (1950.)

[2] *Royal Commission on Population Report*, Cmd. 7695 (H.M.S.O. 1949), p. 159. "Our survey of the history of family limitation leaves us in no doubt that, if these methods were not available, other means would be used, and some of them, e.g. criminal abortion, the prevalence of which is even now distressingly high, are very undesirable."

[3] *Report*, para. 626.

[4] This point is more fully discussed when the question of world population is considered.

nation that does not replace population, providing living standards
are adequate, may justifiably be regarded as in some respects deca-
dent. The revelation by the Royal Commission on Population (1949)
was that the British nation is no longer replacing itself, the deficiency
being in the region of six per cent, is certainly alarming, especially
when the need of the Commonwealth for immigrants is considered.[1]
The prospect of a rapidly ageing population supported by an ever
diminishing portion of younger people is not encouraging. As the
Royal Commission concluded: "It is possible that with a diminishing
proportion of young people the community might lose something
in energy, initiative, enterprise, and other qualities associated with
youth."[2]

Contraception, maintain Catholics, is corrupting to the individual since it reduces self control and its employment in the
majority of cases will be for selfish reasons. Marriage will be de-
graded to a legalized form of prostitution. Furthermore, contraceptives undermine public morality, removing the fear of pregnancy,
which is a powerful deterrent against promiscuous intercourse.[3] An
argument for employing contraceptives can be made for particular
cases, but once they are made generally available, no means exists

[1] *Report*, para. 626. The Report found that 2·2 was the average size of the
British family. "A further spread of the practice of family limitation, and continued improvement in its effectiveness, must be expected to take place and will
tend to reduce average family size, but only slowly." (Para. 630.) The British
birth rate in fact increased from 16·1 in 1950 to 16·5 in 1957, 16·8 in 1958, and
16·9 in 1959. An optimistic view was expressed by Professor P. B. Medawar in
the first Reith lecture for 1959 on *The Future of Man*. "As for replacement," he
said, "I do not know that any demographer, on present evidence, now fears a
serious decline in the population of Great Britain. The latest estimates suggest
that we are just about breaking even. . . . In so far as purely biological pressures
can influence marriage rates and ages, I guess that the present upward turn
may be genuine and not just temporary." *The Listener*, 62:865, November 19,
1959.

[2] *Report*, para. 647.

[3] This contention is born out by the data available. Kinsey found that in his
sample of 5,700 women, fear of pregnancy ranked third in the factors deterring
them from pre-marital intercourse. 89 per cent cited moral objections, 45 per
cent lack of desire, 44 per cent fear of pregnancy, 44 per cent fear of discovery,
22 per cent lack of opportunity, 14 per cent fear of disease. A. Kinsey: *Sexual
Behaviour in the Human Female*, Philadelphia 1953, p. 332. Amongst college
women, investigators have found that fear of pregnancy ranks as a primary
factor—50 per cent. D. D. Bromley and F. H. Britten, *Youth and Sex: A Study
of 1,300 College Students*, New York 1938.

of restricting their use to these cases. These Catholic arguments are countered by those favouring contraception, with a list of benefits accruing from its employment. It prevents overpopulation: avoids the birth of unwanted children: reduces infant mortality and juvenile delinquency: safeguards the mother's health and facilitates early marriage. The argument on this level, however, tends to be artificial. Sociological arguments are employed by Catholics mainly for polemic purposes and as a gloss to illustrate the argument from natural law. Moreover, now that Catholic theologians have sanctioned the use of the safe period as a legitimate method of birth control, a number of the arguments have lost their force. Underpopulation or promiscuity might well result from a wide dissemination of knowledge of the arithmetic of periodic continence. The Catholic attitude to the safe period may here be conveniently considered at greater length.

The Safe Period

For centuries doctors have speculated about the possibility of a sterile period in women, but until this century no reliable means was available to calculate its duration. In 1930, however, two doctors, Dr Ogino of Japan and Dr Knaus of Austria, working independently, published the results of their researches, which, though differing in detail, indicated the same method for calculating the length of the period. A woman's menstrual period is normally twenty-eight days and during this time ovulation occurs only once, the ovum or egg being discharged from the ovary into the Fallopian tubes. Conception can only take place when the egg is present. Thus if the date of ovulation can be accurately calculated, then the commencement of the sterile period can be ascertained. The latest research based on the findings of Ogino and Knaus indicates that ovulation takes place on the fifteenth day before the onset of menstruation. The days must be computed from the beginning of the menstruation following ovulation rather than that before it, since the physiological process is leading up to the new menstruation. The method also assumes that the pattern over a year of a woman's menstrual cycle will be uniform. This does not mean that every period will be of the same length but that variations will remain within constant limits, e.g. twenty-five to thirty days. Once a woman's particular pattern has been established by careful observation then a formula can be worked out which will indicate her sterile period. Allowance must be made for the irregularities in the cycle, a variable factor in different women but constant in the same subject; for the period in which male sperm can survive in the female genital tract, approximately two days; and for the period of life of the ovum, one day. Thus in the case of a woman with an absolutely regular cycle of twenty-eight days the fertile period will be five days.[1]

Use of this method to control conception has a number of advantages. It involves no mechanical contrivance and allows physiological union, it avoids the risk of physical injury which appliance methods may cause, and it demands the exercise of a degree of self control. On the other hand it has obvious disadvantages. First it can only be used after a period of extended observation and the help of a competent physician. Even after the most careful observation a woman can easily make an error of calculation in using her chart. Ovulation exceptionally may take place on days other than the fifteenth or may be brought on prematurely by sexual intercourse. An emotional disturbance may upset the menstruation cycle and after pregnancy a considerable time may elapse before the cycle returns to stability. It requires absolute continence on certain days and some married couples may find this almost impossible.

An alternative method of fixing the date of ovulation is a basal body temperature chart. Directly after ovulation, the basal or lowest normal daily temperature rises and remains at the higher level until shortly before the next period of menstruation. Here again previous observation of the temperature pattern for a considerable period is

---

[1] A formula commonly proposed is as follows: Take 15 and 2 from the minimum length of a woman's cycle, and take 15 from and add 2 to the maximum length and this will give the fertility period. Thus in a woman with a period pattern of 24–29, the fertile period will be from the seventh to the sixteenth day of her cycle. This condensed formula is based on the following data. Menstruation will occur between 24 and 29 days after the onset of the last menstruation. As ovulation occurs on the fifteenth day before menstruation, 14 days must be subtracted from 24 and 39 giving 10 and 15, the dates between which ovulation may occur. From 10 a further 3 is subtracted to allow for survival of fertilizing capacity in the sperm, and one must be added to 15 to allow for the survival period of the ovum. Thus if intercourse takes place from the first to the sixth day of the cycle and from the seventeenth to the twenty-ninth, no conception should occur.

necessary, and mistakes can obviously be easily made. Furthermore, the method provides no protection against conception resulting from intercourse in the two or three days before ovulation has taken place. On the other hand, by combining this method with that of Ogino-Knaus, the number of days on which intercourse must be restricted can be reduced, and this is of especial importance where there is a wide variation in the menstrual cycle.

Yet another method of fixing the time of ovulation has recently been evolved. In order to nourish the egg, the womb secretes sugar, and this sugar is only present at the time of ovulation. When the egg dies, the sugar disappears. A piece of chemically prepared tape can be held against the womb, which turns green if the sugar is present and remains neutral if it is not. A period of four days abstention after the tape shows green is advised.[1] Experiments are also proceeding to develop a drug which will stabilize the menstrual period, and this would be especially helpful for women with highly irregular periods.

Various studies have been undertaken to ascertain the effectiveness of the rhythm method of birth control in practice. In an investigation carried out by the St Louis University Department of Sociology, two thirds of the doctors who replied to a questionnaire thought the method was not too complicated for most women.[2] As to its effectiveness opinion was very divided, ranging from estimates of 5 per cent to 100 per cent, the midpoint in the distribution of estimates being 71 per cent.[3] An investigation of women using the rhythm method at the Free Hospital for Women at Brookline, Massachusetts, revealed that the risk of pregnancy was 14·4 for every

---

[1] *The New York Times*, April 24, 1958. 26. 1. Dr Doyle of Boston carried out the experiments.

[2] G. S. Schnepp and J. Mundi. "What Doctors think of the Rhythm Method", *The American Ecclesiastical Review*, 123:111 (July-December, 1950). The questionnaire was sent to 523 physicians, of whom 273 replied. Catholic doctors comprised 39 per cent. For an estimate of 100 per cent effectiveness see L. J. Latz and E. Reiner, "Further Studies on the Sterile and Fertile Periods in Women", *American Journal of Obstetrics and Gynaecology*, 43:79 (1942).

[3] Schnepp and Mundi, p. 114. "Of the 192 doctors, 171 or about 89 per cent checked this question, and their opinions ranged from 5 per cent to 100 per cent effectiveness. Taking the average of all estimates, or the mean, we found it to be 65·1 per cent with a standard deviation of 25 per cent; the latter indicates a considerable spread of opinions. The median, or midpoint in the distribution of estimates was 71 per cent effectiveness."

hundred years of exposure. For women using contraceptives the equivalent figure was 6-7.[1] Other doctors have estimated that if the rules are strictly observed, the percentage of failure is 3 per cent.[2]

From the medical and other evidence available, one may reasonably conclude that while the safe period as a method of birth control does not merit the contempt with which it has often been dismissed by those advocating the use of appliances, it is by no means foolproof, and exaggerated claims on its behalf are not supported by fact. No contraceptive is wholly reliable, but in the present state of knowledge the margin for error is greater in rhythm than in appliance control. The conclusions of Dr Tietze and others seem justified when they write that the rhythm method offers a satisfactory degree of protection against unwanted pregnancy to "rigorously selected and carefully instructed wives who, with their husbands, are intelligent and strongly motivated. For others and for those to whom pregnancy would be dangerous, the effectiveness of the method in preventing conception is not considered adequate."[3]

Catholic Moral Views on Rhythm

Despite its condemnation by St Augustine,[4] use of the rhythm is now approved of by the highest authorities in the Catholic Church.[5] Pius XII removed all doubt from the matter in two statements, in 1951.[6] The Catholic ideal is one of fertility not of sterility, and, all

---

[1] C. Tietze, S. R. Poliakoff and J. Rock: "The Clinical Effectiveness of the Rhythm Method of Contraception", *Journal of Fertility and Sterility*, 2:444 (1951).

[2] S. Fleck, E. F. Snedecker and J. Rock, "The Contraceptive Safe Period", *New England Journal of Medicine*, 223:1005-9 (1940).

[3] Op. cit.

[4] *On the Morals of the Manichaeans*, XVIII, 65.

[5] The statement of Pius XI in *Casti Connubii* that married couples were not acting unnaturally if they exercised their right to intercourse "although on account of natural reasons, either of time or of certain defects, new life cannot be brought forth" is sometimes quoted as approving the deliberate use of rhythm, but strictly interpreted it only has reference to such situations as sterile marriages and the lawfulness of intercourse during the safe period.

[6] Express approval to employment of the rhythm was given and the circumstances appropriate to its use discussed. See "Address to Italian Catholic Union of Midwives", October 9, 1951, *A.A.S.* 43:835, and "Address to National Congress of the Family Front", November 26, 1951, *A.A.S.* 43:855-60. For an appraisal of the statements see Gerald Kelly, S.J., *Medico-Moral Problems*, St. Louis, 1956, IV, p. 29, and *Linacre Quarterly*, 19:39 (1952).

things being equal, a large family is probably considered preferable, but the Church has not given its approval to indiscriminate breeding. Rather, the practice of family planning is enjoined as a duty, the dispute with contemporaries being confined to the means employed. The general consensus of theologians is that the deliberate use of the safe period as a means of family planning is morally indifferent, and that the morality of its employment will depend on the presence of certain circumstances.[1] Two indispensable conditions are that both parties to the marriage freely agree to its use and both are able to bear the strain which it may impose. In addition there must be some serious reason for its employment. "The matrimonial contract," said Pius XII in 1951, "which confers upon the parties the right to satisfy the inclination of nature, constitutes them in a state of life, the state of matrimony. Now upon the parties who make use of this right by the specific act of their state, nature and the creator impose the function of providing for the conservation of the human race. . . . It follows from this that to enter upon the state of matrimony, to make constant use of the faculty proper to it and only in matrimony allowable, and on the other hand consistently and deliberately, and without serious reason, to shirk the primary duty it imposes would be to sin against the very meaning of married life."[2]

The extent of the duty to procreate the race will clearly vary with external circumstances such as local population and economic conditions. Serious reasons, justifying resort to rhythm, will in most cases, however, be personal, and these may be financial, medical, eugenic, or social.[3] In each case the judgment whether to use rhythm must be conscientiously made by the married partners after a careful survey of the relevant circumstances.

---

[1] For a typical article representing the majority view see J. A. Ryan, "The Moral Aspect of Periodic Continence", *The Ecclesiastical Review*, 89:28 (1938). For a contrary view see N. O. Griese, *The Morality of Periodic Continence*, Washington 1942. His principal conclusion is that to use the safe period systematically in marriage is "objectively unlawful", although it can be justified in individual cases for just cause. It is *"per se illicitum, per accidens autem licitum"*.

[2] Address to Midwives, 1951. *A.A.S.* 43:835–54.

[3] For a discussion of serious reasons, see John L. Thomas, *Marriage and Rhythm*, London 1957, pp. 85–112.

CATHOLICS AND THE LAW

Does Roman Catholic theology require that contraception be banned by law? As has been seen, it is unequivocally condemned as contrary to natural law, but one cannot conclude with some rigorists that the question is immediately answered in the affirmative, since all contraventions of natural law are not fit subjects for legislation. Fornication, adultery, lying, for example, are contrary to natural law, but civil sanctions are not advocated for such offences. Nonphilosophic criteria must be applied before the question can be disposed of. A breach of natural law must be a fit subject for legislation, and injure the common good substantially, before it is forbidden by law. The law must be capable of enforcement and equitable in its incidence. Finally, if it would cause greater evils than those it is intended to avoid, recourse to legislation must be eschewed.

The banning of the *use* of contraceptives by law, as in Connecticut, fulfills none of these criteria. Using a contraceptive is essentially a private act, and though it may have harmful social consequences, it is impossible to isolate any particular act, and demonstrate that harmful consequences flow from it. In practice such a law is obviously unenforceable, and the attempt to enforce it would involve an intolerable interference with the private life of individuals. Private individuals and married couples would have to be subjected to constant supervision, the home would be invaded by investigators, and the police State advanced to a new point.

Banning the sale of contraceptives and the dissemination of birth control information, on the other hand, is a possible subject for legislation, since these are public acts, capable of regulation by law. Certainly such laws are difficult to enforce, but their effect would be far from nugatory, given a climate of moral opinion which approved their content. Thus in a predominantly Catholic country, such laws would not be unreasonable, and are found in countries such as Spain, Italy and Ireland.[1] It might, of course, be maintained that

[1] S. 16 of The Censorship of Publications Act (Ireland: No. 21 of 1929), forbids the sale or publication of matter "which advocates or might reasonably be supposed to advocate the unnatural prevention of conception". S. 17 of the Criminal Law (Amendment) Act, 1935, forbids the sale or importing of contraceptives. Penalties under both statutes, a fine not exceeding £50 or imprison-

moral condemnation renders a law superfluous, but this view is un-realistic since law is closely connected with the moral opinion of the community, and is a powerful, although subsidiary means of main-taining moral standards.

Some would condemn such laws on abstract grounds, namely that they violate the freedom of the individual to make his own choice. But on this abstract level, the argument would not appeal to Catho-lics, who maintain that there can be no right to commit an immoral action. Nor would the contention that condemnation of contra-ception is a specifically Catholic doctrine fare better, since Catholics hold that the prescripts of natural law are binding on all men, and the Church herself is powerless to change them. Protestants and others often argue that to allow the sale of contraceptives in no way diminishes Catholics' rights, since they are under no obligation to use them. In a certain sense this is true, but a society in which contraceptive sales and propaganda is unfettered clearly exerts a strong pressure on its members to use them, or at least makes it very much more difficult for them to abstain from their employ-ment.[1] The plain fact is, that if religion is more than a purely personal and private exercise, if it sets out to provide a *weltan-schauung*, then it is bound to have social effects, which may diminish the freedom of those who reject the faith. To expect a society in which the majority of its inhabitants condemn contraception as a moral and social evil to allow its unfettered spread in the name of a doctrine

ment for not more than six months, or both. In Spain, an Act of January 24, 1941, forbids any form of public instruction on methods of birth control, and the exhibition or offering for sale of contraceptives. Customs regulations forbid the importation of contraceptives. Doctors, however, are not forbidden to prescribe contraceptives, but birth control advice may not be given as part of any public health service and there are no birth control clinics in Spain. The laws appear to be effective. In Italy, birth control propaganda is forbidden, but sale of contraceptives is allowed in pharmacies. No birth control clinics exist and contraception may not be advised by those discharging public health service duties.

[1] This point is illustrated unintentionally by those who produce evidence of Catholics who attend birth control clinics, as part of the argument for lifting legal bans. In fact, as the United Nations Population Commission and others have recorded, while Catholics in the U.S.A. do use contraceptives, they do so less than non-Catholics. See U.N. Economic and Social Council Report, ECN, September 1955, para. 153, and N. E. Himes, *Medical History of Con-traception*, Baltimore 1936, pp. 414–16.

of abstract right is to ask for the impossible. It is only because moral opinion in Britain and the United States accepts contraception as more or less a good, that it is so largely uncontrolled.

Does Catholic theology then oblige Catholics in non-Catholic countries, and specifically in England and the United States, to work for such prohibitory laws or to defend them where they exist? Such a question can certainly not be answered by means of a logical deduction from a natural law premiss, but the particular social situation in the country under consideration must instead be carefully examined. By the constitution and political philosophy of both England and the United States, Catholics certainly have a right to work for the passage of such laws, using all the normal political means, such as public campaigns and lobbying of legislators, to attain their end. By such means in the past, laws restricting gambling, betting and drinking, have been added to the statute book, but not by Catholics. Indeed they reject the doctrinal suppositions which these laws embody, and might argue that their personal freedom was unfairly diminished. The right then exists, but whether Catholics would be wise to follow Protestant precedent and exercise it, is open to considerable doubt.

Laws embodying moral precepts are only enforceable if they are supported by a corresponding moral consensus in the community. The Volstead Act should have made this plain enough. A law forbidding the sale of contraceptives would be effective only if the vast majority of citizens believed their use to be wrongful, and possibly not even then. The laws of Connecticut and Massachusetts on birth control are not in fact enforceable and, save for the exclusion of birth control clinics, are without effect. Even here the presence of clinics over the State lines does much to neutralize their exclusion from the States themselves. Catholics, then, in campaigning for the maintenance of such laws, gain little for public morality. They do, however, increase the fear of Catholicism in the minds of non-Catholics, and increase the likelihood that when Protestants visualize the Church, the image will not be that of a religious body, but of a political power structure. This is a high price to pay for the maintenance of ineffectual statutes. The argument from natural law is unconvincing since outside the Catholic Church even those who accept the concept of natural law are unable to see that it forbids birth control.

While without bearing on the truth or falsity of the natural law premiss, an almost universal scepticism should be treated as relevant when a policy of enforcing the precept by means of civil legislation is considered.

Aside from metaphysics, Catholics could justify a prohibitive law if they could show that demonstrable evils flow from the practice of contraception. If a declining population and a falling standard of life could be traced directly to birth control, then a strong case would have been made out for banning it. On these grounds, birth control has been banned in France, the law being inspired by imperial and sociological rather than theological reasons.[1] In England a similar situation might come about in the foreseeable future, but in the United States such a contingency is remote.[2] Again, if contraceptive methods could be shown to be harmful to health, a prohibitory law might be justified, but as has been noted, the evidence on the point is conflicting and allows no such conclusion. Finally, the argument that recourse to contraceptives increases lust and promiscuity, would, if established, give grounds for a ban, but increase in such vice is not measurable and if it were, it could not be conclusively demonstrated to result from contraception.

In summary, then, one may say that while the prophetic mission of the Church to judge and if necessary condemn society, is not questioned, a strong case exists for the abandonment of Catholic efforts to secure a total legislative ban on contraceptives. Efforts to preserve public morality would be more constructive if confined to measures commanding general support, such as the banning of sales of contraceptives from slot machines, or the restriction of sales to adults.[3] Statutes regulating contraception belong more

---

[1] By a law of July 31, 1920. Use of the mails is restricted by article 91 of the Decree-Act of July 20, 1939. Importation of contraceptive propaganda, etc., is restricted by a decree of February 5, 1946. No birth control clinics operate, nor is advice given under public health services. Exemptions exist for doctors to prescribe contraceptives, such as the danger to a mother's health from further pregnancies.

[2] The U.S. birth-rate is high, the rate of 24·9 per 1,000 in 1954 increased to 25 in 1957, see Table 56. *Statistical Abstract of the U.S.A.* (Washington, D.C. 1958). It declined to 24·3 in 1958. The rate for 1959 was lower, 24·1 (See *U.N. Statistical Bulletins.*) This, however, by any standards, is still a high birth-rate.

[3] Where a prohibitory law is impossible a regulatory law may be desirable even if it "recognizes" indirectly the existence of an evil.

appropriately to the field of public nuisance than to the criminal law proper.

Catholics might also legitimately and prudently oppose laws which in any way commit the State to approve or advocate birth control. Two events in the United States during 1959 raised this issue sharply. In July 1959, the Draper Committee, appointed to study the foreign aid programme, submitted its third interim report to the President.[1] With the report went a covering letter stating that the committee recommended that when requested by aid-receiving nations, the United States should help them to formulate programmes, "to deal with the problem of rapid population growth and should support research leading to better understanding of this problem". Mr Draper agreed with reporters that this reference included the provision of birth control information by the United States, but added, hopefully, that the point should not be unduly stressed.[2] In September, the issue was raised again, when the Senate Foreign Relations Committee published a report by the Stanford Research Centre recommending that the United States should study the possibility of backing large scale foreign tests of birth control devices.[3]

In November, a reaction came from the Roman Catholic Bishops of the United States who announced they would fight any attempt to use foreign aid funds to promote "artificial birth prevention programmes" in underdeveloped countries. Condemning such programmes as a "morally, humanly, psychologically and politically disastrous approach to the population problem", they stated that the logical answer to world population problems was not to decrease the number of people but to increase the food supply, "which is almost

---

[1] U.S. Government Publications, Washington, D.C. 1959, No. 776, publication No. 13550. Letter to President of United States from the President's Committee to study military assistance programme and Committee's third interim report, economic assistance programme and administration.

[2] Facts on File, July 23–29, 1959, p. 240. The Report itself did not stress this point, recommending the provision to requesting countries of "demographic information".

[3] U.S. Government Publications, Washington, D.C. 1959, No. 778, publication No. 16204, U.S. foreign policy, possible non-military scientific developments and their potential impact on foreign policy problems of the United States.

unlimited in potential".[1] This statement caused a political storm. Bishop Pike, the Protestant Episcopal Bishop of Southern California, condemned the statement and asked was it binding on candidates for public office? The reference was clearly to Senator Kennedy, then one of the aspirants for the Democratic nomination, who replied that he thought such policies would be mistaken since they would be interpreted as discriminatory. The United States had never urged them either at home or in Western Europe.[2] If faced with a Bill embodying such a programme, he stated, he would judge the measure by whether "it would be in the interests of the United States". If it became law he would uphold it.[3]

Senator Kennedy's replies were both judicious and constitutionally correct. The Catholic Bishops were also within their rights in making their statement, and it might well be taken as a guide for future Catholic political activity in this area. This should be limited to securing governmental neutrality on the issue, not an ideal objective, but one which recognizes an irreconcilable conflict of moral and social views within the community.[4] The proposition that adoption of an artificial birth control programme should be made a condition precedent of receipt of foreign aid funds would in any event probably command little support. The supply of foreign aid funds at the request of an individual State in order to implement such a programme would, on the other hand, be found unobjectionable by many. But just as Catholics would be wise in recognizing the majority view and refraining from pressing for prohibitive domestic legislation, so the majority favouring contraception would be judicious in refusing such requests, and so recognizing the susceptibilities of the minority. To dub such a policy, allowing the minority to dictate to the majority, is to mis-state the issue. It would be better

---

[1] *The Times*, November 26, 1959.

[2] Mr Stevenson and Senator Humphrey were in favour of providing information on request, only Senator Symington expressing himself unequivocally in favour of birth control. See *The Economist*, December 5, 1959.

[3] *Time Magazine*, December 7, 1959. No U.S. foreign aid money has in fact been spent on this objective.

[4] An example of a State Government exceeding the bounds of neutrality occurred in Pennsylvania in December 1958, when the Board of Public Assistance approved a resolution permitting case workers to refer relief clients to birth control information centres. See *Pittsburgh Post-Gazette*, December 24, 1958, and *Commonweal*, January 23, 1959.

described as a judicious recognition of the existence of a considerable minority opinion, the flouting of which would inevitably lead to serious diminution of civil peace. Reasonable concessions to such opinion offers a better as well as a more effective basis for the working of a democracy than the mechanical application of the principle that the will of the majority must always prevail.

SOME CATHOLIC PROBLEMS

Tax supported hospitals and public health services

The giving of contraceptive advice in tax supported hospitals or as part of public health services has caused sharp conflict between Catholics and Protestants. Catholics claim that since their money is being used to finance public institutions, practices which they consider immoral should not be followed. Protestants and others also claim that since their money is employed, practices which they consider morally acceptable should not be excluded by Catholic veto. In England, as has been noted, advice on contraception may be given as part of a public health service, but is subject to restriction. In the United States, in certain southern States, where Catholics are few, such advice is given in health centres and hospitals, but in many municipally financed hospitals in the north, it is forbidden.

The issue came to a head in New York in 1958, where for many years city hospitals had followed an unwritten rule that advice on birth control should not be given. In July 1958, a Protestant physician, Dr Hillman, employed at Kings County Hospital, announced that he was going to fit a Protestant patient with a contraceptive diaphragm, but was forbidden to do so by Dr Morris Jacobs, a hospital commissioner. A public controversy followed with Protestants and Jews demanding that the ban be lifted in the interests of accepted therapy and preventive medicine, and the Roman Catholic Chancery Office stating that: "It would be extremely unfortunate if our hospitals and medical faculties, aimed for the preservation of life, should be perverted to seek for the prevention of life." On September 17, 1958, the full Hospital Commission ruled in favour of Dr Hillman, and reversed the ban. The Board laid down that municipal hospitals "should provide such medical advice, preventive measures and devices for female patients under their care whose life and health in the opinion of the medical staff may be jeopardized by pregnancy and who wish to avail themselves of such health services". A certificate of medical necessity signed by two physicians must be issued, the consent of the patient and her husband if possible, obtained, and the Board recommends a conference with her spiritual adviser. Physicians, nurses, and other hospital employees who have religious or moral objections to contraceptive procedure are excused from participation in contraceptive procedures. Later the same month, the New York Department of Welfare adopted a similar policy.[1]

The new compromise reached seems reasonably satisfactory. Catholic doctors and patients are in no way obliged to follow procedures violating their moral principles and religious beliefs, while non-Catholics are assured that they will not be denied access to contraceptive medicine where this might endanger health. At the same time the susceptibilities of Catholic taxpayers are recognized by leaving general contraceptive advice to be given by voluntary agencies founded for that specific purpose. This compromise, because the factual situation is different, is not the same as that suggested in connection with the foreign aid programme. The two situations are also theoretically distinguishable, since artificial birth control facilities provided in municipal hospitals within these restricted limits do not commit the municipality to a policy of generally furthering birth control. The foreign aid programme, on the other hand, is an act of policy involving the whole nation as such.

Catholic Hospitals

In Catholic hospitals, birth control advice, unless it relates to the practice of continuous or periodic continence, may not be given.[2] As an internal domestic matter this raises no problem, but controversy has arisen over the position of doctors on the staff of Catholic hospitals who have associated themselves with the work of birth

[1] For an account of this incident see *The New York Times*, September 17, 18 and 23, 1958. Also *America*, October 4, 1958, and for a comment, see *Commonweal*, September 12, 1958, "Controversy in New York", by James Finn. See also A. W. Sulloway, *Birth Control and Catholic Doctrine*, Boston 1959.

[2] See *Ethical and Religious Directives for Catholic Hospitals*, St. Louis 1955, No. 30.

control organizations. Thus, in 1947, six Protestant physicians were dismissed from three Connecticut hospitals for their work—outside the hospital—for the Planned Parenthood League. Again, in 1952, St Francis Hospital, Poughkeepsie, New York, presented seven Protestant physicians with an ultimatum to quit the Planned Parenthood League, or to resign from the hospital staff. Three agreed to resign from Planned Parenthood, but four declined and were suspended. After a number of protests, they were reinstated at the beginning of 1953.[1] Other Catholic hospitals have sought to make it a condition of employment that doctors will not give birth control advice, either in the hospital or in private practice.[2]

To require Protestant doctors employed in Catholic hospitals to refrain from giving advice on birth control in the course of discharging their hospital duties is reasonable enough. A doctor is free to make a contract with any hospital, and if he objects to any specific term, he can make his services available elsewhere. But to extend hospital jurisdiction to private practice or to activities carried on outside the hospital in a personal capacity is a grave infringement of individual liberty. While there might be a case for excluding a Catholic doctor who supported Planned Parenthood, because of the scandal his attitude would give to Catholic patients and hospital personnel, the coercion of a Protestant doctor to go against his conscience is wrong in principle. It also betrays a confusion in practical aims. A Catholic hospital is primarily a hospital and exists to give the best medical treatment available to its patients. If conditions, such as that forbidding Protestant doctors to prescribe contraceptives outside the hospital, were generally imposed, it would materially restrict the medical talent on which the hospital could draw. Apart from this, attempts to dominate a doctor's entire professional life, will be generally construed as tyrannical and can only serve to embitter relations between the Catholic and other local, religious and civic communities.

[1] Connecticut, see *Time Magazine*, April 21, 1947, and *New York Times*, April 8 and May 5, 1947: New York, see *New York Times*, February 1 and 2, 1952 and January 22, 1953. See also *New Republic*, January 22, 1945, for a similar incident at St. Joseph's Hospital, Paterson, N.J.

[2] St Elizabeth's Hospital, Newark, N.J., set such a condition in 1945, *New Republic*, January 22, 1945.

Civic Problems

Catholics often use local political pressure to counter birth control organizations. Thus, in 1952, Planned Parenthood was excluded from membership in the Welfare and Health Council of New York, because the Catholic agencies represented threatened to withdraw.

Six months later, however, the Council voted for admission of Planned Parenthood, whereupon the Catholic agencies resigned, thus handicapping the Council's work.[1] In 1955, Catholics boycotted the Princeton, New Jersey, Community Chest, fund-raising campaign, thus compelling the withdrawal of Planned Parenthood from the Chest.[2] Whatever one may think of the prudence of such actions, and this can only be judged in the context of local conditions, Catholics are well within their democratic social rights in taking them. They hardly, however, seem "necessary" since membership of a co-operative organization does not imply approval of the constituent members. Furthermore, the line between legitimate and illegitimate social pressures can be easily crossed, as was the case in Holyoke Massachusetts in 1940, when, owing to Catholic pressure, Mrs Margaret Sanger was deprived of a public meeting place to state her views, until one was provided at the last moment by the local textile workers union. Such action was clearly against the spirit of the Constitution with its guarantees of freedom of speech and the right to hold orderly public meetings.[3] The hostility aroused against the Catholic community by these tactics would be hard to overestimate; they strengthen in the non-Catholic mind the ever present fear of Catholic power and do much to nullify the persuasive force of Catholic teaching. In proportion to their ill effect their good effect is small, and Catholics would be well advised to abandon them.

[1] See *The New York Times*, January 15, 1953, March 13 and 19, 1953, and May 8, 29 and 30, 1953 and July 1, 1953.

[2] *New York Times*, September 1, 1955.

[3] For a description of Mrs Sanger's experiences in Holyoke see Kenneth Underwood, *Protestant and Catholic*, Boston 1957. The secretary of the local union providing the hall was in fact a Catholic. Catholic pressure also caused the cancellation of birth control exhibits at fairs in Chicago in 1940 (*New York Times*, July 8, 1940) and in New York in 1941 (*New York Times*, August 22, 1941).

The Birth Control Pill

Experiments have been proceeding for some time to develop an oral means of contraception.[1] All women, when pregnant, secrete a natural hormone, progesterone, which prevents ovulation during the pregnancy period. A synthetic substitute for this hormone, progestin, has been developed, which has the same effect of inhibiting ovulation, and can be taken through the mouth. The drug has been used in tests carried out in Puerto Rico and California, and the Puerto Rican experiments have proved successful. The drugs have, however, produced bad side effects such as nausea and dizziness and have proved very expensive. Much remains to be done before they can be put on the market for large-scale sale.[2] Another method inducing temporary sterility has been suggested by Dr Sieve of Boston, who has used phosphorylated hesperedin to form a viscous barrier around the ovum and so prevent penetration by the male sperm. While early experiments met with success, later ones failed.[3] It has been suggested that such drugs would be acceptable to Catholics, since it leaves the physical nature of the sexual act un-

---

[1] An ancient Chinese prophylactic was to swallow twenty-four fresh tadpoles for two days in the spring which was alleged to prevent conception for five years. It has not earned widespread favour. Tests are, however, proceeding on certain plants used by primitive tribes as contraceptives. A full account of progress and remaining difficulties is given in Richard L. Meier's *Modern Science and the Human Fertility Problem*, London 1959.

[2] See *New York Times*, September 19, 1958, where Dr Rock reported figures of 100 per cent success for the experiments. These varied with the results reported in June by Edward Tyler and Henry Olson which showed a 9·3 per cent rate of ineffectiveness. See Robert Sheehan, "The Birth Control Pill", *Fortune Magazine*, April 1958. Also *The Family and Population Control*, Reuben Hill, J. Mayone Stycos, Kurt Back (North Carolina U.P. 1959). See *The Times*, March 31, 1960, for an account of experiments in England which show that although a pill has been developed with a high degree of effectiveness, harmful side-effects persist. Cf. "The Use of Drugs for Contraception", by Our Scientific Correspondent, *The Guardian*, March 22, 1960. In the U.S.A. the Food and Drug Administration has approved the sale of one brand of pill for oral contraception (Enovid) which has been developed from the drug used in Puerto Rico, but only on prescription. See *The Observer*, July 10, 1960.

[3] *Science*, October 10, 1952, pp. 373–85. Yet another drug MER-25 is claimed to prevent implantation of a fertilized ovum in the womb. So far it has been successfully used only on rats. The destruction of a fertilized ovum would be condemned by Catholics and possibly by other Christians. See W. J. Gibbons and T. K. Burch, "Physiologic Control of Fertility Process and Morality", *American Ecclesiastical Review*, 138:261–3 (1958).

impaired, but Catholic moralists have been unanimous in condemning the use of the drugs as a violation of the divine law, since
they prevent the natural end of the sexual act, procreation.[1] The
only justification for their use would be medical rather than a
contraceptive motive, e.g. relief from pain caused by menstruation,
when their employment would be justified on the principle of
double effect. This principle may be invoked to justify the sale
of prophylactics, which, while they may be used to prevent conception, are not sold with that purpose, but rather to prevent
disease. Thus their distribution to members of the armed forces
would be held by some not to be contrary to Catholic moral teaching.[2]

WORLD POPULATION GROWTH
AND CHRISTIAN RESPONSIBILITY

Since the end of the Second World War, first experts, and then the
public in general, have been increasingly aware of the enormous
problems created by the rapid rise in world population. "The
problem of population," states Sir Julian Huxley, "is the problem
of our age."[3] Numerous monographs have been published on the
consequences of the rise, the United Nations has carried out an
important series of investigations into the causes and extent of the
increase, and in 1954 convened an international conference in
Rome, to exchange information.[4] The magnitude of the problem is

[1] See *American Ecclesiastical Review*, 122:225 (1950), 137:50 (1957), John J.
Lynch, "Fertility Control and the Moral Law", *Linacre Quarterly*, 20:83 (1953).
Use of pills to regularize a woman's menstrual cycle would not be contrary to
Catholic teaching. Cf. D. O'Callaghan, "Fertility Control by Hormonal Medica-
tion", *The Irish Theological Quarterly*, 27:1–15 (January 1960). For a statement
by Pius XII, see "Address to Seventh International Haematological Congress",
A.A.S., 50:734–5 (1958).

[2] For an expression of caution lest impression be given that prevention of disease
is more important than avoidance of wrong-doing see *Irish Ecclesiastical Record*,
January 1942, p. 83.

[3] *Scientific American*, March 1956, p. 2.

[4] E.g. *World Population and Resources*, London, P.E.P. 1955; *Four Thousand
Million Mouths*, Le Gros Clark, F. (ed.), London 1951. See also *The Family
in Contemporary Society*, where world population problems are considered at
length. For United Nations publications see the series of Population Studies
(ST/SOA), especially *The Determinants and Consequences of Population Trends*
(No. 17), and *The Future Growth of World Population* (No. 28). The population
estimates quoted are taken from these publications. The British Association for

stated dramatically in the United Nations publication "The Future Growth of World Population", where the author points out that whereas the human race took 200,000 years to reach 2,500 million, it will take only thirty years to add another 2,000 million. If the present rate of increase continues, within 600 years only one square metre of earth will be left for each person to live on. In 1950, world population was 2,500 million; by 1958 it had reached 2,800 million; by 1980 a population of 4,280 million is forecast. World population is expected to double within the next fifty to sixty years, and if current estimates are correct, a world population of between 6,000 and 7,000 million can be expected by the end of the century.

Population growth is a world wide phenomenon, but is taking place faster in the underdeveloped countries of Asia, Africa, and tropical South America, than in the advanced countries of Europe, and even, in some cases, the United States.[1] In some places such as Puerto Rico, the annual increase is in the region of 3 per cent compared with an increase for the United States in 1954 of 1·8 per cent.

In Africa from 1951–5 the population was increasing by 2·2 per cent per year, in Asia, as a whole, by 1·7 per cent, the figure being higher for individual countries, compared with a ·7 annual increase for Europe.[2] Highest rate of increase amongst the developed countries is shown by the United States, where a population estimated at 166 million in 1955 is expected to reach 204 million by 1970. Europe does not reflect this pattern of increase, the 51 million population of the United Kingdom, for example, being expected to be only 53·7 million by 1970, and France's population of 43·3 million will be 47·4 million in that year. By contrast, countries such as China and India will increase from 600 to 799 million, and from 386 to 504 million, in the same period.

Industrial and agricultural revolutions have contributed to this

---

the Advancement of Science sponsored a symposium: *World Food and Population* at Cardiff in September 1960. See *The Times*, September 6, 1960.

[1] From 1950–2000 the population increase of the developed countries is expected to be 74 per cent, of the underdeveloped countries, 180 per cent. See R. M. Fagley, *Population Growth and Christian Responsibility*, New York 1960, p. 21. Only in Ireland has population declined over the past fifty years.

[2] U.N. Economic and Social Council: *Population Commission Report* 1957, p. 4. See also *Background Facts on World Population and Population Trends* (1957, UNESCO).

swift growth, but primary cause is the reduction of disease and a fall in the death rate. Modern medical science has made decline in mortality an almost universal phenomenon, the only exception being Middle Africa where physical and cultural obstacles remain to be overcome.[1]

In Puerto Rico for example, the death rate fell from 11·8 per thousand in 1947 to 7·2 in 1955.[2] The scope for further reduction is illustrated when one considers the infant mortality rates in different countries. In Britain it is now 26·5, but in India, despite improvement, it is 200. Countries appear to pass through a fourfold cycle in relation to births and deaths. First, both birth and death rates are high, and this is followed by a period of high birth rates and falling death rates. Then both birth and death rates fall, and finally the country passes into a period of low birth and death rates.[3]

In the West, stage two of the cycle was not reached until improvements in agriculture and the industrial revolution were under way, but in the East the decline in death and disease has not been similarly matched. Thus, while the advanced countries can maintain and even raise the standard of life for their increased population, the technologically undeveloped countries, where the population by contrast is seriously undernourished, can barely maintain even existing standards, any advance being immediately swallowed up by the increased numbers. In India, for example, the average diet is only 1,590 calories per person—less than half that of the United States—and two thirds of the Indian population is underfed. In all 70–75 per cent of the world's population has insufficient to eat, 70 per cent being concentrated in Asia, and 18 per cent in Africa and parts of South America.[4]

A world in which material resources are so unequally divided, and where the poorest parts are those where the population is increasing most rapidly raises an acute problem for the Christian

---

[1] *The Future Growth of World Population*, pp. 3–5.

[2] *U.N. The Demographic Year Book* (1956).

[3] One would now have to add a possible fifth stage to the cycle to cover "affluent" societies, since in the U.S.A. for example, the birth-rate has been rising, but it is too early to formulate any final conclusions on this.

[4] Speech of Sir Russell Brain to Annual General Meeting of Family Planning Association in London, June 7, 1958. (*Family Planning*, 7:3–5, July 2, 1958).

conscience.[1] The late Pope Pius XII analysed the problem in a number of messages and encyclicals; it was discussed at Lambeth in 1958; and an international Protestant study group met at Oxford in April 1959 at the request of the World Council of Churches to consider the world population problem and the related question of family planning. There is, however, no unanimity amongst Christians as to what action should be taken.

A number of Catholic writers dismiss the population problem as an illusion.[2] They point out that the problem is theoretical rather than practical, since the prophesied catastrophe is dependent on the present rate of expansion of the race continuing into the future. Some resort to ridicule, pointing out that if the egg of every housefly was hatched, the whole surface of the globe would be covered by a mass of flies to a height of three miles within ten years. Again, projecting present population increases into the future, they show that in 5,000 years the weight of human beings would equal the weight of the earth, in 14,000 the weight of the universe, and even given stellar emigration, within a few thousand years the stars themselves would be fully occupied.[3] This *reductio ad absurdum* is hardly helpful, any more than is the attitude of those religious writers who maintain that whatever the figures of expansion, God in due course will provide means of subsistence. Such a total rejection of reason is alien to the tradition of Western Catholicism. Others draw comfort from Thomas Doubleday's law first enunciated in 1837, stating that Nature always counteracts the endangering of the existence of a species by an increase in fertility, and this is especially so when the danger arises from lack of food. Consequently, "the state of depletion or the deplethoric state is favourable to fertility, and that, on the other hand, the plethoric state, or state of repletion,

[1] The disparity is widening. In 1956 the *per capita* gross national product in Western industrial societies was ten times that of underdeveloped countries. By 1976 it will probably be fifteen times as great. See R. M. Fagley, *The Population Explosion and Christian Responsibility*, p. 7.

[2] Professor P. B. Medawar (a non-Catholic), in his first Reith lecture for 1959, "The Fallibility of Prediction", pointed out some of the very grave difficulties in the way of giving an accurate forecast of the future size of world population. See *The Future of Man* by P. B. Medawar, London 1960, chapter I.

[3] See John L. Russell, "Christian Theology and the Population Problem", *The Month*, 19:197 at 198, April 1958. The article as a whole is a serious discussion of the problem.

is unfavourable to fertility in the ratio of the intensity of each state".[1]
Thus, once the general standard of living is raised, the population
problem will solve itself.[2] It is of course arguable that the fall in the
birth-rate amongst the better fed is due not to repletion but to an
accompanying sophistication which leads to the use of contraceptives. It is also pointed out by Catholic writers that important
factors in the present population increase are essentially short-
term.

The growth in life expectancy brought about by a drop in
infant mortality, and the increase in the life span must eventually
come to an end. "Once the ultimate frontier of life expectancy will
have been reached by most of the human race, and will have been
implemented into the various population compositions," writes Fr
Zimmerman, "the explosion of human numbers will dissipate itself
visibly and dramatically, assuming a continuation of present
fertility rates."[3] Given two doublings of human numbers before the
population explosion ends he estimates factual world population at
11 billion, which would then multiply at a much slower pace.

Of course, the raising of the standard of living to the requisite
level will need an intense and concerted international effort, but
Catholic social scientists welcome this. They see the population
problem as a spur driving mankind forward to the development of a
universal community. This positive attitude is evident in the writings
of all Catholic thinkers who recognize the urgency of the problem.
They stress that individual States have no absolute ownership of
territories and natural resources, but hold these on trust for the
whole of the human race. Thus, in his very first encyclical, Pope
Pius XII declared that the human race has a true unity of nature, a
unity of purpose, and a unity of dwelling place on earth, "of whose
resources all men can by natural right avail themselves to sustain

---

[1] Halliday Sutherland, *Laws of Life*, p. 197.
[2] Doubleday's law in modified form has received recent support in Dr
Eversley's *Social Theories of Fertility and the Malthusian Debate*, Oxford 1959.
In the U.S., as noted earlier, the birth-rate has risen, and this may mean a
modification of Doubleday's law. But as regards underdeveloped countries the
prospect of reaching this stage is sufficiently remote to be dismissed at this stage
of the discussion as irrelevant. Chief factors in the higher post-war U.S. birth-
rate are earlier marriage and earlier child-bearing.
[3] *Overpopulation: The "Catholic Viewpoint"*, London 1959, p. 2.

and develop life".[1] The goods created by God should be equitably shared and wealthier countries are bound by principles of justice and charity to share their resources with countries which are less well provided.

It follows, writes Mgr Montini, "that a really adequate study of the relations between population and density and means of subsistence must tend to take place on a world-wide scale, while the problem to which they give rise cannot be solved except on that same scale, through the industrious solidarity of all peoples, so that those artificial barriers which divide them being removed, there may arise a more orderly circulation of peoples, of capital, and of material goods. With this subordination of particular national economic welfare to the common good of the society of nations, frontiers will no longer be valleys which divide, but bridges which unite, and material goods will be free to fulfill their natural function of satisfying everyone's needs."[2] The Protestant and utilitarian approach of reducing population pressure by spreading contraception as a social policy is condemned not only as a violation of natural law, but as a facile avoidance of the true solution to the problem. "What an error it would be," stated Pius XII in his Christmas message of 1952, "to blame the natural law for the present miseries of the world, when it is clear that these derive from the lack of mutual solidarity of men and peoples."[3]

Given then, a high degree of international co-operation to raise living standards, how many people could the earth support? Estimates vary from 5 billion to 28 billion, Colin Clark calculating in 1958 that the world could support 28 billion if cultivation and con-

---

[1] *Summi Pontificatus*, October 20, 1939, *A.A.S.* 21:426. See also letter to Archbishop McNicholas of December 24, 1948, *A.A.S.* 31:60: 69-70 "The Creator of the Universe has provided all His good gifts primarily for the good of all; consequently, the sovereignty of individual States, however much this is to be respected, ought not to be carried so far that access to the earth's bounty, which is everywhere adequate to support multitudes of human beings, should be denied to needy but worthy persons who have been born elsewhere."

[2] Letter to Cardinal Siri on Twenty-sixth Italian Catholic Social Week held at Palermo, September 27, 1953. *L'Osservatore Romano*, September 28-29, 1953.

[3] *A.A.S.* Series 2, 20:42. Mgr Montini in his letter also rejected attempts to solve population problems by contraception. "Such attempts include not only the direct killing of the innocent, but also any defrauding of nature's intentions, which, as such, express the will of the Creator Himself."

servation of agricultural land were to reach Dutch standards.[1] To achieve this a great technological effort would have to be made by the richer nations.[2] More scientists and agricultural experts would have to be trained and made available, new methods of crop rotation and soil management introduced, and more arable land developed by irrigation, possibly using sea water. Genetic improvement of seed and stock would also help to raise yields. World food production has in fact been increasing by approximately 2·7 per cent annually since 1948, almost twice as fast as world population. Japan provides an encouraging example of how food production can be raised. During the last sixty years, food supplies have increased faster than the population, and Japan now supports 3·6 times as many people per hectare of cropland than the rest of the Far East, despite the lower fertility of her land.[3] China has also made extraordinarily rapid progress, increasing food production by 50–100 per cent, according to Lord Boyd Orr, in the past three years. He attributes the increase to a substitution of deep ploughing for the old earth scraping technique and the use of fertilizers and insecticides. "China," says Lord Orr, "has one quarter of the world's population but seems capable of feeding it well."[4] Great areas of forest and scrub land could be cleared and brought under cultivation.[5] New sources of food supplies could be developed from soil-less agriculture and synthetic manufacture, and the oceans themselves could be utilized for the vegetable substances and fungi which they contain. Expansion

[1] *Nature*, May 1958, p. 1236. P.E.P. estimated that an annual increase of 2·25 per cent per annum in food production was essential to provide a minimum diet for all. *World Population and Resources*, London 1955, p. xviii.

[2] The F.A.O. considers it technically possible to achieve the requisite increase in production of food and raw materials to meet world needs for the foreseeable future. See R. M. Fagley, op. cit., p. 63. Crop rotation and fertilizers for example, widely and intelligently used, could increase production by at least 50 per cent, and in many countries by 100 per cent, p. 71.

[3] See A. F. Zimmerman, *Overpopulation*, Washington 1957, p. 32. Japan supports seven times as many people per hectare of cropland as the world average and fourteen times as many as the United States.

[4] *New York Times*, May 14, 1959.

[5] Estimates vary as to how much of the earth is cultivatable, but a common figure is 4,000 million acres, or 12 per cent of the area. Of this, four-fifths is under cultivation (*U.N. Determinants and Consequences of Population Trends*, 1954, p. 182). An increase of 25 per cent is possible and perhaps more. Once pests were cleared from the tropic zones cultivation could proceed rapidly.

of fish breeding and fish catching offers a very promising and comparatively unexploited source of additional food supplies. All this would involve astronomic expenditure, one estimate of the initial capital required by underdeveloped countries being 25 billion dollars.[1] Huge as this figure is, it moves into the range of the attainable, when one considers that the military expenditure of the United States and the Soviet Union is probably at least four times the amount.[2] Utilization of solar and atomic energy could speed this revolution considerably. Better use could be made of Western food surpluses, which, if distributed, could do much to ease world hunger.[3]

A supplementary solution to world population problems stressed by Catholic writers is increased opportunity for emigration. In a letter to the American Bishops in 1948, Pius XII declared that man had a natural right to emigrate, since God had provided material goods for the use of all. "If, then," said the Pope, "in some locality, the land offers the possibility of supporting a large number of people, the sovereignty of the State, although it must be respected, cannot be exaggerated to the point that access to this land is, for inadequate or unjustified reasons, denied to needy and decent people from other nations, whenever this does not hinder the public welfare as measured on honest-weight scales."[4] Immigration laws should be liberalized, but there are obvious limits to this process. If Australia for example were to be peopled by Indians, the maximum that could be absorbed over a long period would be fifteen million, which in 1955 represented the annual increase of India's population

[1] Sir Robert Jackson in *Foreign Affairs*, October 1958. In the article he suggests the creation of an International Aid Authority.

[2] See James J. Norris, "The Population Explosion", *America*, April 25, 1959. Much progress has been made. The F.A.O. Report, 1958–9, notes that during the year world food production rose by 4 per cent and world population by 1·6 per cent.

[3] In 1958 26 per cent of the $4,000,000 total of U.S. exports of farm products was accounted for by the programme for disposal of surplus agricultural commodities. Distribution problems would be solved by a concerted international effort, but the payment problem remains. As the underdeveloped countries become industrialized so they will be able to pay for food imports, but this will not be possible for a considerable period.

[4] Letter dated December 24, 1948. *A.A.S.* 2nd series, 16:69–71. For other statements of Pius XII on migration see "Exsul Familia", *A.A.S.* 2nd series, 19:649–704.

for only three years.[1] Again the capacity of individuals to cross from one culture to another of a radically different nature is clearly limited, and a wholesale immigration would be destructive to the migrants and the social structure of the receiving countries.[2]

Sharing of resources, increase of food supplies, more emigration are the solutions put forward by Catholics for solving the problems created by world population increase. Protestants and others also support these measures, but emphasize them rather less, as they advocate the spread of family planning as a remedy.[3] It should be made clear that while family planning in the long run may have a material effect on population increase, it cannot be adopted quickly enough to stem the minimum increase of one billion which is likely to be achieved by 1980.[4] Contraception is not easily spread amongst primitive peoples because they find the technique of using them difficult to master and they are comparatively expensive. This would be so even if the United Nations used its influence to encourage world wide family planning, but attempts to secure the adoption of such a policy have been blocked by Roman Catholic and Communist countries.[5] Thus, in 1952, the World Health Organization

[1] *World Population and Resources*, p. 180.

[2] For a symposium of emigration problems, see *The Catholic Lawyer*, IV, No. 2, pp. 103–51 (Spring 1958).

[3] E.g. Karl Barth has stated: "It is the duty of Christians, (*a*) to support policies which involve sacrifices by the developed countries on behalf of the underdeveloped ones, and (*b*) to advocate policies designed to increase the mobility of capital and labour between the developed and underdeveloped parts of the world." *The Family in Contemporary Society*, p. 163. For a typical Protestant article advocating family planning, see Theodore A. Gill, "The Demographic Explosion", *Christian Century*, 75:895 (August 6, 1958).

[4] See George L. Zeegers. "The Meaning of the Population Problem of the World", *Cross Currents*, 8:22 (Winter 1958). Also *Simple Methods of Contraception*, New York 1958, p. 11.

[5] Communism maintains that there is no true population problem, but shortage has been created by the capitalist system. This doctrine has not always been rigidly applied in Communist countries, Lenin, for example, allowing contraceptives to be made available, a policy reversed by Stalin in 1936. The last public statement on the Soviet position was made at the Population Conference of 1954 when contraception was condemned. China adopted a birth control programme in 1956–7, but at the end of the year it was rumoured that it had been abandoned. In April 1960, however, it was announced from Peking that Professor Ma Yin-Chu had been dismissed from his post as President of Peking University. The significance of this is that Professor Ma had urged that China's enormous population was an obstacle to progress. It would seem that China has

dropped a Norwegian proposal to study contraception as part of its official programme after opposition from Catholic delegates.[1] The United Nations has accordingly adopted a policy of neutrality on the subject, one of the agreed principles of co-operative action established at the 1954 World Population Conference, being to respect different ethical and religious values and to promote mutual understanding.[2] This attitude of Roman Catholic countries has been severely criticized, but is not unreasonable. The United Nations is not a super-State whose majority decisions are binding on all members, but an agency for co-operation between equal partners. If delegate countries take radically conflicting stands on birth control the only possible line for the United Nations to follow is neutrality. At the same time advice and the services of experts are available to individual States on request.

A way out of the United Nations dilemma, as far as Catholic countries are concerned, might be offered by the rhythm method of birth control. Catholic theologians are generally agreed that a justifying cause for resorting to rhythm would be the social welfare of a particular community which would benefit by a reduction in population.[3] This, of course, would mean a widespread public dissemination of knowledge about rhythm, and many moralists consider that communication should be cautious.[4] On the other hand, these scruples might well be counter-balanced by the knowedge that the alternative would be use of unnatural means of birth control. As early as 1939, Catholic writers were advocating the founda-

now given up controlled population policies and is relying exclusively on increased agricultural production to raise the standard of living. See *The Times*, April 19, 1960. Cf. Stephan Schattmann, "The Case of Mr Ma Yin-Chu", *The Listener*, May 19, 1960.

[1] *New York Times*, May 20, 1952, 13:5.

[2] Opposition to contraception is not confined to Christians. Thus, in Mauritius, Hindu members of the legislature have joined with Christians in declaring their opposition to the propaganda of contraception. See *The Times*, April 29, 1960.

[3] See John L. Thomas, *Marriage and Rhythm*, p. 117. For a discussion see Zimmerman, op. cit. Also *America*, 92:2 (October 9, 1954): *Commonweal*, 62:9 (June 3, 1955) and William Gibbons, "*The Catholic Value System in Relation to Human Fertility*", Studies in Population, Princeton University 1949, pp. 107–34.

[4] For the controversy, see *The Clergy Review*, 13:150, 199, 273, 358 and 14:92, 184, 469 (1937).

tion of Catholic medical bureaux to give rhythm advice, and the need has become very much more urgent since then.[1] From 1952-4, with the help of the United Nations, experiments were in fact carried out in India in the use of the rhythm method. Two locations were selected, Lodi colony, an urban middle-class centre, and Ramangaram, a small rural town in Mysore. The project ended abruptly in 1954. About 75 per cent of the 2,362 married couples in the two centres expressed a desire to learn about family planning, but only 13·6 per cent of the couples in Ramangaram and 28·3 per cent of those in Lodi colony proved capable of learning the method. By the end of March 1954, only 5 per cent and 7·5 per cent respectively were known to be following the method regularly. Difficulties reported were a wide variation in women's cycles, mistakes in calculations, and the reluctance of husbands to agree to long periods of abstinence.[2] On the other hand, Dr Abraham Stone, who went to India to give instruction in rhythm methods under the auspices of the World Health Organization in 1951, reported a success rate of 65 per cent.[3]

India has not confined its activities to propagating the rhythm method, and, like Japan, the other Eastern country with a population policy, has sought to increase knowledge of contraception.[4] The possibilities of wider application of rhythm, however, remain, and as scientific advance renders it a more reliable and simple method of control, it may well be more widely employed. Its major advantage is that it is the only possible method of international family planning, being acceptable to all major world religions, not only Judaism and Christianity, but also Buddhism, Hinduism, Confucianism, and Islam.

[1] E.g. John O'Connell, "Birth Control Clinics Needed", *The Ecclesiastical Review*, 101:246 (1939).   [2] *World Population and Resources*, p. 219.

[3] *New York Times*, October 20, 1951, p. 17.

[4] In India, provisions for giving effect to recommendations from the Panel on Health Programmes of the Planning Commission (1951) that the State should provide facilities for sterilization and giving contraceptive advice, especially where indicated on medical grounds, were included in the first and second Five Year Plans. Japan has also legalized abortion for medico-social reasons by the Eugenic Protection Law of 1948, subsequently amended. The results have been astonishing, 2,679,000 births in 1947 having been reduced to 1,563,000 in 1957, over 70 per cent of the reduction being attributable to abortion. The effects on health have been deplorable and the policy may be modified. 763 health centres in Japan give advice on abortion, sterilization and contraception. See *Family Planning*, Vol. 7, No. 3, October 1958.

CHAPTER THREE

Artificial Human Insemination

Artificial human insemination is the attempt to fertilize a woman by a means which is a substitution for natural intercourse. With the aid of instruments, semen is deposited in a woman's vagina, cervical canal, or uterus, in order to produce a pregnancy. Artificial insemination may be of two kinds, *homologous*, when the semen employed is obtained from the husband (A.I.H.), and *heterologous*, when it comes from a third-party donor (A.I.D.).[1] Sometimes, these two types of insemination are combined, and a mixture of the husband's and donor's semen employed (A.I.H.D.). Conditions calling for the employment of A.I.H. are most commonly, impotence, malformation of the male organ, vaginal spasm, failure to ejaculate, or dyspareunia. A.I.D. may be resorted to where the husband is sterile or suffers from an hereditary disease, or for eugenic reasons.

HISTORY

General interest in artificial insemination is recent, but its history stretches back for centuries into the twilight of legend.[2] It is said to have been used in the fourteenth century as a war stratagem, when

---

[1] The Feversham Report gives an account of experiments which have separated a husband's spermatozoa from their own seminal plasma and combined them with the plasma of a donor, thus increasing their motility. Dr Samuel Rozin of Jerusalem has reported that it has been successful in producing pregnancy in two out of five cases of infertility of long duration, in one of which A.I.H. had previously been attempted unsuccessfully. (*Aeta. Med. Orient.* (1958), Vol. XVII, Nos. 1–2.) There is no report of its use in Great Britain. Since the donor's spermatozoa can be totally excluded from the plasma, thus making it impossible for him to be responsible for conception, the method would rank as A.I.H.

[2] As early as the second century A.D. a hypothetical discussion of the effects of the accidental insemination of a woman while taking a bath appeared in the Talmud. The matter was also discussed in the Rabbinical Academy in Palestine by pupils of Ben Zoma. See Kardimon, "Artificial Insemination in the Talmud", *Hebrew Medical Journal*, 2:164 (1942).

Arab brood mares were impregnated with semen from stallions of inferior physique, so that the offspring would be reduced in speed and stamina.[1] It is heard of again in the seventeenth century when a Leyden physician, Johan Swammerdam, made an unsuccessful attempt to fecundate fish by artificial means.[2] This experiment was brought to a successful conclusion by Ludwig Jacobi in 1742, and he was followed by Lazario Spallanzani of Modena, who fertilized a spaniel bitch in 1780. Ten years later, John Hunter, a well-known English physician, carried out the first successful human insemination, his subject being the wife of a linen draper in the Strand, whose husband suffered from hypospadias.[3] In France, Girault claimed a successful experiment in 1838, and in 1868 published a series of ten experiments, in which he claimed eight successes, including one pair of twins. In the United States, the first human insemination was performed by Marion Sims, who reported the successful experiment in 1866, but who abandoned the work because of the ensuing public outcry.[4] All these cases appear to have been A.I.H.

In 1909, A. D. Hard, an American physician, reported the use of a donor's semen to fertilize a woman whose husband was sterile.[5] Since the beginning of the century the use of artificial insemination for stock breeding and for human purpose has steadily increased, with a notable increase in the latter since the nineteen-twenties.[6] The literature on the subject, until the late nineteenth century, was extremely meagre, but since the publication of Dehaut's pamphlet in Paris, in 1865, this has also grown steadily, especially in recent years.[7] The concern about the growth and extent of artificial

---

[1] *An Inhabitant of Darfur* (an Arabic book of 1322). See H. Rohleder, *Test Tube Babies*, p. 35.

[2] *Historia Insectorum Generalis*. Utrecht, 1669.

[3] Philosophical Transactions of the Royal Society of London (1799), 18:162.

[4] Clinical Notes on Uterine Surgery with special reference to the management of the Sterile Condition, New York 1866.

[5] "Artificial Impregnation", *The Medical World*, 27:163ff (1909). The operation allegedly took place twenty-five years earlier.

[6] For a full history of the subject, see A. M. C. M. Schellen, *Artificial Insemination in the Human*, London 1957, pp. 7–22, and William K. Glover, *Artificial Insemination among Human Beings*, Washington, D.C. 1948.

[7] *De la fécondation artificielle dans l'espèce humaine comme moyen de remédier à certaines causes de stérilité chez l'homme et chez la femme.*

human insemination in the United Kingdom was shown by the appointment of an ecclesiastical commission to investigate the subject in December 1945, and this culminated in a House of Lords Debate in February 1957.[1] The Government then announced that it would appoint a departmental committee to inquire into the practice of A.I.D. and to make any relevant recommendations. The Committee, whose chairman was Lord Feversham, presented its report in July 1960.[2] While the majority strongly condemned A.I.D. and recommended that it should be discouraged, a minority report signed by two members, although against encouraging A.I.D., thought it might be properly employed in a small number of cases. The committee unanimously recommended that A.I.D. should not be declared criminal or regulated by law. The evidence given by the Church of England Committee and the Primate, the Archbishop of Canterbury, was published in January 1960[3] and that submitted on behalf of the Roman Catholic body in England and Wales in March of the same year.[4]

EXTENT

The extent to which artificial human insemination is employed today is very difficult to assess. In England and the United States it seems scarcely to have been used at all until after the First World War. Dr Marie Stopes claimed to have been the first to popularize the notion in 1918. In England, its use has been connected with the work of clinics specializing in the cure of sterility, but from the limited data available its employment still seems to be exceptional. Thus, in the clinic founded by the Exeter and District Women's Welfare Association, A.I.D. by 1948 had been used in only 1 per cent of the cases in which advice had been sought because of involuntary

[1] See *The Times*, February 27, 1958.

[2] *Report of the Departmental Committee on Human Artificial Insemination*, London, H.M.S.O., Cmd. 1105 of 1960. The Summary of the Committee's recommendations is given in Appendix III.

[3] *Artificial Insemination by Donor: Two Contributions to a Christian Judgment.* Church Information Office, 1960.

[4] See *The Dublin Review*, Spring 1960, pp. 21–30. Evidence submitted by a Committee appointed by His Eminence the Cardinal Archbishop of Westminster. The evidence was subsequently published as a pamphlet by the Catholic Truth Society.

sterility.[1] *The British Medical Journal* for January 1945 reviewed
two series of cases. Thirty cases of A.I.H. resulted in nine conceptions, leading to four live births, four miscarriages, and one in
which pregnancy had not reached term at the time the article was
written. Fifteen cases of A.I.D. from the same donor, led to ten
conceptions and eight live births.[2] Few English doctors engage in
this type of work, a few specialists catering for the whole country.[3]
No figures for A.I.H. births are available, but in the House of Lords
debate of February 1958 Lord Blackford stated that 7,000 A.I.D.
births had taken place in the United Kingdom over the last twenty
years.[4] The Feversham Committee concluded that A.I.D. was
practised on a "very small scale" in England. In a memorandum
submitted to the committee, the British Medical Association estimated the number of practitioners known to be regularly engaged
in the practice of donor insemination was less than twenty, but the
Committee thought this an exaggerated figure. They received
evidence from twelve doctors who at one time had practised A.I.D.,
but, of these, five had ceased to do so. The Committee estimated that
the number of A.I.D. children in Britain was unlikely to be more
than 1,150 and that the annual birth-rate for such children was about
100 per year.[5]

In the United States, artificial human insemination is more widespread than in the United Kingdom. Writing in 1928, Dr Schorohowa
described fifty cases and claimed twenty-two successes.[6] In 1941,
30,000 American physicians were circularized to obtain information,

[1] *Artificial Human Insemination.* The Report of a Commission appointed by
His Grace the Archbishop of Canterbury, London 1948, p. 13.

[2] M. Barton, K. Walker and B. P. Wiesner, "Artificial Insemination", *B.M.J.*,
I:40. (January 13, 1945.) Dr Mary Barton declared at a Conference in 1946 that
300 children had been born in Great Britain by A.I.D. in the past five years,
and there were "thousands of cases" of A.I.H. See *Artificial Human Insemination*,
London 1947, pp. 45 and 48.

[3] "The Implications of A.I.D." By Our Medical Correspondent, *Manchester
Guardian Weekly*, January 16, 1958.

[4] The *Times*, February 27, 1958.

[5] *The Feversham Report*, pp. 6–7. Figures supplied to the Committee by six
A.I.D. practitioners indicated that 60–70 per cent of parents conceived successfully, the remaining 30–40 per cent discontinued the treatment because it was
unsuccessful. The number giving birth to live children was between 50 and
60 per cent. *The Report*, p. 10.

[6] *Archbishop's Report*, p. 12.

replies being obtained from 7,642. They reported 9,489 cases of women achieving at least one pregnancy, 5,728 by A.I.H., and 3,510 by A.I.D.[1] The Feversham Committee received information from eight American practitioners that they had been responsible for a total of over 1,000 pregnancies up to 1959.[2] Estimates of the number of persons conceived by this method have been put forward by a number of writers, but they seem little more than inspired guesses. Judge Ploscowe gave a figure of 20,000 in 1951,[3] while four years later the *New York Post* ventured 50,000 for the whole United States, and 10,000 for New York City.[4] *The Scientific American* gave the birth-rate for such babies in 1934 as between 50 and 150, and by 1955 this had risen to between 1,000 and 2,000, according to *McCalls Magazine*.[5] Two sperm banks are found in the United States, one in Iowa and the other in New York.[6] Since the whole process of artificial insemination is necessarily shrouded in secrecy, it seems impossible in the nature of things to obtain accurate figures of the births involved. No doubt exists, however, that the practice is spreading, and the growth in the number of sterile marriages combined with a decline in the number of children available for adoption, has materially increased its demand. Artificial human insemination is accordingly no longer a medical curiosity, but a technique which raises acute ethical, legal and social problems, in the solution of which the whole community has an immediate interest.[7]

[1] F. Seymour and A. Koerner: "Artificial Insemination: Present Status in the United States as Shown by a Recent Survey", *The Journal of the American Medical Association*, 116:2747ff (1941). These figures were trenchantly criticized by C. E. Folsome in "The Status of Artificial Insemination", *American Journal of Obstetrics and Gynaecology*, 45:917ff (1943).

[2] *The Report*, p. 92.

[3] M. Ploscowe, *Sex and the Law* (1951), p. 113.

[4] March 28, 1955, pp. 4. 18. The Feversham Committee, however, thought that 10,000 was the total of A.I.D. births for the whole U.S.A. *The Report*, p. 91.

[5] J. H. Caldwell: "Babies by Scientific Selection", *Scientific American*, 150: 124ff (1934), and *McCalls Magazine*, May 1955, p. 60.

[6] Preservation of semen is only feasible at low temperatures and this may well impair its fertilizing power. See *Feversham Report*, p. 20.

[7] The Feversham Committee concluded that apart from the U.S.A., "It may well be that in proportion to population, Israel is the country where A.I.D. is practised most, in spite of the opposition of the Orthodox Jewish religion." *The Report*, p. 4. Appendix I of the Report considers the law and practice in seventeen countries and indicates that apart from the U.S. and Israel, in none of the countries is A.I.D. more than of very tiny incidence.

A.I.H.

From the legal standpoint, A.I.H. is of only minor importance.[1] The child is undoubtedly legitimate and a legal problem only arises if one party seeks to dissolve the marriage on grounds of non-consummation. Does A.I.H. and the consequent birth of a child bar a nullity decree? An English Court has held that it does not constitute such an impediment and of itself does not ratify the marriage.[2] The Royal Commission on Marriage and Divorce, on the other hand, recommended that the rule should be altered. "Consent to an act which is likely to produce a child of the wife is in our view so fundamental a step that it must be taken to mean that the parties acquiesce in the marriage."[3] At one time such a decree would have bastardized the child, but statute has now prevented this result, both in England and in many American jurisdictions.[4]

[1] A.I.H. is also of very minor medical importance according to a doctor-contributor to *The Practitioner* (August 1960). No fewer than fifty-one of the author's 114 patients gave up after six or fewer inseminations. Of those who had an adequate number of inseminations, 51 per cent became pregnant, but the over-all degree of success is considered to be around 30 per cent. See *The Times*, August 1, 1960.

[2] *R.E.L. v. E.L.* (1949), p. 211. See also *Slater v. Slater* (1953), p. 235, where it was held that A.I.D. of itself did not constitute an impediment to a nullity decree. In both cases it was assumed that artificial insemination would not constitute consummation. At the time she underwent the treatment the wife's knowledge of her legal remedies was too hazy to allow it to approbate the marriage. It seems then that artificial insemination with full knowledge of the facts might be a bar. See also *Q. v. V.* (*The Times*, May 12, 1960) where a wife had given birth to an A.I.D. child and this was held not to constitute approbation of the marriage, since at the time of receiving A.I.D. she had no knowledge of the legal remedy open to her because of her husband's incapacity. In *W. v. W.* (1952) 1 All. E.R. 858, however, it was held that adoption of a child by both spouses debarred either of them from obtaining a nullity decree. For a full discussion of this and allied points see G. W. Bartholomew, "Legal Implications of Artificial Insemination", *Modern Law Review*, 21:236 (May 1958).

[3] Cmd. 9678, paras. 286–7.

[4] *Matrimonial Causes Act* (1950), 14 Geo. 6, c. 25, s. 9. Most American jurisdictions have such statutes but not New York, Iowa, N.A. or the District of Columbia. Roman Catholic canon law holds that in a marriage invalid through impotence, a child conceived through artificial insemination of the husband's seed before both parties realized the invalidity of their union, would be legitimate and would remain so, even if the marriage were later canonically declared to be null.

CHRISTIAN VIEWS

At first sight, A.I.H. would not seem to raise serious problems for the Christian moralist. Since all Christian theologians are agreed that procreation is at least one of the purposes of marriage, A.I.H. might well be dismissed as an additional technical means to bring this about. Roman Catholic theologians have for so long stressed that procreation is the primary purpose of marriage, that they might legitimately be expected to be more favourable to A.I.H. than their non-Catholic brethren, but this is not the case. The Church of England Commission, appointed in 1945 to study both A.I.H. and A.I.D., cautiously commends the former.[1] A.I.H., concludes its report, is morally unobjectionable, where a sufficiently grave cause exists for its use. Thus its employment would be lawful if the husband suffered from a permanent physical disability rendering *coitus* impossible, or from impotence of psychological origin, or if the wife suffered from vaginal spasm. It should only be employed after diligent enquiry and with the greatest caution. An emotional maladjustment between the partners would constitute a serious objection to its use. This view may reasonably be regarded as that generally held amongst non-Roman Catholic Christians.[2]

A.I.H. is not so easily disposed of, however, and theological difficulties arise when the methods of obtaining the semen are considered. The principal methods may conveniently be listed as follows:[3] Masturbation: aspiration of spermatozoa by puncturing a testicle and the epididymis: rectal massage of the prostate gland and

[1] *Archbishop's Commission*, pp. 21–4.

[2] See for example the Report of the Committee on the Family in Contemporary Society adopted by the Lambeth Conference, 1958, which adopts this view. *The Lambeth Conference*, 1958, S.P.C.K. Press, London 1958, 2:148.

In December 1955, the Dutch Protestant Society, "Zedenopbouw", whose views are representative of the Dutch Reformed Church, appointed a commission on the subject which reported in June 1956. This accepted A.I.H. in principle if medical opinion indicated that fertilization could not be achieved in the natural manner. It added: "If the indication for A.I.H. is the lack of natural intercourse, grounded in sentiment, there is this serious objection to it that in such a case the elementary conditions necessary for the education of the child are lacking." See Schellen, op. cit., p. 363.

[3] For this classification I am indebted to W. K. Glover, op. cit., p. 24.

seminal vesicles with pressure on the ampulla of the vas deferens: coitus interruptus: condomistic intercourse: post-coital aspiration of semen from the vagina: post coital use of the "tassette" or similar container.

The Archbishop's Commission discusses the legitimacy of masturbation in this context and concludes that although masturbation impairs the natural unity of the sexual act, its use as a last resort is justifiable.[1] "The act which produces the seminal fluid, being in this instance directed towards the completion (impossible without it) of the procreative end of the marriage, loses its character of self abuse. It cannot in this view, be the will of God that a husband and wife should remain childless merely because an act of this kind is required to promote conception."[2] Not all Anglicans would agree with this proposition[3] and today it is unanimously rejected by Roman Catholic theologians, who regard masturbation as intrinsically evil. In the past, however, the majority Anglican view has received some Roman Catholic support.[4] Such views were not tenable after 1897 when the Vatican officially condemned artificial insemination. The terms of the condemnation are without reservation, and appear to have been determined by the then current view that semen could only be obtained for artificial insemination purposes by means of self pollution.[5] When it became clear that semen could be obtained by means other than masturbation, the discussion was re-opened

[1] *Archbishop's Report*, p. 58. The Reverend R. C. Mortimer, then Regius Professor of Moral and Pastoral Theology at Oxford, and subsequently Bishop of Exeter, disassociated himself from this finding, but later retracted his reservation. See *Artificial Insemination by Donor. Two Contributions to a Christian Judgment*, p. 18.

[2] Ibid., p. 47.

[3] See for example two articles in the *Church Times*, of March 16 and March 23, 1948. Masturbation, declared the writer "is condemned by all Christian moralists because it implies the solitary and essentially individualistic use of sexual activities intended to be used in association. It disregards the truth that with these powers God provides physiological means for exercising them in a joint and common act."

[4] See Ballerini-Palmieri's *Opus Theologicum Morale*, VI:684, n. 1304 (1892 ed.). Also supported by Berardi *Praxis Confessariorum*, n. 1009 (ed. 2a) (1898). Both subsequently retracted their views.

[5] *Acta Apostolicae Sedis*, 29:704 (1897). To the question, *"An adhiberi possit artificialis muliexis foecundatio?"* the Commission of Cardinals replied: *"Non licere. Quod responsum R. Pontifex (Leo XIII) approbavit 26 Aprilis eiusdem mensis et anni."*

amongst theologians and continued until its closure by three statements of Pius XII.

The legitimacy of the second and third methods of obtaining
semen was advocated first by Father Vermeersch in 1919, and
subsequently has received support from other theologians.[1] They
argue that since the methods are employed to further the primary
end of marriage and do not arouse the venereal appetite or involve
venereal abuse, they are wholly legitimate. Distinguishing these
methods from masturbation, Fr Kelly, S.J., writes: "But the puncture of the epididymis involves no use of the sexual *processes*, hence
cannot properly be styled as an abuse, an unnatural sexual act. Of
itself, its intrinsic morality might partake of the nature of a minor
mutilation, somewhat similar to that involved in a blood transfusion.
Moreover, if extraction of seminal fluid from the epididymis were
absolutely wrong (like pollution and onanism), it could never be
allowed and physicians could not resort to it even for examination
purposes."[2] Father Glover and others oppose this view, stating that
the pleasure obtained from the act of masturbation does not constitute its evil, but that the act is evil in itself and so renders the pleasure
illegitimate. Extending this argument to the methods under discussion, they assert that the removal of semen from the male
generative organs is intrinsically evil as this destroys the ordination
of semen to generation required by the natural order. "In order that
the semen be physically ordained to generation it must remain within
the generative organs of either the male or the female."[3] Man, on this
view, has not full dominion over his semen, but merely a right to its
use and then only in relation to generation which is brought about
by an act of natural conjugal intercourse.[4]

Father Kelly asks for proof of this assertion, and maintains that it
ignores the distinction between what is *contra naturam* and *praeter*

[1] *De Castitate* (Prato, 1919), 81, n. 85 and 257, n. 241. Father Gerald Kelly
has been the principal American exponent of this view. See *The Ecclesiastical
Review*, 101:107–18 (1939), also *Medico-Moral Problems*, Dublin 1955, pp. 111ff.
Following the statements of Pius XII, referred to in the text, he has since
modified these views, see *Medico-Moral Problems*, St. Louis 1956, II:14, and
University of Detroit Law Journal, 33:135, 1955–6.

[2] "The Morality of Artificial Fecundation", *The Ecclesiastical Review*, 101:114,
1939.

[3] Glover, op. cit., p. 79.

[4] See Merkelbach *De Castitate*, n. 62 ad 4.

naturam. "Are not the married parties," asks Father Kelly, "in very much the same situation regarding propagation as the individual is in regard to self preservation? He has a natural right to preserve his life, and, failing normal means, he may use abnormal or artificial forms of nourishment. So, it seems that married people, when unable to generate by the normal means of sexual intercourse, may use abnormal means, provided that means be not sinful."[1] Father Kelly's arguments are persuasive, but as will be seen they have been superseded by the direct intervention of Pius XII. The point is of greater theological than practical importance since very few spermatozoa are obtained by testicular puncture and in the case of rectal massage they are present only by chance.

The fourth method of *coitus interruptus* is mentioned briefly in the report of the Archbishop's Commission and presumably a procreative purpose would in the members' view neutralize the sinful character of the act as it does in masturbation. Roman Catholic theologians are unanimous in rejecting this method as sinful, and are supported by those who see in the story of Onan an express Biblical condemnation of the practice.[2] Condomistic intercourse, on the other hand, under these special circumstances has been defended by a minority of Roman Catholic theologians while condemned by the majority.[3] The minority concede that use of a condom divides the act of fecundation into two periods but holds that this does not *per se* render it unlawful. Intimacy is also reduced by this method, but it is distinguished from masturbation by actual functioning of the sexual organs in conjugal union. The situation is admittedly anomalous, but the anomalies are justified by the abnormal circumstances.[4] Further dispute occurs as to whether the condom should be perforated or not, most theologians of the minority view making this a necessary condition of the legitimacy of the procedure, the point being that the instrument should allow a sufficient outflow of semen

[1] The Morality of Artificial Fecundation, *The Ecclesiastical Review*, 101:113, August 1939.

[2] Genesis xxxviii, 7–10. Dispute exists as to whether this text refers to *coitus interruptus*, masturbation, or is confined in its application to the Jewish institution of the levirate.

[3] Salsmans held this view, see Génicot-Salsmans *Casus Conscientiae*, 4th ed. (1922), Casus 1125. Later he withdrew it. See *seventh edition* 1938.

[4] See Canon Tiberghien, Professor of Medical Deontology at Lille, *Mélanges de Science Religieuse*, Lille 1944, pp. 341–2.

to make generation by the natural act at least a possibility.[1] As has been noted, the majority condemn use of the condom in any circumstances as an unnatural act, since "the psycho-physical process leading to sexual orgasm are used in such a way that the orgasm itself takes place outside of *coitus*. It is true that there is an appearance of *coitus* in condomistic intercourse and *coitus interruptus*. But it is only an appearance. The determining factor of true *coitus* is ejaculation into the vagina; and that factor is missing. . . ."[2] Since the condoms now in use are considered by doctors to be spermicidal, the issue of the controversy, at the moment, has little practical significance.

The two methods remaining, post-coital aspiration of the semen from the vagina by means of a syringe or the use of the tassette, are better described as "assisted" rather than artificial insemination. Since the full act of *coitus* precedes the application of these procedures, little theological difficulty arises, although Father Glover and others, faithful to their notion of the unlawfulness of breaking "the ordination of semen to generation", even for a few moments, insist that the syringe must not be withdrawn from the precincts of the vagina.

The general argument of those Roman Catholic theologians opposed to A.I.H. may be summed up by saying that married people have a right to only such sexual intercourse as is performed in the natural manner, and that procreation must be the result of *coitus*. Their views have now been confirmed by Pope Pius XII in three addresses, given in 1949, 1951 and 1956, so that the controversy may be considered at an end.[3] "Artificial fecundation," said the Pope, "exceeds the limits of the rights which spouses have acquired by

[1] The point also arises in connection with sterility tests. Its use here is favoured by some. See J. J. Clifford, "Sterility Tests and Their Morality", *The Ecclesiastical Review*, 108:364ff. (1942).

[2] Gerald Kelly, "Artificial Insemination: Theological and Natural Law Aspects", *University of Detroit Law Journal*, 33:135 (1955–6). For a discussion of the opposing views see the same author, "Moral Aspects of Sterility Tests and Artificial Insemination", *Medico-Moral Problems*, St. Louis 1956, II:14.

[3] Pius XII, "Address to Fourth Convention of Catholic Doctors in Rome" (September 1949), *A.A.S.* 41:557. "Address on Moral Problems of Married Life" (October 29, 1951), *A.A.S.* 43:835 at 850. "Address to Second World Congress on Fertility and Sterility" (May 19, 1956), *The Pope Speaks*, 3:191 (Washington, D.C. 1956–7), *A.A.S.* 48:468.

the matrimonial contract, namely, that of fully exercising their natural sexual capacity in the natural accomplishment of the marital act. The contract in question does not confer on them a right to artificial fecundation, for such a right is not in any way expressed in the right to the natural conjugal act, and cannot be derived from it. Still less can one derive it from the right to the 'child', the primary 'end' of marriage. The matrimonial contract does not give this right, because it has for its object not the 'child' but the 'natural acts' which are capable of engendering a new life and are destined to this end. It must likewise be said that artificial fecundation violates the natural law and is contrary to justice and morality."[1] The only exception admitted by the Pontiff is what I have called "assisted" insemination. He expressly excluded "the use of certain artificial means designed only to facilitate the natural act or to enable that act, performed in a natural manner, to attain its end".[2]

A.I.H., CHRISTIAN MORALS AND THE LAW

Do Christian principles require that A.I.H. should be regulated by the law? The Feversham Committee concluded that it was only rarely resorted to in Great Britain and that it should not be condemned.[3] As has been seen, Christian opinion is divided as to its moral legitimacy, but on neither view would intervention by the courts be justified. The common good is in no way affected by A.I.H., it is not subversive of marriage as the basis of civil society, and raises no intricate legal difficulties. Its use or non-use is a matter for conscientious decision by the parties of the marriage, having carefully considered their own situation and the moral guidance afforded by their denomination. To take the issue out of the forum of the private conscience into that of the courts would constitute

---

[1] *The Pope Speaks*, 3:195 (1956–7).

[2] *A.A.S.* 41:557 at 560.

[3] *The Report*, p. 19. The Committee viewed the possibility of using A.I.H. to produce children of a particular sex by separating spermatozoa into those carrying male and those carrying female genes and thus leading to an increased demand for A.I.H. They concluded that the experiments should be kept under review. Widespread recourse to A.I.H. for this purpose might well upset the balance of the sexes in the community. *The Report*, pp. 20 and 34.

an unwarrantable intrusion into the privacy of the home, which, even on the Roman Catholic view, would create a worse evil than that which a prohibitory law would be designed to prevent. A prohibition might, however, be appropriate in a Catholic code of medical ethics, adopted by the relevant medical association, for presumably no Catholic doctor could in conscience undertake to perform an artificial insemination. Nor would there be any objection to Catholic doctors endeavouring to persuade their medical colleagues of the rightness of their views, and to have such a prohibition inserted in the general code of ethics of the medical profession.[1]

A.I.D. AND THE LAW

Unlike A.I.H., the practice of A.I.D. bristles with social and legal problems. Does A.I.D. constitute adultery, and, if so, within what limitations? Is an A.I.D. child legitimate or illegitimate? What are the property rights of such a child? To these and a host of other problems the law must give answers, in which Christian opinion is vitally interested. As yet the law on the subject is fragmentary, but the tentative decisions reached must be examined as a preliminary to establishing how Christian opinion would shape the law.

A Crime?

Is A.I.D. a criminal offence at common law? Since the common law never contemplated such a contingency the answer must be negative. Is A.I.D. a statutory crime? It could only be so if it constituted adultery. Adultery is no longer punished by the English courts,[2]

---

[1] A subsidiary issue raised by both A.I.H. and A.I.D. is whether birth of such a child validates a marriage invalid from the impediment of impotence. Probably it does not. The Cardinal's committee pointed out that it would not have this effect in Roman Catholic canon law and recommended that the same position be adopted by civil law. The Feversham Committee recommended that if a live child has been born as a result of artificial insemination of a woman with the seed of her husband, or a donor, if both parties have consented, it should be a bar to proceedings by either spouse for nullity of marriage on the ground of impotence. *The Report*, pp. 33 and 82. The Committee reached this conclusion in the interests of the child.

[2] It could theoretically be punished in the ecclesiastical courts, but this is not a practical possibility.

but in most American States it is a statutory crime, although in practice the law is rarely enforced.[1] The statutes punish either adulterous cohabitation or single acts of adultery. A.I.D. would not be punishable under them, however, since a universal rule has been evolved by the courts, that to constitute adultery for criminal purposes, there must be actual contact of the sexual organs and a penetration, however slight, of the female organ by that of the male.[2] Indirectly, A.I.D. might give rise to criminal liability. An agreement to perform A.I.D. might ground an indictment for conspiracy, since a combination to carry out an immoral or unlawful purpose may be a crime, although the purpose in itself may not be criminal. Under certain circumstances an indictment might lie for obtaining property by fraud. These somewhat hypothetical cases apart, an offence might easily arise under a relevant registration statute. Thus, in England, the registration of an A.I.D. child under the Registration Act of 1953 as that of the husband, would probably be a criminal offence under the Perjury Act of 1911, involving a maximum penalty of seven years imprisonment as well as a fine.[3]

Adultery at Civil Law

Does A.I.D. constitute adultery at civil law and thus provide a ground for divorce? The traditional definitions of adultery for this purpose all include the element of sexual intercourse, but since judges and jurists did not have A.I.D. in mind when framing them, the question is not finally disposed of. Adultery gives rise to a divorce suit on two grounds: it violates the exclusive right to sexual intercourse conferred on the spouses by the marriage contract, and it may

[1] See p. 218.

[2] See George Radler, *Marquette Law Review*, 39:146–53 (1955–6). See also *State v. Warner*, 79 Utah 500, 291 Pac. 307 (1930) and others. Cf. *People v. Courier*, 79 Mich. 366, 44 N.W. 571 (1890).

[3] *Perjury Act*, 1 & 2 Geo. 5, c. 6, (1911). It has been suggested that "Father" in the Register of Births means husband of the mother at the time of the birth and not natural father. A.I.D. was not considered when the appropriate statute was drafted in the nineteenth century but adulterous miscegenation was known. A husband who forgave an adulterous wife who had conceived a child and registered himself as the father would probably not be held to have committed perjury. See *Justice of the Peace Journal*, 113:442–3 (1949). Ontario has a Vital Statistics Act of January 1949, which requires all children to be registered under the name of the mother, the name of her husband being placed after it. It is only presumed that the husband is the father of the child. See Schellen, op. cit., p. 311.

introduce a false strain of blood into the family. Adultery might then be defined in terms of carnal union or of impregnation or possibly of both. Until 1921 there had been no case in any common law jurisdiction of a finding of adultery without some element of carnal intercourse, but in that year a departure was made in the Canadian case of *Orford v. Orford*.[1] In that case a wife sued her husband for alimony, and explained the existence of a child, of which admittedly he was not the father, by alleging an operation of A.I.D. The court discounted this, holding that she had committed conventional adultery.

The judge went on to dispose of the point she had raised, namely, that A.I.D. was not *per se* adultery. "The essence of the offence of adultery," said Judge Orde, "consists not in the moral turpitude of the act of sexual intercourse, but in the voluntary surrender to another person of the reproductive powers or faculties of the guilty person; and any submission of those powers or faculties to the service or enjoyment of any person other than the husband or wife comes within the definition of 'adultery'."[2] Having admitted that A.I.D. was a wholly novel procedure which had not been considered by the courts, the Judge stated that even if it had never before been declared to be adultery, then on grounds of public policy the Courts should proceed to do so. These remarks were *obiter dicta* but have received subsequent jurisprudential support.[3] Judge Orde's view that A.I.D. constitutes adultery has been followed in one United States case, *Doornbos v. Doornbos*, an Illinois decision of 1954.[4]

The difficulties raised by Judge Orde's definition of adultery were pointed out by Lord Wheatley in the most recent court decision on A.I.D., a Scottish case of 1958. "In the normal and natural method of performing an act of sexual intercourse," said Lord Wheatley,

[1] 58 D.L.R. 251 (1921).
[2] Ibid., p. 258.
[3] See the legal sections of the *Archbishop's Report*, and the conclusions of the Hon. Justice H. B. Vaisey, D.C.L., and the Rt. Hon. H. U. Willink. These coincide in part with those of Judge Orde, pp. 36–42. See also G. P. R. Tallin, "Artificial Insemination", *Canadian Bar Review*, 34:1 (January 1956). For an opposing view see H. A. Hubbard, "A Reply to Dean Tallin", *Canadian Bar Review*, 34:425 (1956).
[4] N. 54 S. 14981. (Sup. Crt. Cook Co., December 13, 1954). An appeal was taken to the Appellate Court of Illinois but dismissed without any reference to the principal question in the case. 12 Ill. App. 2d. 473.

"there is a mutual surrender of the sexual and reproductive organs. While the primary purpose of sexual intercourse is procreation, in the eyes of the law surrender of the reproductive organs is not necessary to consummate the act of intercourse. Expedients may be used by the parties to secure birth prevention or the woman may have previously undergone an operation by which her reproductive organs were removed, or they may have ceased to function from natural causes and yet the conjunction of the sexual organs involving at least some degree of penetration would constitute intercourse and, in the circumstances under consideration, adultery. Thus, impregnation *per se* cannot be the test of adultery, since, in the eyes of the law, the act of intercourse can be consummated without impregnation either as a result of natural causes or by the parties resorting to artificial expedients."[1]

What then is the test of adultery? Lord Wheatley answered, sexual intercourse or carnal connection, maintaining that "just as artificial insemination extracts procreation from the nexus of human relationships in or outside of marriage, so does the extraction of the nexus of human relationship from the act of procreation remove artificial insemination from the classification of sexual intercourse".[2] *Conjunctio corporum* was the essential ingredient of the traditional definitions of adultery: "the idea that adultery might be committed by a woman alone in the privacy of her bedroom aided and abetted only by a syringe containing semen was one with which the earlier jurists had no occasion to wrestle".[3]

An objection to Lord Wheatley's definition of adultery is raised by the House of Lords case of *Russell v. Russell*.[4] Mrs Russell was fecundated *ab extra*, not by a syringe but by a third party, and this was held by Lord Dunedin to constitute adultery. Lord Wheatley answered this point by saying: "I am satisfied that what his Lordship meant was that where there was a mutual surrender of the bodies to an illicit passion and there was sufficient proximity of the respective

---

[1] *Maclennan v. Maclennan. Scots Law Times*, 1958 (February 8), p. 12, at p. 15. In the English case of *Baxter v. Baxter*, 1948 A.C. 274, it was held that use of contraceptives was not a bar to consummation.

[2] *Maclennan*, p. 17.

[3] *Maclennan*, p. 14. For a definition of adultery see Latey on *Divorce*, 14th ed., p. 74.

[4] 1924 A.C. 687.

organs to enable seed to pass from one to another, it did not preclude the act from being an adulterous one merely because there had
been no penetration."[1] Lord Wheatley's view receives some support
from other cases in common law jurisdictions, but there is also
authority for the proposition that an actual penetration of the
female organ by the male is necessary to constitute adultery.[2]

Applying the principles he had outlined, Lord Wheatley held that
A.I.D. did not constitute adultery, although he stressed that a
woman who allowed A.I.D. to be performed without her husband's
consent, had committed a heinous breach of the marriage contract.[3]
He went on to lay down certain propositions of law:

(1) For adultery to be committed there must be the two parties
physically present and engaging in the sexual act at the same time.

(2) To constitute the sexual act there must be an act of union involving some degree of penetration of the female organ by the male.[4]

(3) It is not a necessary concomitant of adultery that male seed
should be deposited in the female's ovum.

(4) The placing of the male seed in the female ovum need not
necessarily result from the sexual act, and if it does not, but is
placed there by some other means, there is no sexual intercourse.[5]

Lord Wheatley's views that sexual intercourse in the sense of
carnal contact is essential to adultery, and that A.I.D. does not fall
within its definitions, are supported by a number of United States

[1] *Maclennan*, p. 16.

[2] In *Rutherford v. Richardson*, 1923 A.C. 1, at p. 11, Lord Birkenhead stated
that a lesser act than penetration might constitute adultery. In *Sapsford v.
Sapsford*, 1954, p. 394, J. Karminski held that while manual satisfaction of the
co-respondent by the wife was not in itself adultery, taken in conjunction with
the nature of the association, etc., it was. Cf. Two South African cases where
partial penetration or some act short of it sufficed to constitute adultery:
Louw v. Louw, 1946 C.P.D. 117, and *Cayeux v. Cayeux*, 1956 (2) P.H., B. 23 (N.)
For a contrary view, i.e. requirement of some penetration, see *Dennis v. Dennis*,
1955, p. 153.

[3] It should be noted that the birth of a child where there has been no opportunity of access by the husband is *prima facie* evidence of adultery and the onus
of proving an artificial insemination is on the defendant. In this case she declined to provide the necessary information and the case was entered on the
undefended roll.

[4] Elsewhere in his judgment Lord Wheatley postulates "a physical contact
with an alien and unlawful sexual organ" as a necessary element of adultery,
p. 18.

[5] *Maclennan*, p. 17.

cases.[1] In April 1956, a sub-committee of the Michigan State Bar Committee reached a similar conclusion.[2] In the House of Lords on February 26, 1958, Lord Merriman, President of the Probate, Admiralty and Divorce Division of the High Court, referred to Lord Wheatley's decision and affirmed that in his view A.I.D. was not adultery.

Some jurists, including Dr Glanville Williams, have sought to escape from the dilemma of choosing between impregnation and sexual intercourse as the basis of adultery, by treating it as a dual concept based on both.[3] The female genital consist of the organs of sexual intercourse and the organs of reproduction, surrender of either to a third party being adultery. Whether the reproductive organs are surrendered to the syringe of a medical practitioner or to a third party during sexual intercourse is immaterial.

Assuming that A.I.D. is adultery, does it cease to be so if the husband gives his consent? One can argue that it does, since there is no physical intimacy between the wife and a third party, children of a false blood strain are not secretly introduced into the family, and the purpose of the operation is not to weaken the marriage but to strengthen it. On the other hand, if adultery is defined as the surrender of the wife's reproductive powers to another man, the husband has no greater right to consent to A.I.D. than he would to her commission of conventional adultery. In any case, consent would constitute a bar of connivance to a divorce decree.

Lord Wheatley's view that A.I.D. does not constitute adultery seems more in accord with traditional jurisprudence and common-sense than its opposite. It avoids a major difficulty of definition as well as such absurdities as citing the donor and doctor as co-respondents. A.I.D. without consent should certainly be a ground for

---

[1] In *Hoch v. Hoch*, an unreported Illinois case, Judge Feinberg held that A.I.D. was insufficient evidence of adultery to found a divorce decree. In *Cw. v. Moon*, 151 Pa. Super. 555, 30 A 2d. 704 (1943) it was held that "the gist of adultery is voluntary sexual intercourse: it being defined as carnal connection between a married person with any person not his wife or husband". In *Johnson v. Johnson*, 78 N.J. Eq. 507, 80 A. 119 (1911) an element of penetration and connection was held necessary.

[2] See *University of Detroit Law Journal*, 34:473.

[3] This view is adopted by Judge H. B. Vaisey and the Rt. Hon. H. U. Willink. See *Report of Archbishop's Commission*, p. 37. See also *The Practitioner*, 118:349 (1947).

dissolution of marriage and a recommendation to this effect was made by the Royal Commission on Marriage and Divorce in 1956.[1]

Legitimacy of A.I.D. Child

Is a child born of A.I.D. legitimate or illegitimate?[2] Here again the case law is scanty. In *Strnad v. Strnad*,[3] the decision was in favour of legitimacy provided the husband gave his consent, the judge equating the position to that of a child born out of wedlock, who is legitimated by the subsequent marriage of the parties. A contrary decision was reached in *Doornbos v. Doornbos*, decided some years later.[4] Most lawyers are, however, agreed that such a child is not legitimate.[5] It is difficult to see what bearing the husband's consent has on the child's legitimacy, which must be judged by objective rules of law.[6]

Legitimacy is of great personal importance to the child and will also determine such matters as property rights, succession to titles of honour, rights of maintenance, etc.[7] In most jurisdictions, illegitimate children have rights of succession on intestacy to the mother but not to the father. In a number of jurisdictions a father is bound to maintain his wife's illegitimate children, but in others he

---

[1] Cmd. 9678 of 1956, paras. 90, 318.

[2] According to the Cardinal's committee, such a child would be illegitimate by Roman Catholic canon law.

[3] 190 Misc. 786, 78 N.Y.S. 2d. 390 (Sup. Ct. 1948). Judge Greenberg held that a husband had a right of visitation but the mother moved to another jurisdiction where this decision was not followed. See *Indiana Law Journal*, 28:620, n. 3. The position as to property rights was left open.

[4] The consent or non-consent of the husband was held irrelevant.

[5] See reply of Rt. Hon. Henry Willink, then Minister of Health, that such a child is illegitimate. April 19, 1945, *Hansard*, 410:379. Also Glanville Williams, op. cit., p. 118. See also Report of Sub-Committee of Michigan State Bar Association to this effect, April 28, 1956.

[6] The sole test of legitimacy is the existence of a marital bond between the natural parents. The child must be immediately biologically related to its mother's husband.

[7] In a memorandum submitted to the Home Office Committee on artificial insemination, the College of Arms recommended that children born as a result of A.I.D. should not be allowed to succeed to peerages and other dignities and honours. To allow succession would be "a fraud on the Sovereign" and would wrong those who stood lower than the husband of the A.I.D. child's mother. *The Times*, March 22, 1960.

is not, so that legitimacy would again determine the issue.[1] In practice, however, illegitimacy would be difficult to establish. Apart from the secrecy surrounding A.I.D., the law presumes that a child born in lawful wedlock is a child of the marriage, and in England bars declarations of non-access by the father or mother which would bastardize issue born after the marriage.[2]

These two principal issues apart, A.I.D. raises a host of subsidiary legal issues. Is A.I.D. performed without the wife's consent tantamount to rape? Could it under certain circumstances amount to incest? Would insemination with a dead man's semen constitute necrophilia? What is the legal responsibility of the physician who performs A.I.D.? To these and a number of related questions the law provides no certain answer.[3] How the law *should* answer them depends directly on one's view of the nature and purpose of the institution of marriage.

In the controversy over the legitimacy of A.I.D., two conflicting views of matrimony are clearly discernible, and from these different premises, the rival protagonists have drawn radically conflicting conclusions. The traditional Christian view of marriage, reflected in the common law, is that marriage is an exclusive, lifelong, contract,

---

[1] In England the Matrimonial Proceedings (Magistrates Courts) Act, 1960, provides that a magistrate's court shall have power in any matrimonial proceedings brought under the Act to order the payment by the husband of maintenance for any child born to the wife and accepted by the husband as one of the family. This covers A.I.D. children.

[2] This presumption is one of the strongest in English and United States law. In *Ohlsen v. Ohlsen*, Super Crt. Cook County Ill. (unrep.) it was held that the presumption was not overcome by conflicting evidence of artificial insemination. See *Journal of American Medical Association*, 1639 (1955). For the rule as to declarations, see *Goodwright v. Moss* (1777) 2 Cowp. 591. In the United States, generally speaking, the wife has no right to make a declaration, but the husband is not under the same disability. See *Vetten v. Wallace*, 39 Ill. App. 390 (4th Dist. 1890), *Flint v. Pierce*, 136 N.Y. Supp. 1056 (Sup. Crt. 1912), *Anon v. Anon*, 143 N.Y.S. 2d. 221. (Sup. Crt. 1955).

[3] A typical problem which could occur is that raised by the South African "Immorality Act". (Act No. 5 of 1927 as amended by Act No. 21 of 1950). The Act makes it a criminal offence to have illicit carnal intercourse with a non-European female if one is a European male, or with a non-European male if one is a European female. Illicit intercourse is intercourse other than that between husband and wife. Would an appropriate operation of A.I.D. violate this statute? Similar problems could arise under United States miscegenation statutes.

creating a permanent status, necessary for the procreation and education of children and for the stability of the State.[1] Statute has modified this concept: divorce is now easily obtainable both in England and the United States, but the marriage dissoluble by mutual consent is unknown to the law, and it is presumed to be for life, unless certain clearly defined matrimonial offences are committed.[2] Opposed to this traditional notion is the personalist concept of marriage, in which the contract depends for its validity on the mutual consent of the spouses and its purpose is to promote their joint happiness. Once these conditions have ceased to exist, the marriage should be dissolved. Essentially this is a non-Christian view of marriage, but it has received support from individual Christians of various Protestant denominations.

A.I.D.—THE CHRISTIAN VIEW

Marriage, according to traditional Christian theology has three ends, the procreation of children, the promotion of the mutual love of the spouses, and the orderly satisfaction of the sexual instincts. Roman Catholic theologians stress that procreation is the primary end of marriage, but the majority of Anglican and Protestant divines do not distinguish between primary and secondary ends, regarding them as equal in importance.[3] Further dispute centres around the

---

[1] The 1948 Lambeth Conference passed the following resolution: "The Conference affirms that the marriage of one whose former partner is still living may not be celebrated according to the rites of the Church, unless it has been established that there exists no marriage bond recognized by the Church." (No. 94.)

[2] The traditional view of marriage was adopted by the *Royal Commission on Marriage and Divorce* (1956). "The Western world has recognized that it is in the best interests of all concerned—the community, the parties to a marriage and their children—that marriage should be monogamous and that it should last for life. It has always recognized that owing to human frailty, some marriages will not endure for life, and that in certain circumstances it is right that a spouse should be released from the obligations of marriage. . . . By the law of England and of Scotland, marriage is the voluntary union of one man and one woman to the exclusion of all others . . . . We have accepted these views on marriage and divorce as the basis of our approach to the task." Cmd. 9678.

[3] Thus the Lambeth Conference of 1958 stated: "It has been common in Christian theology to mention the procreative function first, as if to say that it is the ruling purpose. So it is, in the sense that no marriage would be according to God's will which (where procreation is possible) did not bear fruit in children.

sacramental character of matrimony, but all Christians are agreed that it is a state specially blessed by the Creator, and that Church and State have duties to protect it by law. Children will not be the fruit of every marriage and the absence of issue in no way invalidates the contract, yet the normal expectation is that children will be born and visibly embody the love of the spouses. The Christian teaching that marriage is monogamous and indissoluble derives fom theological principle and revelation, but it is also based on the natural order which requires these two features not only for the good of the spouses but pre-eminently for that of the children. Parental duty does not end with conception, for the child requires to be nurtured and educated, and this can only take place within the framework of the family.

"Every use of the faculty given by God for the procreation of new life," states Pius XI in his encyclical *Casti Connubii*, "is the right and the privilege of the married state alone, by the law of God and of nature, and must be confined absolutely within the sacred limits of that state."[1] The natural law principle, here invoked, is accordingly not an arbitrary dogma but one based on the essential conditions of human existence. For the Christian, then, the argument that every woman has a "right" to bear a child has no validity, for outside of the married state no such claim is recognized.[2] Those who advocate such a practice, and the development of A.I.D. makes it a practical possibility for all spinsters, spare little thought for the welfare of the child. Yet modern psychiatry confirms what the Church has always known, that a fatherless child is potentially more liable to neurotic and psychological disorders than one brought up normally

---

But it is clearly not true that all other duties and relationships in marriage must be subordinate to the procreative one. Neither the Bible nor human experience supports such a view. Where it has been held, the reason generally lay in a fear of misuse of the sexual relationship or in a false sense that there is, in any sexual relationship, an intrinsic evil." *Report*, 2, 144.

[1] Pius XI. *Casti Connubii*. Encyclical on Christian Marriage. *A.A.S.* 22:546 (1930). The Pontiff quotes St Augustine on Conjugal Honour: "What belongs to either of the parties by reason of this contract sanctioned by the divine law, may not be denied, or permitted to any third person."

[2] Thus Pius XII declared in 1949: "Artificial insemination outside of marriage is to be condemned purely and simply as immoral. According to both the natural law and the divine positive law, the procreation of new life can only be the fruit of marriage." *A.A.S.* 41:557 at 559 (1949).

within the family.[1] Furthermore, Christian teaching denies man absolute sovereignty over his body. "He may not," says the Church of England Report, "use his body, his talents, his powers, just as he pleases: they are to be used in accordance with God's will, made known to man in part by revelation, in part through apprehension, both intuitive and rational, of general moral principles, and in part from the internal structure and inherent purpose of that particular thing of which he has the use."[2]

Within the married state, the right to beget new life belongs to the spouses alone. The Christian view is that the marriage contract gives no absolute right to husband and wife to the conception of children, but confers on them a permanent and exclusive right to sexual intercourse, and the use of each others reproductive functions, which may result in the birth of children. This right cannot be waived even with the consent of both parties, for although the marriage contract is formed initially by free agreement, it creates a status which is not alterable at the will of the parties. Much less can one party change it by unilateral action.[3] As recent theology has emphasized, the act of *coitus* is very much more than a physiological device to beget children, since it involves the deepest emotions of both parties and is an act of spiritual as well as physical love in which the spouses make a mutual and disinterested surrender of themselves. "To reduce the cohabitation of married persons and the conjugal act to a mere organic function for the transmission of the germ life," said Pius XII in his address to the Italian midwives in 1951, "would be to convert the domestic hearth, sanctuary of the family, into nothing more than a biological laboratory. Hence, in our address of September 29, 1949, to the international congress of Catholic doctors, we formally excluded artificial insemination from marriage. The conjugal act in its natural structure is a personal action, a simultaneous and immediate co-operation of the spouses,

---

[1] See St Thomas, *Summa Contra Gentiles*, III:122 (London 1928)

[2] *Archbishop's Report*, p. 44.

[3] "The husband may not demand that his wife receive the seed of another man; nor may the wife demand that her husband authorize the reception of alien seed. By their mutual surrender to each other in the marriage contract, they set up an exclusive union and an exclusive mutual right. Neither has the power to introduce into that union any third party by such means as involve breach of that mutual right." *The Archbishop's Report*, p. 45.

which by the very nature of the participants and the special character of the act, is the expression of that mutual self-giving which, in the words of Holy Scripture, effects the union *in one flesh*."[1] A.I.D., as the Archbishop's Commission pointed out, effectively depersonalizes the sexual act by removing it entirely from the nexus of human relationships.

The rejection of A.I.D. by the Anglican and Roman Catholic Churches has been made on similar grounds by various Protestant denominations.[2] Leading theologians of the Lutheran Established Church in Sweden have stated that A.I.D. constitutes the unwarrantable intrusion of a third party into the marriage relationship. "And there is certainly nothing in the Bible that could be interpreted as suggesting that a woman can fulfil her highest task, motherhood, by the agency of a man other than her husband."[3] Protestantism, declared M. Marchal, Professor of Divinity at Paris, rejects A.I.D. as conflicting with the principle of monogamous marriage.[4] Another French Protestant divine has characterized A.I.D. as a revolt of man against God's creative power and the authority of the scriptures: "For it is precisely by this coming together, this spiritual, sentimental and physical union, that humankind participates in the act of creation; in other words: every authentic creation is consummated in love, that is, through God's love for us, to whom He has given these powers. If we refuse to recognize this love and this unity, we are committing an offence against life and against divine love."[5] At the Methodist Conference in England in 1958, the secretary of the Department of Christian Citizenship also condemned A.I.D.[6]

---

[1] October 29, 1951, *A.A.S.* 43:835 at 850 (1951). The Pope repeated these views on May 19, 1956. See *The Pope Speaks*, 3:191 (1956–7), *A.A.S.* 48:468.

[2] A diocesan council of the diocese of Northern Indiana (Protestant Episcopal) passed a resolution condemning A.I.D. as contrary to God's will, of an adulterous nature, and harmful to the sanctity of family and individual life. See Joseph Fletcher, op. cit., p. 110.

[3] A. M. C. M. Schellen, op. cit., pp. 361–2.   [4] Ibid., p. 362.

[5] J. Bosc. "La Fécondation Artificielle": *Reforme Hebdomodaire Protestant Française* (June 26, 1948), 4: No. 171. The Dutch Protestant Society "Zedenopbouw" already referred to, stated that A.I.D. violated the integrity of conjugal intercourse.

[6] *The Observer*, July 13, 1958. For another Free Church condemnation of A.I.D., see the paper by the Rev Dr T. G. Dunning in *Artificial Insemination*, Report of a Conference held by the Public Morality Council (London 1947).

Jewish views vary, but most Rabbinical authorities agree that it is sinful.[1]

Adultery from the Christian Standpoint

A.I.D., as has been seen, is regarded by Christians as sinful, but what kind of sin is it? Does it constitute adultery? Adultery in the traditional Christian definition must include bodily union between two persons one of whom is married to another.[2] Other sexual acts, short of union, may be sinful, but do not amount to adultery.[3] This lack of bodily contact is stressed by those who argue that A.I.D. is not morally adultery. Adultery, they add, injures the other partner, disrupts the family and harms society, but A.I.D. with the consent of both spouses does none of these things. Adultery, in essence, is a betrayal of the other partner and the giving way to lustful pleasure, but neither occur in A.I.D. As to harming society, the harm arises from the deception required by present laws and these could easily be altered.

The argument that A.I.D. is not adultery because it involves no sensual pleasure may be summarily disposed of. As the Archbishop's Commission pointed out: "Adultery is not wrong because people enjoy it. The enjoyment is sinful because the adultery is wrong. . . . Fornication, adultery and (ordinarily) masturbation are wrong because they are all disordered uses of the sex function: the function is ordered away from its proper end."[4] The evil in adultery is the surrender of the body to one who has no right to receive it. It derogates from the exclusive right to sexual intercourse given by

---

[1] The Chief Rabbi of Algeria has stated that A.I.D. is adultery according to mosaic law. In agreement are the French Chief Rabbi and Rabbi Weinberg of Berlin. See Schellen, op. cit. For conflicting Rabbinical *responsa* see *Syracuse Law Review*, 7:104 (1955).

[2] See St Paul: *Romans* vii, 3; 1 *Corinthians* vi, 15 and 16. Canon law gives no definition of adultery but the moral theology books do. Thus Henry Davis, S.J., defines adultery as "copula inter virum et feminam, quorum alterutra est conjugata. Hoc peccatum est contra castitatem et iustitiam". *Moral and Pastoral Theology*, II:238 (sixth edition, London 1949). A similar definition is given by Father Prummer, O.P., in *Vade Mecum Theologiae Moralis*, p. 283, s. 523 (1923 ed.).

[3] Adultery may be committed in the "heart", see *Matthew* v, 28. Even here, however, the desire for bodily union is present, and the consenting to that desire constitutes the sin. Adultery of this type would have no canonical effect.

[4] *Archbishop's Report*, p. 50.

the marriage contract. A.I.D. is similar to adultery in that the reproductive organs are surrendered to the use of one who has no right to them, the exclusive right to their employment being vested in the husband. In neither case does the consent of the husband or wife alter the immorality of the act, since the rights conferred by matrimony are not alienable.[1] A.I.D. and adultery then, are of the same genus but not the same species. Technically, A.I.D. is not adultery since there is no bodily contact, but it partakes of the malice of adultery since it violates the exclusiveness of the married state.[2]

Should A.I.D. be Prohibited by Law?

Whether or not A.I.D. should be a ground for divorce is not a question on which Christian opinion is relevant, since the authority of the State to dissolve the marriage contract is not recognized.[3] A.I.D. without the consent of both spouses should, however, constitute a ground for judicial separation, since it fundamentally breaches the marriage contract, and, of this, canon and civil law should take cognisance.[4] The Church is not, on the other hand, indifferent to the question whether A.I.D. should be made a crime, since she is

[1] Thus the late Cardinal Griffin declared on April 8, 1945: "No consent of husband and wife can remove the immorality from the act nor render the child legitimate." Cf. Canon 1081, s. 2, which defines matrimonial consent as "an act of the will by which each partner gives and receives permanent and exclusive bodily rights for the performance of acts fitted of their very nature for the generation of children".

[2] The reasons for the exclusive character of the matrimonial state are discussed by St Thomas Aquinas in his *Summa Contra Gentiles*, III:CXXIV, London 1928.

[3] Nevertheless the Church of England committee advising the Feversham Committee recommended that A.I.D. by the wife without her husband's consent should be made a new ground for divorce. This recommendation was, of course, limited to secular law and made without prejudice to theological views.

[4] Cf. The Royal Commission on Marriage and Divorce which with one dissentient (Lord Keith of Avonholm) recommended that A.I.D. without consent should be a ground for judicial separation. Cmd. 9678, p. 91. This recommendation was also made by the Cardinal's committee, which suggested that the inseminator and donor should be liable for costs and damages. Whether donation of semen by a husband without a wife's consent should be a ground for judicial separation or divorce is more debatable. The wife is undoubtedly injured by this, but not as gravely as the husband by the wife's impregnation without his consent.

interested in maintaining the common good of the community which
A.I.D. must necessarily affect, either for good or evil. The Archbishop of Canterbury's Commission, with one dissentient, concluded that A.I.D. was so harmful to society that it should be prohibited, a view upheld by the Archbishop himself speaking in the
House of Lords and elsewhere.[1] On the setting up of the Feversham
Committee in 1958, the Archbishop appointed a second committee
to formulate the Church of England's attitude to artificial insemination and advise the Feversham Committee. This committee, while
expressing its broad agreement with the report of the earlier commission, recommended that although A.I.D. should be treated as
unlawful, in the sense of not being countenanced by the law, it
should not be made a criminal offence. In the committee's view,
A.I.D. should be equated with adultery or fornication according to
circumstances, and this should be declared if necessary by legislation.
The Archbishop stood by the conclusions of the earlier commission
and therefore submitted his own personal memorandum on A.I.D.
to the departmental committee. In 1960 both memoranda were
published by the Church Information Office under the title "Artificial Insemination By Donor: Two Contributions to a Christian
Judgment". The Cardinal's committee came to a similar conclusion
but recognized that such a course might be impracticable. In that
event the Committee suggested that the maintaining of semen banks
of donors and the sale of semen should be made illegal.[2] In reaching
its conclusion, the Archbishop's Commission laid great stress on the
fraud and perjury to which A.I.D. at present gives rise. A false

[1] In January 1958, in his presidential address to the Convocation of Canterbury, the Archbishop called for a legal ban on A.I.D. The subject was fully
debated in the House of Lords (February 26, 1958) on Lord Blackford's motion
declaring: "That in the opinion of this House artificial insemination of a married
woman by a donor other than her husband is tantamount to adultery, that it
should be sufficient ground for divorce and that all children so conceived are
illegitimate." The motion was by leave withdrawn. The Archbishop of York
condemned A.I.D. as immoral but did not think it should be made a crime, a
view shared by the Bishop of Exeter. Lord Denning also condemned A.I.D.:
"It seems to me that if this practice becomes widespread it will strike at the
stability and security of family life, at the roots of our civilization."
[2] Recommendation 2. See *The Dublin Review*, Spring 1960, p. 28. The
Cardinal's committee also suggested that in the case of A.I.D. being carried out
without the husband's consent, the husband should have an action against the
inseminated donor for damages and costs.

registration of the child's father must be made, and the child itself may inherit property to which it has no natural or legal right. Society has a right to knowledge of each individual's identity, and here again there is perpetration of a fraud.[1] The Commission pointed out that any widespread use of A.I.D. would undermine public confidence in the genuineness of family ties and records of parentage and increase the possibilities of involuntary incest. "The increased likelihood of the marriage of half-brothers to half-sisters unknown to each other is certainly not to be ignored when the potential offspring of one donor is reckoned in thousands: and even where an arbitrary limit of 100 children *per* donor has been imposed, the possibility of marriage between two of them is not very remote."[2]

All these results flow from the secrecy which at present shrouds operations of A.I.D., and the validity of the Commission's objections accordingly depend on how far secrecy is essential. On this question the members were not in doubt: "It is axiomatic for the champions of A.I.D. that secrecy shall be absolute and continuous; and this, in a matter which touches the very springs of physical life, the family's pride in its stock, and the community's concern for its future genetic constitution, is contrary to the established and unvarying tradition of every known society."[3] But is secrecy an absolute necessity? Presumably it has a threefold basis. It protects the spouses from harmful comment and gossip, safeguards the donor's reputation and frees him from risk of blackmail, and protects the psychological security of the child. Exposure to the first might well be a risk which a childless couple would be prepared to take, and the donor could be protected by a register with restricted access. Whether secrecy is essential for the child is open to conjecture since there is no evidence of the effects of such a revelation on the psyche. Accidental discovery of the truth by the child might be so

---

[1] The Feversham Committee doubted whether society at large had any such right, since in most dealings it is of no consequence to know who the parties' fathers were, and society allows the use of any surname at will. However, it conceded that within a fairly wide circle of friends and relations the assumption is usually made that the mother's husband is the father of the child. A.I.D. will thus usually involve the permanent deception of a considerable number of people. *The Report*, pp. 66–7.

[2] *Archbishop's Report*, p. 34.

[3] Ibid., p. 34.

harmful that it would be better deliberately to inform him. In the exceptional case of A.I.D. being resorted to because of an heredi-tary disease of the father, knowledge of his origin would, however, be of positive advantage to the child. The solution of providing a compulsory register of A.I.D. births with a number in place of the donor's name is then at least a possibility, and if this were adopted the objections on the grounds of perjury, deceit and fraud, would be overcome. On the other hand, most psychologists agree that know-ledge of the manner of its birth would be harmful to the child and possibly traumatic.[1]

Christian teaching presents a more fundamental objection to A.I.D. than that of contingent fraud and deception. Our whole social system is based on the institution of the family and the mono-gamous character of marriage. A.I.D. practised on any appreciable scale would effectively subvert this order and substitute a different pattern of relationships.[2] This was the principle consideration leading the Feversham Committee to condemn A.I.D. The committee added: "Anything which tends to weaken the estate of marriage threatens the security of children everywhere."[3] As the Archbishop's Commission points out, the claim that A.I.D. creates a family is false, for the essential structure of the family is "the community of parents and the children begotten by them". A.I.D. creates a quite different association with another set of relationships. With the abandonment of the principle that child bearing is only lawful with the co-operation of the parties to the marriage contract, the way would be opened for the bearing of children by unmarried women. In this way a dissolvent would be introduced into the social system and the common good seriously damaged. The Christian moralist

[1] Thus Dr Mary Barton refers to the "most appalling damage" which would be done to a child by the discovery that the man thought to be the father was in fact no relation. *Artificial Human Insemination*, London 1947, p. 45. The Archbishop's Commission accepts this view and rejects a register as a practical solution, adding that it might be dishonestly used. *Report*, p. 42.

[2] Thus the Rev K. Glover writes: "The reason why marriage is an essential condition for the lawful use of the generative faculty is because of the harm which would come to the offspring and to society in general were the parties not united in the permanent and exclusive bond created by marriage. The obligation, therefore, to the right use of the generative faculty is an obligation of social (legal) justice, so that any abuse of the faculty involves some kind of injustice against society." Op. cit., p. 139–40.   [3] *The Report*, p. 66.

and sociologist can thus legitimately call for the practice of A.I.D. to be forbidden by law.

It may be asked why Christian teaching requires legislation against A.I.D. when it does not demand legal suppression of adult homosexual practices.[1] The question can only be answered by considering the common good. A.I.D. constitutes a direct attack on the family, whereas homosexual practices between adults do not. The law, by removing penal sanctions from homosexual behaviour in certain clearly defined circumstances, in no way approves of homosexuality, but merely states that the problem is better dealt with in the internal forum of conscience, the confessional, or the doctor's consulting room, rather than in the courts. With A.I.D. the situation is different, since the law cannot ignore the problem and do nothing, but must either equate it with the birth of children by natural parents or forbid it altogether. The first course would give legal approval to A.I.D. by institutionalizing it. The true parallel in relation to homosexuality would be a proposal that homosexuals could contract a legally binding "marriage" which would have social and legal effects. A final distinction of some importance is that most homosexual acts are rooted in passion and weakness of the will, whereas A.I.D. is not the fruit of a masterful concupiscence, but a deliberate and carefully considered act, taken after full consideration of the issues involved.

A further objection is that the Christian view in England and the United States is that of a minority and the Church has no right to impose her particular theological teaching on the majority. Whether the Christian view on this particular issue is a minority one is by no means certain and can only be determined after the fullest public discussion and debate.[2] The conclusions and reasoning of the Feversham Committee indicate that the Christian view of A.I.D. is that generally accepted in England. Setting aside this open question, the

[1] See pp. 223-5.

[2] 247 students at Colorado University were asked (1) Would you yourself make use of artificial insemination with your husband as donor if you wanted a child and could not have one by normal sex relations? (2) Would you yourself make use of artificial insemination using an unknown donor if you wanted a child and your husband was sterile? 10 per cent answered *no* to question (1), but 50 per cent gave a negative answer to question (2). See Greenberg, "Social Variables in Acceptance or Rejection of Artificial Insemination." *American Sociological Review*, 16:86 (1951).

objection is fallacious since the Church possesses no political means of imposing her will on a hostile majority. Any proposal to ban A.I.D. would need the consent of a democratically obtained majority in the legislature. Christian action would thus be limited to persuading the legislators and electors that the Christian view was right and its implementation in the best interests of the country, and in pursuing this end would be entitled to use any of the normal political means for securing assent. In a country officially recognizing one particular religion, different considerations might apply.[1]

The premiss that A.I.D. is morally wrong does not, as has been noted, entail the conclusion that it should be prohibited by law. The Feversham Committee condemned A.I.D. but decided against a legal ban because it doubted whether the practice could be effectively prohibited, and held that its extent and social consequences were too small to justify making it into a new offence. The committee concluded that while the prohibition of A.I.D. might deter some of those at present engaging in the practice, others would not be so deterred, and their activities would be extremely difficult to detect. The committee also felt that A.I.D. might fall into unscrupulous hands if prohibited, and increased scope be given for blackmail.

Successful implementation of the law would require the whole-hearted co-operation of the medical profession, and it has been maintained that this would not be forthcoming, but the evidence is conflicting.[2] Given a complaisant doctor and a consenting husband the law would be wholly ineffectual. These arguments have some

[1] That is in States where an established Church is co-equal with the State or to a substantial degree independent of it, not in States such as England where the Church is subject to Parliament. Thus on July 17, 1956, the *Osservatore Romano*, official Vatican newspaper, took the Tribunal of Rome to task for some passages in a judgment holding that a husband could repudiate a child born to his wife by A.I.D. performed with his knowledge and consent. The judgment stated that a religious evaluation was *obviously* not the basis of the secular system of law. "We must not only take into account ethical considerations, but also the fundamental law of the country and the general judicial conscience. And so our decision must be squared to the fundamental principles of our particular law." Such a distinction, declared *L'Osservatore*, was not consistent with the fact that in a Catholic nation, in which the State officially proclaims the Catholic religion, the public system of law cannot prescind from Catholic morality.

[2] In England, the Feversham Committee concluded from the evidence submitted that A.I.D does not have the general support of the profession (*The Report*, pp. 67–8). Those condemning the practice included committees of the

weight but show an undue pessimism about the deference of doctors and others to the law. Some doctors would undoubtedly defy it, but they would be a small minority. No law is completely enforceable and the legislature would have officially expressed its disapproval of A.I.D., which for many Christians would be worthwhile in itself.[1]

The Committee also justified non-intervention on the grounds that A.I.D. was only practised by a tiny minority, but this is hardly a convincing argument since the very smallness of its incidence makes a ban practicable, and the ban might well stop the practice from spreading. The report also referred to the role of the criminal law as outlined by the Wolfenden Committee and stressed that since A.I.D. is not offensive to public order or decency a ban would be an encroachment on individual liberty. But the appropriate test to apply here is not that of personal liberty but of the common good. The libertarian argument ignores the harmful social effects of A.I.D. and the ambiguous position of the resulting child. It is clear that from the Christian view any curtailment of liberty involved by prohibiting A.I.D. would be more than compensated for by the benefit accruing to society from preventing its wider spread.

Despite its rejection of A.I.D. the Church is not indifferent to the problems raised by childless marriages, yet cannot accept the argument that a barren marriage is bound to fail. A constructive approach to the problem would be an extension of the adoption facilities now available, especially those for foreign adoption.[2] A precaution that

Royal College of Physicians, the Royal College of Surgeons, Edinburgh, and the Royal College of Obstetricians and Gynaecologists. The Council of the British Medical Association referred to a "substantial body of opinion in the profession" which regards the practice as undesirable, although in the Council's opinion it did not "contravene any of the accepted principles of scientific medicine". However, in the U.S., opinion is in conflict. E.g. at a convention in Atlantic City in 1955, 500 medical specialists in problems of sterility declared A.I.D. to be a "completely ethical, moral and desirable form of medical therapy". *New York Times*, June 5, 1955. For a resolution to the contrary by the Federation of Catholic Physicians Guilds representing 4,000 Canadian and U.S. doctors, see *The Register*, Denver, Colorado, June 19, 1955, p. 1.

[1] Cf. the Christian attitude to the laws prohibiting abortion.

[2] One million applications for adoption are made annually in the United States, but only 75,000 babies are available. See *New York Times*, April 5, 1952, p. 18. Another obstacle is fear of the child's antecedents, which may lead to anti-social or criminal developments. By careful selection of the donor, risks can be minimized in A.I.D.

might well be taken by those about to marry would be a thorough medical examination, so that those especially anxious to have children would be spared subsequent unhappiness and frustration.

A.I.D. AND UTILITARIAN–LIBERAL CHRISTIAN VIEWS

Those who favour A.I.D. are for the most part utilitarians supported by a number of "liberal" Christians, both groups being concerned with the greatest happiness of the greatest number rather than with any theological presuppositions of the nature of the married state. Their *summum bonum* is the relief of suffering and the satisfaction of human needs. As Lord Chorley stated in the Upper House: "A.I.D. could do much to relieve suffering, misery and frustration among a small number in the community and should, to that extent, be encouraged and made readily available, rather than proscribed."[1] They stress that A.I.D. would only be employed in a few instances, and that provided the married couple and their doctor have conscientiously considered all the relevant circumstances of their marriage and the implications of the use of A.I.D., most of the objections to its use would fall to the ground.[2]

Fundamental to the conclusions of many protagonists of A.I.D. is the postulation of every woman's inherent right to bear a child. Adoption is no answer to the problem, for the experience of pregnancy, birth and lactation are of profound physical and psychological importance to a woman, and adoption does not provide these. A.I.D. thus becomes the right not only of sterile couples but of unmarried women. No one seems especially concerned with the effect of fatherlessness on the child. "In artificial insemination," writes Dr Alfred Koerner, "the best interest of all involved demands that the

---

[1] See *The Times*, February 27, 1958.

[2] The circumstances when A.I.D. might legitimately be used were detailed by an anonymous writer in *The Manchester Guardian Weekly*, February 27, 1958. They are the physiological improbability that the husband can father a natural child, a thorough study by the couple of A.I.D. and its implications, a strong wish by both to have a child by this means, a stable and secure marriage and shared religious belief. The assessment of these factors requires a doctor experienced in the field and a good judge of character. With such safeguards concludes the writer: "It is hard to see what social objection can be valid or what religious objection can be embodied in civil law."

principal concern should be for the sterile couple. Once they have
decided that the process meets their moral code, who can take
exception to it?"[1] The Rev Dr Soper would rather that a child knew
the fervent love of a mother, than of neither parent.[2] The Church,
while compassionate to those who desire children and are unable
to have them, cannot but consider the demand for children at any
price, as *inordinate* in the theological sense, one that transcends all
legitimate bounds. "On what rational ground," asks the Archbishop's Commission, "is it urged that while *sexual* desires ought
not to be indulged at will, *parental* desires may be? And are the
results of indulgence in the latter case likely to be quite different, in
their total effect on the personality, from those which are known to
follow in the former?"[3]

Those Christians who favour A.I.D. reject the natural law theology
of marriage, substituting in its place a purely *personal* bond. Thus
Dean Matthews, in his dissent from the Archbishop's Report, remarks tartly that as he is a Christian and not a Stoic he must judge
A.I.D. from the standpoint of the Christian ethic and not from that
of the law of nature. This ethic is based on the notion that God is
Love, and every law, including that of nature is to be judged by the
supreme law of love. The Reverend Joseph Fletcher, a Protestant
Episcopal clergyman, adopts a similar view in his book, *Morals and
Medicine.* He asserts that the fidelity of marriage is based on a
personal bond between husband and wife, not on a legal contract,
and that parenthood is a moral rather than a material or physical
relationship. "The claim that A.I.D. is immoral," he writes, "rests
upon the view that marriage is an absolute generative, as well as

----

[1] "Medicolegal Considerations in Artificial Insemination", *Louisiana Law
Review*, 8:484 (1947-8). Cf. Charles Neville, "Is it adultery?" *McLean's Magazine*, February 15, 1949: "Artificial Insemination provides the unmarried
business woman with a decent and moral method of acquiring the children
nature intended her to bear."

[2] Dr Soper has been President of the Methodist Conference in England,
but on this, as on many other topics, speaks mainly for himself. For his views see
Time Magazine, 80:50, February 17, 1958.

[3] *The Report*, p. 50. The Cardinal's committee points out that insatiable
desire of a woman for a child or the desire of a husband to escape from a sense
of inferiority indicate a lack of adaptive capacity "which is the hall-mark of the
inadequate personality". A.I.D. would place further stress on adaptive capacity,
op. cit., p. 27.

sexual, monopoly; and that parenthood is an essentially, if not solely physiological partnership. Neither of these ideas is compatible with a morality that welcomes emancipation from natural necessity, or with the Christian ethic which raises morality to the level of love (a *personal* bond), above the determinism of nature and the rigidities of the law as distinguished from love."[1]

The Dean of St Paul's denies that the law of love is too vague to form the basis of moral judgments, but in relation to A.I.D. it appears to be so. At any rate it leads to conflicting conclusions. Dean Matthews, applying the law of love, concludes tentatively that A.I.D. is an attack on our conception of personality but that there may be special circumstances in which its employment is morally justified.[2] Applying the same law, Joseph Fletcher gives it a warm and much more enthusiastic welcome. Finally Dr Soper, starting from the same premiss, concludes that A.I.D. should be made available to spinsters.[3] "I agree that the ideal condition is that a child should be born in wedlock, but wedlock is itself an omnibus word which covers a multitude of relationships that have very little love in them. Many people don't know the love of a father now. I would rather . . . that a little child knew the fervent love of a mother. Is it a better thing to impose loneliness and frustration on women who haven't the decorative values to attract a male, and therefore can't get married and have children?"[4] In practice, to apply "the law of love" is to abandon the attempt to find a rational principle to judge A.I.D. and to leave it to the sensibilities of each individual to determine its legitimacy.

Some non-Christian utilitarians go even further and welcome A.I.D. not merely as a technical device to fructify the sterile, but as a

[1] *Morals and Medicine*, p. 139.

[2] See *The Archbishop's Report*, pp. 59–63: "And finally I recur to the thought with which I began. It may be that the employment of any mechanical aids to procreation strikes a blow at the integrity of the human personality and the intimate union of body, mind and spirit, and, therefore, would have in the long run, a disastrous effect on the health of society."

[3] The Feversham Committee concluded that English doctors decline to inseminate single women. *The Report*, p. 15.

[4] The Modern Churchman's Union in evidence submitted to the Home Office departmental committee expressed its hesitation in joining in the condemnation of A.I.D. as sinful. It recommended that it should not be forbidden by the law. *The Times*, July 11, 1959.

desirable means of separating the reproductive and personal aspects of marriage. The combination of the modern techniques of birth control and A.I.D. opens a new era of opportunity for the eugenist. "It is now open to man and woman," writes Julian Huxley, "to consummate the sexual function with those they love, but to fulfil the reproductive function with those whom on perhaps quite other grounds they admire."[1] Dr Glanville Williams expresses himself in similar fashion.[2]

Leaving these prognostications aside, one must return to the facts. From the utilitarian point of view, A.I.D. must be judged by its results. As has been noted, the information on these is not extensive. The obvious beneficial result of A.I.D. is that it enables a sterile marriage to be transformed into a fruitful one. It fulfils a woman's dearest wish of bearing a child, even if that child is sired by a stranger and not by the man she loves. The husband also benefits by the partial satisfaction of his paternal instincts. Society benefits by an increase in the population. By means of A.I.D., a marriage heading for breakdown because of its childlessness may well be saved.

Against these advantages must be placed the effect of A.I.D. on the institution of marriage. Practised on any wide scale it would clearly break up the traditional pattern of the family on which Western society has up to this time been based. Those favouring A.I.D. dismiss this objection by stressing that in the nature of things only a tiny minority will make use of A.I.D. Yet we know that a large number of marriages are infertile. In the U.S.A. it is estimated that 10 per cent of the marriages are sterile. In England, medical opinion estimates the proportion of sterile marriages as between 7 per cent and 9 per cent. In 30 per cent of these the husband may be solely responsible.[3] The problem is thus not as miniscule in its

---

[1] *The Uniqueness of Man*, pp. 78–9.

[2] Dr Williams writes: "It opens the way for separating the procreative from the companionate and sexual elements in marriage. A woman can now choose one man as the biological father of her children, and another as her lover and companion, and as the father of her children by adoption. It offers the possibility, too, of immensely increasing the number of women whom it is practicable for one man regarded as of good stock to fertilize. The exploitation of this invention to its full effect would certainly involve a revolution in our social and moral ideas which is unlikely but not totally impossible." *The Sanctity of Life and the Criminal Law*, New York 1957, p. 115.

[3] The Feversham Report, p. 17.

social impact as is suggested. Indeed, one of the principal arguments used to justify A.I.D. is this very prevalence of sterility in our society. A second anti-social effect of A.I.D. might well be the siring of an excessive number of children by a single donor. It might be employed as part of a eugenic policy by a totalitarian State and even in a liberal society any extensive use of a single donor materially increases the risk of incest.[1] A third objection to A.I.D. on social grounds is that it would immeasurably increase the pace at which contemporary society is being depersonalized. Christian views on this point have already been analysed, but it is not only Christians who will recoil from the prospect of the brave new world outlined so enthusiastically by Dr Huxley and others.

The beneficial psychological effects of A.I.D. in relieving child-lessness may well be counterbalanced by subsequent complications. Paternal authority may be undermined and the husband suffer from acute feelings of inferiority, resulting in hostility to the child. The wife may transfer her affections from the husband to the donor. Even if these feelings are largely unconscious, the child may sense them and exhibit neurotic symptoms. If the child is informed of its origins either by design or by chance, then it may suffer a psycho-logical trauma of incalculable effects. A further risk is that the hus-band's attitude to the child may alter: if, for example, it develops abnormal tendencies, he may wish to disclaim paternity. Feelings of guilt and shame may develop in both parties and effectively destroy their happiness as well as that of the child.[2]

These objections are largely conjectural, but are by no means unreasonable, and the answers that may be made to them cannot claim any greater scientific accuracy. Follow up studies on A.I.D. children and their parents over a number of years and on an exten-sive scale are the only means of obtaining reliable information. Un-fortunately these would be very difficult to obtain, both because of

[1] The Feversham Committee concluded that the danger "is at present mini-mal". "We have been informed that if 2,000 live children per year were to be born in Great Britain as a result of the successful use of A.I.D. and if each donor were responsible for five children, an unwitting incestuous marriage is unlikely to occur more than once in about fifty to a hundred years", p. 12.

[2] *Vaginismus* and impotence, to remedy which A.I.D. may be sought, are themselves indications of neurosis. Such couples may well be unfit to bring up children.

the secrecy surrounding A.I.D., and the undesirability of subjecting an A.I.D. family to an inquisition which might create or increase emotional strain. The evidence that is available on A.I.D. families is on balance more favourable than not.[1] Writing in the *Manchester Guardian*, a physician engaged in this work has declared that he and a number of his colleagues have kept in touch with their cases over a number of years and failed to find any defect in the children. Their physical and mental health was sound, and a high proportion turned out to be above the average in intelligence. "I and my colleagues have no evidence whatsoever that the use of A.I.D. disrupts the family or produces psychological problems, and I am sure that this is because candidate couples are selected with care, as, of course, are the donors."[2]

Dr C. P. Blacker, Secretary of the English Eugenics Society, has personal knowledge of eight cases of A.I.D., in all of which the results have been successful. The children are happy and the legal fathers "feel towards the children (they say) more warmly than stepfathers in general would feel towards their step-children because here the child believes that legal father to be the real father."[3] Other favourable evidence adduced from personal experience has been given by Dr A. Stone, Editor of the American journal, *Human Fertility*, who has inseminated 100 couples, ten of whom returned for a second child.[4] Dr R. L. Dickinson, Chairman of the National Committee on Maternal Health, New York Academy of Medicine, also reports satisfactory results, with the incident of artificial impregnation soon forgotten.

All these statements must be received with some reserve, since the majority of A.I.D. children are still very young, and complications may well appear at a later stage. They must also be read in conjunction with the conflicting experience of other A.I.D. practitioners. Dr Eustace Chesser, for example, has stated in the *British Medical Journal*, that experience and reflection have caused him to renounce his practice of A.I.D., because of its serious psychological

---

[1] The Feversham Report states: "The information received by this means [follow-up studies] has hitherto been almost entirely favourable but it normally covers only the first few years of the child's life." p. 16.

[2] *Manchester Guardian Weekly*, February 13, 1958: "A.I.D.—a Physician's View." By a medical correspondent.

[3] *The Archbishop's Report*, p. 17.   [4] Ibid., p. 29.

dangers, among which he lists the feelings of inferiority on the husband's part after the birth of the child, anxieties about the status of the child, and the mental attitude of the wife towards the donor.[1]

The Feversham Committee reported a few cases where a woman who had received A.I.D. or her husband or child subsequently showed signs of unhappiness or instability. Some of the cases illustrate the danger of undertaking A.I.D. where the couple are not completely stable.[2]

The legal objections to A.I.D., already discussed, are as serious for the non-Christian as the Christian and can only be overcome by the same means, the abandonment of secrecy. Provision could be made for a donor register, and the entry of a number on the child's birth certificate would close the door to fraud in the devolution of property and titles of honour. With the abandonment of secrecy the way would be open for further regulation of A.I.D. by law. There are, however, weighty objections to such a register, which were pointed out in the Feversham Report, and led the committee to reject the suggestion.[3] The record would not be conclusive proof that a birth had in fact resulted from A.I.D. This could only be established by the provisions of detailed particulars of the blood groups of the husband, the donor, and the child, which would probably not be made available. The record would almost certainly be incomplete since many couples would have powerful reasons for avoiding registration. Unless there was some reason to suspect that a child was of A.I.D. origin, the record would, in many cases where consultation was called for, not in fact be consulted. Furthermore, the record would increase the danger of an A.I.D. child getting to know of his

[1] *British Medical Journal*, I:738 (1947).

[2] *The Report*, p. 17. "In the first case the husband suffered from a congenital defect which made normal intercourse impossible, and the wife from cerebral dysrhythmia. They were refused adoption on account of the wife's condition, and after A.I.D. had been tried several times without success the husband had a nervous breakdown. In the second case, the wife attempted to treat the doctor as the father. In another an A.I.D. child was followed by two children of the husband and tension developed in the family because the husband viewed the A.I.D. child differently from the other two. In the fourth case, the wife of an infertile husband became so desperate that she attempted to commit suicide; A.I.D. was performed and resulted in pregnancy; but six months later the wife again attempted suicide; one year later the husband was himself a patient in a mental home", p. 17.

[3] *The Report*, pp. 54–7.

origin and would constitute an additional threat to his security. Another difficulty would be the necessity of supplying incorrect information for the public register, unless the principal of registration was changed so that particulars given related to the "mother's husband" rather than to the "father".

Legitimacy presents a major legal problem. Christian opinion would not be in favour of legitimizing the child, as this would equate A.I.D. in one important respect with normal birth and to that extent would approve it. The Feversham Committee rejected the suggestion that A.I.D. children should be given legitimate status on this ground, and also because they thought such a change would lead to an increase in those resorting to A.I.D.[1] Two members of the committee, however, in a minority report, favoured the legitimizing of A.I.D. children, stating that it was wrong to depress the status of the child as a means of discouraging the resort to A.I.D. They made the telling point that if the community was prepared to tolerate A.I.D. it had a duty to protect the interests of the resultant children. As illegitimate children are tolerated by the community— their conception is not a criminal act—the argument entails the removal of all distinctions between legitimate and illegitimate children, a position acceptable to the signatories of the minority report but not to the majority.[2]

Those favouring A.I.D. could bring about legitimacy in a number of ways, the simplest of which would be a statute declaring that all A.I.D. children are legitimate. Bills along these lines have been introduced into the legislatures of New York, Indiana, Virginia, Wisconsin and Minnesota, but have met with no success.[3] An alternative method would be to extend existing adoption legislation. A number

[1] *The Report*, pp. 50 and 51.
[2] When the Legitimacy Bill of 1959 was being debated in the House of Commons, a new clause was proposed by which "any child born to a married woman, and accepted as one of the family by her husband", would have been deemed to be a child of the marriage. The proposal was defeated. (House of Commons Official Report, May 8, 1959, col. 760.) Although the concept of legitimacy has been extended, English law still requires that a child to be considered legitimate must be born of parents who were or have become married or who have gone through a ceremony of marriage.
[3] The Bill introduced into the legislature of the State of New York by Senator Friedman on January 26, 1948, provides as follows: (a) "A child born to a married woman by means of artificial insemination with the consent of her

of States including Arizona, California, Idaho and Utah, have statutory provisions similar to the following: "The father of an illegitimate child, by publicly acknowledging it as his own, receiving it as such with the consent of his wife, if he is married, into his family, and otherwise treating it as if it were a legitimate child, thereby adopts it, and such a child is thereupon deemed for all purposes legitimate from the time of birth."[1] Statute could provide that such legislation should cover any child of a man's wife.[2] Given the consent of the husband to the operation, adoption could be made compulsory by statute, or the husband deemed to have adopted the child if he recognized it.[3]

Amongst other modifications of the law would be the provision of adequate protection for the doctor. The written consent of husband, wife, and donor, should constitute a complete defence to any civil or criminal proceedings connected with A.I.D. save for negligent performance of the operation. As a counterbalance it might be made a criminal offence for a doctor to perform A.I.D. without consent in this form. A further criminal offence might possibly be the artificial insemination of an unmarried woman. A.I.D. without the consent of the husband could be made an additional ground for divorce, a course recommended by the Feversham Committee.[4]

husband shall be deemed the legitimate, natural child of both the husband and his wife for all purposes and such husband and wife shall sustain towards each other the legal relation of parent and child and shall have all the rights and be subjected to all the duties of that relationship including the rights of inheritance from each other. (b) The consent of the husband contemplated by subdivision 1 of this section is one which is in writing, duly executed and acknowledged by the husband, and duly filed in the office of the clerk of the county in which such husband and wife reside. Each such consent so filed shall be sealed by the clerk's office and shall not be subjected to inspection by any person or received in evidence in an action or proceeding, except pursuant to an order of a court of competent jurisdiction. The fee of the county court for filing and sealing such consent shall be one dollar."

[1] C. G. Vernier, *American Family Laws*, IV, 178–80. Other States with such legislation are Montana, North and South Dakota, and Oklahoma.

[2] Judge Ploscowe makes this suggestion. See "Your Test Tube Baby may be illegitimate", *Law Guild Review* (November–December 1948), 8:496–500.

[3] An obstacle here would be that some American States do not allow couples to adopt their natural children.

[4] *The Report*, p. 36. A Cincinnati Court in 1947 granted a divorce on this ground. A soldier returned from the war to find his wife pregnant by means of A.I.D. A divorce was granted as the husband had not given his consent.

It has also been suggested by the Law Society in a memorandum to the Feversham Committee that failure on the part of a donor to obtain his wife's consent to his acting as a donor should be a new ground for divorce, at the instance of the wife.[1] The Feversham Committee rejected this, however, on the ground that the act was not in itself serious enough to justify dissolution of the marriage and that it would be difficult to define exactly the new ground for divorce.[2]

If A.I.D. is not to be made into a criminal offence, should it be regulated by law? The Church of England committee which submitted advice to Lord Feversham's committee, as has been noted did not think it should be made a crime, but considered that it should rank as an unlawful act, unrecognized by the law and therefore unregulated. The committee, however, also concluded that if despite its advice the practice was made lawful, it should be regulated, preferably by some professional medical body such as the Royal College of Obstetricians and Gynaecologists, and in the last resort by the law itself. Such regulation should provide for the securing of the written consents of the woman to be inseminated, of her husband if any, of the donor, and if married, of the donor's wife. Other matters to be dealt with should be the selection of donors and the limitation of the number of inseminations to be obtained from them, the conditions under which the operation should be performed, and the registration and certification of the birth of the resulting child.[3]

These and other suggestions for regulation were considered by the Feversham Committee, which recommended against any legal regulation.[4] Statutory provisions regulating the medical techniques of insemination, concluded the committee, were unnecessary and would be unenforceable. It also rejected proposals that A.I.D. should be undertaken by certain practitioners only, and that advice should be available under the national health service. The committee rejected various proposals to control the non-medical aspects of A.I.D., such as the keeping of a central record of inseminations or the screening of A.I.D. applicants by a special com-

[1] See Memorandum published in the *Law Society's Annual Report* for 1959–60 at pp. 50–8.
[2] *The Report*, p. 60.
[3] *Artificial Insemination by Donor*, p. 23.
[4] *The Report*, pp. 72–8.

mittee. A suggestion that A.I.D. for single women, or for married women, without their husband's consent, should be forbidden, was also turned down. Many witnesses suggested to the committee that persons other than medical practitioners should be forbidden to perform A.I.D., but the proposal was rejected as premature since there was no evidence to show that this was taking place.

The committee justified non-intervention on a number of grounds. They thought that regulation of A.I.D. by law or through a professional body would be impracticable, and that any regulations made would be impossible to enforce.[1] They also feared that regulation would imply some degree of recognition and hence approval of the practice. There undoubtedly would be difficulties in the way of effective regulation, but some may think that the committee allowed them too much weight in reaching their conclusion that nothing should be done.

One need, not considered by the committee, was that for public health regulations governing the obtaining and distribution of semen. Presumably it was ignored because no such trade exists in England. The situation is apparently different in the United States where New York doctors were startled in 1947 to receive an unusual circular. Drawn up by a young science graduate it announced: "We offer semen drawn from healthy and investigated professional donors. Suitable types for your patients' specifications. Active specimens guaranteed and delivered daily. Confidential service- office hours 5.30-7.30 p.m."[2] Alarmed at this development New York forbade such enterprises by its sanitary code.[3]

[1] No country in the world has yet passed legislation dealing with human artificial insemination. A German commission on penal law has, however, recommended that the new criminal code should include an article prohibiting A.I.D. but permitting A.I.H. In Norway, Sweden and Denmark, committees have reported favouring the legal approval of A.I.D. under certain safeguards, but these recommendations have not been implemented. For details of the safeguards proposed see Appendix I of the Feversham Report, pp. 90-1. The Norwegian committee suggested limitation to married women and specially qualified doctors; consent of the husband in writing; and a minimum age for husband and wife of 25. The child would be granted the ordinary legal rights of a child born after normal conception.

[2] See "Symposium on Artificial Insemination", *Syracuse Law Review*, 7:96 (Fall, 1955). Article by Abner I. Weisman.

[3] S. 112. Sanitary Code. (1947:1950). These regulations are reproduced as Appendix II below.

Conclusion

Between the traditional Christian view of marriage and its person-alist-utilitarian counterpart, little common ground can be found. It is not surprising then that starting from such disparate premisses, radically conflicting conclusions should be drawn as to the manner in which A.I.D. should be dealt with by law and society. As there is no moral consensus on the status and purpose of the institution of marriage, there can be no agreement on the practical issues raised by A.I.D. Since no agreement is possible, one or other view must prevail, and if it is argued that Christians have no right to impose their views on society as a whole, they are entitled to give the secularists a *tu quoque* reply. Which solution is finally adopted is of course a political decision which must be made through the ordinary democratic machinery of the liberal State. Public debate on the subject will continue for some time, but legislative action is inevitable. An understanding of the conflicting principles involved will not lead to agreement but is indispensable for rational discussion. The rival protagonists may well remain locked in argument, but this is preferable to the exchanges of mutual recrimination and abuse, which so often masquerade as public discussion of moral issues in our contemporary pluralist society.

CHAPTER FOUR

Human Sterilization

Sterilization of human beings is a surgical operation which deprives a man or woman of the ability to procreate. Unlike castration it in no way desexes the individual, nor does it preclude participation in sexual intercourse. Its one indubitable physiological effect is to prevent the conception of children. Various sterilizing techniques have been developed by medical science, but those most commonly employed are salpingectomy for the female, and vasectomy for the male. Salpingectomy prevents conception by cutting or tying the Fallopian tubes between the ovaries and the womb. Vasectomy is an even simpler operation, which by ligating and resecting a small portion of the vas deferens, cuts off a portion of the seminal fluid and renders it sterile. Reversal is a theoretical possibility, but in practice it cannot always be brought about.[1] Other methods of sterilization such as oophorectomy (removal of the ovaries), of hysterectomy (removal of the womb), are irreversible in all cases.

Sterilization may be employed for a number of purposes. Therapeutic sterilization is performed for health reasons, the most common subjects being women for whom a further pregnancy would prove dangerous. Eugenic sterilization is performed as a means of racial improvement, to prevent the birth of physically deformed or mentally abnormal children. Sterilization has also been employed as a punitive measure in connection with sexual offenders. Its use may be purely contraceptive when an individual or couple for reasons of personal convenience wish to avoid conception of children. Finally, sterilization may be indirect, when it results unintentionally from an operation performed to preserve life or health for other reasons.

As an organized movement, sterilization has been closely connected with eugenics, a science founded by Sir Francis Galton in the latter part of the nineteenth century to study the influences that

[1] See V. J. O'Connor, *Journal of the American Medical Association* 136:162 (1948), who reports a successful reversal rate of only 35–40 per cent.

improve the inborn qualities of a race, and those which develop them to the greatest advantage. The United States has taken the lead in developing sterilization techniques and their implementation by the law. Vasectomy was perfected in 1889 by Harry C. Sharpe of the Indiana State Reformatory, and after unsuccessful attempts to pass sterilization statutes in Michigan and Pennsylvania, the first act became law in Indiana in 1907. Since that date thirty-three States at different times have had sterilization statutes in force. In 1926 the Human Betterment Foundation was established in New York with a principal purpose of furthering eugenic sterilization. In Nazi Germany a comprehensive sterilization statute was passed in 1933, and in its first year of operation 56,244 sterilizations were ordered.[1] In England, a departmental committee was appointed in June 1932, "to examine and report on the information already available regarding the hereditary transmission and other causes of mental disorder and deficiency: to consider the value of sterilization as a preventive measure, having regard to its physical, psychological and social effects and to the experience of legislation in other countries permitting it: and to suggest what further enquiries might usefully be undertaken in this connection". The Committee in its Report, presented in 1934, recommended the legalizing of voluntary sterilization.[2] This recommendation has not been implemented.

STERILIZATION AT COMMON LAW

In the absence of statutory authorization, compulsory sterilization is clearly a criminal offence at common law. Is voluntary sterilization a crime? Therapeutic sterilization, performed to save a patient's life or to benefit his health, is legally unobjectionable. In 1934 the Supreme Court of Minnesota affirmed that such an operation is not against public policy and that medical necessity constituted adequate grounds for its performance.[3] A similar decision was arrived

[1] *Eugenics Review*, 29:9 (1937-8).
[2] 1934. Cmd. 4485. The Report is known from the name of its chairman as "The Brock Report".
[3] *Christensen v. Thornby*, 255 N.W. 620 (Minn. 1934). The plaintiff's wife having been advised that her life would be endangered by bearing another child, her husband agreed to the performance of a vasectomy upon himself. The wife later became pregnant and the doctor was sued for failure to secure sterility.

at in a Californian case of 1952, where a doctor in the course of an operation discovered that his patient's Fallopian tubes were infected and removed the diseased portions. Judgment for the doctor was upheld on appeal.[1]

Where sterilization is carried out for eugenic or contraceptive purposes the common law position is obscure. It is well established that no one has the right to consent to the infliction of bodily harm on himself amounting to a maim, unless he has a just cause or excuse. Thus Lord Coke records a case at Leicester in 1604 where a "young strong and lustie rogue, to make himselfe impotent, thereby to have the more colour to begge or to be relieved without putting himself to any labour, caused his companion to strike off his left hand".[2] Both were found guilty of a criminal offence and fined. Is sterilization a maim? Castration was explicitly held to be a maim[3] and if it is equated with sterilization the question is answered. Dr Glanville Williams denies that sterilization is a maim, pointing out that the essence of a maim was that it lessened a person's ability to fight, and the belief that castration had this effect led to its classification under this heading.[4] Sterilization has no such effect and therefore should not be held a maim. Another jurist has pointed out that the law of maim did not apply to women and would still be inapplicable today.[5]

Even if sterilization is not a maim the question is not disposed of, for sterilization might well be classified as an assault and battery, and here again consent without a justifying cause is no defence.

In *Bravery v. Bravery*, a Court of Appeal case of 1954, Lord Justice Denning stated *obiter* that sterilization came within this

A demurrer to the complaint was sustained. The wife survived the pregnancy. For a discussion of what constitutes "medical necessity" see James V. Campbell, *Western Journal of Surgery*, 58:371 (1950).

[1] *Danielson v. Roche et al.* 241 Pac. 2d. 1028 (Calif. App. 1952).
[2] Co. Litt. 127a and 127b: 1 Hawk. P.C. 108.
[3] I Hawk. P.C. 107.
[4] *The Sanctity of Life and the Criminal Law*, p. 104.
[5] See L. Minty, *Medico-Legal Journal*, 24:54 (1956). Stephen in his Digest defines a maim as "bodily harm whereby a man is deprived of the use of any member of his body or of any sense which he can use in fighting, or by the loss of which he is generally and permanently weakened, but a bodily injury is not a maim merely because it is a disfigurement". See Article 290 (7th ed., London 1926).

definition. "Take a case where a sterilization operation is done so as to enable a man to have the pleasure of sexual intercourse without shouldering the responsibilities attaching to it," said Lord Denning. "The operation then is plainly injurious to the public interest. It is degrading to the man himself. It is injurious to his wife and to any woman he may marry, to say nothing of the way it opens to licentiousness; and unlike contraceptives, it allows no room for a change of mind on either side. It is illegal, even though the man consents to it . . ."[1] No judicial statement has been made on the validity of a consent given for a sterilization operation on eugenic grounds, apart from a remark made *obiter* by Lord Denning in *Bravery v. Bravery*, that sterilization to prevent transmission of an hereditary disease would be lawful.[2] Dr Glanville Williams also opines that voluntary eugenical sterilization is legitimate.[3] The Brock Committee, on the other hand, concluded that eugenic sterilization of mental defectives was legal but not that of normal persons. The position at common law would seem to be that therapeutic sterilization is lawful, contraceptive sterilization is unlawful, and the position of eugenic sterilization is doubtful. If the patient dies as a result of an unlawful sterilization operation, the physician is guilty of manslaughter.

Consent may be irrelevant to the criminal liability of the surgeon, but it is of importance in any civil litigation. If both spouses consent to the operation, no tort action will lie on the principle of *volenti non fit iniuria*. If, on the other hand, only one spouse consents and there are no grave medical reasons for the operation, then the physician is in danger of a suit from the other spouse for interference with marital rights. There is no case directly in point, but in *Murray v. McMurchy*, a Canadian case of 1949, 3,000 dollars

---

[1] *Bravery v. Bravery*, 1954, 3 All E.R. 59, at p. 68. The other two judges left the question open.

[2] The lawfulness of eugenical sterilization of mental defectives at common law is supported by the Baltimore case, *Ex parte Eaton* (Baltimore City Circuit Court, 1954). Baltimore has no sterilization statute but a decree was issued ordering the sterilization of Georgia Eaton on petition of her husband, relatives, and Incompetent Committee. Two Catholic lawyers intervened as *amici curiae* to procure rescinding of the decree on grounds of public policy but their application was denied.

[3] Op. cit., p. 106. Cf. For an opposite opinion Wharton, *Criminal Law*, 12th edition, sec. 182. "Consent cannot cure such operations on women as prevent them from having children."

damages were awarded to a woman, whose surgeon performed a sterilization during a caesarian operation.[1] The husband had consented to the operation and "any further surgical procedure found necessary by the attending physician". On the facts, the Court held that such a drastic operation without express consent was not justifiable. Sterilization by one spouse without the consent of the other and without serious medical cause would be a ground for dissolution of marriage, and could be equated with cruelty or treated as constructive desertion.[2]

Many States in the United States have sterilization statutes providing for the compulsory sterilization of mental defectives and others, and the existence of such statutes may affect public policy, so that it would favour voluntary sterilization, at any rate on eugenic grounds. Some of the statutes contain a provision stating that nothing in the statute shall prevent a sterilization being performed for therapeutic reasons.[3] Other States, while allowing a defence of medical necessity, forbid any form of sterilization other than that authorized by the statute, under pain of fine and imprisonment.[4]

---

[1] British Columbia Supreme Court (1949), Dom. L.R. 442, vol. 2. In England the medical defence unions decline to indemnify surgeons for performing sterilization operations. For full discussion, see H. W. Smith, "Antecedent Grounds of Liability in the Practice of Surgery". Rocky Mt. L. R. 14:233 at 276–84 (1942), also Richard C. Donnelly, "Liability of Physicians for Sterilization in Virginia", *Virg. Med. Monthly*, 78:25 (January 1951).

[2] For cruelty, see remarks of Sir Raymond Evershed and Lord Justice Hodson in *Bravery v. Bravery*, at p. 61. See also *Kreyling v. Kreyling*, 23 Atl. 2d. 800 (1942). For desertion, see H.R.H. "Sterilization as ground for the dissolution of marriage", *South African Law Journal*, 72:198 (May 1955). "Since the act in itself is evidence of an intention to put an end to the normal marital relationship, it is submitted that the other spouse would be entitled to a divorce on the ground of constructive desertion", at p. 201. See also *Cackett v. Cackett* (1950), p. 253.

[3] E.g. Arizona, Mississippi. See Appendix V for these and others.

[4] Connecticut, Kansas, and Utah statutes contain such provisions. See Appendix V. In those States forbidding birth control, contraceptive sterilization would presumably be against public policy. In 1938 a New York Court refused to grant a licence to exhibit a film dealing (unfavourably) with sterilization, the judge describing it as "an illegal practice, which is, as a matter of common knowledge, immoral and reprehensible according to the standards of a very large part of the citizenry of the State". The decision was reached by a majority of 3 to 2. *Foy v. Graves*, 3 N.Y.S. 2d. 573 (1938).

STERILIZATION STATUTES

No sterilization statute exists in England, but in twenty-eight of the American States sterilization statutes are in force. Sterilization is not dealt with directly by federal law. All these statutes have a eugenic purpose and are designed to restrict the spread of insanity, mental deficiency, feeble mindedness, epilepsy etc., through preventing the birth of children from parents suffering from these afflictions. Some declare that their purpose is also to benefit the health and well being of the sterilized person, both directly and by enabling him to be released from his institution. Vasectomy for males and salpingectomy for females are the operations most generally authorized or recommended, although other techniques such as the irradiation of the gonads may be employed. Castration is expressly excluded in one State, West Virginia, and authorized in another, Nebraska. The Nebraska provision applies to male inmates of certain named institutions who have been committed for rape, incest, and crimes against nature.[1] It is the only example in the sterilization statutes of an obviously punitive provision.

In twenty-three States sterilization is compulsory and the consent of the defective person is not required. In two, it is voluntary and the consent of the person, his spouse or guardian, is a necessary condition of performing the operation. Three States provide both voluntary and compulsory procedures.[2] In fourteen States the compulsory provisions are mandatory and in twelve permissive. Application of the laws is limited to the inmates of designated institutions in twenty States, but in eight they also cover defectives and others who are at large. Six distinct classes of persons who may be sterilized are covered by the statutes. The feeble minded are included in all statutes and the insane in the majority. Two-thirds of the statutes designate epileptics as subjects for sterilization, and over one-third include criminals. Moral degenerates and sexual perverts are mentioned in one quarter of the statutes, and one State, Georgia, provides for sterilization of those suffering from physical disease.

[1] See Appendix V.
[2] For a complete chart of this and other classifications, see Appendix IV.

In most States the sterilization procedure is set in motion by the head of the institution where the person is confined. Administrative boards rather than judicial tribunals make the decisions to sterilize. In six States special eugenic boards have been set up. In most States the person to be sterilized must be served with notice of the proposal and is entitled to appear at the hearing where he has a right to be heard.[1] Appeal to the courts is provided for in the majority of States.[2]

STERILIZATION AND CONSTITUTIONAL RIGHTS

Until 1925 all sterilization statutes challenged in the courts were held unconstitutional, but in that year the Supreme Court of Michigan upheld the State statute, although the sterilization order was vacated.[3] In the same year, the Virginia Supreme Court of Appeals, upheld the validity of the Virginia sterilization statute in the case of *Buck v. Bell*.[4] The point was taken to the Supreme Court of the United States and the judgment affirmed by Justice Oliver Wendell Holmes in 1927.[5] From that date until 1942 judicial policy favoured sterilization statutes, but in that year the Supreme Court in *Skinner v. Oklahoma* held that the Oklahoma statute violated the equal protection clause of the 14th amendment. Since the decision in that case the constitutionality of all the sterilization statutes has been in some doubt.[6]

I. The Police Power

The first question which must be answered is whether sterilization for eugenic purposes is wrong in principle and violates the fundamental rights to life, liberty and the pursuit of happiness enunciated in the Declaration of Independence. Or, to put the question the other

[1] States without such provisions include Alabama, Connecticut, Delaware, Maine and Oregon. In Maine and Oregon, rights of appeal are granted. In Wisconsin, notice of the finding of the Board must be given but there is no right to appear at the hearing. See Appendix V.

[2] Alabama, Connecticut, Delaware and Wisconsin confer no right of appeal. See Appendix V.

[3] *Smith v. Command. (Wayne)*, 231 Mich. 409, 204 N.W. 140 (1925).

[4] 143 Va. 310 (1925).

[5] 274 U.S. 200 (1927).

[6] 316 U.S. 535 (1942).

way round, is a State sterilization statute a valid exercise of the police power entrusted to the different States of the union? In 1918 the Supreme Court, Albany County, New York, held that the State sterilization statute was not a proper exercise of the police power, since it was designed to save expense in operating eleemosynary institutions.[1] *Smith v. Command*, as has been seen, upheld the constitutionality of the Michigan sterilization statute, but a vigorous dissent attacked the whole principle of sterilization as being unconstitutional. "The inherent right of mankind," declared the judge, "to pass through life without mutilation of organs or glands of generation needs no declaration in constitutions, for the right existed long before constitutions of government, was not lost or surrendered to legislative control in the creation of government and is beyond the reach of the governmental agency known as the police power."[2]

The decision in *Buck v. Bell*, however, made it plain that eugenic sterilization, even if compulsory, is not in principle unconstitutional. In that case, Carrie Buck, an eighteen year old feeble minded white woman, the daughter of a feeble minded mother, and the mother herself of an illegitimate feeble minded child, was ordered to be sterilized by the Virginia courts. She appealed to the Supreme Court. "We have seen," declared Justice Holmes, "more than once that the public welfare may call upon its best citizens for their lives. It would be strange if it could not call upon those who already sap the strength of the State for these lesser sacrifices, often not felt to be such by those concerned, in order to prevent our being swamped with incompetents. It is better for all the world, if instead of waiting to execute degenerate offspring for crime, or to let them starve

---

[1] *In re Thomson*, 103 Misc. Rep. 23; 169 N.Y. Supp 638 (1918). *Osborn v. Thomson*, 185 App. Div. 902; 171 N.Y. Supp. 1094 (1918).

[2] 231 Mich. at 436, 204 N.W. at p. 149. With this may be compared the majority judgment. "What are the legal rights of the class of citizens as to the procreation of children? It is true that the right to beget children is a natural and constitutional right, but it is equally true that no citizen has any rights superior to the common welfare: measured by its injurious effect upon society, what right has any class of citizen to beget children with an inherited tendency to crime, feeble mindedness, idiocy or imbecility. . . . Under the circumstances it was not only its (the legislature's) right but its duty to enact some legislation that would protect the people and preserve the race from the known effects of the procreation of children by the feeble-minded, the idiots, and the imbeciles."

for their imbecility, society can prevent those who are manifestly unfit from continuing their kind. The principle that sustains compulsory vaccination is broad enough to cover cutting the Fallopian tubes.
(*Jacobson v. Massachusetts*, 197 U.S. 11.) Three generations of imbeciles are enough."

Justice Holmes made it plain that in cases involving sterilization
of defectives, personal rights must be subordinated to the general
welfare of the community and this principle has been followed in
subsequent cases. Thus in *State v. Schaffer*, a Kansas decision of
1928, Judge Burch declared: "The interest of the individual invaded by the statute is of the highest order, and the invasion can be
justified only as a necessary protection to some more important
interest. Reducing this problem of reconciliation of personal liberty
and governmental restraint to its lowest possible biological terms,
the two functions indispensable to the continued existence of human
life are nutrition and reproduction. Without nutrition, the individual
dies; without reproduction, the race dies. Procreation of defective and
feeble minded children with criminal tendencies does not advantage,
but patently disadvantages, the race. Reproduction turns adversary
and thwarts the ultimate end and purpose of reproduction. The race
may ensure its own perpetuation and such progency may be prevented in the interest of the higher general welfare."[1]

II. Equal Protection

The fourteenth amendment to the American Constitution provides
that no State shall "deny to any person within its jurisdiction the
equal protection of the laws".[2] This amendment does not automatically forbid all statutes which apply to one class only, and they
may be held valid if the class has a reasonable and not an arbitrary
basis, and the law applies alike to all persons similarly situated.[3] In
the first decision rendered on the validity of a State sterilization sta-

[1] 270 Pac. 604. (Kansas) (1928). See also *Clayton v. Board of Examiners*,
120 Nebr. 680, 234 N.W. 630 (1931). "We think it is within the police power of
the State to provide for the sterilization of feeble minded persons as a condition
pre-requisite to release from a State institution", at p. 632. Cf. *Board of Eugenics
v. Troutman*, 50 Idaho 673, 299 Pac. 668 (1931).
[2] Proposed June 16, 1866, declared ratified July 21, 1868.
[3] See *Hayes v. Missouri*, 120 U.S. 68, 7 Sup. Ct. 350 (1887); *Lindlsey v.
Natural Carbonic Gas Co.*, 220 U.S. 61, 31 Sup. Ct. 337 (1910).

tute, *Smith v. Board of Examiners*, in 1913, the New Jersey Act was held invalid as failing to furnish equal protection of the law.[1] It applied only to the inmates of institutions and not to the population at large. The New York statute was held invalid on similar grounds in 1918.[2] Michigan followed suit in the same year.[3]

Justice Holmes departed from this line of reasoning in *Buck v. Bell* (1927), rejecting the contention that the statute failed because it applied only to inmates of named institutions and not to the multitudes outside as "the last resort of constitutional arguments". The answer to the argument, he declared, is that "the law does all that is needed when it does all that it can, indicates a policy, applies it to all within the lines, and seeks to bring within the lines all similarly situated so far and so fast as its means allow. Of course, so far as the operations enable those who otherwise must be kept confined to be returned to the world, and thus open the asylum to others, the equality aimed at will be more nearly reached." State courts followed the *Buck v. Bell* ruling until 1942.[4]

In 1942 the Supreme Court was called upon for a second time to consider the validity of a sterilization statute.[5] Acting unanimously, the court invalidated an Oklahoma statute authorizing the compulsory sterilization of habitual criminals convicted of "felonies involving moral turpitude". A criminal, Skinner, who had been convicted of three felonies, two robberies with firearms and one offence of chicken stealing, was ordered to be sterilized by the Supreme Court of Oklahoma. He appealed to the United States Supreme Court claiming that the statute violated the fourteenth amendment. Justice Douglas declared that the statute failed to meet the equal protection clause of the amendment, pointing out that embesslement could not be visited with sterilization but larceny could. "When the law lays an unequal hand on those who have committed intrinsically the same quality of offence and sterilizes one and not the

---

[1] 85 N.J.L. 46, 88 A. 963 (1913).
[2] *In re Thomson*, 103 Misc. Rep. 23, 169 N.Y. Supp. 638 (1918). *Osborn v. Thomson*, 185 App. Div. 902, 171 N.Y. Supp. 1094 (1918).
[3] *Haynes v. Lapeer*, 201 Mich. 138, 166 N.W. 938 (1918).
[4] *Davis v. Walton*, 74 Utah 80, 276 P. 921 (1929). *State v. Schaffer*, 126 Kans. 607, 270 P. 604 (1928). *State v. Troutman*, 50 Idaho 673, 299 P. 668 (1931). See also *In re Salloum*, 236 Mich. 478, 210 N.W. 498 (1926).
[5] *Skinner v. Oklahoma*, 316 U.S. 535 (1942).

other, it has made as invidious a discrimination as if it had selected a particular race or nationality for oppressive treatment."[1]

III. Due Process

No State, declares the fourteenth amendment, shall "deprive any person of life, liberty, or property, without due process of law". In substantive law, due process is a standard of reasonableness, and thus constitutes a limitation on the exercise of the police power. In procedural law, it requires that those threatened with deprivation of rights should have both notice of this intention and opportunity to be heard. Here we are concerned with due process in its second and procedural sense.

In 1914, the Iowa sterilization statute was held invalid for failing to provide the plaintiff with a hearing.[2] "In the case at the bar," said the judge, "the hearing was a private hearing, and the prisoner first knew of it when advised of the order. Due process of law means that every person must have his day in court, and this is as old as Magna Charta; that some time in the proceedings he must be confronted by his accuser and given a public hearing."[3] In 1933 the North Carolina statute was struck down for failing to provide a hearing upon notice for the individual to be sterilized. Human rights, declared the courts, as well as property rights, require a forum with notice and hearing.[4] *Skinner v. Oklahoma*, as has been seen, nullified the sterilization statute for failing to afford equal protection, but the due process point was also raised and stressed by Chief Justice Stone. The erection of a class condemned to an invasion of personal liberty, with no opportunity for individuals to show that they were not members of the class, was a violation of due process. "And so," said Chief Justice Stone, "while the State may protect itself from the demonstrably inheritable tendencies of the individual which are injurious to society, the most elementary notions of due process would seem to require it to take appropriate steps to safe-

[1] At p. 541.

[2] *Davis v. Berry*, 216 F. 413 (1914). The Court also stated that the law amounted to a Bill of Attainder which it defined as "a legislative act which inflicts punishment without a jury trial".

[3] This reasoning was applied and the case quoted with approval in *Williams v. Smith*, 190 Ind. 526, 131 N.E. 2 (1921).

[4] *Brewer v. Valk*, 204 N.C. 186, 167 S.E. 638 (1933).

guard the liberty of the individual by affording him before he is condemned to an irreparable injury in his person, some opportunity to
show that he is without such inheritable tendencies."

Where such an opportunity has been afforded, the statutes have
been upheld, and the argument that they violated the "due process"
provision rejected. Thus in *Smith v. Command* (Michigan 1925), the
court upheld the statute, pointing out that the law required notice
of the time and place of the hearing to be served on the individual
concerned, as well as affording him a judicial enquiry and opportunities for defence and appeal. "Nothing further," said the court,
"is required by the 'due process of law' clause of the constitution."[1]
In *Buck v. Bell*, Justice Holmes carefully reviewed the procedure
laid down by the Virginia statute and declared: "There can be no
doubt that so far as procedure is concerned the rights of the patient
are most carefully considered, and as every step in this case was
taken in scrupulous compliance with the statute and after months of
observation, there is no doubt that in that respect the plaintiff in
error has had due process of law."[2]

The validity of each statute when challenged under "due process"
is thus a matter of individual construction of the act concerned. The
minimum requirements for compliance with the fourteenth amendment would seem to be a hearing on reasonable notice before a duly
constituted tribunal where the person to be sterilized has a right to
appear. If this tribunal is not in itself a court then a right to appeal to
a court for judicial review must be included. The model Bill drafted
by the Human Betterment Association includes these safeguards and
detailed provisions of the form they should take.

IV. Cruel and Unusual Punishment

The eighth amendment to the American Constitution forbids the
infliction of any "cruel and unusual punishment", and sterilization
statutes have been challenged as violating this provision.[3] Most

[1] For a later Michigan case, adhering to this ruling, see *in re Salloum*, 236
Mich. 478, 210 N.W. 498 (1926).

[2] Other cases reaching similar conclusions and approving *Buck v. Bell* are:
State v. Schaffer, 126 Kans. 607, 270 P. 604 (1928). *State v. Troutman*, 50 Idaho
673, 299 P. 668 (1931). *In re Main*, 162 Okla. 65, 19 P. (2d.) 153 (1933).

[3] The first ten amendments were proposed by Congress on September 25,
1789, and ratified by the requisite number of States by December 15, 1791.

State constitutions embody similar prohibitions.[1] In *Davis v. Berry*, an Iowa statute of 1913, which ordered the sterilization of any inmate of a penal institution, twice convicted of felony, was invalidated.[2] Having reviewed the history of castration as a punishment for crime, the court equated it with sterilization. A similar decision was reached in *Mickle v. Henrichs*, where a vasectomy performed on a man convicted of statutory rape was held to be ignominious and degrading, involving mutilation of the human body and destruction of its normal functions.[3] The court in *Thomson*'s case (New York 1918) distinguished between sterilization as a punishment and as a eugenic measure. Its application to defectives was held to be non-punitive, and the validity of its application to criminals left an open question.[4] In *Smith v. Command*, sterilization of defectives was again held to be non-punitive. "The only purpose of this constitutional provision," said the court, "is to place a limitation on the power of the legislature in fixing punishment for crime. There is no element of punishment involved in the sterilization of feeble minded persons. In this respect it is analagous to compulsory vaccination. Both are non-punitive. It is therefore plainly apparent that the constitutional inhibition against cruel or unusual punishment has no application to the surgical treatment of feeble minded persons. It has reference only to punishment inflicted after convictions of crimes."[5]

The validity of sterilization statutes in relation to the eighth amendment seems then to be first a matter of construction. Provided their language is not punitive, the validity of their application to non-criminal groups is clear. If their intent is unambiguously eugenic, statutes applying to criminals should on principle be equally valid, but of this there is considerable doubt. When adjudicating on statutes containing sections applicable to both criminals and defec-

---

[1] Not Connecticut, Illinois and Vermont.

[2] 216 F. 413 (1914).

[3] 262 Fed. 687 (D. Nev. 1918). However, in *State v. Feilen*, 70 Wash. 65, 126 P. 75 (1912) a contrary decision was reached.

[4] Cf. *Haynes v. Lapeer*, 201 Mich. 138, 166 N.W. 938 (1918).

[5] 231 Mich. 409, 204 N.W. 140 (1925). Cf. *Buck v. Bell*, 143 Va. 310, 130 S.E. 516 (1925), *Davis v. Walton*, 74 Utah. 80, 276 P. 921 (1929), *State v. Troutman*, 50 Idaho 673, 299 P. 668 (1931). *In re Clayton*, 120 Nebr. 680, 234 N.W. 630 (1931). *In re Main*, 162 Okla. 65, 19 P. (2d.) 153 (1933).

tives, judges have been careful to limit their remarks to the sections dealing with defectives. A typical case is *Clayton v. Board of Examiners*.[1] The Nebraska statute applied not only to insane persons and the feeble-minded, but also to habitual criminals and sexual perverts. The court throughout the opinion referred only to the feeble minded and drew attention to the "pointed observation" of the trial court that "the only part thereof that could or should be held constitutional would be the part relating to the sterilization of feeble minded persons".

The Constitutional Position Today

By careful drafting, statutes can escape the perils presented by the necessity of equal protection, procedural due process, and the prohibition of cruel and unusual punishments. *Buck v. Bell* appeared to have ensured the validity of sterilization in principle but this judgment must now be considered in the light of the second Supreme Court decision of *Skinner v. Oklahoma*. As has been seen, the statute was struck down principally for its violation of the equal protection clause but the remarks of the judges indicate a change in judicial policy with regard to the sterilization principle. Thus Justice Douglas declared procreation to be "one of the basic rights of man", and warned that the power to sterilize if exercised, "may have subtle, far-reaching and devastating effects. In evil or in reckless hands it can cause races or types which are inimical to the dominant group to wither and disappear. There is no redemption for the individual whom the law touches. Any experiment which the State conducts is his irreparable injury. He is forever deprived of a basic liberty." Chief Justice Stone stressed the necessity of provisions to safeguard individual rights. Justice Jackson went even further, declaring that: "There are limits to the extent to which a legislatively represented majority may conduct biological experiments at the expense of the dignity and personality and natural powers of a minority—even those who have been guilty of what the majority define as crimes."[2]

---

[1] 120 Nebr. 680, 234 N.W. 630 (1931).
[2] For an opinion that sterilization statutes are now of doubtful constitutional validity, see H. Kalven: "A Special Corner of Civil Liberties", in a symposium, "Morals, Medicine and the Law", *N.Y.U. Law Review*, 31:1157 (1956), p. 1234.

THE PRACTICE OF STERILIZATION—ITS EXTENT

No figures are available for voluntary sterilization in either the United Kingdom or the United States. In the United Kingdom, therapeutic and indirect sterilization apart, it would seem to be comparatively rare, and compulsory sterilization is unknown. Sterilization figures are available for the United States, the majority being compulsory, but a small proportion, coming from those States which provide voluntary procedures, are voluntary.[1] The total number of sterilizations reported since the enactment of the first American sterilization law in 1907 up to January 1, 1958, is 60,166, of which 24,008 are male and 36,158 are female. Mental deficients account for 31,038 of these, those suffering from mental illness for 26,922, the remaining 2,206 being made up of epileptics, criminals etc. California has carried out by far the highest number of sterilizations, with a grand total amounting to 19,998. Virginia ranks next with 6,811, and two other southern States have higher than average figures, North Carolina (4,777) and Georgia (2,578). Other States with high figures are Indiana (2,354), Iowa (1,738), Kansas (3,025), Michigan (3,597), Minnesota (2,325), Oregon (2,200) and Wisconsin (1,799). Figures for the eastern States are uniformly low. All figures represent a very small percentage of the total population.

In the past fifteen years the number of sterilizations reported has steadily declined. Thus in the five year period from Janurary 1941 to January 1946, 9,200 sterilizations were reported; for the following period from 1946 to 1951, this had dropped to 7,100; and in the next five years from 1951–6 it had fallen to 6,100.[2] The figures for 1957 show a further decline. Of the thirty States listed in Appendix I, three statutes had been declared unconstitutional and hence no sterilizations were reported. Seven other States where the sterilization statutes are still theoretically in force made no use of them; eight States carried out less than ten sterilizations in the year; four less than twenty; and five less than fifty. Only three States, Georgia, North Carolina, and Virginia carried out sterilizations numbering

[1] For full figures for the various States, see Appendix I.
[2] See James B. O'Hara and T. Howland Sanks: "Eugenic Sterilization", *Georgia L.J.*, 45:20 (1956).

above 100. These represented 7 · 09, 6 · 78, and 3 · 37 sterilizations per 100,000 of the population, respectively. In California the percentage had fallen to · 09. The grand total of sterilizations for all States was 909 in 1956 and 973 in 1957.

Psychological, social, and religious reasons account for this flight from sterilization. Both sexes have deep seated fears about sterilization and these are stronger in men than in women. Moya Woodside reports that of seventy-four welfare institutions in North Carolina which answered a question on this point, fifty-four stated that the resistance of men was greater than women.[1] The use of sterilization in Nazi Germany as a means of race extermination has immensely increased this revulsion from sterilization, and re-inforced the arguments of Roman Catholic and certain Protestant theologians against its employment. The medical profession has been traditionally reluctant to employ sterilization, and this conservative view has been strengthened by recent researches showing the uncertainty of many principles of heredity which had hitherto been accepted as axiomatic. Shortage of hospital beds, doctors and nurses, has also contributed to the reduction in sterilizations. A further reduction in numbers of sterilizations seems likely in the future.

COMPULSORY EUGENIC STERILIZATION
—ITS UTILITY

"I think," wrote Justice Holmes, "that the sacredness of human life is a purely municipal ideal of no validity outside the jurisdiction. I believe that force mitigated so far as may be by good manners, is the ultimate ratio."[2] Such an approach to law excludes all question of fundamental, inalienable rights, inhering in human beings, and simplifies the approach to compulsory sterilization by prescinding from any consideration of a right to bodily integrity. Sterilization statutes must be judged solely on their utility, by a consideration of their results. In essence there is no distinction between animal breeding and human breeding, and just as one has been improved by the development of scientific techniques, so should the other. "There is a striking contrast," notes Dr Glanville Williams re-

---

[1] *Sterilization in North Carolina*, Chapel Hill: University of North Carolina Press, 1950, p. 66.

[2] *The Common Law*, supra note 5 at 36.

gretfully, "between human fecklessness in our own reproduction and the careful scientific improvement of other forms of life under man's control. No rose-grower, pigeon-fancier or cattle-breeder would behave as men do in their own breeding habits."[1]

The primary benefit claimed to result from schemes of compulsory sterilization is racial improvement. Insanity, feeble-mindedness, epilepsy, sexual perversion and certain forms of criminality, runs the argument, are on the increase. They are all heritable characteristics, and since defectives propagate at a higher rate than normal persons, the danger of being "swamped by incompetents" is a real and growing one. State resources are limited, and the economic burden of maintaining an ever increasing number of defectives in institutions is not one that can be permanently sustained. Consideration of the common good apart, sterilization benefits the individual concerned. It prevents the birth of children who will pass through life permanently handicapped and is beneficial or at least harmless to the health of those upon whom it is performed. Finally it enlarges individual freedom by enabling those who would otherwise have to be confined in institutions to be released. These claims must be further examined.

No evidence exists to support the contention that insanity and mental defect are increasing.[2] The numbers in mental homes and hospitals have certainly grown in recent years, but the growth is explicable on quite other grounds. Diagnosis of mental diseases has greatly improved, medical knowledge of the mental causes of physical disease has increased, and standards of medical care are higher. Many who were in need of mental treatment and could not obtain it, now have facilities at their disposal. The contention that defectives breed faster than normal people is equally baseless, despite its constant repetition.[3] The Brock Committee reported that neither their own enquiry nor the statistics made available on the size of families

[1] *The Sanctity of Life and the Criminal Law*, p. 82.
[2] See Abraham Myerson: "Certain Medical and Legal Phases of Eugenic Sterilization", *Annals on Internal Medicine*, 18:580 (1943). See also Report of the American Neurological Association on Sterilization (1936).
[3] Thus J. P. Hinton and J. E. Calcutt in their work *Sterilization: A Christian Approach*, London 1935, cite an isolated table from the Brock Report to support their claim that defective families are larger than normal families, ignoring the Report's rejection of the conclusion, p. 18.

of known defectives showed a higher birth-rate. "The supposed abnormal fertility of defectives is, in our view, largely mythical and results from the accident that from time to time distressing exceptions to the general rule find their way into the Courts and are noticed in the Press."[1] In fact mental defectives have a lower marriage rate and a higher divorce rate than normal people. Their death-rate is higher and their birth-rate lower than the average, and their sexual drives are also reduced.[2] Offspring of defectives have considerably less chance of survival than those of normal parents. The Brock Report records an investigation into 3,733 cases where the mother was defective in 3,247 and the father in 486. These marriages produced 8,841 children of which 22·5 per cent died before reaching the age of seven.[3]

Sterilization would undoubtedly enable a certain number of mental defectives to be released from institutions, but the proportion would not be high since only those capable of looking after themselves could be set at liberty. The Brock Committee estimated that between 3 and 5 per cent of the institutional defectives in England could be released.[4] Furthermore, the benefit to the individual might well be counterbalanced by an increase in promiscuity and hence of venereal disease. Sterilized defectives, no longer deterred by fears of pregnancy, and no longer presenting this threat to others, could easily be exploited for the basest purposes. After-care, even if available, would only be a limited answer to this problem.

Whether sterilization is beneficial to health is still an open question. A number of case studies have been carried out, but the evidence is not conclusive. Popenoe reported a series of cases of vasectomy in 1929. Of thirty-six persons suffering from mental diseases and vasectomized, twenty-two declared that they noticed no change in their sexual life: nine reported an increase in sexual activity and five a decrease. Only two of another sixty-five persons who had undergone a vasectomy experienced any decrease in virility.[5]

[1] Cmd. 4485 of 1934, p. 18.
[2] See Abraham Myerson, "Certain Medical and Legal Phases of Eugenic Sterilization", *Yale Law Journal*, 52:618–33 (1943).
[3] Pp. 16–17.   [4] *The Report*, p. 31.
[5] P. Popenoe, "Effect of Vasectomy on the Sexual Life", *Journal of Abnormal and Social Psychology*, 24:251–68 (1929). Amongst those interviewed, the time elapsed since the operation varied between three months and twenty years.

Popenoe also investigated the effect of salpingectomy on women. Of 108 psychotic women sterilized, seventy-eight experienced no change in their sexual lives, twenty-two greater satisfaction, and eight less.[1] None of the men experienced any deterioration in their general health. Some thought it had improved.

Moya Woodside's researches also indicate that sterilization has no serious physical or psychological effects in the majority of cases. A follow-up study of forty-eight married women, not mental defectives, who had undergone a therapeutic sterilization, showed that the health of twenty-four had improved, twenty-one were unchanged, and three were worse. Thirty-three reported no change in libido, six an increase, and eight a decrease. In one case no data was available. Interviews took place on an average about one and a half years after the operation. "It was in the psychological sphere," reports Moya Woodside, "that the greatest difference had been wrought through removal of fear of pregnancy. Freed from recurrent anxiety, sexual and marital relationships were felt to be improved, and women individually were much happier. Of equal importance was the physical relief from constant child-bearing and the alleviation of economic worry. Husbands were said to approve the operation in three-quarters of the cases. In the few instances where unfavourable results were observed, they were associated with neurotic personality and maladjustment in the life situation. To the group as a whole, sterilization had conferred great practical and psychological advantage and could have been even more constructive if earlier undertaken in a number of cases."[2] The Brock Committee also concluded that vasectomy and salpingectomy had no harmful results when performed on normal persons or mental deficients, although it expressed a doubt where operations on those suffering from mental diseases were concerned.[3]

Whatever the effects on the individual may be, the utility of

[1] P. Popenoe, "Effects of Sterilization on the Sexual Life", *Eugenics*, 1:9–15 (1928). See also by same author, "Menstruation and Salpingectomy among the Feeble Minded", *Pedagogical Seminary and Journal of Genetic Psychology*, 35:303–11 (1928). For other cases showing that sterilization has few physiological effects, see J. H. Landman, *Human Sterilization*, New York 1932, pp. 230–1.

[2] *Sterilization in North Carolina*, Chapel Hill 1950, pp. 115–49.

[3] *The Report*, p. 29.

eugenic sterilization must principally depend on medical knowledge of heredity. The whole sterilization movement has been based on the belief that insanity, feeble mindedness, mental defect and criminality are hereditary. The validity of these assumptions must be carefully investigated.

Criminality

Criminality as such is not a biological concept but a social and legal construct. Lombroso put forward a biological theory of crime, claiming that criminals as a class were marked by a certain stigmata of degeneration and claimed to have discovered a significantly higher proportion of vestigial and atavistic characters amongst criminals than were displayed by the normal population, but his work is now generally agreed to lack an adequate scientific basis.[1] In the absence of a satisfactory biological theory of criminality, the suggestion that it can be inherited falls to the ground. Accordingly there can be no justification on eugenic grounds for sterilizing criminals.[2] "Most writers agree," concludes the sterilization committee of the American Neurological Association, "that while there may be a constitution which in its reaction to the milieu appears as criminal conduct, the effort to breed it out by any eugenical measures is, in the present state of our knowledge, not to be recommended and that more fruitful approaches to crime are to be found in social measures of one type or another."[3]

Mental Disease: Mental Defect: Feeble Mindedness

Mental disease on the one hand, and mental defect and feeble mindedness on the other, are distinct clinical entities, although an agreed medical terminology is lacking. Mental disease is a generic term covering all the disorders affecting the mind, which before the onset of the disorder has been functioning normally. Mental defect is a state of mental retardation or incomplete development. The

---

[1] Lombroso still has some followers, e.g. Professor E. A. Hooton, see *The American Criminal: An Anthropological Study*, Harvard U.P. 1939.

[2] See M. F. Montagu, "The Biologist Looks at Crime", *Annals of the American Academy of Political and Social Science*, 217:46 (1941), and P. Popenoe, "Sterilization and Criminality", *American Bar Association R.* 53:575 (1928).

[3] *The Report* (1936), p. 152.

Brock Report defines it as "arrested development of mind, whether congenital or induced by injury or disease before development is complete. It is in almost all cases a permanent condition and in the present state of knowledge is beyond real cure, though much benefit may result from skilled training."[1]

The degree to which mental disease and defect are inherited is a matter of continuing dispute amongst doctors, and the layman may be excused a certain bewilderment as he ploughs his way through the welter of conflicting theories and conclusions reached by the medical profession. The science of heredity is still in its infancy and the areas of ignorance remain disconcertingly wide. Mendel's laws, although modified in certain aspects, are still the basis of contemporary investigation. Mendel's first law, that of dominance, demonstrated that when two pure bred plants with contrasting characters are cross bred, all the offspring of this first mating will show only one of two characters. The character apparent in the offspring is dominant, that which is hidden, recessive. His second law declared that the characters which appear in the original organism are transmitted to the offspring without being changed or lost. Finally he established that a hidden recessive character in a hybrid offspring may re-appear in a later generation. From the mating of two hybrids, the distribution of any unit character will be pure dominant 25 per cent: hybrid 50 per cent: pure recessive 25 per cent. The ratio is thus 1 : 2 : 1, and this is the same for later generations of hybrids.[2]

Corresponding to every inherited character, claimed Mendel, are certain determiners or genes. The early students of heredity, by assuming that a defective mind corresponded with a single defective gene, greatly oversimplified the problem. Later research has shown that there are a multiplicity of genes, whose absence or combination may result in defect or disease. The relevance of Mendel's discoveries to sterilization procedures are obvious. To eradicate mental defect it would be necessary to sterilize not only the defectives but also all "carriers", who themselves are normal but whose organism contains recessive genes, which will appear as defect in later generations. Carriers far outnumber defectives, so that the amount of

[1] At p. 7.
[2] For an account of Mendel's theories see *Encyclopaedia Britannica*, XI: 484 (1954) and *Collier's Encyclopaedia*, XIII:385 (1953).

disease and deficiency which can be eradicated by the present sterilization measures is extremely small.

Carriers apart, the problem of eradicating mental disease and defect by sterilization is made practically insoluble by ignorance of the genesis, physiological basis and pathology of mental defect and many diseases, and the non-hereditary quality of others. No hereditary factor is discoverable in arterio-sclerotic dementia, senile dementia, general paresis, or in alcoholism.[1] The pathology and physiology of schizophrenia and manic-depression are still uncertain, although prevailing opinion is that they are constitutional and hereditary.[2] Epilepsy is thought to be hereditary but research is at too elementary a stage to establish this beyond doubt.[3] Similar ignorance surrounds mental defect and feeble-mindedness, although a *prima facie* case has been made out that these are caused by genetic factors. Here again "carriers" complicate the problem. Robert Hatton having fully discussed the medical evidence concludes that 50 per cent of feeble-mindedness is inherited, but of that 50 per cent, only 11 per cent is inherited from feeble-minded parents, 89 per cent from parents who appear normal but are in fact carriers. Thus the proportion of the feeble-minded inheriting their deficiency from feeble-minded parents is only 5.5 per cent.[4]

The Brock Report concludes that heredity plays "a large part" in mental disorders, but immediately goes on to say that except in the case of Huntington's chorea and myclonus epilepsy, both rare

[1] See Abraham Myerson: "Sterilization", *Atlantic Monthly*, 186:52 (1940, II, 5).

[2] Ibid. See also J. H. Landman, *Human Sterilization*, New York 1932, p. 164. While stating that a number of mental diseases are hereditary according to the preponderance of medical opinion, he points out that the study of the causes of the diseases and of mental deficiency has been practically "fruitless". See also Walter Wheeler Cook, "Eugenics or Euthenics", *Illinois Law Review*, 37:287–332 (1943) for a discussion of the medical evidence; Myerson, "Certain Medical and Legal Phases of Eugenic Sterilization", *Annals on Internal Medicine*, 18:580 (1943), also *Yale Law Journal*, 52:618 (1943). L. J. Doshay concludes: "The possibility of the inheritance of mental diseases is practically nil." "Evolution disproves heredity in the Mental Diseases", *Medical Journal and Record*, 131:143–8, 194–7, 248–50 (1930).

[3] See above articles and *Kentucky Law Journal*, 23:523 (1935).

[4] Ibid., p. 525. Cf. Estimate given by Fisher, "Elimination of Mental Defect", *Journal of Heredity*, 18:529 (1927), where he concludes that 89 per cent of all feeble-minded children come from normal parentage. See also Myerson, *American Journal of Medical Jurisprudence*, 1:253 (1938).

diseases, there is no conclusive evidence that inheritance follows mendelian ratios, and the part played by heredity varies widely between different types.[1] "It is impossible," states the Report, "in the present state of our knowledge about the causation of mental defect to forecast with certainty whether a child of any given union will exhibit mental abnormalities. It can, however, be shown that, whether the cause be bad heredity or adverse environmental conditions, or both, the children of parents one or both of whom are mentally defective are, on the average, below the normal, and our enquiry shows that nearly one third of such children as survive are likely to be defective, and more than two fifths must be expected to exhibit some degree of mental abnormality."[2]

Moral Degeneracy and Perversion

A quarter of the American sterilization statutes provide for the sterilization of moral degenerates and perverts. Whatever these terms may mean, and they are nowhere defined, no evidence exists that they are inheritable characteristics. Medical opinion increasingly favours environmental explanations of homosexuality and the congenital theories once widely held are now discredited save in relation to a tiny minority. Sterilization of such people might conceivably be justified on punitive grounds but not on those of eugenics.

Conclusions

The case for compulsory sterilization can only be sustained on utilitarian grounds if it can be clearly shown that mental defect and disease are hereditary. As Dr Landman has put it, "the human sterilization movement is as strong as our scientific knowledge concerning the inheritance of human qualities. Logically, therefore, those socially inadequate persons in our midst, the heredity of whose undesirabilities is doubtful, should not be subjected to sterilization until we are more certain as to which are inherited."[3] As has been

[1] *The Report*, p. 27.
[2] Ibid., p. 21. For views that mental deficiency is heritable, see Clarence Gamble, *American Journal of Mental Deficiency*, 57:123 (1952), Walter E. Southwick, *Journal of Mental Science*, 85:707 (1939), B. S. Johnson, *American Journal of Mental Deficiency*, 50:437 (1946).
[3] Op. cit., p. 247.

seen, medical knowledge is so fragmentary in this sphere, and the dispute over the nature of the hereditary processes so fundamental, that scientific knowledge cannot be said to have reached the degree of certainty requisite to justify a policy of compulsory sterilization. It is even doubtful whether the vast majority of the sterilization statutes satisfy the requirements of substantial due process, which requires their provisions to bear a reasonable relationship to existing medical knowledge of heredity. It may of course be argued that the statutes are justified on environmental rather than hereditary grounds, for if they do not eradicate hereditary defect, they do prevent children being brought up in unsuitable homes and by inadequate parents. Construed as they are written, most of the statutes could not be upheld on this ground, and even in those that lay down "social" reasons for sterilization, the avoidance of environmental hardship would probably not be considered a sufficient justification for such a drastic step as sterilization.

This conclusion has been reached by several authoritative committees. Thus the Brock Report states: "We assume that the Legislature would not feel justified in compelling any persons to submit to sterilization, unless it could be shown beyond reasonable doubt that some at least of their offspring would either be mentally defective or would develop mental disorder. In the present state of knowledge no such proof can be produced."[1] A special committee appointed by the British Medical Association on November 12, 1930, reached a substantially similar conclusion. Sterilization, it decided, might be advisable for a small number of mental defectives who were not in need of institutional care, provided they were carefully selected and adequate supervision exercised to prevent promiscuous intercourse and the spread of venereal disease.[2] The American Neurological Association has also recommended the abandonment of a compulsory sterilization programme. Genetics, stressed the Report, is still an experimental science, and no thorough-going application of its laws to the mental and personality diseases is possible. "We do not believe that society needs to hurry into a programme based on fear and propaganda. Although the problem of mental

---

[1] At p. 37.
[2] See *The British Medical Journal Supplement*, June 25, 1932, where the Report is printed.

disease and defectiveness is enormous, there exists no new social or biological emergency."[1] The danger of cutting off the assets as well as the liabilities that may be transmitted to posterity must also be born in mind.[2] What is needed now is an institute to carry out a long range programme into the nature of human heredity.

With compulsory sterilization laws ruled out, the alternative of voluntary sterilization remains. The Brock Report justified this by laying down the principle that "no person, unless conscience bids, ought to be forced to choose between the alternative of complete abstinence from sexual activity or of risking bringing into the world children whose disabilities will make them a burden to themselves and society".[3] Voluntary sterilization would accordingly be available only for eugenic and not for contraceptive reasons. The Brock Report suggests three classes of people for whom voluntary sterilization should be available:

(a) Those who are mentally defective or have suffered from mental disorder;

(b) Those who suffer from, or are believed to be carriers of grave physical disorders which have been shown to be transmissible;

(c) Those who are believed to be likely to transmit mental disorder or defect. To carry out this operation the authorization of the Ministry of Health would be required as well as the support of two medical practitioners. A small advisory medical committee should be set up to advise on doubtful cases.[4] A major difficulty in the way of establishing such a programme would be to show that it was indeed voluntary. Many defectives would be quite incapable of giving a true consent, since they would be unable to grasp all the implications of a sterilizing operation. The opportunity of exercising un-

---

[1] *The Report of the American Neurological Association* (1936), p. 183. For Summary of the Report see *American Journal of Medical Jurisprudence*, 1:253–7 (1938).

[2] See Myerson, "Sterilization", *Atlantic Monthly*, 186:52, p. 55. Referring to an investigation in Massachusetts he writes: "In many groups we found feeble mindedness for one or two generations, but we also found collaterals who reached distinction and were respected in the community. On the other hand, we found no family tree, however distinguished, which did not have hanging from its branches, the mentally sick, the defective, the alcoholic, the failure, the ne'er-do-well, and the social misfit", p. 55.

[3] Op. cit., p. 90.

[4] *The Report*, p. 57.

due influence would be great and it would be difficult to provide safeguards against its employment. Any voluntary sterilization statute would have to tackle this problem, which cannot be dismissed in the words of the Brock Report as "mere casuistry".[1]

STERILIZATION—THE TRADITIONAL CHRISTIAN VIEW

Traditionally, Christian theology has condemned all forms of direct sterilization, whether compulsory or voluntary. This condemnation derives from the Christian view of the creatureliness of man. Man is not absolutely master of his own body: he has no "dominium" over it, but holds it in trust to use for God's purposes as shown in the design of nature. Man's procreative faculty is one of his most important endowments and he cannot do away with it at will. Steriliaztion is more than a mutilation of the body, it involves the deprivation of a major faculty and its gravity is to be measured more by its effect than by the actual surgical operation, which today can be of the simplest. The Christian view can be traced back to the teaching of the Church Fathers. In the early Church, certain zealots, misinterpreting the gospel passage "there be eunuchs which have made themselves eunuchs for the kingdom of heaven's sake" (*Matthew* XIX, 12), castrated themselves. These practices were condemned in both canon law and the writings of the Fathers.[2] The body, they taught, could only be mutilated if a portion were diseased and it was essential for the welfare of the body as a whole that the diseased portion be severed. Self-castration in order to preserve chastity failed in its object and was also contrary to Christian doctrine since it posited the body as intrinsically evil and denied the use of man's free will.

These arguments were developed in the Middle Ages by St Thomas Aquinas and other ecclesiastical writers. A man who mutilates his body without cause sins in three ways: he violates the natural law of self-preservation and proper self-love; he offends against the community of which he is a part; and he commits an offence against God. The motive of curbing unchastity may be laudable but the

[1] *The Report*, p. 42.
[2] See Conc. Nic., Can I: Apost. Can. 21-4, Chrys., *Hom. lxii in Matt.*

method is both ineffective and disproportionate. Control of evil thoughts, not mutilation, is the remedy. To this law there is only one exception. "If, however, the member be decayed and therefore a source of corruption to the whole body, then it is lawful with the consent of the owner of the member, to cut away the member for the welfare of the whole body, since each one is entrusted with the care of his own welfare. The same applies if it be done with the consent of the person whose business it is to care for the welfare of the person who has a decayed member; otherwise it is altogether unlawful to maim anyone."[1]

The traditional teaching was re-affirmed by Pius XI in his enyclical on "Christian Marriage" when he declared: "Christian teaching establishes, and the light of human reason makes it most clear, that private individuals have no other power over the members of their bodies than that which pertains to their natural ends; and they are not free to destroy or mutilate their members, or in any other way render themselves unfit for their natural functions, except when no other provision can be made for the good of the whole body."[2] Pius XII confirmed his predecessor's teaching.[3] The Church of England Moral Welfare Council stated the same underlying principle in 1951: "Man does not belong to himself. He was created by God and for God, and therefore belongs to God. Consequently he has not an unqualified right to dispose of himself as he wishes; his right is limited by the laws of his Creator (which are also the laws of his own nature), and by the nature of his destiny."[4] All direct sterilization was forbidden by a decree of the Holy Office of February 21, 1940.[5]

---

[1] *Summa Theologica*, London 1929, II–II lxv.

[2] *Casti Connubii*, New York 1931, p. 33.

[3] See address to Italian Midwives (*A.A.S.* 18:43): "Direct sterilization, that which aims at making procreation impossible as both means and end, is a grave violation of the moral law, and therefore illicit." Cf. Statement to Italian Urology Society. (*L'Osservatore Romano*, October 10, 1953).

[4] *Human Sterilization: Some Principles of Christian Ethics*, published for the Church of England Moral Welfare Council by the Church Information Board (1951), p. 3.

[5] See Decree of February 1940, *A.A.S.* 32:73. Cf. 1951 *A.A.S.* 43:844.

STERILIZATION AND THE STATE

St Thomas Aquinas discusses the right of the State to use sterilization as a punitive measure. He concludes quite simply that since the State may take the life of a guilty person for the good of the community, *a fortiori*, it may impose the lesser penalty of mutilation.[1] Whatever the soundness of this view in principle, humanitarian sentiments would prevent any Christian from putting it forward as a just and appropriate penalty today. Moral theologians reject sterilization as a punishment for sexual offences on the grounds that it is unreasonable. It might well not be a punishment for the type of individual concerned, and since the sexual urge is not diminished it does not protect society.

May the State enforce a compulsory eugenic sterilization policy? Applying the principles just outlined, the conclusion must be negative. A man's right to bodily integrity is only invasible if he cuts himself off from the community by the commission of a grave crime. Mental and physical defect are misfortunes but they are neither crimes nor sins. Public authority has no right to prescribe sterilization, declared Pius XII, "or to have it carried out to the harm of the innocent".[2] Similarly, the committee on the family at the Lambeth Conference of 1958 stated that all were agreed that "any government policy of compulsory sterilization as a means of population control is unacceptable to the Christian conscience, at least in our present state of knowledge and understanding; some indeed felt that such a policy could never be justified".

It has been argued by Justice Holmes, amongst others, that just as the State has the right to call on its citizens for the sacrifice of their lives in war, so it may require a surrender of their reproductive functions from those who would harm society by procreation. The analogy with war does not hold good on the Christian view, for while every citizen is under a duty to defend the State against unjust aggression, there is no moral duty to submit to sterilization in

[1] *Summa Theologica*, II–II lxv.

[2] *A.A.S.* 18:443. See also decree of Holy Office of March 21, 1931, issued with approval of Pius XI condemning eugenic sterilization.

order to improve the national stock.[1] There may be a moral duty to abstain from intercourse if one knows one is likely to transmit a serious defect, but that is another matter. The analogy with vaccination is also erroneous since vaccination does not deprive the individual of any important faculty and protects the community not by mutilating the individual but by protecting him. The compulsory sterilization argument is based on the assumption that only the strong and the fit have a right to live a human life in the full sense of living it unmaimed. It is only a short step from this assumption to the further conclusion that such people have no right to life at all. Such an approach is profoundly un-Christian for it substitutes for the Christian attitude of loving care for the physically and mentally unfortunate, one of calculating utility which would eliminate them in "the national interest".

In the past, Catholic writers have advocated compulsory sterilization by the State.[2] They have justified sterilization on grounds of necessity in order to protect the community from inundation by criminals and defectives. For their arguments to apply, two conditions of fact would have to be fulfilled. First, the threat to the State from defectives would have to be so serious as to threaten its survival: second, segregation would have to be ruled out as a practical possibility. Neither of these conditions pertain today. This view appears irreconcilable with a condemnation of sterilization as evil in itself.[3]

---

[1] The mere power to procreate cannot be in itself an attack on the State as is the assault of an enemy. Thus the analogy breaks down on a second point. Nor does the State in war intend the killing of its citizens or itself carry it out.

[2] For a discussion of these writers and their views, see Joseph B. Lehane, *The Morality of American Civil Legislation concerning Eugenical Sterilization*, Washington D.C. 1944. See also S. M. Donovan, *The Ecclesiastical Review*, 42:271 (1910). Other Catholic writers supporting this view have been Fr. J. A. Ryan, Dr Mayer and Dr Bruehl. Such views would not be tenable by Catholics today.

[3] A further difficulty is raised by the custom of castrating singing boys of the Sistine Choir to preserve their treble voices. St. Alphonsus records two contrary opinions on this point, one condemning it and the other justifying it as being for the common good. (*Theol. Mor.* III n.374). Benedict XIV condemned the practice but provided that such persons were not to be expelled from the choir. (*De Synodo Diocesena*, XI, cap. 7, n.4). See E. J. Mahoney "Sterilization—A Difficulty", *The Clergy Review*, 4:71.

Voluntary Sterilization

Christian opinion is less unanimous when voluntary instead of compulsory sterilization is considered. Both the Roman Catholic and
Anglican Churches recognize the validity of therapeutic sterilization
as morally justified if it is the only means of securing the welfare of
the body as a whole. Thus if vasectomy and salpingectomy are the
only means of curing a disease, their use is legitimate. Their employment would fall within the exception mentioned by St Thomas
Aquinas in connection with mutilation. Neither communion, on the
other hand, countenances the use of sterilization where a woman's
health would be gravely endangered by a further pregnancy. Dr
Glanville Williams finds such a view "astonishing" but it is not unreasonable.[1] Sexual intercourse is not a necessity and the woman can
adequately safeguard her future either by abstention, or in the view
of many Anglicans by the use of contraceptives. Such sterilization
is not strictly speaking therapeutic but contraceptive. In the case of
subnormal couples, incapable of handling contraceptives efficiently,
the case for employment of sterilization is stronger, but only of
course amongst those who regard the use of contraceptives as
legitimate. The latter might extend sterilization as a legitimate
procedure from defectives in danger of physical injury through
pregnancy, to defectives who would be placed under overwhelming
strain through further child-bearing. As the Church of England
Moral Welfare Council points out, this conclusion may prove
difficult even for those who approve of contraception. Sterilization
might well be considered too grave a course to employ save directly
for the cure of a disease. Furthermore, while in sterilization of a
defective wife whose health would be threatened by pregnancy, and
where intercourse can be regarded as inevitable, the causal connection between the operation and the result aimed at is very close;
in the second case, where the burden of looking after children is the
main concern, the connection is remote. A further complication in
this latter case is that there is no indication which of the parents
should be sterilized.[2]

A second form of sterilization recognized as lawful by both Communions, may conveniently be called "incidental" or "indirect".

---

[1] Op. cit., p. 100.
[2] See *Human Sterilization* (1951), pp. 7–9 and 15.

The category is created by applying the principle of double effect.[1]
The principle, familiar to students of moral theology, states that an
action, not in itself intrinsically evil, followed by both a good and a
bad result, may be performed, provided that the good and not the
evil effect is directly intended, that the good effect is not produced
by means of the evil effect, and a grave reason exists for permitting
the evil to occur. The distinction between "direct" and "indirect"
intention, is that between foreseeing a consequence and desiring it,
and merely foreseeing it while desiring some other consequence. An
example will make the working of the rule clearer. It can justify
the performance of hysterectomy. The consequence directly intended by the removal of a diseased womb is the saving of a woman's
life, that indirectly intended is her sterilization. All the conditions of
the principle of double effect are fulfilled so the operation is legitimate.

Voluntary sterilization for eugenic reasons is not countenanced by
the Roman Catholic Church. The Church of England Committee
puts forward the argument that a normal couple who know that one
partner is a carrier of defect may regard the sexual organ as "diseased", in that the genes it secretes are defective, and given circumstances of "necessity", may resort to sterilization. This argument is
answered by pointing out that the organ is not diseased in relation
to the parental body but only to the hypothetical child. What constitutes "necessity"? Here the couple have two alternatives; they can
abstain or they can use contraceptives. Accordingly sterilization
would not be justified in their case.[2]

One is then faced, once more, with the problem of the sub-
normal couple, incapable of using contraceptives efficiently or of
abstaining from intercourse. Here the Commission expresses doubt
whether any genuine voluntary sterilization can arise and points to
the uncertainty of all the children being defective. The final conclusion is so subtly phrased that for fear of misleading it must be
quoted in full. "With a mentally normal couple who decide that the
risk of handing on a disease to children is so grave that there must be
no children, but that contraceptives are not sufficiently infallible to

[1] See J. T. Mangan, S.J., "An Historical Analysis of the Principle of Double
Effect", *Theological Studies*, 10:41. St. Thomas Aquinas, *Summa Theologica*,
II–II lxiv. For a further discussion of the principle see E. Healey, *Medical
Ethics*, Chicago 1956, and A. Bonnar, *The Catholic Doctor*, New York 1950.
[2] *Human Sterilization*, pp. 11–12.

make avoidance of the risk absolutely certain: some would say they may resort to sterilization, others would say that a decision can only be arrived at after distinguishing between a *certainty* and a *probability* that the disability would affect someone in the family."[1] Curiously enough the Report makes no mention of segregation as an alternative solution to the problems raised by mental defect.

The Lambeth Conference of 1958 formulated a somewhat obscure statement on voluntary sterilization. The Committee appears to have been greatly influenced by the present irreversibility of sterilization in declaring it an abdication of an important area of responsible freedom and "a violation of the human body".[2] Presumably this judgement would be revised if sterilization could be reversed. The Committee evidently concluded that in some circumstances sterilization is justifiable for it recommends "prayerful and serious consideration" before a decision to be sterilized is taken. The circumstances are not specified.

STERILIZATION AND THE LAW
—CHRISTIAN VIEW

A State policy of compulsory sterilization conflicts radically with Christian morals and social policy. It violates the fundamental rights of the human person, and confers powers on the State to which it has no claim. The maintenance of State authority is in no way incompatible with the presence within the community of unsterilized mental defectives and others. As has been established, the uncertainty shrouding the whole hereditary process, the ignorance of the pathology of mental diseases and defect, and the high proportion of the population who would have to be sterilized for a eugenic policy to have substantial effect, must result in the rejection of compulsory sterilization on the level of practical ethics. Christians, accordingly, have not only a right but a duty to resist the legislative sponsoring of such projects, and to work for their repeal where they have been enacted. The experience of Nazi Germany has convinced many of the validity of the Christian contention that once sterilization powers have been conferred on the State, the danger of their ruthless

[1] *Human Sterilization*, pp. 15–16.
[2] *The Lambeth Conference*, 1958, 2:149.

exploitation is a real one. A Christian campaign on this issue could accordingly expect general public support. It is a little surprising to observe that the Catholics of Connecticut who have fought so fiercely for the retention on the statute book of a birth control statute which invades the privacy of the home, should have acquiesced for all practical purposes in the presence of sterilization provisions in the State Code which can be invoked without hearing or appeal.

Segregation is sometimes put forward as an alternative to sterilization to check the increase of mental defect. Here again, the paucity of medical knowledge would be a powerful inhibiting factor, but even assuming the predictability of transmission of defect, grave objections are raised by the Christian conscience. The State has the right to impose restrictions on the individual person only when they are proportionately necessary for the preservation of the common good. Since deprivation of liberty is in many ways a more fundamental deprivation of fundamental human rights than sterilization, it could only be justified if the community was in danger of innundation by defectives, and of this no evidence exists. Segregation for the eugenic benefit of the State alone must be ruled out, but if it can be shown that those concerned are a danger to others, or else a danger to themselves because of their irresponsibility, it is legitimate. What of those who do not come within these categories? No person has a moral right to procreate if he has no reasonable assurance that he can beget healthy offspring and make reasonable provision for them. The State may accordingly forbid the marriage of such persons in defence of the common good. Some American States already forbid the marriage of habitual criminals or drunkards:[1] others deny it to insane and feeble-minded individuals who may pass the condition on to their children.[2] Nearly all the States require evidence of freedom from communicable syphilis before a marriage may be contracted. As to procreation by such persons outside of marriage, this could be restricted by the criminal law.

[1] E.g. Virginia, Washington, Delaware and Ohio.

[2] E.g. Michigan, Nebraska and South Dakota. No system for the registration of the insane and feeble minded exists and the provisions are easily evaded. See Glanville Williams, op. cit., p. 95. This, however, could be remedied. For a discussion of Catholic principles involved, see J. P. O'Brien, *The Right of the State to make disease an impediment to marriage*, Catholic University of America Press, 1952.

Yet another alternative to compulsory sterilization is a voluntary procedure. Those who regard sterilization as wrong in itself would clearly oppose any campaign for its extension conducted by official authority. Even those who do not subscribe to this judgment might well conclude that until further medical research has been carried out on both the mechanism of heredity and the effects of sterilization, such a campaign would be premature. Does the Christian conscience require all sterilization to be forbidden by law? Many would agree with Pius XII that public authority has no right to permit sterilization "under the pretext of any 'indication' whatsoever", and that apart from the established exceptions of therapeutic and indirect sterilization, it should be legally banned. This, however, is not the only conclusion compatible with Christian belief.

Most Christians would agree that a contraceptive sterilization undertaken solely for reasons of personal convenience should not be tolerated by the law. At common law this is probably the present legal position. The justification for such a prohibition is that sterilization directly injures the common good when it deprives the community of potentially healthy stock. Again contraceptive sterilization by removing fear of pregnancy might well increase immorality and the consequent spread of venereal disease. Furthermore, those who wish to avoid children may resort to contraceptives, and even those Christians who condemn contraception would rather see their employment than the greater evil of sterilization.

When voluntary sterilization for eugenic purposes is considered, different considerations arise. If those who have good reason to think that they will transmit disease or mental defect are permitted to sterilize themselves it is difficult to see how the common good suffers. The possibility of loss to the community is at least balanced by that of possible gain. A law which permitted such sterilization provided that competent medical authority certified that it was being employed for well founded eugenic reasons would not *ipso facto* be unacceptable to Christians. The decision whether to employ it would be left to the individual taking into account the tenets of his particular denomination. The alternative choices of abstention from sexual intercourse or the use of contraceptives would still be available. The State would in no way be approving of sterilization but would merely be stating that in the restricted circumstances outlined the final decision should be left to the individual rather than the State.

Some, however, would oppose even this concession on the grounds that it would only be the thin end of the wedge, and would lead to legalizing other forms of sterilization.[1] They might also raise the objection that in countries where there is a government health service, the State would be promoting an immoral practice. This difficulty could be surmounted by excluding the facilities from the service.

SPECIFIC CATHOLIC PROBLEMS

Sterilization in Catholic hospitals

In both England and the United States the Roman Catholic Church is responsible for the administration and staffing of a number of hospitals. Although they perform a public service, these hospitals are essentially private institutions, and apply the religious principles already discussed in the treatment of their patients. Practice in Catholic hospitals is conveniently summed up in a recent publication *Ethical and Religious Directives for Catholic Hospitals*.[2] Procedures that induce either permanent or temporary sterility may only be employed when:

"(a) they are immediately directed to the cure, diminution, or prevention of a serious pathological condition;

(b) a simpler treatment is not reasonably available; and

(c) the sterility itself is an unintended and, in the circumstances, an unavoidable effect." These principles allow the performance of the routine vasectomy carried out in many hospitals after certain operations, but Father Gerald Kelly points out that in patients of the younger age group, it should only be employed where there is a special reason for its use.[3] The development of the anti-biotic drugs may soon render this routine vasectomy unnecessary.

The above conditions, based on ethical considerations, are not

---

[1] Thus the Italian Penal Code (art. 552) prohibits acts directed to render a person impotent to procreate.

[2] Published by the Catholic Hospital Association, St. Louis, Missouri (1955).

[3] See Gerald Kelly, "Vasectomy with Prostatectomy", *Medico-Moral Problems*, II:35, St. Louis 1956.

open to objection in a pluralist society. They are not imposed on patients against their will, for Catholic practice is of reasonably common knowledge, and the average patient expects certain ethical limitations to medical procedure when he enters a Catholic hospital. If he wishes he can always transfer to another hospital where sterilization operations may be more readily available. Every patient certainly has the moral right to be informed if an operation beneficial to his health cannot be performed for ethical reasons. He clearly cannot compel the doctor to perform an operation to which the latter morally objects, but the decision not to employ it should be shared by the patient so that he may have an opportunity of exercising responsible assent. The information will create a liberty in practice to go elsewhere, but its exercise need not be the primary purpose of the communication. Knowledge may be a dangerous thing but the patient has a right to it. Whether the physician has an obligation to inform the patient where the operation can be carried out is more open to question and must be decided by the individual doctor considering all the circumstances of the case.[1]

Catholic doctors, nurses, etc., in non-Catholic hospitals

Catholic doctors or officials in charge of hospitals may not "formally" co-operate in sterilization operations. Formal co-operation, according to Catholic theologians, occurs when one acts with another in performing an external act which is wrong in itself with or without internal assent, or where assistance is given to one performing an immoral act by an act in itself indifferent but with the intention of promoting the evil action.[2] Material co-operation is the performance of an indifferent act helping another's evil act but with no intention of forwarding it. Material co-operation is licit provided a grave reason exists for co-operating. Loss of employment by a nurse or doctor would constitute such a reason. Thus it would never be lawful for a Catholic doctor to perform a sterilization operation under any

[1] I would say that such an obligation does exist. The doctor is primarily concerned with the health of the body and not of the soul. In informing his patient of the availability of alternative facilities he is in no way advocating their employment but discharging his duty of making all relevant information available without which the patient cannot come to a considered decision.

[2] Performance of an act wrong in itself with no internal assent is sometimes separately classified as "immediate" co-operation.

circumstances, but an anaesthetist might give the anaesthetic before such an operation, if his refusal would cause grave inconvenience, without violating his conscience. An elaborate casuistry has been built up in the literature on the subject, but few difficulties arise in practice, since most non-Catholic hospitals are careful to defer to the scruples of their Catholic medical staff, and excuse them from operations to which they morally object.[1]

Catholic judges

Catholic judges, like any others, are bound to uphold the law of the country, but they, like their medical colleagues, may find themselves in difficulty when dealing with an application for sterilization. It is arguable that the judge is not responsible for the state of the law, that he only administers it and takes it as he finds it. He neither approves nor disapproves of particular provisions but applies them in accordance with the instructions of the legislature. There is a sphere of judicial discretion, but it is limited, and a judge who consistently enforced the dictates of his own conscience rather than the law would be guilty of betraying his office. Thus the correct attitude for a Catholic judge when faced with a sterilization application would be to set his own pre-possessions aside, and in a case which fell clearly within the relevant statute, to apply the law.

Against this it may be said that a judge may never oblige anyone to commit what he considers an intrinsically immoral act, for in doing so he becomes a "material" co-operator. Such is the conclusion of Father Davis in his book, *The Moral Obligations of Catholic Civil Judges*. "The judge in such cases," he writes, "cannot throw responsibility from his shoulders, nor can he render a decision obliging a person to commit an act intrinsically evil. Therefore the Catholic judge can never in his judicial action render a decision putting the law of eugenical sterilization into effect."[2] Since the judge is obliged by his position to enforce the law, he is left with no alternative save that of arranging not to hear the case, or if this proves impossible, to resign from office. The withdrawal of Catholic judges

---

[1] See A. Bonnar, op. cit., pp. 50-1, Edwin Healey, op. cit., pp. 103-6, and J. B. Lehane, *The Morality of American Civil Legislation concerning Eugenical Sterilization*, Washington 1944, pp. 96-7.
[2] Washington 1953, p. 147.

from office would doubtless be considered an evil, from the Church's point of view, but the avoidance of this evil would not be considered a justification for taking part in an intrinsically evil act.

LIBERAL CHRISTIAN VIEW AND THE LAW

Not all Christian denominations accept the traditional Christian view on sterilization, but owing to the paucity of the literature on the subject and the custom among the sects of leaving such matters to be decided by the individual conscience, it is almost impossible to formulate their views precisely. In 1954 a questionnaire was circulated in the United States among some thirty-six denominations of which thirty replied.[1] Roman Catholics and Moslems were the only denominations to condemn sterilization in general, twenty denominations had not defined their attitude on medical and voluntary eugenical sterilization, and twenty-two took no stand on sterilization for social or economic reasons. Seven approved eugenical sterilization and one disapproved. Judaism's general position seems clear. Sterilization is prohibited.[2]

Joseph Fletcher in his book, *Morals and Medicine*, commends the legalizing of voluntary sterilization. He agrees with the authors of *Sterilization—a Christian approach*,[3] that the foremost concern of Christianity is personality, and that divine rights and duties are not expressed through natural or physical necessities but only through personal human experience and decision. To them it is blasphemy to say that God wills that stunted and defective children should be born. They emphatically reject the view that to exist without taint is better than not to exist at all. When there is a reasonable cause to eliminate the possibility of reproduction, then the Christian has not only a right but a responsibility to do so. Like the utilitarians, this group would welcome the legalizing of voluntary eugenic sterilization.

---

[1] See Theodore W. Adams, "Thoughts on the Control of Postpartum Sterilization: Presidential Address", *Western Journal of Surgery*, 62:101 (1954).

[2] See Emanuel Rackman, "A Jewish View" in Symposium on Morals, Medicine and the Law, *New York U. Law Review*, 31:1211 (1956).

[3] By J. P. Hinton and J. E. Calcutt, London 1935.

CHAPTER FIVE

Homosexuality

THE LAW

In neither England nor the United States is the state of homosexuality a crime, nor does it confer any special status in law, but
homosexual acts between males are criminal offences. English law
does not punish homosexual acts between women, but similar acts,
between men, whether they take place in public or private, are contrary to the law. Punishment varies with the type of act committed.
Thus buggery or sodomy is a felony punishable by life imprisonment,
the attempt carrying a penalty of ten years imprisonment.[1] Other
sexual acts between consenting males are classified under the general
heading of gross indecency, and are punished by a maximum of two
years imprisonment.[2] Persistent soliciting or importuning carries
the same maximum penalty if proceeded against by indictment, but
on summary trial the maximum is reduced to six months. Offences
of a minor nature against local by-laws are punished by a fine of £5 in
magistrates' courts.

United States law derives directly from English law, but varies
considerably from State to State.[3] Homosexual acts between males
are offences in all jurisdictions, but the type of act punished is
variable. Certain States, such as Arkansas, punish only sodomy, and
this is strictly defined. Others have a similar position by statute, but
judicial interpretation has considerably extended its effect.[4] A
third group of States punishes a variety of sexual acts, defined by the
actual wording of the statutes and within this group, some punish
any form of unnatural intercourse.[5] Finally, it should be noted that
Vermont is unique in not punishing sodomy. *Lewdness* is an offence,

---

[1] *The Sexual Offences Act*, 1956, 4 and 5 Eliz., 2, c. 69, s. 12, schedule 2 (3).
[2] Ibid., s. 13. Indecent assaults by males on males are punishable with a
maximum of ten years' imprisonment (s. 15 [1]). Similar offences against
females carry a maximum of only two years' imprisonment (s. 14 (1)).
[3] See Appendix I for a summary of the laws in different States.
[4] E.g. Georgia, Indiana, Kansas, Nebraska, Nevada and North Carolina.
[5] E.g. Arizona, Colorado, Louisiana and New Hampshire.

but this is narrowly defined.[1] Some States punish sexual acts between women, but others do not.[2] In the United States, as opposed to England, sodomy is probably also a common law offence.[3]

In English law a fairly clear order of penalties is established for homosexual offences, sodomy being singled out for the severest punishment. By contrast American law is chaotic, with no consistent penal policy. Penalties may be as low as one year, with a maximum of three as in Virginia, or as high as a minimum of seven years (Rhode Island), or a maximum of sixty years (North Carolina). The District of Columbia may deal with a case by imposing a fine of 1,000 dollars, but in Indiana it can be as low as 100 dollars.[4] Certain States distinguish between types of offences, and penalties are graded according to which offence is committed and whether there are aggravating circumstances.[5] Thus, New York recognizes three degrees of sodomy. First degree sodomy is defined as intercourse *per anum* or *per os*, without the consent of the other party, or where consent is impossible by reason of mental or physical weakness, or immaturity, etc., and is punished by twenty years' imprisonment or an indeterminate sentence. Second degree sodomy is committed when one of the parties is under eighteen, and the aggravating conditions of first degree sodomy are absent, and is penalized with a maximum of ten years' imprisonment. Other sodomy offences are classified as in the third degree and rank as misdemeanours.[6] Some States provide an additional penalty for sodomy in the form of infamy or loss of civil rights.[7] A curious legal provision in certain jurisdictions provides that no particulars of the alleged sexual acts need be furnished in the indictment. The District of Columbia code con-

[1] I.e. copulation *per os*. Other acts are only subject to the law if open and gross. *Revised Statutes*, 1947. 8480 and 8478.
[2] Thus Arizona and Washington penalize such behaviour but Mississippi does not.
[3] See *State v. Vicknair*, 52 La. Ann. 1921, 28 So. 273 (1900). In England sodomy was under the jurisdiction of the ecclesiastical courts until the Henrician statute of 1533 (25 Hen. 8, c. 6).
[4] See Appendix X for details of penalties.
[5] E.g. California, Florida, Massachusetts, New Jersey, Vermont and Georgia. Youthfulness of one party is normally an aggravating circumstance.
[6] *Consolidated Laws* 1944, as amended, 690.
[7] E.g. Colorado (Revised Statutes 1953), 39.10.18 and Illinois (Revised Statutes 1957), 38. 587.

tains such a provision but allows them to be obtained by the accused on motion of request.[1] Soliciting or importuning in public places is sometimes specifically dealt with by statute, but otherwise comes within the numerous disorderly conduct, lewd behaviour, or vagrancy statutes.

LAW ENFORCEMENT

In England the Wolfenden Report has shown that the English laws are by no means dead letters. Indictable cases rose from 390 in 1931 to 2,504 in 1955.[2] The statistics do not show how many cases were those involving acts between consenting adults taking place in private, but the majority of cases probably included some element of duress or were of a public nature. For the three years ending in March 1956, 300 adult offenders were convicted solely for offences committed in private with other consenting adults.[3] As can be seen from the table reproduced below, this is only a small percentage of offenders brought before the courts. Of these 300, seven were absolutely discharged, seventy-four bound over, sixty-six placed on probation and thirty-four fined. Only 116 were sentenced to imprisonment, the sentences ranging from twelve months or less for sixty-four of the offenders, to a maximum of five years for one offender.

No comparable figures for the United States as a whole are available, and this is a field where research into the number of prosecutions and convictions and the type of sentence imposed, should be especially valuable. In the nature of things, however, only a very small percentage of acts taking place in private can come to the

[1] Code 1951, 22. 3502.
[2] *Report of the Committee on Homosexual Offences, etc.*, London, H.M.S.O. Cmd. 247, September 1957, p. 131.

Proceedings re indictable homosexual offences.

Year	Buggery	Indecent Assault	Gross Indecency	Total
1931	57	212	121	390
1939	63	361	171	595
1947	130	585	302	1,017
1955	428	1,081	995	2,504

[3] Wolfenden Report, Table VI.

notice of the police.[1] In New York City for example, in 1948 there were only 146 arrests for sodomy, and in 1949 the figure was 112.[2] One of the few detailed investigations into sexual offences was that undertaken by a California committee, set up in 1950, to investigate offences within the State. The committee found that very few persons were prosecuted in California superior courts for sodomy, only four cases being disposed of in 1951 in twenty-three counties, and only eight in 1952 in the entire State. Prosecution for other types of homosexual offence, on the other hand, was more common.[3] From 1950–54 only eighty-nine sodomy cases were reported in the United States, of which twenty-seven were in California, nine in Texas, and five in New York. Fifty-three of the cases were distributed amongst five States. Nearly all of these cases involved some public element.[4] Enforcement of the law against female homosexuals seems to be so rare as to be of no social importance. The records, for example, of the Indiana state prison for women show only one conviction of a woman for a homosexual offence and that took place in an institution.[5] From 1930 to 1939 in New York City, only one case of female homosexual sodomy was reported, and from 1946–56 only three, all of them dismissed.[6]

HISTORY OF THE LAW AND JUDAEO-CHRISTIAN INFLUENCE

Jewish law and custom rejected any form of homosexual conduct as contrary to the law of God. In this it was similar to Zoroastrianism and to later Christianity. The peculiar abhorrence in the Jewish mind for homosexual conduct has been traced to the Lot story in *Genesis*. The traditional interpretation of the story is that the men of Sodom demanded intercourse with two angels, the guests of Lot, and the

---

[1] See D. W. Cory (pseud.) *The Homosexual in America*, New York 1951, pp. 53 and 54.

[2] M. Ploscowe, *Sex and the Law*, New York 1951, p. 208.

[3] Report of California Sexual Deviation Research Committee, January 1953, p. 18.

[4] See Karl M. Bowman and Bernice Engle, "A Psychiatric Evaluation of Laws of Homosexuality", Temple L. Q., 29:273 (Spring 1956), p. 296.

[5] Ibid., p. 281.

[6] Ibid. Cf. A. Kinsey, *Sexual Behaviour in the Human Female*, London 1953, p. 484.

city was destroyed for this attempted sacrilege.[1] The basis of this view is that the demand of the citizens to "know" the angels is a demand to debauch them. This is supported by the offer to the citizens of Lot's daughters. It looks as though he is offering them a heterosexual experience with his daughters as a substitute for homosexual intercourse with his guests. This interpretation has been challenged. Dr G. A. Barton has suggested that the interpretation of "know" in the coital sense is not necessary and that it may mean to "get acquainted with".[2] Recently this view has been expounded with great learning by the Anglican scholar, Dr D. S. Bailey.[3] He employs three arguments to show that the Hebrew verb *yādhá* (to know) in this particular context means not to engage in *coitus* but to make the acquaintance of. He points out that while *yādhá* is a common verb, its use in a coital sense is exceptional, and its reference always heterosexual and not homosexual. The citizens are thus demanding to meet the men, probably to investigate their *bona fides*. Dr Bailey supports his interpretation by appealing to external evidence and points out that the sin of Sodom is not considered homosexual in *Ezekiel* or the *Apocrypha*. Furthermore, none of the passages in the Bible which refer to homosexuality mention Sodom, a strange omission if Sodom's sins were of this nature. Dr Bailey disposes of the offer of Lot's daughters as being merely the most tempting bribe which he could offer to appease the angry crowd, alarmed at his entertaining of two friends who might have designs against the city.

If this view is correct how has Sodom come to be connected with homosexual practices? Dr Bailey finds the connection between sodom

---

[1] *Genesis* xix, 4–8. The angels were sent to investigate the situation in Sodom, and were received by Lot. "But before they lay down the men of the city, even the men of Sodom, compassed the house round, both old and young, all the people from every quarter: and they called unto Lot, and said unto him, Where are the men which came into thee this night? Bring them out unto us that we may know them. Lot went out at the door unto them, and shut the door after him. And said, I pray you, brethren, do not so wickedly. Behold now, I have two daughters which have not known man; let me, I pray you, bring them out unto you, and do you to them as is good in your eyes; only unto these men do nothing; for therefore came they under the shadow of my roof."

[2] "Sodomy", *Encyclopaedia of Religion and Ethics*, XI:672.

[3] *Homosexuality and the Western Christian Tradition*, London 1955. See also, "The Homosexual and Christian Morals" in *They Stand Apart*, symposium, edited by J. Tudor Rees and Harley V. Usill, New York 1955.

and sexual transgressions in the Palestinian Pseudepigrapha, a development beginning with the *Book of Jubilees* of the second century B.C.[1] Here the emphasis is shifted to sexual but not to homosexual sins. It is only in the first century A.D. that explicit references are found to Sodom as the centre of unnatural vice, although the connection was probably established considerably earlier.[2] The homosexual interpretation of the Sodom story is accordingly not an unbroken tradition but an illustration of the reaction of the Jewish people against the pagan world where homosexual practices were so prevalent. This view of the Sodom story does not mean that the Jewish people did not condemn homosexual practices, of which there is abundant evidence in the Bible and in Rabbinical literature.[3] Nor does it in any way affect the influence of the traditional interpretation in shaping Christian attitudes, but it may well be of importance in assessing what the contemporary Christian attitude to homosexuality ought to be.

The Sodom story apart, homosexual practices are condemned in the *Book of Leviticus:* "Thou shalt not lie with mankind, as with womankind: it is abomination." (*Lev.* xviii 22.) A subsequent passage lays down the penalty as death. (*Lev.* xx. 13.)[4] The method of execution was by stoning. Passive minors and active minors, if the passive partner was under the age of nine, were exempted from

---

[1] *Jub.* xiii, 17; xvi, 5–6; xx, 5–6; vii, 20–21.

[2] E.g. *The Book of the Secrets of Enoch*, a Hellenistic-Jewish work, written in Egypt before the middle of the first century A.D. and itself based on a lost work, the *Writing of Enoch*, reference to which is made in certain additions to the *Testaments of the Twelve Patriarchs* of the period 70–40 B.C. The passage in Enoch is 2 *Enoch*, xxxiv, 2. Dr Bailey concludes that by approximately 50 B.C. at the latest, the interpolators of the *Testaments* viewed the sin of Sodom as unnatural vice. Of course this attribution may have been earlier. See Bailey, op. cit., p. 20. Cf. Philo, *De Abrahamo*, xxvi, 134–6.

[3] Rabbinical literature, however, only once links homosexual acts with Sodom, see the Midrash on Genesis (*Gen. Rabbah*. 1. 5. 7).

[4] *Deut.* xxiii, 17, also condemns sodomy in a passage taken to refer to temple prostitution. Other associated passages are 1 *Kings* xiv, 22–24, 1 *Kings* xv, 12, 1 *Kings* xxii, 46 and 2 *Kings* xxiii, 7. Westermark, Kinsey and others have read these passages as condemnatory of homosexual practices but this is challenged by Dr Bailey who maintains that the Hebrew words *qadhesh* and *qadheshim* have been mistranslated in the authorized and revised versions as sodomite and sodomites, op. cit. p. 53. He further dismisses *Judges* xix as a doctored text, consciously assimilated to the Sodom story and therefore of little evidentiary value.

the law, others were liable to the death penalty, but there is no evidence that this was ever imposed. A final point of Rabbinical law which may be noted, is that female homosexuality was not penalized save for a disqualification from marriage with a priest.[1]

Summing up the evidence from the Old Testament and other sources, the Jewish people's condemnation of homosexuality is clear, but even if one does not accept all Dr Bailey's conclusions, later writers and commentators have exaggerated Jewish abhorrence of this sin. Homosexual sins were denounced, but adultery, fornication and other sexual sins were condemned with much greater frequency. The law against homosexual practices was severe, but in the absence of evidence of its enforcement, it would be rash to assume that the Jews regarded them with the vindictive horror that many have thought them to have possessed.

The New Testament and the Fathers of the Church

In the New Testament the most unequivocal and best known condemnation of homosexual practice is made by St Paul in his *Epistle to the Romans*. Referring to the sins of the Gentiles, he writes: "For this cause God gave them up unto vile affections: for even their women did change the natural use into that which is against nature: and likewise also the men, leaving the natural use of the women, burned in their lust one toward another; men with men working that which is unseemly, and receiving in themselves that recompence of their error which was due." (*Romans* i, 26–7.[2]) A passage in the epistle of Jude is of interest in connecting Sodom with homosexual sins. This connection was elaborated with vigour by the Church Fathers, their denunciations probably being prompted by the state of the contemporary Roman world, where homosexuality was widely practised. Tertullian, John Chrysostom, Justin, Eusebius, Lactantius, Salvian, and Augustine, were in agreement in con-

---

[1] Bab. Shab., 65a.
[2] Other Pauline references are 1 *Corinthians* vi, 9–10, and 1 *Timothy* i, 9–10. Two passages in St John's *Revelations*, xxi, 8 and xxii, 15, have been supposed by some commentators to refer to homosexual practices but this is disputed. *Jude* 7, is referred to in the text, cf. 2 *Peter* xi, 6–8. The only other new Testament passage on the matter is *Eph.* v, 12, but this is highly ambiguous and capable of other interpretations.

demning all such activites.[1] Such vices, declared Tertullian, should be banished "not only from the threshold but also from all shelter of the Church, for they are not sins so much as monstrosities".[2] St Augustine, in his *Confessions*, declared that sins which are against nature, "like those of the men of Sodom, are in all times and places to be detested and punished. Even if all nations committed such sins, they should all alike be held guilty by God's law which did not make men so that they should use each other thus. The friendship which should be between God and us is violated when nature— whose author He is—is polluted by so perverted a lust."[3] His condemnation was repeated in the *City of God*.[4]

These fiery denunciations naturally influenced ecclesiastical law, and also the secular law, when the Empire became Christian. It should not, however, be forgetten, that laws punishing homosexual conduct, were not a novelty, and had first been passed under the Republic.[5] These were not enforced in the pagan Empire, and in 342 a change of attitude was demonstrated by a prohibitory law of Constantius and Constans, preserved in the Theodosian Code.[6] In 390, Valentinian ordered that sodomists should be burned, but it is dubious whether this penalty was enforced.[7] Justinian issued two *novellae* on the subject, but they are more remarkable for their exhortation to repentance than for their penal character.[8] Both attribute all manner of disasters to homosexual conduct, including famine, pestilence, and earthquakes, and their chief importance lies in their influence on later theologians and lawyers in their attitude to the problem.

Church Councils and Synods imposed penalties on sodomists.

[1] Justin, 1 Apol. xxvii, Eusebius, *Theoph.* ii, 81 and *Demonstr. Evang.* iv, 10, Lactantius, *Instit.* v, 9 and Salvian, *De Gubernat. Dei*, vii, 7. See also Chrysostom, *In epist. ad Rom.* iv, *In Matt. hom.* lxxxiii, 3, Ad Pop. Antioch. hom. xix, 7. There are numerous other references.

[2] *De pudic*. iv. At this time he was a Montanist.

[3] viii, 1-15.

[4] III xvi, 30. Cf. *De Mend.* vii (10), *Contr. Mend.* ix, 20, 22, xvii, 34.

[5] The *Lex Scantinia* was passed after the scandal associated with C. Scantinus Capitolinus came to light. The Lex Julia de Adulteriis, 17 B.C. originally was confined to heterosexual offences but was later extended by *interpretatio* to include homosexual offences.

[1] *Cod. Theod.* ix, vii, 3.

[7] Ibid., ix, vii, 6.

[8] Novel 77 of 538 and Novel 141 of 544.

Thus the Council of Elvira, meeting in Southern Spain (305–6), forbade communion to be given to *stupratores puerorum*. In 314 the Council of Ancyra (Asia Minor) passed two canons condemning homosexual practices and bestiality. Sporadic legislation was passed in the following centuries. The State also intervened, King Kindasvinth of Spain, for example, issuing an edict in 650 prescribing the punishment of castration for offenders.[1] In 693 the Council of Toledo laid down whipping and banishment as penalties for homosexual acts and to these, castration was later added by royal order.[2] Spain apart, the most vigorous action against homosexual activity was taken in Palestine, where the Council of Naplouse, held in January 1120 under the auspices of King and Patriarch of Jerusalem, laid down a system of comprehensive penalties.[3] The Church was not opposed to the punishment of homosexual offences by the secular arm, but the emphasis was as much on their character as sins as crimes, and repentance if genuine could secure a remission of penalties.

In medieval times, the polemics of the Church Fathers were echoed by Peter Damiani (1007–72), in the *Liber Gomorrhianus*, in which he claimed that homosexual practices were prevalent amongst the clergy and called for severe penalties. The book's violent tone was much criticized and led to a modification by Leo IX of his earlier approval. Of far greater significance was the treatment of the subject by St Thomas Aquinas in his *Summa Theologica*.[4] His discussion of the problem is notably temperate, but his condemnation of homosexual acts is uncompromising. St Thomas taught that they were against nature as being contrary to "right reason" and "contrary to the natural order of the venereal act as becoming to the human race". The purpose of the sexual act is procreation and this end is directly frustrated by homosexual practices. There is nothing novel about St Thomas's teaching, but it does develop fully the Pauline teaching on their unnatural character.

With the composition of the *Summa Theologica*, Christian teaching on homosexuality assumed a definitive form. St Thomas's character-

---

[1] *Lex Visigoth*, III, v, 4.
[2] *Conc*. XVI. Toletan 3.
[3] *Conc. Neapolitan* 8.
[4] II-II, q. 153 art. 2, q. 154 arts. 1, 11 and 12.

ization of such acts as unnatural, together with the traditional
interpretation of the Sodom story, have been the determining factors
in the Christian viewpoint up to the present day. These moral ideas
have been reflected in the law, but it would be false to think that the
Church vindictively persecuted offenders. Councils continued to
condemn homosexual activity, ecclesiastical penances were imposed,
and heresy was in some cases associated with homosexual conduct,
but the Church consistently emphasized the sinful character of
homosexual acts rather than their illegality. Dr Kinsey's assertion
that medieval times provide "abundant records" of imposition of
the death penalty is not supported by adduced evidence.[1] In England,
homosexual conduct was within the principal although not exclusive
jurisdiction of the ecclesiastical courts, and it was not until the
sixteenth century that the State assumed full jurisdiction over such
offences.

HISTORY OF ENGLISH LAW

Early English legal treatises contain references to homosexual conduct. Thus in *Fleta*, dating from 1290 in the reign of Edward I,
burying alive is prescribed as the penalty for sodomy.[2] Shortly after-
wards, another treatise, *Britton*, gives burning as the right punishment.[3] Glanville, however in *De Legibus et Consuetudinibus Regni
Angliae*, makes no reference to the subject. It is highly unlikely that
these penalties were enforced, and the preamble to Henry VII's
statute of 1533 complained that there was "not yet sufficient and
condign punishment" appointed by law "for the detestable and
abominable vice of buggery committed with mankind or beast".[4]

Non-enforcement of ecclesiastical law was one reason for assumption of jurisdiction, but it was part of the general policy of Henry
VIII in extending the royal supremacy. The statute deprived the
ecclesiastical courts of their jurisdiction and transferred it to the
royal courts. After various vicissitudes, the Act was revived by

[1] See Kinsey, op. cit., p. 484.
[2] *Fleta, seu Commentarius Juris Anglicani*, London 1735, p. 84, xxxviii, 3.
[3] *Britton*, ed. F. M. Nichols, Oxford 1865, I:41–2.
[4] 25 Hen. 8, c. 6.

Queen Elizabeth and remained in force for the next 275 years.[1] The law was certainly enforced spasmodically, although present evidence does not allow a final judgment to be formed. The first trial of a person of social prominence under the statute took place in 1631 when the Earl of Castlehaven was charged with the rape of his wife and sodomy with his servants.[2] He was condemned and executed. During the eighteenth century, according to Mr Montgomery Hyde, the law was consistently enforced: "The Old Bailey and Middlesex Sessions papers abound with trials for sodomy at this time, and many death sentences are recorded, although the law seems to have been very fairly, if severely applied."[3] Among cases reported in the eighteenth century were those of the Reverend Robert Thistlethwaite of Wadham College, Oxford for assaulting a pupil (1739), Samuel Foote, the actor, for assaulting a servant (1776): and of Margaret Clap in 1742 for "keeping a sodomitical house off Holborn".[4] Nineteenth century trials include those of a private soldier for offences with the Hon. Percy Jocelyn, Bishop of Clogher, the former being executed and the latter fleeing the country (1822); of William Bankes, M.P. (1833), who was acquitted; and of Oscar Wilde in 1895.[5]

After the passing of the Henrician statute, which it should be remembered applied only to sodomy strictly defined, the offence was referred to by English legal writers in terms of severe condemnation. Thus Coke in his *Institutes* denounces it as a "detestable and abominable sin, amongst Christians not to be named", and one of the sins crying out to heaven for vengeance.[6] Blackstone is equally censorious: "This the voice of nature and of reason, and the express law of God, determine to be capital. Of which we have a signal instance long before the Jewish dispensation, by the destruction of two cities by

---

[1] 5 Eliz. 1, c. 17. The Act was renewed in 1536 and 1539 and was made permanent in 1541, but was abolished by Edward VI in 1547 who consented to renewal in 1548, although lands and goods were not to be forfeited and an indictment was to be brought within six months. Mary repealed the Act in the first year of her reign, jurisdiction returning to the ecclesiastical courts.

[2] III *State Trials*, 402–6.

[3] *The Trials of Oscar Wilde*, London 1948, p. 379.

[4] *Select Trials at the Session House of the Old Bailey*, III, 37.

[5] Wilde was not tried for sodomy, but under the Criminal Law Amendment Act of 1885.

[6] *Third Part of the Institutes*, London 1817, chap. X, pp. 58–9.

fire from heaven; so that this is an universal, not merely a provincial precept." He did, however, include a warning against the danger of unjust convictions, describing it as a crime "which ought to be strictly and impartially proved, and then as strictly and impartially punished. But it is an offence of so dark a nature, so easily charged, and the negative so difficult to be proved, that the accusation should be clearly made out; for, if false, it deserves a punishment inferior only to that of the crime itself."[1] Blackstone's views were of wide influence both in England and the United States, owing to the employment of the Commentaries as the basis of the system of legal education and instruction.

No change was made in the law until the nineteenth century. Although few were charged with the offence, most of those proceeded against were hanged up to the 1830's.[2] In 1823, assault with intent to commit an unnatural offence was made punishable by fine or imprisonment to which hard labour might be added.[3] In 1828 the Elizabethan statute was repealed by a consolidating statute, but the offence remained a felony and the death penalty was still incurred.[4] It was not until 1861 that under the influence of Victorian humanitarianism the death penalty was finally abolished and a term of penal servitude from ten years to life substituted.[5] The minimum penalty for sodomy was abolished in 1891 by the Penal Servitude Act,[6] but the maximum remained unchanged.

In 1885 the Criminal Law Amendment Act provided that any male person, guilty of committing or procuring, or attempting to procure, an act of gross indecency with another male, "in public or private", should be guilty of a misdemeanour, punishable with a maximum term of two years imprisonment, with or without hard

[1] *Commentaries on the Laws of England*, London 1826, IV:215. Cf. R. Burns, *Ecclesiastical Law*, London 1788, I:234.

[2] E.g. four of five convicted in 1810. See *The Times*, January 14, 1958, "Homosexual Laws in History".

[3] 3 Geo. 4, c. 114.

[4] 9 Geo. 4, c. 31, ss. 1 and 15. The statute provided that the offence was complete on proof of penetration only, s. 18.

[5] 24 & 25 Vict., c. 100. Attempted crimes were to be punished with from three to ten years' penal servitude or imprisonment for not more than two years with or without hard labour. Assaults with intent to commit the crime were to be similarly punished, s. 62.

[6] 54 & 55 Vict., c. 69.

labour.[1] The circumstances in which this clause was passed are of some interest. The original purpose of the Bill was to protect women and girls, and no mention of homosexual practices was made until it reached the committee stage in the House of Commons. The new clause was introduced early in the morning by Henry Labouchere and agreed to without discussion or debate. Labouchere himself spoke only one sentence and that was ambiguous, saying that it was intended to protect men as well as boys against "assault". It is extremely doubtful whether the Members appreciated that they were radically altering the law by adopting this clause. Since 1885 the law has remained substantially unchanged. In 1921 the House of Lords rejected a Bill to penalize female homosexuality.[2] In 1954, partly as the result of a notorious trial, a special departmental committee, under the chairmanship of Sir John Wolfenden, was appointed to consider the whole problem, and their report was published in September 1957.[3] Their recommendations, the chief of which was that private homosexual acts between consenting adults should no longer be criminal offences, were not discussed by the House of Commons until three years later. On June 29, 1960, a Labour Member, Mr Kenneth Robinson, moved a motion in the House of Commons calling on the Government to implement the relevant sections of the Wolfenden Report, but after debate the proposal was defeated by 213 votes to 99. Party whips were withdrawn for the debate, a contrary proceeding for private members' motions, and members were able to vote according to their consciences. A new consolidating statute dealing with sexual offences was passed in 1956.[4] The Act repeals and re-enacts the relevant statutes using neutral language to describe homosexual offences.

SOCIOLOGICAL, MEDICAL, SCIENTIFIC KNOWLEDGE AND CHRISTIAN THOUGHT

Christian moral ideas may transcend sociological and scientific fact, but they are not independent of such data, and moral ideas may well have to be modified to bring them into relation with new discoveries.

[1] 48 & 49 Vict., c. 69, s. 11.
[2] "Homosexual Laws in History", *The Times*, January 14, 1958.
[3] H.M.S.O. Cmd. 247.
[4] 4 & 5 Eliz. 2, c. 69.

The development of the social sciences on mainly secularist lines does not invalidate their usefulness for the Christian ethicist and legal philosopher. When the Christian attitude to homosexuality was formed, no accurate information was available as to its extent and little was known of its causes. Today this has to some extent been remedied and the traditional Christian attitude needs re-appraisal in the light of this new knowledge.

Extent of Homosexuality

Westermarck stressed the universality of homosexuality, and its occurrence sporadically among every race of mankind.[1] Ancient Greece is the best known example of a society where homosexual activity was incorporated into the pattern of the general mores. Ford and Beach conclude that in forty-seven of the seventy-six societies, other than our own, for which information is available, homosexual activities are considered normal for certain members of the community.[2] Hirschfeld estimated that inverts in Germany numbered 2 per cent of the population, and another 4 per cent had some form of homosexual inclination. In England, Havelock Ellis estimated the proportion as 2 per cent of the population. These figures were not based on what would nowadays be considered acceptable scientific research. The Wolfenden Committee confessed that they could establish no precise figure for homosexual activity in Great Britain, the only figures relating to the systematic examination of a normal sample being provided by a psychologist who had examined 100 male undergraduates and found that thirty of them had had homosexual trends and fantasies at some time in their lives, and five of them still retained these over the age of twenty.[3] The Committee was unable to decide whether homosexual activity had increased in England in recent years. It is certainly more talked about than in the past, and the number of homosexual offences known to the police has increased, but this is not evidence of an actual increase.

In the United States a number of research projects have been

---

[1] *Origin and Development of the Moral Ideas*, London 1908, II, p. 456.
[2] C. S. Ford and Frank A. Beach, *Patterns of Sexual Behaviour*, New York 1951, pp. 129–30.
[3] *Wolfenden Report*, p. 18.

carried out investigating the extent of homosexual practices.
Katharine Davis found that over 50 per cent of a group of college
women graduates, five years out of college, had experienced intense
emotional relationships with other women, and 26 per cent had taken
part in overt physical practices.[1] Dr Hamilton, who carried out
research in a group of 100 married men and a similar number of
married women, found that seventeen men and twenty-six women
had taken part in homosexual activity since reaching the age of 18.[2]
G. V. Ramsey and F. W. Finger have also carried out investigations
in this field.[3] The best known work, and probably the most thorough,
is that undertaken by Dr Kinsey and his associates in the course of
preparing their two reports on male and female sexual behaviour.

While Dr Kinsey's assumptions, methods, and conclusions are
controversial, his findings undoubtedly throw some light on the
problem. In the first of his reports, that on the male, published in
1948, Kinsey used case histories of 12,000 men. He rejected the
question how many people in a given group are homosexual, since
homosexual contacts are not confined to a homogeneous homosexual
group. Taking as his standard "physical contact to the point of
orgasm", he concluded that 37 per cent of the male population of the
United States had had some homosexual experience between the
beginning of adolescence and old age. For males who had remained
single until the age of thirty-five, the figure rose to 50 per cent.
25 per cent of the male population had more than incidental homosexual experience or reactions for at least three years between the
ages of sixteen and fifty-five. 10 per cent of the males were more or
less exclusively homosexual for at least three years between the ages
of sixteen and fifty-five. 8 per cent of the males were exclusively
homosexual for at least three years within these age limits, and 4 per
cent of the white males were exclusively homosexual throughout
their lives after the onset of adolescence.[4] All these figures, it should

[1] *Factors in the Sex Life of Twenty-two Hundred Women*, New York and London, 1929, p. 277.
[2] *A Research in Marriage*, New York 1929, p. 497.
[3] "The Sexual Development of Boys", *American Journal of Psychology*, 56:217–34 (1949), "Sex Beliefs and Practices among Male College Students", *Journal of Abnormal and Social Psychology*, 42:57–67.
[4] A. C. Kinsey, *Sexual Behaviour in the Human Male*, Philadelphia and London 1948, pp. 623, 650–1.

be remembered, are cumulative over a lifetime, but even allowing for this, they are startling. Kinsey and his colleagues were themselves surprised at the results, but an elaborate system of checks yielded the same figures.

A number of minor conclusions of Dr Kinsey are of interest. He established that contrary to popular belief, homosexual activity is not the prerogative of a highly educated, artistically inclined coterie, but occurs at every level of society, a conclusion reached independently by the Wolfenden Committee.[1] Rural groups, are however, less prone to homosexual practice than corresponding groups in cities. Religion is related to homosexual activity, in that devout Catholics, Orthodox Jews, and active Protestants, are less prone to homosexual contact than non-Churchgoers.[2] Kinsey also concluded that homosexual conduct is less frequent among women than men, and that women were less promiscuous in their choice of sexual partners.[3]

What conclusions can one draw from his two reports? Kinsey denied that he was assessing moral questions and claimed that he had divorced his studies from both morals and customs, but these assertions are not born out by the texts themselves. Kinsey was a taxonomist, and an entomological approach to human beings characterizes all his work. Such an approach involves moral assumptions about man's nature which at times become explicit. "Whatever factors are considered," he writes in his study of male homosexuality, "it must not be forgotten that the basic phenomenon to be explained is an individual's preference for a partner of one sex, or for a partner of the other sex, or his acceptance of a partner of either sex. This problem is, after all, part of the broader problem of choices in general: the choice of the road that one takes, of the

[1] Report, p. 17. "Among homosexuals will be found not only those possessing a high degree of intelligence, but also the dullest oafs."

[2] Op. cit., p. 631. Kinsey found the same relation in women. See *Sexual Behaviour in the Human Female*, Philadelphia and London 1953, pp. 464–5.

[3] Homosexual responses "had occurred in about half as many females as males, and contacts which had proceeded to orgasm had occurred in about a third as many females as males. Moreover, compared with the males, there were only about a half to a third as many of the females who were, in any age period, primarily or exclusively homosexual. A much smaller proportion of the females had continued their homosexual activities for as many years as most of the males in the sample", op. cit., p. 475. 71 per cent of the women restricted themselves to one or two partners, the figure for men being 51 per cent, ibid.

clothes that one wears, of the food that one eats, of the place in which one sleeps, and of the endless other things that one is constantly choosing. A choice of a partner in a sexual relation becomes more significant only because society demands that there be a particular choice in this matter and does not so often dictate one's choice of food or clothing."[1] This is a moral judgment clearly opposed to Christian teaching.

Dr Kinsey further argues that since individual conduct bears no relation to the law, the law should be changed. Once again, for the Christian, this is not a conclusive argument. The Christian cannot agree that because aberrations exist they are therefore right, for this would be to deny any objective moral law. Christian thought must, however, be affected by the reports, for it can no longer treat the problem of homosexual conduct as one of isolated cases of perversion. It must henceforth see it as one of far wider social significance.

Causes of Homosexuality

Medical and psychological opinion is in conflict as to the causes of homosexuality and the voluminous literature on the subject cannot be fully discussed here. But the presumed causes of homosexuality must be briefly examined, for they are relevant to the formation of an adequate Christian attitude to the problem. A primary distinction, generally accepted, is that between transient homosexuality and sex inversion. Conclusive evidence shows that all human beings pass through a conscious or unconscious phase of homosexuality in child-hood or adolescence, from which a transition is made to hetero-sexuality. Some, however, do not succeed in making this transition and become inverts. Inversion is the direction of the psycho-sexual impulse more or less exclusively towards persons of the same sex in persons who should have reached psycho-sexual maturity. Apart from such inverts there are also perverts who have turned to homosexual practices and who have no such determined condition. Traditional Christian thought has been ignorant of inversion and has regarded the whole problem as one of perversion without extenuating circum-stances. The views of St Paul, St Augustine and St Thomas, have therefore to be modified in the light of subsequent knowledge.

[1] *Sexual Behaviour in the Human Male*, p. 661.

While this will not make homosexual conduct morally right, for the will is still free, it should lead to less stress on the *unnatural* character of such acts, for as far as the genuine invert is concerned, homosexual acts are at any rate *subjectively* more in accord with his nature than heterosexual activity. It further raises the question as to whether censure and punishment is the best way of dealing with such conduct.

As has been noted, experts are not agreed about the causes of homosexuality, but certain broad groupings can be made. First, some doctors regard it as a congenital anomaly. Homosexuals are born such and their condition is directly traceable to physical causes, glandular secretions etc. A second school regards homosexuality as a psychogenetically acquired misdirection of the sexual impulse. Opinions as to the cause of this misdirection vary widely in the group. Thus Freudians attribute homosexuality as failure to resolve the Oedipus complex. Adlerians interpret it as a manifestation of inferiority in males who distrust their own virility and ability to dominate the opposite sex. Others associate homosexuality with a traumatic experience suffered in early years. Dr Kinsey is of this school, although he adds certain personal views such as the individual's ability to respond to any form of sexual stimulus, depending on circumstances. Ford and Beach incline to the same view: "Physical or physiological peculiarities that hamper the formation of heterosexual habits may incline certain individuals to a homosexual existence. But human homosexuality is not basically a product of hormonal imbalance or *perverted* heredity. It is the product of the fundamental mammalian heritage of general sexual responsiveness as modified under the impact of experience."[1]

Both St Paul and St Augustine suggest that homosexual sins are a *recompense* for other sins, the result of a wider sinfulness and an abandonment of moral standards.[2] These views have been strikingly confirmed by contemporary research workers, for, in many, although not all, homosexual "case" histories, there is a background of parental divorce, separation, or estrangement. If homosexual practices are in fact increasing, may not the cause be traced further back to broken homes and the decline in standards of heterosexual morality?

[1] Op. cit., p. 259.
[2] Rom. i, 27; Augustine de nat. et grat., xxii.

Is homosexuality a disease? This is often the way in which it is described by those who wish to see changes in the law and are sympathetically disposed towards homosexuals. The Wolfenden Committee suggested three criteria for deciding the question, the presence of abnormal symptoms, caused by a demonstrable pathological condition, itself the result of some other "cause". All should be linked in a chain, one being necessarily antecedent to the next. The committee concluded that none of the criteria could be established and that a classification as a "disease" has no scientific foundation.[1]

SUGGESTED CHANGES IN THE LAW IN ENGLAND AND THE UNITED STATES

On both sides of the Atlantic it has been suggested that homosexual acts taking place in private between consenting adults should no longer be subject to the criminal law. This was the principal recommendation of the Wolfenden Report in 1957. A similar recommendation was made by the Model Penal Code reporters, to the Council of the American Law Institute in March 1955, supported by a unanimous advisory committee.[2] The proposal was rejected by the Council. However, in May 1955 the members of the American Law Institute in turn rejected the decision of the Council and voted to exclude sodomy from the list of crimes included in the Code.[3] Were this recommendation to be followed, the law in England and America would be brought into conformity with the law of the majority of European States. Only Austria and Germany punish such offences, while in Norway the law although technically punitive, is not enforced. Thus in Belgium, homosexual acts are not punishable unless there are circumstances of indecent assault, relations with minors, abuse of authority or violation of public decency.[4] A similar situation obtains in Denmark and Sweden. In France, homosexual acts between consenting adults are not offences unless they involve abuse of authority, fraud, public indecency or soliciting. They are not mentioned in the Code Napoleon, in force in France since 1810.

[1] *Report*, pp. 14–15.
[2] American Law Institute, *Model Penal Code*, p. 276. Draft No. 4, 1955.
[3] The vote was 35–24 in favour of removing sodomy from the list of crimes. *Time Magazine*, May 30, 1955, p. 13.
[4] Penal Code (1867).

In Italy and Spain, both Catholic countries, private acts between adults are not offences. The same is true of the Netherlands, Switzerland and Greece.

One's view of the proposed change will naturally depend on one's concept of the role of the criminal law. No modern State assumes this to be co-extensive with morality, although the two are closely connected, and most serious criminal offences are also moral offences. In both morals and the common law there is a further assumption that mature adults are responsible for their actions unless the contrary is proved.

The role of the law, it would be generally agreed, is to protect the common good. What is *not* agreed is whether the removal of penal sanctions against private, adult, homosexual, activities would be harmful to the public good. Those favouring the present law maintain that homosexual activities undermine the health of society, have damaging effects on family life, and that those allowed to maintain relationships with other men would inevitably turn their attention to boys. These points were considered by the Wolfenden Committee, who found no evidence to support the view that homosexuality caused the decay and demoralization of civilizations. The Committee pointed out that homosexual behaviour was no more damaging to family life than adultery, fornication or lesbian behaviour, yet none of these was subject to the criminal law. Having considered expert evidence, the Committee concluded that men who have homosexual relations with adult partners seldom turn to boys, and vice-versa.[1]

Some further arguments for retaining the existing law were put forward in a dissenting minority report by a member of the Committee, Mr James Adair. He maintained that the removal of criminal sanctions would destroy a principal motive influencing homosexuals to consult medical advisers, and deprive the police of opportunities to carry out preventive work. Further, it would deprive young adult employees in occupations and professions "where the practices are particularly rife", of a strong defence against corrupt approaches. These arguments are rather slight, but a further contention that change in the law would be tantamount to giving approval to homo-

[1] *Wolfenden Report*, pp. 10, 22, 23.

sexual practices, is of considerable weight.[1] In England, and to some extent in the United States, the law has always been given a moral significance lacking in most other countries. There is, however, a distinction between removing a legal sanction against an action, and positively approving of it by law. A way out of the dilemma, has been suggested by Quentin Edwards in a recent pamphlet, where he recommends that any repealing statute should contain a declaration that such conduct is unlawful, although criminal sanctions will not be imposed.[2]

Subsidiary factors influencing the Wolfenden Committee in their decision were the anomalies of punishing male but not female homosexuality, and of leaving adultery unpunished.[3] The argument that since the law does not punish adultery or fornication, it should not penalize homosexual activity, is not *prima facie* applicable to the United States, where thirty-seven States punish fornication, and only five have no laws punishing adultery. However, in all States, with the possible exception of Massachusetts, these laws are not in practice enforced.[4] The Wolfenden Committee maintained that the present law gave rise to blackmail, and supported this contention with some figures for 1950, when thirty-two of the seventy-one cases reported to the police for blackmail were connected with homosexual offences.[5] Some years earlier, speaking in the House of Lords, Lord Jowitt, formerly Lord Chancellor, disclosed that when he was Attorney General, 95 per cent of the blackmail cases coming to his attention, arose from homosexuality.[6] In the United States,

[1] *Wolfenden Report.*, p. 120.
[2] *What is Unlawful?* Church of England Moral Welfare Council, London 1959. Adultery, prostitution, slander are in this category of unlawful acts which are "without the countenance or sanction of the law and contrary to the fundamental principles on which the law rests", p. 5.
[3] This point might be answered by punishing female homosexuality as well, but this hardly seems a practical possibility. In those countries or States which do penalize female homosexuality, the law is not enforced.
[4] In 1948 Boston had 242 arrests for adultery. See Ploscowe, *Sex and the Law*, New York 1951, p. 157. Only eighteen of the thirty-seven States punish a single act of intercourse, others requiring an "open and notorious" or continuous relationship. The five States not penalizing adultery are Arkansas, Louisiana, Nevada, New Mexico and Tennessee. No punishment for adultery or fornication is included in the Model Penal Code.
[5] See *Report*, p. 40.
[6] Debate in the House of Lords of May 19, 1954.

the law also lends itself to blackmail. Judge Ploscowe reported that in 1940 the New York District Attorney broke up a blackmailing ring that had been operating for twenty years in and around New York City. Twenty-three members of the ring were sent to prison.[1] Opportunity for blackmail would not by itself be a sufficient ground for changing the law, but it is clearly an evil which removal of criminal sanctions would reduce, although not abolish. The Wolfenden Committee recommended that unless there was some grave reason, homosexual offences incidentally revealed in the course of investigating allegations of blackmail should not be punished.

The proposal to exempt private homosexual acts between adults from penal sanction appears simple enough, but raises some tricky problems of definition. The Wolfenden Committee recommended that standards of "consent" should be the same as those applied in heterosexual cases. "In private," it defined negatively, by excluding acts "where members of the public may be likely to see and be offended" by them.[2] As to the age when a man is to be treated as an adult, various suggestions were made to the Committee ranging from sixteen to sixty, but the members eventually decided on twenty-one as an age at which a person could be regarded as sufficiently adult to make decisions for himself and take the consequences. They emphasized that it was not their intention that proceedings should be taken in every case where a person or persons under twenty-one were involved in a homosexual offence, but only where aggravating circumstances, such as abuse of authority, were found. They finally recommended that save for prosecutions initiated by the Director of Public Prosecutions no proceedings against persons under twenty-one should be taken without the consent of the Attorney General.

Like the Wolfenden Committee, the American Law Institute has recommended in its model code, that sexual relations of a homosexual nature between consenting adults should no longer be subject to law, provided they take place in private. Its reasons for coming to this decision are very similar to those influencing the Wolfenden Committee: the lack of harm to the secular community; the unenforceability of the penal law; the opportunities created for black-

[1] Op. cit., p. 209.
[2] *Report*, p. 25.

mail; the unsuitability of imprisonment for offenders; the undue interference in personal affairs; and the strain placed by the law on limited police resources. Law enforcement, concluded the Institute, was practicable only in cases of violence, corruption of minors, and public solicitation.

Certain differences between the two approaches should be noted. While both bodies recommend a statutory limitation on prosecutions, the American draft limits it to six months as opposed to the twelve suggested by the Wolfenden Committee. Adulthood, in the American view, should for this purpose commence at eighteen, not twenty-one. The Institute had considered sixteen as a suitable age but rejected it on the grounds that emotional instability was greater among males than females, that protection was needed during the period of secondary education, and that at sixteen homosexual experience was more likely to precipitate a fixed pattern of sexual behaviour than at eighteen. The draft code applies the law equally to men and women, and does not distinguish between different modes of sexual intercourse. Whatever the age of the parties, an offence only occurs if there is some form of penetration of the body.[1] The Wolfenden Committee conceded the illogicality of a classification of punishments based on the type of sexual intercourse, but nevertheless recommended a higher penalty for buggery with a boy under sixteen than an act of gross indecency under the same circumstances. Otherwise, its classification of penalties depends on the age of the parties and the employment of force.[2] A final point of contrast

---

[1] Deviate sexual intercourse, the act penalized under prescribed circumstances by the code, is defined under s. 207.5 as "penetration by the male sex organ into any opening of the body of a human being or animal, other than carnal knowledge within s. 207.4 and any sexual penetration of the vulva or anus of a female by another female or by an animal".

[2] The suggested classification of offences is given in a table. (*Report*, pp. 34-5.)

(a) Buggery with a boy under 16: Life imprisonment.

(b) Indecent assault (all acts against the will whatever the age of victim, also acts of gross indecency with boys under 16): Ten years.

(c) Buggery or gross indecency committed by a man over 21 with a person between 16 and 21, in circumstances not amounting to indecent assault: Five years.

(d) Buggery or gross indecency in any other circumstances: Two years.

Some members dissented from the distinction between buggery and other homosexual offences, suggesting only two categories of offences, indecent assault and gross indecency. See *The Report*, pp. 123-6.

concerns public soliciting. The American Law Institute suggests that soliciting should only be punished if the person soliciting had no previous acquaintance with the person solicited, whereas the Wolfenden Committee recommends that public soliciting should be an offence under any circumstances.[1] The American Law Institute has drafted a complicated series of clauses to punish offences involving different degrees of duress or violence, and these are reproduced in a separate appendix.[2]

For learned bodies and committees to make recommendations is one thing; to pass such measures into law is another. Despite widespread public support for a change in the law in England, the Government is unwilling to introduce legislation to implement the recommendations of the Wolfenden Committee.[3] This was made plain by the Lord Chancellor when the Report was debated in the House of Lords in 1957.[4] If the law is to be altered, then it will probably have to be done by a private member's Bill. Public opinion in the United States seems much less prepared to accept this change in the law than its equivalent in England.[5] In any case, legislation would have to be passed separately in every jurisdiction and this would present formidable difficulties. Since 1951 certain States have modified their laws. Thus Arkansas has reduced the minimum penalty for sodomy from five years to one; Colorado has reduced the maximum penalty from life to fourteen years; Nevada has reduced the minimum from five to one year; New York has reduced the

[1] The Wolfenden Report does recommend that "procuring or attempting to procure an act with *himself* which is not a criminal offence under the reform no longer to be an offence but to be so if a third party procures or attempts to procure an act of gross indecency", p. 44.

[2] See Appendix IV.

[3] Support for the Wolfenden Report has come from the Archbishop of Canterbury, the Bishops of Birmingham and Exeter, Lord Attlee and Lord Pakenham, amongst others.

[4] See *The Times*, December 5, 1957.

[5] In Connecticut, for example, a confidential questionnaire circulated to all Upper House legislators and ninety-three Lower House representatives, showed that over half (57·5 per cent) favoured no change in the law, while 23·5 per cent favoured some amelioration. In Connecticut, sodomy can be punished with thirty years' imprisonment, *Yale Law Journal*, 63:895 (1954). The Report of the Congressional Sub-Committee on "Employment of Homosexuals and other Sex Perverts in Government" is not a liberal document. (Res. 280, 81st Congress, 2nd Session) Doc. 241, December 15, 1950.

penalties in certain cases and graded them; Wisconsin has set a new maximum term of five years. On the other hand, some States have made their laws more severe. Thus California has increased the maximum penalty for sodomy, as has New Jersey in certain cases. Oregon has abolished its maximum penalty for the offence and West Virginia has increased its maximum.

CHRISTIAN AND OTHER MORAL OPINION

Most of Bentham's followers would be in favour of repealing the laws punishing private adult homosexual acts, on the ground that they do not affect society as a whole, and there is accordingly no justification for inflicting punishment. The dominant utilitarian view is well expressed by H. A. Hammelmann: "Repressive measures of the criminal law are justified only by their social necessity; they are obviously never in themselves desirable, least of all in the case of a behaviour whose physiological and psyclogical causes are still largely obscure."[1] Dr Kinsey's views are similar save that he emphasizes that variations in sexual intercourse are a matter of personal taste, a view shared by Judge Learned Hand.[2] Those moralists who regard moral judgments as based on emotive reactions also favour a change in the law. Indeed, their concept of the nature of moral judgments receives strong support from the average re-action to homosexual conduct, which is more often emotional than rational.

The Christian attitude to homosexual practices has already been outlined historically. How has it been modified by new knowledge? The importance of Dr Bailey's interpretation of the Sodom story is at once apparent. If it be correct, then homosexual sins have not been singled out for special punishment by the Creator, and the Christian theologian and moralist is free to evaluate them employing the criteria of moral philosophy, leaving this specific revelatory interlude out of consideration. Contemporary medical knowledge of the state of inversion must also modify traditional Christian views. In the United States, Christian thinkers have given little attention to the problem of homosexuality. In England, however, both the Church of

[1] *They Stand Apart*, New York 1955, pp. 180-1.
[2] See *Proceedings of the American Law Institute*, May 19, 1955, p. 129.

England and the Roman Catholic Church were requested to give
evidence before the Wolfenden Committee, and their respective
reports are useful guides to contemporary Christian thought.

The Anglican Viewpoint

In its report, "Sexual Offenders and Social Punishment", the Church
of England Moral Welfare Council emphasizes that the state of
inversion is in no way sinful, and equally that all homosexual acts
are grave sins.[1] Reason shows that the sex organs are the means of
establishing *henosis*, and also of conceiving children, and accordingly
sexual relations are only permissible in a heterosexual, marital,
relationship. Homosexual love may be an elevating experience but
it cannot, without sin, be expressed in sexual acts. Dr Bailey points
out that not every homosexual act is formally sinful, since the subject may be in a state of invincible ignorance concerning their
wrongfulness.[2] The Report then draws a sharp distinction between
sin which transgresses the law of God, and crime which is conduct
of which the law disapproves. The Church has the prerogative of
dealing with sin as such, whereas the State is limited in its jurisdiction to those sins which also constitute offences against public
morality.

Accordingly the Report recommends that homosexual acts
between consenting adults in private should no longer be criminal
offences, and that the State should punish male or female homosexual acts, which involve minors, public nuisance, assault, violence
or duress.[3] Adult age should be fixed for this purpose at seventeen.
Apart from its general philosophic distinction between sin and crime,
the committee put forward a number of subsidiary reasons for its
suggestion of a change in the law including the anomaly of leaving
adultery and fornication unpunished; the suicides caused by the law;
the opportunities created for blackmail and police corruption; and its
creation of an aggrieved and self conscious minority. The Committee's proposals have been supported by the Archbishop of

[1] Ed. E. S. Bailey. Published for the Church of England Moral Welfare
Council, London 1956.
[2] See his treatment of the subject in *They Stand Apart*, pp. 55-6.
[3] *Church of England Report*, pp. 40-1. Appendix III, gives the substance
of a 1954 interim report by the Church on homosexuality. The conclusions are
the same save that the age for commencement of adulthood is given as 21.

Canterbury, and in November 1957 the Church Assembly by a majority of seventeen (155–138) gave a general approval to the similar recommendations of the Wolfenden Committee.[1]

Roman Catholic Viewpoint

The Roman Catholic Church adheres to its traditional condemnation of homosexual acts as sinful, and also lays down canonical penalties for those found guilty of homosexual crimes.[2] The late Cardinal Griffin appointed a special committee to advise the Wolfenden Committee on Catholic teaching, and its report was published in the *Dublin Review* in 1956.[3] Its conclusions were virtually identical with those of the Anglican Commission, and it posited the same jurisprudential rule that moral evils, so far as they do not affect the common good, are not the concern of human legislators. "The criterion of what is meant by the public good," said the Report, "is to be sought in the fact that from a particular mode of conduct there can proceed effects morally harmful to the members of the community who do not possess the necessary power to resist such influences." In addition the Committee found that the present law is ineffectual, inequitable in its incidence, gives scope for blackmail, and imposes severities disproportionate to the offence committed. Accordingly it recommended that the criminal law should be amended to restrict penal sanctions for homosexual offences to prevent the corruption of youth, offences against public decency, and the exploitation of vice for the purposes of gain. Adulthood should begin at twenty-one.

In December 1957, the Archbishop of Westminster made a statement on homosexuality and the law. He pointed out that certain private acts may affect the common good and therefore may rightly be subject to the civil law. If it could be shown that toleration of

---

[1] See *The Times*, November 15, 1957. On May 20, 1960, *The Friend*, the English Quaker paper, published an article under the names of an important group of Quakers which presumed the need for a change in the law in the Wolfenden sense.

[2] See canons 2357 and 2359.

[3] The committee was presided over by the Catholic Chaplain to London University, Mgr G. A. Tomlinson, and included a professor of moral theology, a parish priest, a queen's counsel (later a judge), a psychiatric social worker and a welfare officer. See *The Dublin Review*, No. 471, pp. 60–5, Summer 1956.

homosexual acts by the law would lead to their increase, then they might be legitimately punished by the State. But this, the Archbishop pointed out, was a disputed question of fact, together with the allied question of whether by taking cognisance of private acts of homosexuality, the law creates worse evils than those which it avoids. Accordingly Catholics are left to make up their own minds on the matter.[1] The tone of the Archbishop's message is guarded, but the Committee Report indicates that the weight of educated Catholic opinion in England favours a change in the law.[2] It is probable, however, that Catholic opinion in the United States would be less liberal.[3] Neither group, nor indeed any Christian society, would favour giving social or legal recognition to homosexual relationships.

TREATMENT OF HOMOSEXUALS

Imprisonment is the normal treatment meted out to homosexual offenders, but it is extremely dubious whether this is in the best interests of either the offender or society. From the point of view of cure it is as futile as hoping to rehabilitate a chronic alcoholic by giving him occupational therapy in a brewery.[4] In England, in 1955, 30 per cent of those found guilty of homosexual offences were sent to prison. Other methods used by the English courts are absolute or conditional discharge, binding over, fining, or placing on probation. Probation, at present, probably offers the best method of dealing with homosexual cases where there are no aggravating circumstances such as violence or duress.[5] The Courts, on medical evidence, may make the reception of medical treatment a con-

---

[1] See statement of Archbishop Godfrey. *The Tablet*, 210:523, December 7, 1957.

[2] This would be in accord with opinion in Roman Catholic countries on the Continent. In Belgium, in 1950, a small group of Catholic politicians suggested that homosexual acts taking place in private between adults should be made punishable by law but the suggestion aroused widespread disapproval and was dropped. See *They Stand Apart*, p. 157.

[3] For a moderate article, however, see J. R. Connery, S.J., "A Theologian Looks at the Wolfenden Report", *America*, 98: 485-6, January 25, 1958.

[4] See Benjamin Karpman, "Sex Life in Prison", *Journal of the Institute of Criminal Law*, 38:475-86, January–February 1948.

[5] 24 per cent of homosexual offenders were placed on probation in 1955.

dition of probation, even if the offender is not suffering from a disorder serious enough to justify certification under the Mental Health Act. Younger offenders may be dealt with by imposing a period of borstal training or commitment to an approved school or detention centre.[1] Committal to the care of a fit person, or attendance at a disciplinary centre may also be ordered by the courts.[2] Persistent offenders may be sentenced to corrective training and, in the last resort, to preventive detention, for the protection of the public. The Wolfenden Committee drew attention to the unsatisfactory disparity in sentences for similar offences, but was unable to suggest any remedy, save for a recommendation that courts should deal dispassionately with homosexual offences, "giving proper weight to the reformative as well as to the deterrent or preventive aspects".[3]

A minimum reform is the requirement in every case involving homosexual conduct of a medical report, to be furnished after conviction but before sentence. Curiously enough this was not recommended in the Wolfenden Report which confined itself to suggesting a compulsory report where the convicted person is under twenty-one. Major obstacles to the successful medical treatment of homosexual offenders are shortage of psychiatrists and ignorance of the aetiology of homosexuality. A re-orientation from complete homosexuality to complete heterosexuality is hardly a practical possibility. The Wolfenden Committee could find little medical evidence of such changes. Their pessimism is born out by general medical opinion. Some authorities such as Ernest Jones, Stekel, and Clifford Allen are hopeful of the effects of psycho-analysis but Freud himself was doubtful. In a letter to the mother of a homosexual he wrote: "In general we cannot promise to achieve cure. In a certain number of cases we succeed in developing the blighted germs of heterosexual tendencies which are present in every homosexual. In the majority of cases it is no more possible. It is a question of the quality and age of the individual. The result of treatment cannot be

[1] Ages for Borstal training are 15–21, for detention 14–21, approved school, under 21. The object of Borstal training is to develop character and the moral, mental, physical and vocational capacities of the offender, with particular emphasis on the development of responsibility and self control.

[2] Committal under 17, attendance 10–17.

[3] *Report*, p. 61.

predicted."[1] Treatment, however, can be directed towards securing a better adaptation to life and strengthening powers of self control.

The weakest part of the Wolfenden Report is precisely the sections dealing with cure and treatment of homosexuals, and this reflects a wider medical ignorance. Constructive research is required to bridge this gap, and the Wolfenden Committee suggest the establishment of a research unit of psychiatrists, criminologists, geneticists and others, based on an establishment such as a university department with experience in socio-medical research.

Some countries have resorted to castration as a means of solving homosexuals' and other sex offenders' problems. The Scandinavian countries have carried out both voluntary and compulsory castration.[2] Nazi Germany employed this method and it has been used in Holland and Iceland. Castration has been carried out in California on petition of individuals who have committed serious sex crimes.[3] The effect of castration is medically disputed, and although the sexual urge may be reduced, this effect does not always follow. The Wolfenden Committee accordingly rejected castration as a solution to the problem.[4] The Roman Catholic Committee expressed its "abhorrence" of castration procedures.[5]

A milder method of lessening the sexual drive is the taking of hormones. Oestrogens and stilboestrol are both effective for this purpose, and produce no permanent or bad effects. The Wolfenden Committee approved of this method, provided the agreement of the prison medical officer was secured, and the Roman Catholic Committee saw no objection on moral grounds, provided a serious pathological condition was present, other remedies had proved ineffectual, and the patient consented.[6] Incorrigible offenders might benefit from this treatment, and they might also be dealt with, if mentally sub-normal although not certifiable, by confinement in a maximum security—minimum discipline establishment. The

[1] See *They Stand Apart*, p. 126.

[2] See K. Bowman and B. Engle, "The Problem of Castration as a Treatment of Sex Criminals", in Report on California Sexual Deviation Research, 1953, p. 123.

[3] Final Report on California Sexual Deviation Research, March 1954, 20:12.

[4] *Report*, p. 72.

[5] Roman Catholic Report, *Dublin Review*, Summer 1956, p. 64.

[6] *Wolfenden Report*, p. 72. Roman Catholic Report, p. 65.

Wolfenden Committee rejected the suggestion of an institution confined to homosexuals, recommending that the problem of recidivists
should be tackled as part of penal policy as a whole, any institution
being set up, taking only a quota of homosexuals.[1]

SEXUAL PSYCHOPATH LAWS

The concept of the criminal as a diseased person in need of medical
attention rather than a moral offender who should be punished has
had many beneficial results, but has also presented a threat to
individual liberty. The common law doctrine of personal responsibility at least assured that a term was set to deprivation of liberty,
and this was fixed by the public conscience acting through the
medium of the courts. Humanitarian and reformative theories of
punishment tend to take the decisions on liberty away from the
courts and place them in the hands of technical experts. The extreme examples of this development are the statutes which authorize
deprivation of liberty of those classified as "sexual psychopaths".
In England the Royal Commission on Mental Illness of 1957
concluded that a satisfactory definition of "psychopath" was impossible, but recommended that compulsory powers of treatment
should be made available to the courts to be applied to those convicted prisoners who were in need of it.[2]

In the United States, on the other hand, at least twenty-three
States have passed sexual psychopath laws, although many of them
have never been invoked. Michigan was the first State to pass such a
law in 1937, but it was held unconstitutional the following year.[3]
Other States were not deterred by the decision and went on to pass
this type of legislation.[4] The laws vary greatly from State to State,

[1] *Report*, p. 71.
[2] H.M.S.O. 1957, Cmd. 169, p. 173.
[3] *People v. Frontezak*, 286 Mich. 51, 281 N.W. 534, 1938. Cf. *Malone v.
Overholzer*, 93 F. Supp., 647, 1950, where it was held that a statute defining
sex psychopaths and providing for commitment is not unconstitutional if it
takes place after a judicial hearing and after a finding by a court or jury.
[4] Alabama, California, District of Columbia, Illinois, Indiana, Massachusetts,
Michigan, Minnesota, Missouri, Nebraska, New Hampshire, New Jersey, New
York, Ohio, Pennsylvania, Vermont, Wisconsin, Washington, are included.
In Illinois, New Hampshire, Indiana and Vermont they are rarely used. In
Massachusetts, Michigan, Wisconsin and Washington, they are inoperative.

but two main types may be discerned, those which require a criminal conviction before they can be brought into operation, and those which require only a process set in motion by a State official, without a previous conviction and sometimes without any criminal charge having been brought. In at least five jurisdictions a person may be assigned to the category of sexual psychopath without the facts of any crime being shown. Definition of the term "sexual psychopath" is often vague. Thus in New Hampshire a sexual psychopath is "any person suffering from such conditions of emotional instability or impulsiveness of behaviour, or lack of customary standards of good judgment, or failure to appreciate the consequences of his acts, or a combination of any such conditions as to render such person irresponsible with respect to sexual matters and thereby dangerous to himself or to other persons".[1] Procedures for the release of psychopaths vary. Many States will not release a prisoner until medical evidence shows that commission of a further sex offence is unlikely. Some States, such as California, provide for a review of the case with jury trial. Release may be absolute or conditional. In Pennsylvania the parole is life-long, but a five year period is more common.

These laws have been subjected to continual criticism. Some States have amended their laws to meet objections, other have been content to leave them as dead letters. Thus the Massachusetts statute (1947) has been twice amended.[2] In 1954 the term "sexual psychopath" was dropped and provision made for a treatment centre for prisoners after conviction. The statute was not to operate until the Commissioner of Mental Health certified that the centre was adequate to carry out its work.[3] The centre has never been set up. A further amendment of 1957 provided for indeterminate sentences for sex deviates.

As Paul Tappan has pointed out, these statutes rest on a number of invalid assumptions.[4] They presuppose that the behaviour of a sex

[1] See Revised Statutes 1955 (as amended to 1957) 173: 2, 3, 1–16, 579: 9. Definitions in the District of Columbia Code (1951, 22: 3503–11) and in the Revised Code of Washington (1957, 71.06.010, 71.06.020–71.06.260) are equally vague.
[2] Mass. Ann. Laws, c. 123, A. ss. 1–6 (1949).
[3] Ibid., ss. 1–10. (Supp. 1956).
[4] "Sentences for Sex Criminals", *Journal of Criminal Law, Criminology, and Police Science*, 42:332, 333–4 (1951).

offender is more dangerous to society than that of other criminals, and that he is more likely to repeat his offence or go on to more serious ones. They also presume that effective treatment can be given to sex offenders if indefinite time is available. Finally, most fundamental assumption of all, they posit the existence of the necessary resources of institutions and personnel to carry out the treatment, and in most States these do not exist. Given that adequate facilities for treatment can be provided, the statutes might be retained, provided that they are amended to safeguard individual freedom. Minimum safeguards are that assignment to an institution should take place only after conviction of a crime, and that the period spent there should be no longer than the maximum term which the offender might have received for the crime of which he was convicted.[1]

THE MINISTRY OF THE CHURCH

The Church can clearly do much to aid the homosexual in adapting himself to society or in rehabilitating him should he be unfortunate enough to have come before the courts. This role was stressed by the Church of England in its report in a special appendix, *Pastor and Homosexual*. It recommended that this ministry should be conducted by priests equipped with the necessary psychiatric knowledge. Understanding and sympathy are essential if the priest's work is to be fruitful and the report points out the unique position of the invert: "For the heterosexual who desires marriage there is generally at least something more than a vestige of hope, but for the homosexual there is none. It is one thing to grow reconciled to the fact that the chance of marriage is gradually receding, or to accept chastity in response to a vocation which may perhaps be fortified by vows of celibacy; it is another to know from the outset that one's condition excludes the legitimate satisfaction of sexual desires which are none the less clamant for being disorientated. No good is done by pretending that the invert's position is other than it really is: it is a

[1] In March 1949 a special commission to examine the problems raised by the sex offender was set up in New Jersey in response to a Senate resolution. In its report, formulated by Paul Tappan, it recommended the inclusion of these safeguards. In addition a special institution with medical, psychiatric and custodial features should be set up and voluntary facilities extended. (Report and Recommendations 1950.)

tragic situation and he must be aided and encouraged to face it with the heroism that it demands."[1]

Unhappily the literature on homosexuality written from the pastoral point of view is both meagre and often misleading. There are signs, however, that this situation is changing. Father Harvey's "Homosexuality as a Pastoral Problem", published in *Theological Studies*, is intelligently sympathetic, and the same may be said of Dr Buckley's *Morality and the Homosexual*.[2] The naturalistic approach to homosexuality can be of small practical help in the present state of our society, and a combination of religious and psychological insights offers the best means of adjustment for the homosexual.

[1] *The Report*, p. 96.

[2] John F. Harvey, *Theological Studies*, 16:86–108, March, 1955. Michael J. Buckley, *Morality and the Homosexual*, London, 1960.

CHAPTER SIX

Suicide

In both England and the United States, suicide is a grave social problem. In England, over 5,000 cases of suicide and a similar number of suicide attempts were known to the police in 1956, but the real figures are probably very much higher.[1] Figures for attempted suicide are especially unreliable, since the attempter or his family may well conceal the act. Some estimates have put the attempted suicide rate in England as high as 30,000 p.a.[2] Figures released by W.H.O. in 1956, give a suicide rate for the United Kingdom of 10·8 per 100,000, that for men being 14·2 and for women 7·6.[3] In the United States, since 1900, suicides have averaged 17,000 p.a., the highest figure being recorded in 1932 and the lowest in 1944.[4] 100,000 is the estimated annual figure for attempted suicide.[5] The United States suicide rate in 1953 was 10·1, according to W.H.O., the figure for men being 16·1, and for women 4·3. Suicide was less common among coloured people than white, 3·8 as opposed to 10·8. With these figures may be compared those for Denmark, 24·1, the highest in the world, and Ireland, 2·3, the lowest. France, West Germany, and Japan have higher suicide rates than England and America; Italy, Spain, and the Netherlands, lower. How does the law in England and America deal with this problem, and what attempts does it make to reduce the suicide rate? To answer these questions one must first examine the history and background of the English common law.

[1] See the *British Medical Journal*, June 28, 1958, p. 1535 and *Ought Suicide to be a Crime?* London 1959, p. 5. In 1959 4,980 cases of attempted suicide were known to the police, *The Times*, October 21, 1960.

[2] *Ought Suicide to be a Crime?* p. 5.

[3] *Time Magazine*, 68:35, August 13, 1956. The figures are for 1953.

[4] B. C. Bosselman, *Self-Destruction*, Springfield, Illinois 1958, p. vii. Cf. *Science Digest*, 42:28, August 1957, which gives 16,200 suicides in the U.S. for 1955, compared with 7,840 homicides. For some fuller, but older statistics. see Chapters I and II of A. D. Frenay's *The Suicide Problem in the U.S.A.* Boston 1927. See also *Encyclopaedia Britannica*, 21:532–3 (1958).

[5] *New York State Journal of Medicine*, 41:1720 (1941).

HISTORY OF ENGLISH LAW

Suicide originally fell under the jurisdiction of the ecclesiastical courts, being condemned by the general canon law of the Church, accepted into England by the Council of Hereford in 673. The penalty was denial of burial rites, and this was laid down in a canon of King Edgar of 967. To this ecclesiastical penalty, popular custom added a further punishment of dishonouring the corpse, which eventually became incorporated as part of the law. Blackstone recorded that burial was in the highway, not in the churchyard, and that a stake was driven through the body.[1] This last practice was a pagan vestige to keep the ghost from returning to the earth. It was common to bury the corpse at a cross-roads so that the malign influence of the body might be diffused and rendered harmless. Burial took place at night. These practices were followed throughout the eighteenth century, and in 1755 when a suicide, Barlow, who had killed himself in prison after murdering his child, was buried unobtrusively, his body was dug up and reburied at Moorfields cross-roads, impaled with the requisite stake.[2] In 1784 John Wesley is found writing to Pitt, urging him to discourage suicide, by hanging the suicide's corpse in chains.[3]

By the early part of the nineteenth century the practice had lapsed, although isolated instances occurred, the last to be recorded being that of Griffiths, who was buried without a stake, but at the junction of Kings Road, Eaton Street, and Grosvenor Place, London, at 1.30 a.m., in 1823.[4] In the following year, the practice was abolished by statute, which provided that burial was to be in a churchyard at night but without religious rites.[5] In 1882, suicides were allowed to be buried in daylight hours.[6] Suicides, if of sound mind, may still not be buried with full Anglican rites, a prohibition not laid down directly by canon law, but by a rubric in the prayer book.[7] If, how-

[1] *Commentaries*, Oxford 1775, IV:190.
[2] L. Radzinowicz, *History of English Criminal Law*, London 1948, I:196.
[3] W. E. H. Lecky, *History of England*, London 1904, III:139–40.
[4] John Ashton, *The Dawn of the Nineteenth Century in England*, London 1866, II:283.   [5] 4 Geo. 4, c. 52.   [6] 45 & 46 Vic., c. 19.
[7] Cripps, *Church and Clergy*, London 1937, 8th edition, pp. 576–7. Under an Act of 1880 anyone not in orders may read the burial service.

ever, the coroner holds that the suicide's mind was unbalanced at the time of the act, the prohibition does not apply.

Suicides were also subject to civil penalties which took the form of forfeiture of land or goods. The exact date of introduction of this sanction is unknown, but Edgar's canon of 967 lays down that a suicide's goods shall be forfeited to his lord, unless he was driven to the act by madness or illness. Bracton, in the mid-thirteenth century, seems to have been doubtful about the precise status of the rule, but concludes that if the suicide were committed to avoid punishment or conviction for a felony, then his lands escheat and his chattels are forfeited. The same results if he committed suicide without any cause. If, however, he committed suicide from "weariness of life or impatience of pain", then the lands descend to his heir and only his chattels are forfeited. If he was insane at the time, then he is guiltless and loses neither.[1] Forty years later, Fleta confines escheat for suicide to cases of previous felony, and a little later Britton does not mention it at all, making the penalty forfeiture of chattels only.[2] The practice of forfeiting chattels in all cases, where a sane man committed suicide, gradually established itself, but lands were not lost. During the eighteenth century, the crown limited forfeiture of goods to cases where it was committed to avoid conviction for felony, and an 1870 statute recognized the existing situation by abolishing forfeiture altogether.[3]

The forfeiture of goods and chattels played an important part in the development of the law, since it led to the view that suicide was a felony. The point was, as it were, argued backwards.[4] Thus by the fourteenth century it was settled that a person of sound mind who

---

[1] Bracton does not state who takes the goods, i.e. whether it is the king or the lord. He first discusses suicide in folio 130, and again in folio 150. At one moment he favoured confining *felo de se* to criminals who killed themselves to avoid execution for felony. For a discussion of Bracton's views, see William E. Mikell, "Is Suicide Murder?" *Columbia Law Review*, 3:379, January 1903. Also, F. Pollock, and F. W. Maitland, *The History of English Law*, London 1898, II:488. The reason why a special rule of escheat was needed was that lands were only forfeited to the king after judgment of felony, impossible in suicide cases.

[2] Implicitly, from the text, to the crown. Fleta. I cap. 36, De Infortuniis. Britton, cap. 7, De Aventure.

[3] 33 & 34 Vic., c. 23.

[4] See T. Plucknett, *A Concise History of the Common Law*, 5th ed., 1956, p. 445.

intentionally took his own life was guilty of felony.[1] The rule was consistently followed and repeated by the major legal writers in succeeding ages, including Coke, Hale and Blackstone.[2] In 1563, in an investigation into the alleged suicide of a judge, Sir James Hale, Judge Brown outlined the reasons for treating suicide as a crime.[3] They are interesting as illustrations of the influence of Christianity on the law. Echoing St Thomas Aquinas, the judge first declared that suicide is against nature, "because it is contrary to the rules of self-preservation, which is the principle of nature, for everything living does by instinct of nature defend itself from destruction, and then to destroy one's self is contrary to nature, and a thing most horrible". He went on to repeat the Augustinian argument that it is an offence against God, "in that it is a breach of His commandment, *Thou shalt not kill;* and to kill himself, by which act he kills in presumption his own soul, is a greater offence than to kill another". Judge Brown's third reason for condemning suicide was that the king lost a subject, "he being the head has lost one of his mystical members". Chief Justice Dyer added a reason of social policy for punishing suicide, in that it set an evil example which might be followed by others. Punishment, in his view presumably, acted as a deterrent.[4]

Blackstone also, stresses the religious heinousness of suicide: "And also the law of England wisely and religiously considers, that no man hath a power to destroy life, but by commission from God, the author of it: and, as the suicide is guilty of a double offence; one spiritual, in invading the prerogative of the Almighty, and rushing into his immediate presence uncalled for; the other temporal, against the king, who hath an interest in the preservation of all his subjects; the law has therefore ranked this among the highest crimes, making it a peculiar species of felony committed on one's self."[5] He adds that an accessory before the fact is guilty of murder. An admitted exception is where the suicide is of unsound mind, but Blackstone adds a caution: "But this excuse ought not to be restrained to that length,

---

[1] See W. Holdsworth, *A History of English Law*, III:315–16 (1923).

[2] Coke, *Institutes*, 3:54, London 1797; M. Hale, *Pleas of the Crown*, London 1678; W. Blackstone, *Commentaries*, IV:189, Oxford 1775.

[3] *Hales v. Petit*, 1 Plow. 253, 75 E.R. 387 (C.B. 1563).

[4] 1 Pl. 262, 75 E.R., at p. 400.

[5] *Commentaries*, IV:189.

to which our coroner's juries are apt to carry it, viz. that the very act of suicide is an evidence of insanity; as if every man, who acts contrary to reason, had no reason at all: for the same argument would prove every other criminal *non compos*, as well as the self-murderer."[1]

Attempted suicide was first recognized as a crime in 1854, and the practice of punishing such attempts is now firmly established.[2] This was the only change in the law of suicide in the nineteenth century, apart from the provision of an Act of George IV that attempts to commit felonies were to be punishable with hard labour, the Army Act of 1881, which placed suicide in the armed forces on a statutory basis, and provisions for burial already mentioned.[3] In 1879, the Criminal Code Commissioners, in their report, suggested that aiding and abetting suicide and attempts to commit suicide should be made specific statutory offences, punishable with penal servitude for life, and two years' imprisonment with hard labour, respectively. These recommendations have never been acted upon.[4]

PRESENT ENGLISH LAW

Suicide, under English law, still ranks as a felony, a species of self-murder, although no criminal sanctions are imposed. The only legal effects are the possible denial of the Anglican burial service, and the avoidance of a life insurance policy. Such a policy is avoided if a person of sound mind commits suicide, on the principle that a man may not profit by his own criminal act. Premiums are not recoverable as of right, although many companies in practice, make *ex gratia* payments to the heirs. If the suicide was insane at the time, then the contract is not avoided in the absence of a specific clause in the contract providing for this. Most policies provide that suicide shall be a disqualification for payment if committed within the first year. Others provide that suicide of an insane person shall be treated as a surrender of the policy and the premiums are returned.

[1] Cf. Hale, 1 *Pleas of the Crown* 412.

[2] *Regina v. Doody*, 23 L.T.O.S. 12, 6 Cox c.c. 463. Followed in the later decisions of *Regina v. Burgess*, L. and C. 258, 169 E.R. 1387 (1862) and *Regina v. Mann* 2 K.B. 107 (1914).

[3] Hard Labour Act (1822), 3 Geo. 4, c. 114, Army Act (1881) 44 & 45 Vict., c. 58, s. 38.

[4] Report, London, 1879. Cmd. 2345: s. 183 Aiding, etc., s. 184 Attempting.

Attempted suicide is regarded as a form of attempted murder, and treated as a common law misdemeanour.[1] Attempted murder has been made a felony by statute, but the courts have held that attempted suicide does not fall within this category.[2]

Suicide can be committed constructively, when a person accidentally takes his own life in the course of committing an unlawful or felonious act.[3] One who accidentally killed another, while endeavouring to kill himself, was guilty of murder up to 1957.[4] The doctrine of constructive malice in the law of murder was in that year apparently abolished by statute, so that the greatest crime that should arise under these circumstances should be manslaughter, which itself requires criminal negligence.[5]

One who aids and abets a suicide, at the very time the act is committed, is a principal in the second degree to the crime of murder.[6] If he counsels or persuades the suicide to commit the act, and is not present at the crime, then he will be implicated as accessory before the fact. At one time, however, he escaped liability owing to the rule that an accessory could not be convicted before the conviction of the principal. In 1861 the rule was abolished, but the courts held that the Act was not intended to apply to accessories to suicide.[7] Later, the opposite view was taken, so that accessories may now be tried.[8] Participants in suicide pacts, if they survived, were

---

[1] *Regina v. Doody*, 6 Cox C.C. 463 (1854).

[2] Offences Against the Persons Act, 24 & 25 Vict., c. 100 (1861). Interpreted in *R. v. Mann*, 10 Cr. App. R. at p. 32 (1914). Cf. *R. v. Burgess*, 2 L and C. 258 (1862).

[3] See Hale, 1 Pleas of the Crown, 411, 412, 413. Also Hawkins, 1 Pleas of the Crown 102. 4.

[4] *R. v. Hopwood*, 8 Cr. App. R. 140 (1913); *R. v. Spence*, Crim. L.R. 188, 41 Cr. App. R. 80 (1957).

[5] Homicide Act 1957, 5 & 6 Eliz. 2, c. 11, s. 1, ss. 1, but the House of Lords decision in *D.P.P. v. Smith* [1960], 3 All E.R. 161 has reduced the effect of this sub-section.

[6] Under the Homicide Act of 1957, 5 & 6 Eliz. 2, c. 11, principals in the second degree are not capitally punished, but liable to life imprisonment. Accessories before the fact cannot be guilty of capital murder, as for this crime, one must personally employ force against the deceased (s. 5 (2)).

[7] Accessories and Abettors Act, 24 & 25 Vict., c. 94 (1861). For the old rule, see *R. v. Russell*, 1 Mood. 356, 168 E.R. 1302 (1832).

[8] *Rex v. Croft*, K.B. 295 (1944). Cf. *Regina v. Gaylor*, D and B 288, 169 E.R. 1011 (1857).

formerly treated either as murderers, principals in the second degree, or accessories, according to the circumstances.[1] The Gowers committee recommended that survivors of such pacts should not be treated as murderers. Two courses were considered by the committee, to remove such cases from the murder category, and to treat them as cases of manslaughter or specific offences, or to provide for an alternative verdict, leaving the jury to convict of the lesser offence. Finally, the committee recommended that a separate offence should be created of aiding, abetting or instigating the suicide of another, with a maximum penalty of life imprisonment. A case where one party to a pact actually killed the other party would not fall within this category, and the committee thought it should be dealt with by the exercise of the prerogative of mercy.[2] In the event, the legislature was somewhat bolder, and the survivor of a suicide pact, whether he kills the other party or not, is by the Homicide Act of 1957, now guilty only of manslaughter.[3]

During 1960 it was indicated by the Home Secretary that the government might be willing to consider revision of the suicide laws to remove suicide and attempted suicide from the list of criminal offences. In October 1960 the Criminal Law Revision Committee published a report on the subject.[4] Their terms of reference were to consider what consequential amendments should be made in the law if legislation were introduced to abolish the crimes of suicide and attempted suicide, and it was assumed that inciting another to commit suicide would remain a criminal offence. The committee recommended that aiding, abetting, procuring etc. the suicide of

[1] *Regina v. Alison*, 8 Car. and P. 418, 173 E.R. 557 (1838); *Rex v. Dyson*, Russ: and Ry: 523, 168 E.R. 930 (1823); *R. v Croft*, K.B. 295, 29 Cr. App. R. 161 (1944). The death sentence was normally commuted.

[2] *Report of the Royal Commission on Capital Punishment*, Cmd. 8932 of 1953.

[3] S.4 of the Act. The Act further provides: "Where it is shown that a person charged with the murder of another killed the other, or was a party to his killing himself or being killed, it shall be for the defence to prove that the person charged was acting in pursuance of a suicide pact between him and the other." It also defines suicide as "a common agreement between two or more persons having for its object the death of all of them, whether or not each is to take his own life, but nothing done by a person who enters into a suicide pact shall be treated as done by him in pursuance of the pact unless it is done while he has the settled intention of dying in pursuance of the pact".

[4] *Second Report* (*Suicide*), London H.M.S.O. Cmnd. 1187 of 1960. The committee was appointed in November 1959.

another should be an offence punishable with a maximum of four-teen years imprisonment. The committee considered making this offence manslaughter which they said would have the attraction that, while securing that the suicide or would-be suicide would no longer be guilty of a criminal offence, "the law would otherwise con-tinue to insist on the sanctity of human life, since the essence of the solution would be that the killing would remain an unlawful killing except in the case of the suicide himself". This solution was re-jected because the committee thought it undesirable to create a new and special kind of manslaughter. The committee published a draft bill giving effect to their recommendations as part of their report.[1]

ENGLISH PRACTICE

Since the eighteenth century, coroners have in practice, avoided the effect of denying the Anglican burial service, by holding that the deceased took his own life, while the balance of his mind was dis-turbed. This verdict is not always returned, but is frequently brought in on very slender evidence. The verdict of *felo de se* is accordingly comparatively rare. In 1935 the committee on coroners recommended that this verdict should be abolished, and be replaced by a simple statement that the deceased died by his own hand.[2] The onus of deciding whether to use the Anglican service would thus be shifted to the clergy, who even under existing law must sometimes exercise discretion. The verdict has not been abolished, but some coroners have used the new verdict on their own authority.

Before 1916, imprisonment was the normal punishment for attempted suicide, but in that year, with the approval of the Secre-tary of State, the Metropolitan Police inaugurated a new policy for London, which has since been adopted all over the country. If an

[1] Various amendments are detailed in the Bill. S.4 of the Homicide Act 1957 (see p. 238 n. 3) would have to be amended to avoid overlap. The committee recommended omission of the italicized words as follows: "It shall be man-slaughter, and shall not be murder, for a person acting in pursuance of a suicide pact between him and another to kill the other or be a party to the other *killing himself or* being killed by a third person."

[2] Cmd. 5070 of 1935, paras. 82–3. Cf. Coroners Rules 1953. Third schedule, Form 18, n. 5 (b).

attempted suicide is apprehended, and he has relatives or friends prepared to accept responsibility for him, he is placed in their custody and no charge is preferred, unless there are special reasons for doing so, e.g. the commission of another crime, a previous attempt to commit suicide, or some definite indications of insanity. In 1921, the practice of the Metropolitan Police was drawn to the attention of other police forces in a Home Office circular, and its adoption recommended.[1]

If a charge is preferred, imprisonment or fine is not the only method of dealing with attempted suicides. Under the Criminal Justice Act of 1948, he may be placed on probation for up to twelve months, provided a medical practitioner gives evidence that while not certifiable his mental condition is such as to require and be susceptible to treatment.[2] By the Mental Health Act of 1959, a person convicted of attempted suicide at Assizes or Quarter Sessions, may be detained in hospital or placed under a guardianship order.[3] If he is brought before a magistrate's court, the court may make similar orders without recording any conviction. The Act further provides for temporary committal to hospital or guardianship without recourse to the courts, if the attempter is suffering from a mental disorder, and may be a danger to himself or to others.[4] Under the Magistrates' Courts Act of 1952, a charge of attempted suicide may be tried summarily, and the accused may be discharged absolutely or conditionally, or placed on probation.[5]

The criminal statistics show that the policy of both police and courts is moderate, but that a considerable number of persons are still sent to prison for attempted suicide. Thus from 1946 to 1955, 5,794 attempted suicide cases were tried by the courts, 5,447 being

[1] Reply of the Home Secretary, Mr R. A. Butler, to Mr Kenneth Robinson, M.P., in the House of Commons, March 13, 1958, reported in *British Medical Journal*, March 22, 1958, p. 719. The formula recommended was not to prosecute unless there was some circumstance calling for punishment or the court constituted the only refuge for one too weak to stand alone.

[2] 11 & 12 Geo. 6, c. 58, s. 4.

[3] 7 & 8 Eliz 2, c. 72, s. 60. Evidence of mental illness must be given by two medical practitioners, detention must be warranted and be the most suitable form of treatment. The Act also provides constables with power to remove an attempted suicide to a place of safety, s. 136.

[4] S. 60, 2.

[5] 15 & 16 Geo. 6 & 1 Eliz. 2, c.55, s.19.

found guilty, and 308 sentenced to imprisonment without the option of a fine. Yet the total number of cases known to the police during this period was 44,946.[1] Prison sentences normally range from one to six months, but heavier sentences are sometimes passed. Statistical tables are reproduced below.[2] The most unsatisfactory feature of the law is that the treatment of the convicted person is entirely within the discretion of the individual magistrate or judge.

UNITED STATES LAW

Unlike some branches of the common law, no general adoption of the English law on suicide took place in the United States. It is true that in 1660, Massachusetts passed a statute proscribing Christian burial for suicides and directing that they should be buried in the highway with a cartload of stones laid on the grave as a mark of infamy, but the statute was not copied in other States, and eventually fell into disuse and was repealed in 1823.[3] In most States suicide is not a crime. "Whatever may have been the law in England," said a Texas judge in 1902 in a typical statement, "or whatever that law may be now with reference to suicides, and the punishment of persons connected with the suicide . . . it does not obtain in Texas.

---

[1] *The Law and Practice in Relation to Attempted Suicide in England and Wales.* Report by a joint committee of the British Medical Association and the Magistrates' Association, London 1958, p. 5. 484 persons were found guilty of attempted suicide in 1959. *The Times*, Oct. 21, 1960.

[2] Figures for five-year period 1952–6 for convictions of attempted suicide:

	Number	Percentage of Total
Imprisonment		
Up to 1 month	31	1·1
Over 1 month and up to 3 months	76	2·6
Over 3 months and up to 6 months	84	2·9
Over 6 months	3	0·1
Probation Order	1,842	63·0
Conditional or absolute discharge, bound over	819	28·0
Fine	21	0·7
Otherwise disposed of	46	1·6
Total	2,922	100

In 1955, 572 persons were found guilty of attempted suicide and of these 46 were imprisoned without option of a fine: for 1956 the figure was 559 of whom 37 were sent to prison. (Figures taken from B.M.A. Report above, pp. 5–7.)

[3] *Mass. Col. Laws* (ed. 1672) 137. Repealed by Statutes 1823, c. 143.

So far as the law is concerned, the suicide is innocent."[1] Other
States do not go as far as this, and while holding it to be a crime or
unlawful act, declare it to be unpunishable.[2] New York and Oregon
hold that suicide is not a crime, but stigmatize it as a grave public
wrong involving moral turpitude.[3] A few States adopted or still
adopt the English position, notably Massachusetts and South
Carolina.[4] The definition of suicide, generally adopted, is the same
as in England. There must be the intentional taking of his own life
by one of sound mind and of the age of discretion.[5] If self destruction results from insanity or accident, no suicide takes place.[6]

Attempted suicide is dealt with in different ways in the various
States, but in the majority it is not a crime.[7] In those States where
suicide is not a crime, attempted suicide is not criminal either.[8] It

[1] *Grace v. State*, 44 Tex. Cr. R. 193, 194–5, 69 S.W. 529, 530 (1902). Cf.
Burnett v. People, 204 Ill. 208, 68 N.E. 505 (1903) ". . . we have never regarded
the English law as to suicide as applicable to the spirit of our institutions." See
McMahan v. State, 168 Ala. 70, 53 So. 89 (1910) for a statement of a policy
against forfeiture of goods or ignominious burial. See also *Royal Circle v.
Achterrath*, 204 Ill. 549, 68 N.E. 492 (1903); *Prudential Life v. Rice*, 222 Ind.
231, 52 N.E. 2d. 624 (1944); *State v. Campbell*, 217 Iowa 848, 251 N.W. 717
(1934); *Darrow v. Family Fund Soc.*, 116 N.Y. 537, 22 N.E. 1093 (1889).

[2] See *Penn. Mutual Life Ins. Co. v. Cobbs*, 23 Ala. App. 205, 123 So. 94 (1929);
Wallace v. State, 232 Ind. 700, 116 N.E. 2d. 100 (1953).

[3] *Hundert v. Comm. Trav. Mut. Acc. Ass. of America*, 244 App. Div. 459,
279 N.Y. Supp. 555 (1st Dept. 1935); *Wychoff v. Mutual Life Insurance Co. of
N.Y.*, 173 Or. 592, 147 P. 2d. 227 (1944).

[4] For Mass. law see *Cw. v. Bowen*, 13 Mass. 356, 7 Am. Dec. 154, where
suicide was held to be a felony. After repeal of the 1660 Statute it was doubted
whether suicide was still technically a felony, but it was held to be unlawful
and criminal as *malum in se*. *Cw. v. Mink*, 123 Mass. 422, 25 Am. Rep. 109. For
S. Carolina law see *State v. Levelle*, 34 S.C. 120, 13 S.E. 319 (1890).

[5] *Southern Life and Health Insurance Co. v. Wynn*, 29 Ala. App. 207, 194 So.
421 (1940). New York Penal Law (1944), 2300, defines suicide as "the intentional
taking of one's own life".

[6] *John Hancock Mutual Life. Ins. Co. v. Moore*, 34 Mich. 41 (1876).

[7] Thus it is not punishable in Indiana (*Prudential v. Rice* (1944)), Iowa (*State
v. Campbell* (1934)), Maine (*May v. Pennell*, 101 M.E. 516, 64 A. 885 (1906)),
Pennsylvania (*Cw. v. Wright*, 26 Pa. Co. Ct. 666 (1902)), Ohio (*Blackburn v.
State*, 23 Oh. St. 146 (1872)), Illinois (*Burnett v. People* (1903)), Texas (*Grace v.
State* (1902)).

[8] *Cw. v. Wright* (Pennsylvania 1902): Arnold, P. J. "A consideration of the
subject involves the question whether suicide is a crime in this State. If it is not,
then an attempt to commit suicide is not a crime; for it cannot be a crime to

might have been made a separate statutory offence, but none of these States has followed this course.[1] In Massachusetts, although suicide is criminal, attempted suicide is not punishable, since the statute law on attempted crimes does not expressly include it.[2] In a minority of States, where suicide is criminal, but not punishable, attempted suicide is a punishable crime, a position reached by interpretation of common law or statute. In New Jersey, attempted suicide has been held to be a crime, by a combined interpertation of statute and common law. "Suicide," said the judge in *State v. Carney*, "is none the less criminal because no punishment can be inflicted. It may not be indictable, because the dead cannot be indicted. If one kills another and then kills himself, is he any less a murderer because he cannot be punished?"[3] It should be noted, however, that statute provides that "all other offences of an indictable nature at common law, and not provided for in this or some other act of the legislature, shall be misdemeanours, and be punished accordingly". In States where suicide is criminal, attempted suicide sometimes constitutes a separate statutory offence.[4] Finally it may be noted that in many jurisdictions, prosecution for attempted suicide is rare.[5]

If suicide itself is not a crime, then, theoretically, aiding and abetting it should not be either, but the majority of States have shrunk from following the point to its logical conclusion. Texas at first had no such scruples, the judge in *Grace v. State* reasoning that if suicide was not a crime, then furnishing the means was not criminal either. "We have no statute denouncing suicidal acts; nor does our law denounce a punishment against those who furnish a suicide

attempt to commit an act which, if it is accomplished is not a crime", pp. 666–7. Cf. *Prudential v. Rice* (1944 Indiana), Shake J.: "We have no common law crimes in this State and there is no statute declaring an attempt to commit suicide a public offence", p. 238.

[1] See *May v. Pennell* (Maine 1906).

[2] *Cw. v. Dennis*, 105 Mass. 162 (1870).

[3] 69 N.J.L. 478 at 480–1, 55 A. 44 (1903).

[4] E.g. *Washington* (Revised Code 1951, 9.80.020), penalty not more than two years imprisonment or fine of not more than one thousand dollars. *North Dakota* (Revised Code 1943, 12–3302), one to two years or fine of not more than one thousand dollars or both. *Oklahoma* (Ann. Stat. tit. 21, p. 812, supp. 1945), not more than two years, fine not more than one thousand dollars or both, 818.

[5] See *Villanova Law Review*, 1:321 (1956).

with the means by which the suicide takes his own life."[1] In a later case, the judge modified his position, by holding that a direct killing at the suicide's request would be murder.[2]

The Texan position is a minority one, and in most States, assisting a suicide is a crime, either murder, or a separate offence. In those States where aiding a suicide is held equivalent to murder, the rationale is that consent to an unlawful act in no way alters the nature of the act. Thus in a Michigan case, a man who placed poison within reach of his wife was held guilty of murder, even though she requested it.[3] Again in the Massachusetts case of *Cw. v. Bowen*, where the accused had obtained a rope for a prisoner to hang himself in goal, he was found guilty of murder: "Now if the murder of one's self is felony, the accessory is equally guilty as if he had aided and abetted in the murder of A by B, and I apprehend that if a man murders himself, and one stands by, aiding in and abetting the death, he is as guilty as if he had conducted himself in the same manner where A murders B; and if one becomes the procuring cause of death, though absent, he is an accessory."[4] In Oregon, it has been held that the active assisting in the act which causes death, such as shooting or stabbing the victim, is murder, even if it was done pursuant to a mutual suicide pact.[5]

Again in a Tennessee case where the defendant entered into a

[1] Tex. Cr.R. 44:193, 194-5.

[2] *Sanders v. State*, 112 S.W. 68 (1908): "However a party would not be justified in taking the life of the party who desires to forfeit his life by shooting the would-be destroyer at his request, for in that case it would be the direct act of the accused, and he would be guilty of homicide, although he fired a shot at the request of the would-be suicide. So it would be with reference to poison. If the suicide obtains the poison through the agency of another, that other knowing the purpose of the suicide to take his own life, the party furnishing it would not be guilty, yet if the party furnishing it knows the purpose of the suicide, and he himself gives the medicine or poison by placing it in the mouth or other portions of the body, which would lead to the destruction of life, then it would be the act of the party giving, and he would not be permitted to defend against the results of such act," at p. 70. See also *Aven v. State*, 102 Tex. Crim. 478, 277 S.W. 1080 (1925).

[3] *People v. Roberts*, 211 Mich. 187, 178 N.W. 690 (1920). Cf. *State v. Jones*, 86 S.C. 17, 67 S.E. 160 (1910) and *McMahan v. State*, 168 Ala. 70, 53 So.89 (1910) (Alabama).

[4] 13 Mass. 356, 7 Am. Dec. 154 (1816), p. 221.

[5] *State v. Bouse*, 199 Or. 676, 264 P. 2d. 800 (1953). Merely inciting to suicide is manslaughter by Statute. Oregon Rev. Stats. (1953) 163.050.

compact with the deceased to commit suicide, and after killing her
by shooting at her request, ran away, he was found guilty of first
degree murder. "Murder is no less murder," said the judge,
"because the homicide is committed at the desire of the victim. He
who kills another upon his desire or command is . . . as much a
murderer as if he had done it merely of his own head."[1] A similar
decision was reached in the Ohio case of *Blackburn v. State*, where,
in pursuance of a suicide pact, the accused gave the deceased some
port wine mingled with strychnine at her request. The judge
pointed out that the criminal act was not the suicide but the administration of the poison.[2] Again in the Illinois case of *Burnett v.
People*, while the judge held that the English law of suicide did not
apply, he ruled that one who furnished a suicide with morphine
might be charged with murder, and whether or not suicide was a
crime was irrelevant to the issue.[3] The point was made yet again in a
Maryland case in 1940. The common law crime of suicide or attempted suicide is not known in Maryland, but the judge stressed that the
accused was not being indicted for suicide but for active participation in another's murder.[4] No statute is thus required to bring
assisted suicide within the law of homicide, but in some States this
has been done.[5] The alternative method of treating assisted suicide
as a separate crime has commended itself to some States. Thus in
New York it is manslaughter to encourage or assist another to
commit suicide or to attempt to do so.[6]

Some States apply the law of transferred malice to cases in-

---

[1] *Turner v. State*, 119 Tenn. 663, 108 S.W. 1139 (1908).

[2] 23 Ohio St. 146, 163 (1872). Whether material was furnished for the act,
or merely persuasion, was held to involve equal guilt.

[3] 204 Ill. 208, 68 N.E. 505 (1903).

[4] *State v. Williams.* (Circ. Court for Ann Arundel Co. Balt.) *Daily Record*,
November 27, 1940. *Maryland Law Review*, 5:324–31 (April, 1941). He was
held guilty of second degree murder and given a suspended sentence of five
years.

[5] Penal Law, ss. 2304, 2305. In Missouri it is also treated as manslaughter,
Rev. Stats. 1939, s. 4383, and see *State v. Ludwig*, 70 Mo. 412 (1879) and
State v. Webb, 216 Mo. 378, 115 S.W. 998 (1908). See also, California Penal
Code, s. 401 (1949), Minnesota Ann. Statutes, 619:02 (1947), Mississippi Code,
2375 (1942), Wisconsin Criminal Code, s. 940:12, N. Dakota Rev. Code,
12:3302 (1943), Washington Revised Code, 980:020 (1951).

[6] Penal Law, ss. 2304, 2305.

volving suicide, and thus one who accidentally kills another in the course of a suicide attempt, will be held guilty of either manslaughter or murder. Thus, in the South Carolina case of *State v. Levelle*, Judge Aldrich laid down that: "In the eye of the law, self destruction – suicide – is an offence; it is an unlawful act, and if a man with a deadly weapon undertakes to take his own life, he is doing an unlawful act, and if in the commission or attempted commission of that act he takes the life of an innocent party, standing by, then in the eye of the law, that is murder."[1] Iowa is an example of a State where the opposite view is taken, murder being defined by statute, and requiring malice aforethought.[2]

THE FORMATION OF THE
WESTERN VIEW OF SUICIDE

Suicide is regarded by Western man with instinctive horror and revulsion. In part this is clearly a legacy of centuries of Christian teaching, but Christianity only served to confirm a basic human impulse of self preservation. Even those societies which have tolerated suicide have sought to confine it within fixed categories, of which the religious suicides of Japan, and the "noble" suicides of the ancient world, provide examples. It is often sweepingly asserted that suicide was generally approved in the Greco-Roman world, but this is a distortion of the real position. Both Thebes and Athens denied funeral rites to suicides, and Attic law directed that the hand of a suicide should be cut off and buried away from the rest of the body.[3] Plato condemned suicide in general, although he excepted from his censure those who took their own lives through intolerable stress or because of a major disgrace.[4] Suicides outside these categories were to be buried alone: "They must have no com-

---

[1] 34 S.C. 120, pp. 122–3. Cf. *Cw. v. Mink*, 123 Mass 422 (1877), where the judge stated: "It is not disputed that any person who in doing or attempting to do an act which is unlawful and criminal, kills another, though not intending his death, is guilty of criminal homicide, and at the least of manslaughter." Professor Glanville Williams points out that this was a case of constructive homicide, op. cit., p. 289. See also *Wallace v. State*, 232 Ind. 700, 116 N.E. 2d. 100 (1953).

[2] *State v. Campbell*, 217 Iowa 848, 251 N.W. 717 (1934).

[3] See Viazzi, "Suicidio". *Enc. Giuridica Italiana* (Ed. Mancini), XV, p. 689.

[4] Book IX of *The Laws*. He also excepted those who took their lives by express command of the State.

panions whatsoever in the tomb; for they must be buried ignomin-
iously in waste and nameless spots on the boundaries between the
twelve districts, and the tomb be marked by neither headstone nor
name."[1] Aristotle also condemned suicide as an act of cowardice
and an offence against the State.[2] Minority schools of philosophers
such as the Epicureans and the Stoics gave a general approval to
suicide as a reasonable exercise of human freedom, but this did not
become the dominant view.

Roman law contained no general prohibition of suicide, but it did
punish it in particular instances. Thus a suicide's goods were forfeited if he took his own life to escape conviction of crime.[3] Again,
a soldier who committed suicide for no adequate reason or to avoid
military duty was guilty of infamous conduct, and if he made an
unsuccessful attempt was punished with death. If, on the other hand,
he was driven to the act through depression, sorrow or madness, his
punishment was less severe.[4] Roman writers were divided over
suicide in the same manner as the Greeks. In different degrees,
Virgil, Apuleius, Caesar and Ovid, all condemned suicide. Cicero
disapproved of it on religious and social grounds.[5] The neo-
Platonists condemned suicide because it disturbed the soul and
hindered passage to the after life.[6] On the other hand, the Roman
Stoics extolled suicide, and pointed to Cato as a noble example of the
ideal. "Human affairs," reflected Seneca, "are in such a happy
situation, that no one need be wretched but by choice. Do you like
to be wretched? Live. Do you like it not? It is in your power to
return from whence you came."[7] Pliny maintained that the power of
dying when one pleased was God's best gift to man amidst the
sufferings of life.[8] The prevalence amongst a minority of similar
views and the general tolerance of suicide made it increasingly
common under the Empire.

[1] Plato, *The Laws*, IX:873 (Trans. A. E. Taylor, London 1934).
[2] *Nic. Ethics*, V:11. Cf. III:8.
[3] Justinian's *Digest*, 48.21.3.
[4] Ibid., 48.19.38 and 49.16.6.
[5] *De Finibus*, II:30; *De Republica*, VI:10. Cicero permitted suicide where
"God himself has given a valid reason", *Tusculanarum disputationum*, I, xxx:74.
[6] Plotino, *Enneadi*, I:9; II:9, 18. Porfirio, *De Abstinentia*, II:47; Apuleio, *De
dogmate Platonis*, II:622. Macrobio, *Comment. ad somnium Scipionis*, I:13.
[7] *Epistolae*, 70. Cf. *De Ira*, iii:15.
[8] Pliny, *Historia Naturalis*, ii:5 (7).

Christian Views and Their Influence

Counteracting the Stoic view of suicide under the Empire, and eventually establishing its unchallenged supremacy, was the Christian condemnation of the practice. In the Bible there is no very clear statement of ethical principle on suicide. In all, eight cases of suicide are mentioned.[1] In no case is there an express condemnation of the act, and Saul and Razis are actually praised for their conduct. The suicides of Abimelech, Samson, and Ahithophel, are neutrally described, the last two being, however, buried in their ancestral tombs. On the other hand, the suicides of Zimri and Judas are treated as punishments for their sins, and the attempted suicide of Paul's jailor is a mere act of terrified cowardice, and is restrained by the saint. Too much need not be made out of this lacuna since the Jewish creed with its positive emphasis on the value of life would have treated suicide, save in exceptional circumstances, as anomalous. Suicide, after the exile, was condemned by Jewish writers, who made some strained interpretations of various texts to uphold their views.[2]

The Christian doctrine on suicide was formulated by St Augustine in *The City of God*, and by other early Fathers of the Church.[3] Augustine condemned suicide on three grounds, that it violated the commandment "Thou shalt not kill", which applied to all innocent lives, one's own as much as another's; that it precluded any opportunity for repentance; and that it was a cowardly act. He gave Job as an example of the better way to bear affliction. He even condemned

---

[1] *Judges*, ix, 54 (Abimelech): To save disgrace of being killed by woman at a siege. *Judges*, xvi, 30 (Samson): Destroyed the Philistines with him. Double effect? 1 *Sam.*, xxxi, 4 (Saul): Fell on his sword. 2 *Sam.*, xvii, 23 (Ahithophel): Hanged himself because his counsel was rejected. 1 *Kings*, xvi, 18 (Zimri): Burnt himself in his house. 2 *Mac.*, xiv, 41 (Razis): Chose suicide rather than fall into enemy hands. *Matt.*, xxvii, 5 (Judas): Hanged himself with a halter from despair. *Acts*, xvi, 27: Jailor of Paul attempted suicide fearing prisoners had escaped.

[2] E.g. Genesis, ix, 5; Exodus, xx, 13; Deuteronomy, iv, 9; Job, ii, 9 and 10. For condemnation of suicide see Midrash Rabbāh 34 and Josephus B.J. III:viii. Sĕmahōth, ii, 1, provides that no rending of garments or formal mourning shall take place for suicides.

[3] *City of God*, I, chapters XV-XXVI. Cf. St Cyprian *De charitate inter fratres* (C.S.E.L. 4, p. 737): St Ambrose *In Psalmum enarrato*, XXXVI (P.L. 14, p. 975): St Irenaeus, *Advers. Haereses*, XXIII (P.G. 18, p. 729): St Athanasius, *De Operibus Charitatis* (P.G. 18, p. 880).

those virgins and others who took their own lives to save their virtue, pointing out that since chastity was a virtue of the mind and will, it was not lost if one was compelled by force to yield to the lust of another. He also condemned the practices of the Circumcelliones, a sect whose members took their own lives, in order to avoid the defilement of sin. The only exception he allowed was to those who took their own lives under divine inspiration, a concession made necessary by those honoured by the Church as saints, who had taken this course.

These views found eventual expression in Church law.[1] In the fifth century, the Council of Arles (452) denounced suicide as a diabolical inspiration. The Synod at Auxerre (578) decreed in its seventeenth canon that no offering should be received from one who had taken his own life.[2] The Council of Braga (563) denied full funeral rites to suicides, and the *Capitula* of Theodore, Archbishop of Canterbury, provided that mass was not to be said for suicides, but only prayers and alms to be offered (c. 63). Attempted suicide was punished by the Council of Toledo (693. c. 4) with exclusion from Church fellowship for two months. In 1284 the Synod of Nimes refused burial in consecrated ground to suicides. These punishments and interdicts are severe, but they are notable for the absence of the barbarous customs of stake impaling etc, which established themselves by popular custom.

St Thomas Aquinas, and other scholastics, elaborated Church doctrine on suicide during the Middle Ages.[3] Thomas based his condemnation of suicide on its opposition to nature and to proper self love. He added that God alone had control over life and death, and in deciding the moment of his own death, a suicide was usurping God's power. Echoing Aristotle, he also condemned it as an offence against the community, by depriving it of one of its members. On suicide to preserve chastity, he follows the opinion of Augustine,

[1] See *Neander's General History of the Christian Religion and the Church*, Vol. V, p. 141, from which the following facts in the text are taken.

[2] This was a more severe position than that taken up by the Second Council of Orleans (533), which allowed oblations to be received from those who (to escape execution?) had taken their own lives (c. 15).

[3] *Summa Theologica*, II-II, q. 64, art. 5. See also Abelardo, *Sic et Non*, P.L. 178, 1603-6. Alessandro d'Hales, *Summa Theologica*, q. 34, art. 2. Bonaventure, III Sent., dist. 28, dub. 2.

and explains the suicide of Samson as possibly committed under divine inspiration.[1] The influence of Thomist thought on English law is clearly seen in the case of *Hales v. Petit*, and in Blackstone's dicta on the subject.[2]

The Augustinian-Thomist position remains to this day that of orthodox Catholicism, and indeed of Christianity in general. Suicide is condemned as a violation of the fifth (sixth) commandment, as contrary to nature, a usurpation of God's prerogative, and a social wrong. Exclusion of repentance is also a constantly given reason for Christian condemnation. Death, and its acceptance, play a special part in Christian thought, both as "the wage of sin", and the opportunity for a final display of confidence and courage. "The Christian therefore accepts death," writes the Anglican committee on suicide, "as that signal occasion when he is finally to prove the love and power of God in Christ. He sees death as the last and crucial occasion for the testing of his faith, where victory is to be won in Christ and his redemption fulfilled."[3] Protestantism, possibly because of its rejection of the doctrine of purgatory, has been no less uncompromising in its condemnation of suicide than Catholicism. Contemporary canon law in the Roman Catholic Church penalizes both suicide and its attempt.[4]

Christian thought allows certain exceptions to its general condemnation of suicide. That covered by a particular divine inspiration has

[1] Q. 59, art. 3.

[2] See p. 235.

[3] *Ought Suicide to be a Crime?* London 1959, p. 28. For an Anglican restatement of the Thomist position, see Bishop R. C. Mortimer, *Christian Ethics*, London 1950, pp. 123–4. For a Catholic criticism of Thomist arguments see A. Kolnai, "Ethics of Suicide", *The Tablet*, 207:42, January 14, 1956. The writer points out that inclinations of nature do not necessarily ground rules of morality, that it is questionable how far man owes himself love, and equates suicide in relation to society with emigration. P. L. Landsberg also rejects the traditional position but rejects suicide as an attempt to escape the Christian vocation of suffering. *The Experience of Death: The Moral Problem of Suicide*, London 1953.

[4] C. 985 imposes "irregularity" for attempted suicide; c. 1240 denies ecclesiastical burial for those who commit suicide "*deliberato consilio*": c. 1241 denies mass, etc. Cf. Canons 2339, 2350 and 2256, n. 2. Anglican canon law does not penalise suicide directly but canon 68 excludes from Christian burial those guilty of "crime without repentance". In the past this has been interpreted to cover suicide.

already been noted.[1] Another exception arises where suicide is the method imposed by the State for the execution of a just death penalty. A third exception is *altruistic* suicide, of which the best known example is Captain Oates. Such suicides are justified by invoking the principle of double effect. The act from which death results must be good or at least morally indifferent; some other good effect must result: the death must not be directly intended or the real means to the good effect: and a grave reason must exist for adopting the course of action.[2]

The Challenge to Christian Views

The Renaissance, with its revaluation of the ancient world, led to a revival of pagan views on suicide. Thomas More, in *Utopia*, suggested that in his imaginary community, where Christian revelation was unknown, those suffering from incurable and painful disease, would be allowed to take their own lives, provided they did so with the consent of priests and magistrates. It was not, however, until the seventeenth century that a comprehensive defence of suicide was published, John Donne's *Biathanatos*, published posthumously in 1644, although written when Donne was a young man in 1608, before his conversion. It was designed to prove that suicide was not incompatible with the law of reason or of God. It provoked some replies, but does not appear to have exercised wide influence.[3]

During the eighteenth century, however, rationalist views gained ground. On the continent, Voltaire showed a tolerant attitude to suicide, Montesquieu attacked the penal law, and Beccaria equated suicide with emigration. In 1790 France repealed the sanctions against suicides. In England, Hume, in a posthumous essay, argued that God had given man control over all matter, including the period of his own life. By retiring from the arena, man did no positive harm, but merely ceased to do good.[4] These views were

[1] See "Suicide", *Catholic Encyclopaedia*, by A. Vander Heeren, New York 1912, vol. 14, pp. 326–8.

[2] For a discussion of "altruistic" suicide, see "Self Sacrifice and Suicide", *The Clergy Review*, 40:170–4, March 1955, and 40:534–7, September 1955. Also *The Irish Ecclesiastical Record*, 82:340–3, November, 1934. "Suicidio" in *Enciclopedia Cattolica*, Vatican 1953, XI:1490–4.

[3] See *Pelecanicidium or Christian Advertiser against Self Murder* by Sir William Denny (1653).

[4] See Hume, *Essay on Suicide* (Ed. of 1789).

challenged by Charles Moore's "Full Inquiry into the Subject of Suicide", published in 1790. The controversy continued into the nineteenth century, Schopenhauer, becoming the apostle of suicide, portraying life as an unpleasant dream, the sooner ended the better.[1] Madame de Staël, on the other hand, in her *Réflexions sur le Suicide* (1814), condemned suicide as inconsistent with the moral dignity of man, and stressed that suffering is essential for spiritual growth.

Later in the century, William James rejected suicide on pragmatic grounds, and a similar line of thought has been developed by Albert Camus, in modern times.[2] A number of contemporary writers such as Harry Roberts, Romilly Fedden and Helen Silving, have relegated the whole question to the field of purely personal choice, suicide requiring no moral justification.[3] Dr Glanville Williams is more cautious and limits himself to the statement that suicide is justified under certain circumstances.[4] The rejection of Christian doctrine has thus failed to result in a consistent view of suicide amongst non-Christian thinkers, but it has led to a demand for a change in the law. Individualists, humanitarians, and utilitarians, have combined to argue that the criminal law should no longer concern itself with suicide, but should relegate it to the private forum. Are such proposals acceptable to the Christian conscience? Before answering this question, recent medical research into the causation of suicide must be briefly examined.

CAUSES OF SUICIDE

Traditional Christian theology has been developed on the basis that suicide, in general, is a perverse act of the will, and a conscious flouting of God's authority. Insanity has always been considered to

[1] See J. Gurnhill, *The Morals of Suicide*, London 1900.

[2] William James, *Is Life Worth Living?* Philadelphia 1896. "Believe," concludes James, "that life *is* worth living, and your belief will help to create the fact." Camus in *The Myth of Sisyphus*, London 1955, admits that life is "absurd" but argues that this must be accepted. "Thus I draw from the absurd three consequences which are my revolt, my freedom and my passion. By the mere activity of consciousness I transform into a rule of life what was an invitation to death—and I refuse suicide", p. 55.

[3] See Roberts, *Euthanasia and Other Aspects of Life and Death*, London 1936; Fedden, *Suicide*, London 1938, and Silving, "Suicide and the Law", in *Clues to Suicide* (Ed. Shneidman and Farberow), New York 1957.

[4] Op. cit., p. 268.

absolve from guilt, but apart from this exception, the Church has not taken into account the causes of suicide. Such neglect is hardly surprising in view of past ignorance of the complexity of suicidal acts and the paucity of medical knowledge. This knowledge, despite recent advances, is still limited, but its existence raises the problem whether the traditional Christian attitude to suicide is one on which contemporary social and legal policy can be based.

One group of suicides is already exempt from censure by Church or State, those who take their lives when insane.[1] Contrary to popular belief, this group is small, if insanity is limited to a condition arising from an identifiable disease of the mind, such as schizophrenia or depression psychosis.[2] Doubtless, nearly all suicides act under considerable emotional stress, but this cannot be equated with insanity. Another, even smaller group, is made up of those who take their lives after a deliberate and fully rational consideration of the issues involved. Thus a person might decide to take his own life if he discovered that he was suffering from an incurable and painful disease, or if he faced public disgrace or conviction of crime, or financial ruin.[3] Considerable research has been carried out to explain suicides which do not fall within these two categories, and actuarialists have attempted to relate suicide to particular factors such as climate, race, age, sex, religion etc.[4] They have put forward no general hypothesis to explain suicide. Others have developed theories to explain suicide, and two schools may be distinguished, that of the sociologists, following Durkheim, and the psycho-analysts, based on Freud.[5]

Durkheim, whose pioneer work on suicide was published in

[1] Thus Roman Catholic canon law provides that ecclesiastical penalties shall only apply if suicide is committed *deliberato consilio* (c. 1240).

[2] See J. A. Harrington and K. W. Cross, "Cases of Attempted Suicide admitted to a General Hospital", *British Medical Journal*, September 19, 1959, p. 463, and J. M. A. Weiss, *Psychiatric Quarterly*, 28:225 (1954).

[3] The connection between the suicide rate and the business cycle has been established by a number of researchers. See A. F. Henry, *The Nature of the Relation between Suicide and the Business Cycle*. (Unpublished dissertation for Ph.D., Department of Sociology, University of Chicago.)

[4] See Louis I. Dublin and Bessie Bunzel, *To Be or Not to Be*, New York 1933.

[5] For a survey of various theories, see N. L. Farberow, "Personality patterns of suicidal mental hospital patients", *Genetic Psychology Monographs*, 42:3–79 (1950).

France in 1897, and his followers treat suicide as a phenomenon caused by social conditions.[1] Egotistic suicide results from the lack of integration of the individual into society, the suicide rate increasing with the degree the individual is thrown on to his own resources. This explains why at a period of national crisis, such as war, suicide rates fall, since the emergency provides greater opportunity for participation in the life of the community. Altruistic suicides, on the other hand, occur amongst those who are too closely identified with society, and occur in groups where individuals are rigorously governed by custom and habit. A third group of suicides, anomic, is made up of those whose needs are closely regulated by society, and who are unable to adapt themselves when a social breakdown occurs.

Durkheim's theories were based on extensive research and have been supported by subsequent investigations. Thus, it has been discovered that the suicide rate in certain large American cities, such as Chicago, Seattle, and Minneapolis, is highest in the central, socially fluid and disorganized sectors.[2] Urban suicide rates are higher than rural, and the suicide rate of married persons lower than that of the single, widowed, and divorced.[3] Those of higher social and economic status seem more prone to suicide than those in lower social groups. They have, according to Alpert, twice the chance of dying by their own hand, and two-thirds less chance of being slain, than their social inferiors.[4] Suicide rates in Catholic countries tend to be lower than in Protestant countries, measuring the higher degree of social integration offered by the Catholic religion.[5]

With Durkheim's work as a point of departure, a number of

---

[1] *Suicide*, London 1952. (First English translation.)

[2] See A. F. Henry and J. F. Short, Jr., "The Sociology of Suicide" in Shneidman's *Clues to Suicide*, p. 61.

[3] Ibid., pp. 61–2.

[4] Harry Alpert, "Suicides and Homicides", *American Sociological Review*, 15:673 (1950). Cf. A. F. Henry, op. cit., p. 67.

[5] See A. D. Frenay, *The Suicide Problem in the U.S.A.*, Boston 1927, pp. 165–70. He refers to suicide figures for Switzerland 1881–90 to illustrate his point. That for Catholics was 13·2. for Protestants 28·0, p. 165. See also Franco Ferracuti, "Suicide in a Catholic Country", in Shneidman's *Clues to Suicide*, p. 70. On the other hand J. M. A. Weiss in his study of suicides in New Haven, Conn. (1936–50), found religious affiliation of limited importance, *The Psychiatric Quarterly*, 28:225, April 1954.

ecological studies of suicide have been made.[1] Sainsbury's "Suicide in London", a study of suicide in twenty-eight London boroughs, lends support to Durkheim's approach. The west-end boroughs, he established, have the highest suicide rates, while the lowest are found in working class boroughs. Curiously enough, he found no important correlation between social status and suicide, but a close connection between the suicide rate and the factors of social isolation and mobility. Social disorganization, in the sense of divorce and illegitimacy, is also connected with a high suicide rate. Sir Alan Rook has also shown the influence of situation on suicide by compiling suicide statistics at the ancient universities for the ten year post-war period. He found that Oxford had the highest rate, 30·5, and Cambridge 21·3, both substantially higher than that for other comparable groups. With these may be compared the suicide rate for Yale students over the past thirty-five years, 13·0.[2]

Opposed to the sociological school is the psycho-analytic school of Freud and his followers. Freud's hypothesis of a death wish, described in "Beyond the Pleasure Principle", as a compulsion to reverse the evolutionary process and return to the equilibrium of death, is not today widely accepted. His explanation of suicide, however, as the outcome not of immediate social conditions, but of long pent-up aggressive and guilt feelings in an emotionally immature person, commands wide support.[3] Suicide and murder, on this view, spring from the same basic impulse, but in suicide the aggression is turned inward, upon the self. In his monograph "Man Against Himself", Karl Menninger has explored and developed this theory of suicide.[4]

A reasonable conclusion is that while attributes of personality and experience pre-dispose to suicide, these are developed by specific social conditions. Accordingly both psychological and social factors

[1] E.g. R. S. Cavan, *Suicide*, Chicago 1926; H. Gruhle, *Nervenarzt*, 13:337 (1940), a study of suicide in different parts of Germany, relating it to social and cultural variables; P. Sainsbury, *Suicide in London: An Ecological Study*, London 1955, and "Social Aspects of Suicide in London", *Howard Journal*, 9:202 (1956).
[2] "Student Suicides", *British Medical Journal*, March 7, 1959, p. 599. Cf. H. M. Parrish, *Yale Journal of Biological Medicine*, 29:585 (1957).
[3] See "Mourning and Melancholia", *Collected Papers*, IV, London 1925.
[4] London 1938.

should be taken into account when framing a social policy on suicide.

Attempted suicide has also been the subject of research and it is now established that many so-called attempts are not so much genuine efforts to end life as appeals for help. This view has been expounded by Professor E. Stengel and Miss Nancy Cook in recent studies.[1] They show that of the suicides investigated, only a small proportion had made previous attempts, and follow-up studies of selected groups of those who have attempted suicide, indicate that very few subsequently carry it out.[2] Accordingly it seems probable that many of the cases coming before the courts are not legal attempts at all, since there is no real intention of carrying out the act. The rarity of attempted suicide in communities hostile to its members, such as concentration camps, is further indication of its appeal function.

However different the approach of research workers investigating the suicide problem, their work leads ineluctably to one conclusion, the irrelevance of the criminal law to its solution. Whether it is hoped to reduce the suicide rate by changing the social structure or providing psychiatric help to potential suicides, the criminal law can do nothing to help. In England, this conviction has steadily grown amongst doctors, so that at present the medical profession is virtually unanimous in demanding a change in the law. Two committees of the British Medical Association have reported in favour of abolishing criminal sanctions for suicide and attempted suicide, and have been supported by the medical and secular press.[3] The

---

[1] See *Attempted Suicide: Social Significance and Effects*, London 1958. Also E. Stengel, "The Reactions of Society to Attempted Suicide", *Howard Journal*, 9:199 (1956). Cf. Similar views of J. M. A. Weiss, op. cit., p. 128, and Moya Woodside, *British Medical Journal*, August 16, 1958, p. 411.

[2] "Recent Research into Suicide and Attempted Suicide", *Journal of Forensic Medicine*, I:252 (1953–4). In an investigation of suicides in N. London, in 1953, they found that only 13 per cent had made a previous attempt. Patients admitted to the mental observation ward of a London hospital from February 1, 1946, to January 31, 1947, were made the subject of a follow-up study. Of the 138 patients, only one had committed suicide by the end of 1952. A similar study of 72 patients at the Bethlem Royal Hospital and the Maudsley in 1949, revealed that three years later only two had taken their lives. Of course the risk of those who have attempted suicide, actually committing it, is higher than for the general population.

[3] Report of a committee of magistrates and doctors set up by the B.M.A. in June, 1946. (*British Medical Journal Supplement*, May 17, 1947, p. 103.) Report of a similar committee in 1958: *The Law and Practice in Relation to Attempted Suicide in England and Wales*. (For summary, see *B.M.J*, May 24,

only justification for making suicide a crime would be if it acted as a deterrent, but of this there is no evidence.

From the Christian point of view it can be argued that the criminal sanctions against suicide represent an upholding by the State of the Christian tradition that life is of value and is also a trust, of which man has not the absolute disposal. Were the laws stigmatizing suicide as a felony repealed, a step back would be taken, towards the pagan societies of the past where suicide was more favourably regarded. A repeal of the laws would be a victory for the forces of secular individualism. Against this a number of telling counter arguments can be made. In the first place, the natural instinct of self-preservation is so deeply rooted in human nature, and especially in Western man, that it could hardly be affected by the abolition of an unenforceable legal rule. As was earlier pointed out, the acceptance of suicide in the classical world was not as widespread as has been suggested, and even in an Eastern society, such as Japan, suicide is confined by ritualistic rules of religion.[1] Furthermore, the experience of the majority of European countries, and those American States where suicide is not a crime, indicates conclusively that no dire results would follow from abolition. In Scotland, where suicide, if technically criminal, is never treated as such, the suicide rate is considerably lower than in England, where the rigours of the law apply. Change in the law would in no way be a condonation of the individualist claim that man has the right to dispose of his own life, but the recognition that while suicide is an anti-social act, the criminal law is not the best means of dealing with it. If necessary, a repealing statute could include a declaration to this effect.

Rather more important, for practical purposes, is whether attempted suicide should continue to be criminally punished. The first point to note is that, as has been recorded earlier, the law is only enforced in a small minority of cases. Attempted suicide is a mis-

1958, p. 1233.) Meeting at Brighton in 1956, the representative body of the B.M.A. passed a motion without dissent, calling for a change in the law. (*B.M.J. Supplement*, July 21, 1956, p. 62.) See leading articles in *The Lancet*, March 15, 1958, and *The Times*, February 26, 1958, and correspondence in *The Times*, February 11, 20, 24 and 25, 1958.

[1] Japan has three principal types of suicide: Harakiri, a method of punishment; Shinju, a suicide pact of lovers; and Junshi, a means of following a dead "lord" into the next world.

demeanour, and accordingly no obligation exists to report it to the police. English doctors make it a practice never to do so. Nevertheless, some people are sent to prison for attempted suicide, the cases being selected on no rational principle, but through the exercise of discretionary powers by policeman or judge. A second point is the clumsiness of the law as an instrument of social policy. Attempted suicide may be nothing more than a demonstration, may be an appeal for help, or may be a genuine effort to end life, but it is virtually impossible for the courts to distinguish between these categories, which require different treatment.

Two arguments are advanced for the retention of the crime of attempted suicide, that it acts as a deterrent, and that it enables treatment to be given to the attempter. It is difficult to see what deterrent value the law has, and it seems more likely to ensure that the person genuinely attempting to end his life will make a good job of it. Imprisonment may well retard recovery, and does nothing to stop a second and successful attempt on release. Furthermore the knowledge that attempted suicide is a crime may discourage an attempter from seeking help, or lead his relations and friends to conceal it. Publicity in the Press may be harmful to the accused person and will be painful to his relatives. Invoking the criminal law may be a means at present of providing the accused person with treatment, but it hardly seems a necessary one. Those suffering from a mental disease can be given compulsory treatment without recourse to the courts under the Mental Health Act (s. 60), and the vast majority of those who have no such affliction, are willing to accept voluntary aid.

The only gap left by abolition of the criminal offence would be that of a small suicidal minority, uncertifiable but unwilling to accept treatment. They could be dealt with by giving the courts power to make temporary "guardianship" orders so that rehabilitation treatment could be given.[1] Not the least merit of changing the law would

---

[1] This course was recommended in the report of the first B.M.A. committee in their report of 1947. It suggested that on the analogy of the Children and Young Persons Act of 1933, adults "in need of care and protection" should be brought before a magistrate's court so that an order for treatment could be given. Individual liberty would be safeguarded by making the order of temporary duration, e.g. 28 days. Cf. A similar suggestion made many years ago by Wilbur Larremore in the *Harvard Law Review*, 17:331 at 340 (1904). For

be to impress on local health authorities the urgency of discharging their responsibilities to potential suicides. A reform of the law in this sense should be welcomed by Christians not only on grounds of social policy but of charity. This is not to subscribe to what Bishop Hensley Henson called "the extravagant sympathy with wretchedness which characterizes an age both selfish and sentimental",[1] but to apply the Christian doctrine of love to suffering fellow beings. The Archbishop of Canterbury's commission on suicide, came to this conclusion and recommended that attempted suicide should cease to be a crime, and that "consideration should be given" to abolishing the felony of suicide.[2]

Amendment of the law in this sense would give rise to a number of additional problems. It might be necessary to restrain those who attempted suicide in a public place, or staged a series of such attempts to the public annoyance. They could be dealt with as disturbers of the peace, and punished as public nuisances, a course followed in Scotland, or bound over conditional on their receiving medical treatment. What of those who incite suicide, or aid and abet it? It was suggested by the Italian positivist, Enrico Ferri, who maintained that man has a right to dispose of his own life, that he had a consequent right to consent to his own destruction. In the absence of fraud or malice, he concluded, those assisting a suicide should not be punished.[3] Ferri's suggestion has been incorporated into the Swiss Criminal Code, which provides that whoever instigates the suicide of another, or assists him, is punishable only if he is actuated by "selfish motives".[4] Assessment of such motives would be such a difficult task for a court, and would involve such risk of fraud, that it could be rejected on these grounds alone.

In the Christian view, Ferri's proposal must be rejected since it involves acceptance of a postulate, the right to dispose of one's own life, directly opposed to Christian teaching. Christians recog-

another such suggestion at a meeting of the American Psychiatric Association in San Francisco (1958) by a New Hampshire physician, O. R. Vail, see *Science Newsletter*, 74:89, August 9, 1958.

[1] See H. H. Henson, *Suicide*, Oxford 1897.

[2] *Ought Suicide to be a Crime?* London 1959, p. 34.

[3] Ferri's monograph on suicide, *L'Omicidio-Suicidio*, was published in Italy in 1883. For a favourable assessment of his views, see Helen Silving, "Suicide and the Law" in Shneidman's *Clues to Suicide*, pp. 88–9.

[4] Code of 1937, art. 115.

nize suicide as a sinful and anti-social act, and their support for changes in the law is based not on individualist philosophy, but on the inadequacy of the criminal law to deal with the social problem of suicide. Suicide should certainly be discouraged and the situation would be best resolved by making it a separate offence to incite, aid, or abet the suicide of another.[1] Survivors of suicide pacts would be guilty of this offence. It has been suggested that a distinction should be drawn between a survivor who actually killed the other party and one who merely helped him to kill himself, but such a rigid distinction might well result in separate classes of offences, divided from each other by technicalities. In a pact to commit suicide by gas, for example, the distinction would turn on the irrelevant detail of which party actually turned on the tap. The English Homicide Act of 1957, which holds the survivor of a suicide pact guilty of manslaughter, makes no such distinction. Given a maximum punishment for the offence, the courts could take into account features of individual cases, when fixing the length of sentence. There is no good reason for classing an accidental killing during an attempted suicide as murder, and this should be dealt with as manslaughter, provided the necessary degree of criminal negligence was present.

Two other changes should be made in the law. First, an alternative burial service should be provided for suicides, its use being left to the discretion of the individual minister. As the Archbishop's committee pointed out, the use of the normal Anglican burial service is unsuitable, but there is no excuse for providing no burial service at all. The alternative form of burial service included as an appendix to the report might well be copied or adapted by other denominations.[2] Second, coroners should abandon the fictitious rider that the balance of the mind of the suicide was disturbed, which can be damaging to the family, and either return a simple verdict that the deceased died by his own hand, or one including a brief description of the circumstances of death.[3]

---

[1] As, for example, in the *Canadian Criminal Code*, 2–3 Eliz. 2, 1953–4, c. 51, an offender is liable to imprisonment for 14 years. Cf. *Indian Penal Code*, s. 306.

[2] Appendix E, pp. 52–6 of the Report.

[3] The Anglican committee recommended that Coroners' verdicts should contain reference to "other significant conditions", contributing to the death of the suicide. Report, p. 34. See also Appendix B of the Report, pp. 39–42, "Coroners' Verdicts and Riders".

With the legal question disposed of, the way would be open for the adoption of additional measures to prevent suicide. Psychiatric treatment should be made more easily available through local hospitals and health services. Research into the causes of suicide should be intensified and this might well be subsidized not only by government, but by the insurance companies who have a direct financial interest in ameliorating the problem. The public should be better educated on the subject so that suicidal symptoms would be more often recognized. In the majority of cases a warning is given by the suicide before he commits the act, and if this were taken more seriously by friends and relatives, the suicide rate would be substantially reduced by the provision of psychiatric aid. Priests and ministers should be given some elementary training so as to be able to cope better with suicidal cases they come across in the course of their ministry. Doctors also might be made more alert in diagnosing illness, to the symptoms of suicide, such as insomnia, loss of appetite, interest in life, and drive, which are present in many cases. The indiscriminate prescription of barbiturates, which puts an easy way of ending life in individual's hands, and addiction to which may cause depression, might well be checked. Care should be taken that patients admitted to hospital for attempted suicide are not discharged prematurely. Lay associations like the American "Save a Life League", the English "The Samaritans", and the suicide bureaux of the Salvation Army, should expand their work of giving immediate aid to the emotionally depressed. The Swedish experiment of an emergency clinic for depression, which has been set up in Stockholm, might be imitated in other cities.

These measures are all, of course, to some extent, mere palliatives, and the increasing rate of suicide in Western countries points to some deep seated malaise. In the final analysis the most hopeful way of reducing suicide is the provision of emotionally secure conditions in childhood in the context of a happy family life, and in adulthood the opportunity for greater dedication to the social or religious ideal of service to others.

CHAPTER SEVEN

Euthanasia

Euthanasia is in origin a Greek word, meaning happy death.[1] It has become associated with a particular social policy, the killing of those suffering from incurable disease, old age, or serious physical malformation. For some decades an organized campaign for legal authorization of euthanasia has been conducted in England and the United States, and has received particular impetus from the growing number of old people found in both countries, and the increase in the incidence of certain diseases, especially cancer.

In neither country is euthanasia countenanced by the law. If an ill person takes his own life, he is guilty of suicide. Doctors or others who assist such persons to take their lives are held responsible as aiders and abetters or principals in the second degree, to the self-murder of another. They are principals in the first degree to murder if they administer the fatal dose themselves, whether or not the patient has given his consent.[2] A relevant rule is stated by Hale: "If a man is sick of some disease which, by the course of nature might possibly end his life in half a year, and another gives him a wound or hurt which hastens his death, by irritating or provoking the disease to operate more violently and speedily, this is murder or other homicide according to the circumstances in the party by whom such wound or hurt was given. For the person wounded does not die simply *ex visitatione Dei*, but his death is hastened by the hurt which he received; and the offender is not allowed to apportion his own wrong."[3]

---

[1] Eu: happy. Thanatos: death.

[2] While technically guilty of murder, they may be held guilty only of manslaughter. Thus in *Regina v. Murton*, 3 F. & F. 492, 176 E.R. (1862), Byles J. said: "If a man is suffering from a disease which in all likelihood would terminate his life in a short time, and another gives him a wound or hurt which hastens his death, this is such a killing as constitutes murder or at least manslaughter." Under the Homicide Act of 1957, such a killing would be very unlikely to be capital murder, (s. 5).

[3] *Pleas of the Crown*, 428.

Such is the law in strict theory, but its administration is more lenient. Long before the English Homicide Act of 1957, distinguishing capital from other types of murder, it was customary to reprieve those held guilty of murder by mercy killing, the Royal Commission on Capital Punishment referring to it as "a foregone conclusion".[1] A typical English case was the trial of Mrs Brownhill in 1934. She had undergone a serious operation and was worried about the future of her thirty-one-year-old imbecile son, whom she killed by gassing and administering aspirin. She was sentenced to death with a strong recommendation for mercy. Two days later she was reprieved, and after three months received a pardon.[2]

Juries, also, mitigate the harshness of the law by bringing in verdicts of acquittal or convicting of a lesser offence than that charged in the indictment. In 1947, for example, Repouille, an American, killed his imbecile, blind child, and was indicted for manslaughter in the first degree. The jury brought in a verdict of manslaughter in the second degree, with a recommendation for "the utmost clemency". The judge imposed a sentence of 5–10 years imprisonment, and placed him on probation.[3] In 1960 an English officer, Major George Johnson, killed his three-month-old mongol son. He was acquitted of murder but found guilty of manslaughter and sentenced to twelve months imprisonment.[4] Verdicts of temporary insanity are also returned.[5] Sometimes a jury will bring in a verdict which hardly accords with the facts. Thus in 1950 when a physician had admitted causing the death of a cancer patient by injecting air into the veins, an admission which he denied at the trial, the jury refused to recognize this as the cause of death.[6] Quite often

[1] Report, 1953, London, H.M.S.O. Cmd. 8932, para. 37.

[2] *The Times*, October 2, December 3, December 4, 1934 and March 4, 1935. The operation was successful. Cf. The case of Long, who gassed his imbecile seven-year-old daughter, and was sentenced to death but reprieved a week later, the death sentence being commuted to one of life imprisonment, *The Times*, November 23 and 29, 1946.

[3] *Repouille v. U.S.*, 165 F. 2d. 152 (2nd cir. 1947). Also *New York Times*, October 13, 1939, and December 6 and 10, 1941.

[4] See *The Daily Telegraph*, July 3, 1960.

[5] See case of Mr Braundsdorf who shot his daughter and tried to kill himself, and was found not guilty by reason of temporary insanity, *New York Times*, May 23, 1950.

[6] *State v. Sander*, New Hampshire 1950. See *New York Times*, February 24 and March 10, 1950, *Michigan Law Review*, 48:1197. Also Helen Silving

mercy killers in the United States are not indicted at all.[1] In the nature of things, it should be remembered, a charge against a doctor is very difficult to prove.

In refusing to give legal sanction to euthanasia, the English and American legal systems are in accord with those of nearly every other country.[2] In both countries, however, movements exist to secure the acceptance of euthanasia by the law. Broadly speaking, those advocating acceptance of euthanasia fall into three groups. First, there are the supporters of euthanasia for the aged, the incurably diseased, and the insane. A second group would limit its operation to monstrosities and defectives in the early stages of life. Euthanasia in both cases would be compulsory. Thirdly, there are those who limit their advocacy to voluntary euthanasia for the dying.

Compulsory euthanasia on eugenic or utilitarian grounds was advocated in the ancient world. Abandonment of the aged was common in primitive societies, but does not seem to have been practised in Greece or Rome.[3] Disposal of defective children, on the other hand, did take place, and was advocated by Plato, and also by Aristotle.[4] "As to exposing or rearing the children born," wrote Aristotle, "let there be a law that no deformed child shall be reared; but on the ground of the number of the children, if the regular customs hinder any of those being exposed, there must be a limit fixed to the procreation of offspring."[5] Seneca advocated the more limited form of euthanasia: "If one death is accompanied by torture, and the other is simple and easy, why not snatch the latter? Just as I

"Euthanasia", *University of Pennsylvania Law Review*, 103:350 (1954). Cf. *Cw. v. Bowen*, 13 Mass 356 (1816), where in spite of a direction for conviction by the judge, the jury acquitted the accused.

[1] See *Michigan Law Review*, 48:1199, 1200 (1950).

[2] In Germany, Norway and Switzerland, a compassionate motive or homicide upon request, operate to reduce the penalty. Only Uruguay excuses the act if both features are present. See Yale Kamisar, "Some non-religious views against proposed 'mercy-killing', legislation", *Minnesota Law Review*, 42:6 (May 1958). The Swiss Penal Code also exempts physicians, etc., for actions performed in discharge of professional duty. (January 1, 1942, art. 32.)

[3] See L. Simmons, *The Role of the Aged in Primitive Society*, London, Oxford 1945, p. 225.

[4] In Sparta, for example. See Plutarch's *Lives*, XVI, London 1914. Plato's views were expressed in *The Republic*, V, IX, and Aristotle's in his *Politics*, VII, 15, 10.

[5] In *Politics*, above.

shall select my ship, when I am about to go on a voyage, or my house
when I propose to take a residence, so shall I choose my death when
I am about to depart from life. Moreover, just as a long-drawn-out
life does not necessarily mean a better one, so a long-drawn-out death
necessarily means a worse one."[1]

Only in this limited sense is euthanasia advocated in England and
the United States at the present time. Compulsory euthanasia for
the aged or incurably ill or insane was supported by some before the
Second World War, but the appalling experience of Nazi Germany
has discredited the idea. The Nazi policy of compulsory euthanasia
was inaugurated by a secret order of Hitler of September 1, 1939.
At first confined to Germans, it was later extended to foreigners.
Altogether 275,000 people perished in German euthanasia centres.
Very many of these were foreign slave labourers alleged to be
suffering from incurable tuberculosis. Euthanasia of foreign citizens has been held to be a crime against international law.[2]

Legalizing euthanasia was discussed in the nineteenth century,
but the project made little headway.[3] In the 1930's Dr C. K. Millard
made it a public issue by advocating mercy-killing in his presidential
address to the Society of Medical Officers of Health (1932), and
by writing about it in the Press.[4] The Voluntary Euthanasia Legalization Society was formed in England in 1936 under the presidency
of Lord Moynihan, a past president of the Royal College of Surgeons,
who was succeeded by Lord Ponsonby, and subsequently by Lord

---

[1] *Epistolae Morales*, LXX, 11.

[2] See *War Crime Trials*, vol. IV, The Hadamar Trial, London 1949. The trial
is fully discussed by M. Koessler in "Euthanasia in the Hadamar Sanatorium
and International Law", *Journal of Criminal Law*, Chicago, 43:735–55 (March–
April 1953). The trial of the officials of the Sanatorium took place before the
United States Military Commission at Wiesbaden, October 8–15, 1945. The
seven defendants were all found guilty, and three executed. The tribunal
proceeded on the postulate that no State has the right to deprive a foreigner of
his life except after conviction of a crime carrying the death penalty, before a
properly constituted tribunal.

[3] A shocked account of a discussion of the New York Medico-Legal Society,
where a doctor present admitted the practice of euthanasia, was published in the
Law Quarterly Review. Stephen: "Murder from the Best of Motives", L.Q.R.
5:188 (1889).

[4] See Glanville Williams, op. cit., p. 330, and C. K. Millard, "The Case for
Euthanasia", *Fortnightly Review*, 136:701 (1931).

Denman.[1] In that year, the Society introduced a Bill into the House of Lords to legalize euthanasia, which was defeated.[2] A further debate took place in the House of Lords in 1950, four members only speaking in favour of euthanasia, and the debate was not pressed to a division.[3] In the United States, a society similar to that in England was formed in 1938, by the Reverend Charles Potter, which adopted the English Bill as the model for a measure of its own. The Bill was introduced into the Nebraska Assembly in the same year, but failed to secure acceptance. An attempt to introduce the Bill into the New York Assembly also failed. The American society had at first intended to include compulsory euthanasia for monstrosities and imbeciles in its programme, but as a result of unfavourable replies to a questionnaire sent to physicians in New York State in 1941, decided to limit it to voluntary euthanasia.[4]

In 1946, 1,776 physicians joined a committee in New York State to work for legalizing voluntary euthanasia, and in the following year, the majority signed a petition to the legislature to amend the law. Other petitions were presented in 1940 by 379 Protestant and Jewish ministers, and in 1952 by 2,000 voters. In 1952 a joint petition of English and American clergymen, doctors, and scientists, requested the United Nations to amend the declaration of human rights, to include the right of incurable sufferers to voluntary euthanasia. The most recent petition, signed by 166 physicians, some of whom later denied their signature, was presented to the New Jersey legislature in 1957.[5] The general public seems to have little interest in euthanasia proposals. An Institute of Public Opinion poll, in 1937, indicated that 54 per cent of Americans were in favour of mercy-killing, but a Gallup poll, of two years later, gave a figure

[1] Supporters of the Society included Dr Julian Huxley, Sir James Jeans, the Dean of St Paul's (Dr W. R. Matthews), Dean Inge, and Dr Norwood (President of the Free Church Council), and Dr Rhondda Williams (Chairman of the Congregational Union).

[2] *House of Lords Debates* (5th s.) 103:465–506 (1936).

[3] *House of Lords Debates* (5th s.) 169:551–76 (1950).

[4] See *Outline of the Euthanasia Movement in the United States and England*, published by the Euthanasia Society of America. See also, for history of movement, Glanville Williams, op. cit., pp. 330–2. In 1949 a Connecticut society was formed.

[5] *America*, February 23, 1957, 96:573.

of only 46 per cent as opposed to 68 per cent in Great Britain.[1] A poll of American general practitioners in 1947 showed that only 37 per cent favoured euthanasia.[2] When the topic was debated in the House of Lords, the professions of the Church, Law and Medicine, were virtually united in condemning it.

THE PROPOSALS

Three different ways of amending the law have been put forward. The Euthanasia societies favour a scheme of State authorized euthanasia, including appropriate safeguards. The English Bill of 1936 requires that the patient shall be twenty-one years old, of sound mind, and suffering from a fatal and incurable disease, accompanied by severe pain. A formal application is to be signed by the patient in the presence of two witnesses and submitted to the "Euthanasia Referee", an official appointed by the Minister of Health, together with two medical certificates, one from the attendant doctor and the other from a specially qualified practitioner. The referee is to conduct a personal interview of the patient and establish that he fully understands what he is doing. Euthanasia is to be administered by a licensed practitioner in the presence of an official witness, such as a minister of religion or justice of the peace. The Bill sponsored by the Euthanasia Society of America is very similar, but provides for application to the courts for a certificate, the courts being empowered to appoint a committee of physicians and others to investigate the case.[3]

This approach to euthanasia has been criticized as cold bloodedly formal and cumbrous, and Dr Glanville Williams has suggested that a more acceptable proposal would be to provide that no medical practitioner should be guilty of any act done intentionally to accelerate the death of a seriously ill patient, "unless it is proved that the act was not done in good faith with the consent of the patient and for the purpose of saving him from severe pain in an illness believed

---

[1] I.P.O. poll see *New York Herald Tribune*, January 17, 1937. Gallup poll, *New York Times Index* (1939), p. 1414.

[2] *Senior Scholastic*, 55:13 (January 11, 1950).

[3] See Appendix I.

to be of an incurable and fatal character".[1] Discretion, as at present, would be left to the individual doctor, but if he killed a patient on request he would be protected by law. The proposal is also recommended by Dr Williams in that it substitutes for the question "Do you approve of euthanasia?", the milder query, "Do you think euthanasia so clearly wrong that a doctor should be punished for administering euthanasia to end hopeless pain even though he thinks his act to be required by the most solemn duty of his profession?"[2] This, claims the writer, is to leave the subject to the individual conscience.

A third line of approach is to rationalize existing practice, by providing lesser penalties for euthanasia, while still forbidding it by law. This, as Helen Silving has pointed out, may be achieved in two ways.[3] The legislature could classify different types of homicide, leaving it to the courts to assign particular cases to the various categories, or it could provide that punishment should be determined by motive. Reprehensible motives would lead to severe punishment, compassionate or humanitarian motives would provide grounds for more lenient treatment.

THE UTILITARIAN VIEWPOINT

Utilitarians advocating euthanasia take as their basic premiss that pain is an absolute evil. Accordingly, provision of euthanasia for the dying sufferer is not only morally permissible but mandatory.[4] The literature distributed in support of the cause stresses the horror of physical suffering, some may think to an excessive degree. The following is a typical piece of descriptive writing: "She was sodden with cancer; every nerve fibre responded hourly to pressure pain that sapped her strength and gave her relentless torment . . . 'Doctor,' she said, and reached her yellow hand to claw mine, 'the pain is dreadful and I am only a misery to my folks. Cannot Doctor put me out of my misery?' As it was, I could do little. Her look when

---

[1] Op. cit., p. 340.
[2] Ibid., p. 341.
[3] See "Euthanasia: a study in comparative criminal law", *University of Pennsylvania Law Review*, 103:350 (1954), p. 386.
[4] Glanville Williams, op. cit., p. 311.

I left her was one of reproach."[1] A death of dignity and repose is
demanded in place of the "shrieking, groaning and cursing" which
is said to continue, "until breath fails".[2] The pain caused to relatives,
awaiting the end, is also emphasized.

This argument is supplemented by the postulation of a right to
die, inherent in the individual. The notion that life is an absolute
value is rejected as a metaphysical fantasy, the value of life being its
quality, not its quantity. The assumption behind this view is clearly
stated by Horace Kallen: "The human person ceases when awareness goes out and unawareness comes in, and awareness goes out
when it becomes intolerable to itself. Death is only the lasting, as
sleep, anaesthesia, and narcosis are the intermittent extinctions of
consciousness."[3] In place of the right to live, a criterion of the
value of an individual life to the community is substituted. What
social interest, asks Dr Williams, is there in preventing the sufferer
from choosing to accelerate death?[4]

These sentiments have been echoed by individual Christians.
Supporters of voluntary euthanasia have included Dr W. R. Matthews, the Dean of St Paul's, Dr Norwood, the President of the
Free Church Council, Joseph Fletcher, an episcopalian minister,
and Canon Peter Green.[5] The petition of the Protestant and Jewish
ministers of New York states the principle clearly: "We believe in
the sacredness of the human personality, but not in the worth of
mere existence or 'length of days'. We no longer believe that God
wills the prolongation of physical torture for the benefit of the soul
of the sufferer. For one enduring continual and severe pain from an
incurable disease, who is a burden to himself and his family,
surely life has no value. We believe that such a sufferer has the right
to die, and that society should grant this right showing the same

[1] Rev C. F. Potter, "The Case for Euthanasia", *Reader's Scope* (May 1947),
pp. 111–14 at 112–13.
[2] Ibid., p. 113.
[3] *New York University Law Review*, 31:1168 (1956).
[4] "Mercy Killing Legislation—A Reply", *Minnesota Law Review*, 43:1–12
(November, 1958).
[5] See Peter Green, *The Problem of Right Conduct*, London 1931. W. R.
Matthews, *Voluntary Euthanasia: the Ethical Aspect*. Address delivered at the
annual meeting of the Voluntary Euthanasia Society, May 2, 1950 (published by
the Society). Joseph Fletcher, "Euthanasia", in *Morals and Medicine*, Princeton
1954.

mercy to human beings as to the sub-human animal kingdom. 'Blessed are the merciful'."[1]

CHRISTIAN VIEWS

Whatever the opinions of some individuals, the overwhelming weight of Christian tradition and teaching condemns euthanasia. Much has been made by euthanasia supporters of the passage in Thomas More's *Utopia*, which states that those suffering from "torturing and lingering pain", would, with the consent of priests and magistrates, be allowed to take their own lives. To deduce from this that Thomas More advocated euthanasia is to ignore the whole purpose of his book and the context in which it was written. More's intention was to depict the institutions likely to exist in a community which lacked any assistance from Christian revelation. The purpose of the book was satirical and to show that some Christian societies were worse than heathen communities. Despite the popular connotation now inseparable from the word "Utopia", it was not intended to depict an "ideal" community, much less one which reflected More's own social views.

The Roman Catholic Church has made clear its rejection of any form of euthanasia. In his encyclical, *Mystici Corporis*, Pius XII unequivocally condemned compulsory euthanasia. "Conscious of the obligations of our high office," said the Pope, "we deem it necessary to reiterate this grave statement today, when to our profound grief we see the bodily-deformed, the insane and those suffering from hereditary disease, at times deprived of their lives, as though they were a useless burden to society. And this procedure is hailed by some as a new discovery of human progress, and as something that is altogether justified by the common good. Yet what sane man does not recognize that this not only violates the natural and Divine law written in the hearts of every man, but flies in the face of every sensibility of civilized humanity? The blood of

[1] Published by the Voluntary Euthanasia Society of America. Cf. Fletcher: "For the man of moral integrity and spiritual purpose, the mere fact of being alive is not as important as the terms of living. As every hero and every martyr knows, there are some conditions without which a man refuses to continue living. Surely among these conditions, along with loyalty to justice and brotherhood, we can include self-possession and moral integrity." Op. cit., pp. 186–7.

these victims all the dearer to Our Redeemer because deserving of greater pity 'cries to God from the earth'."[1] Voluntary euthanasia has also been rejected by the Pope as contrary to Christian teaching. "It is never lawful to terminate human life," he said in an address to Italian doctors, "and only the hope of safeguarding some higher good, or of preserving or prolonging this same human life, will justify exposing it to danger."[2]

Speaking in the House of Lords debate of 1936, the Archbishop of Canterbury denied that any man was entitled to take his own life. His rejection of euthanasia was repeated by the Archbishop of York in the 1950 debate.[3] In 1950 the Church of England's Hospital Chaplains' Fellowship expressed its corporate condemnation of euthanasia.[4] The general secretary of the American Council of Christian Churches, representative of fundamentalist Protestants, has denounced the ministers who supported the voluntary euthanasia bill.[5] In 1952, the General Convention of the Episcopal Church in America passed a resolution opposing the legalizing of euthanasia "under any circumstances whatsoever".[6]

Christians put forward three arguments for condemning euthanasia. The basis of the Christian position is not, as is sometimes stated,

[1] *A.A.S.*, 35:239 (1943). Cf. Reply of Holy Office, approved by Pius XII, December 2, 1940. "*Quaesitum est ab hac Sacra Congregatione: num licitum sit, ex mandato auctoritatis publicae, directe occidere eos qui, quamvis nullum crimen morte dignum commiserint, tamen ob defectus psychicos vel physicos nationi prodesse iam non velent, eamque potius gravare eiusque vigori ac robori obstare censentur? In generali concessu . . . respondendum mandarunt: Negative, cum sit iuri naturali ac divino positivo contrarium.*" *A.S.S.*, 32:553. *The Clergy Review*, 21:55 (1941). For a full statement of the Catholic position, see Franz Walter: *Die Euthanasie und die Heiligkeit des Lebens*, Munich 1935.

[2] Address of May 25, 1948, to Italian Congress of Medical Men. *L'Osservatore Romano*, May 23, 1948. Cf. Address of February 24, 1957, on religious and moral aspects of pain prevention in reply to questions raised by the Italian Society of Anaesthesia. *A.A.S.*, 49:129–47. Also, address of September 9, to "Collegio Internationali Neuro-Psycho-Pharmacologico", *L'Osservatore Romano*, September 13, 1958.

[3] 103 H.L.Deb. (5th s.), 465–506 (1936). 169 H.L. Deb. (5th s.), 551–76 (1950).

[4] *The Times*, May 30, 1950.

[5] Glanville Williams, *The Sanctity of Life and The Criminal Law*, New York 1957, p. 332.

[6] *Journal of the General Convention of the Protestant Episcopal Church*, 1952, p. 216. For a typical Protestant article condemning euthanasia, see W. Hordern, "Reflections on Euthanasia", *Christianity and Crisis*, 10:45–6, No. 6, 1950.

that life has an absolute value, but that the disposal of life is in God's hands. Man has no absolute control over life, but holds it in trust. He has the use of it, and therefore may prolong it, but he may not destroy it at will. A second point made by Christians is that no man has the right to take an innocent life. "The innocent and just man thou shalt not put to death", says *Exodus* (23: 7): "The innocent and just thou shalt not kill", is found in *Daniel* (13: 53).[1] The only occasion when a Christian may take the life of a human being, is when he is an unjust aggressor against an individual or the common good.

Suffering for the Christian is not an absolute evil, but has redeeming features. It may be an occasion for spiritual growth and an opportunity to make amends for sin. Lord Horder in the House of Lords debate in 1950 drew attention to this aspect of pain. "To call the function of a doctor who helps a patient to achieve that degree of elevation of spirit an intolerable burden—as the euthanasia advocate is apt to call it—seems to me to be disparaging one of the very important duties that a doctor has to perform."[2] At the same time the Christian recognizes suffering as an evil in the natural order, and is under a duty to relieve it where possible, although not at any price.

Some writers have represented the Christian attitude towards suffering as sadistic, but how far this is from the truth is indicated in a passage from Pius XII's address to the Italian anaesthetists. He points out that there is no obligation for the sick and dying to endure physical suffering. "Now the growth in the love of God and in abandonment to His will does not come from the sufferings themselves," said the Pope, "which are accepted, but from the intention in the will, supported by grace. This intention, in many of the dying, can be strengthened and become more active if their sufferings are eased, for these sufferings increase the state of weakness and physical exhaustion, check the ardour of soul and sap the moral powers instead of sustaining them. On the other hand, the suppression of pain removes any tension in body and mind, renders prayer

---

[1] The prohibition applies only to human life. See *Genesis* i, 26 and 29. It may be carried out under divine inspiration, *Genesis* xxii, 11, Abraham and Isaac; *Exodus* xii, 29, the slaying of the firstborn of Egypt.

[2] *House of Lords Debates* (5th series), 169:568 (1950).

easy, and makes possible a more generous gift of self. If some dying persons accept their suffering as a means of expiation and a source of merits in order to go forward in the love of God and in abandonment to His will, do not force anaesthetics on them. They should rather be aided to follow their own way. Where the situation is entirely different, it would be inadvisable to suggest to dying persons the ascetical considerations set out above, and it is to be remembered that instead of assisting towards expiation and merit, suffering can also furnish occasion for new faults."[1]

Two other practical points should be recalled when considering the problem raised by pain. Medical science now has at its disposal a wide range of drugs to alleviate pain in all save a few exceptional cases. The incidence of pain in disease can also be exaggerated. The cases for which euthanasia is most strongly urged are those of cancer, but, as Lord Dawson of Penn has pointed out, in less than half the cases of fatal cancer is pain an outstanding feature.[2] The question must also be asked, whose suffering is to be alleviated, that of the patient or that of the relatives? The scope for self-deception is considerable, and an apparently humanitarian motive may be only a cloak for selfishness. Helen Silving has stressed, "that no consideration whatever should be given to euthanasia where it is administered for the benefit of a person or persons other than the suffering patient. This belief is based on the tenet of the equal value of all human beings, which bars the sacrifice of one individual, however useless and burdensome, for the benefit of another or others, however useful."[3]

A third cause of Christian opposition to euthanasia is the "wedge" argument. In its strict form, this states that an act which if raised to a general line of conduct would injure humanity, is wrong even in an individual case. In its more popular sense, it means that once a concession about the disposability of innocent life is made in one sphere, it will inevitably spread to others. The recognition of voluntary euthanasia by the law would at once be followed by pressure to extend its scope to deformed persons and imbeciles, and eventually to the old and any who could be shown to be "burdens"

[1] Address of February 24, 1957, on religious and moral aspects of pain prevention, *A.A.S.*, 49:129–47, p. 144.

[2] *House of Lords Debates* (5th s.), 103:481 (1936).

[3] Op. cit., p .388

to society. That the point is far from academic is shown by the statement of the treasurer of the American Euthanasia Society at its first annual meeting in 1939. Some of the members wished to enlarge the scope of the Society's Bill, and the treasurer pointed out that it was limited purposely to voluntary euthanasia since that was all public opinion was prepared to accept. He went on to add that the Society hoped finally to legalize compulsory euthanasia for those beyond the help of medical science.[1] Dr Glanville Williams does not advocate the euthanasia of hopelessly defective infants, but his discussion of the problem leaves little doubt that he is sympathetic to the proposal.[2] Nor is the reason he gives for abstaining from killing insane adults, namely that such a practice "would greatly increase the sense of insecurity felt by the borderline insane and by the large number of insane persons who have sufficient understanding on this particular matter", particularly reassuring.[3] It offers a somewhat shaky basis on which to build respect for the sanctity of life.

The "wedge" argument certainly has wide appeal and is accepted by many who would reject the arguments of the Christian theologian. It is put forward by Professor Yale Kamisar in his article, "Some non-religious views against proposed 'mercy-killing' legislation", the fullest statement of argument against euthanasia from the non-Christian viewpoint.[4] He outlines the dangers inherent in giving such a power to the average physician. A mistake in diagnosis is quite possible, and, once made, the consequences would be irreparable.[5] He also points out that a cure for the disease may well be established within the life expectancy of the patient. Finally, he

[1] *New York Times*, January 27, 1939.

[2] Op. cit., pp. 349–50.

[3] "Mercy Killing Legislation—A Reply", *Minnesota Law Review*, 43:1, p. 11 (November, 1958).

[4] *Minnesota Law Review*, 42:969–1042 (May, 1958).

[5] "If the range of skill and judgment among licensed physicians approaches the wide gap between the very best and the very worst members of the bar—and I have no reason to think it does not—then the minimally competent physician is hardly the man to be given the responsibility for ending another's life", op. cit., p. 996. Cf. Lord Horder who stated that the incurability of disease is only an estimate based upon experience, "and how fallacious experience may be in medicine only those who have had a great deal of experience fully realize", *House of Lords Debates* (5th s.), 103:492 (1936).

stresses the difficulty of establishing a true consent, when the patient is suffering from severe pain. As Lord Horder earlier pointed out, the mental clarity of those supporting euthanasia bills has no counterpart in the alternating moods and confused judgments of the sick man.[1] Furthermore, how many people really desire death? The answer is probably very few.[2]

A final objection to euthanasia is that it would undermine the relationship of confidence between doctor and patient. At present, the medical convention, based on the Hippocratic oath and the code of medical ethics, obliges the doctor to do all he can to preserve the life of the patient.[3] The knowledge that the doctor will fight for his life is of great importance to the patient in helping him play his part in resisting the advance of illness and strengthening the will to recover. Doctors themselves recognize this, and have protested against the role allotted to them by the supporters of euthanasia.[4]

While Christian and medical ethics agree that the doctor's first duty is to preserve his patient's life, two modifications of the principle are generally recognized. Catholic theologians point out that while both patient and doctor are under an obligation to use all ordinary means to save life, there is no absolute obligation to employ extraordinary means.[5] Ordinary means have been described as "all medicines, treatments and operations which offer a reasonable hope of benefit, and which can be obtained and used without excessive expense, pain or other inconvenience". Extraordinary means, on the other hand, are those which do involve these factors, or

[1] *House of Lords Debates* (5th s.), 103:493 (1936).

[2] See J. J. Walsh, "Life is Sacred", *The Forum*, 94:333 (1935), and A. L. Banks, "Euthanasia", *Bulletin New York Academy of Medicine*, 26:297 (1950).

[3] The Hippocratic oath: "I will give no deadly medicine to anyone if asked, nor suggest any such counsel." The International Code of Medical Ethics, adopted by the third general assembly of the World Medical Association (London, October 1949), states that "a doctor must always bear in mind the importance of preserving human life until death", *Linacre Quarterly*, 22:56 (May, 1955).

[4] See *The Spectator*, 184:502 (April 14, 1950).

[5] See address of Pius XII to international audience of physicians, *The New York Times*, November 25, 1957, *A.A.S.* 49:1027-33. Cf. Gerald Kelly, "The duty of using artificial means of preserving life", *Theological Studies*, 11:203-20 (1950). Ibid., *Medico-Moral Problems*, St Louis, V:6 (1956), E. F. Healy, *Medical Ethics*, Chicago 1956, p. 77.

which, if used, would not offer a reasonable hope of benefit.[1] The patient is obliged to use all ordinary means but not the extraordinary ones, unless his life is of some special value to the community, or their employment is necessary for his spiritual benefit. The doctor is under an obligation to use all ordinary means and also those which the patient reasonably wishes to be used. Both are of course free to use any available means to prolong life if they wish.

The distinction between ordinary and extraordinary is relative, and will vary with time, place, and circumstances. Penicillin, for example, which at one time would have been considered extraordinary, is today a normal feature of medical practice. The rule is basically one of common sense, preventing a patient from reducing his family to penury, for instance, for the sake of a brief prolongation of life or the pursuit of a vague hope of recovery. The good doctor, said Lord Horder, is aware of the distinction between prolonging life and prolonging the act of dying.[2]

The other modification concerns the administration of drugs to relieve pain which also have the effect of shortening life. Provided the patient consents, and the intention of the doctor is to relieve pain, not to kill the patient, their use is morally unobjectionable. The point was discussed by Pius XII in 1957. Speaking of drug injections to reduce pain, the Pope said: "If there exists no direct causal link, either through the will of interested parties or by the nature of things, between the induced unconsciousness and the shortening of life—as would be the case if the suppression of the pain could be obtained only by the shortening of life; and if, on the other hand, the actual administration of drugs brings about two distinct effects, the one the relief of pain, the other the shortening of life, the action is lawful. It is necessary, however, to observe whether there is, between these two effects, a reasonable proportion, and if the advantages of the one compensate for the disadvantages of the other. It is important also to ask oneself if the present state of science does not allow the same result to be obtained by other means. Finally, in the use of the drug, one should not go beyond

---

[1] Gerald Kelly, "The Duty to Preserve Life", *Theological Studies*, 12:550 (1951).

[2] *House of Lords Debates* (5th s.), 103:490 (1936). Cf. Dean Willard Sperry, *The Ethical Basis of Medical Practice*, New York 1950, p. 134, for a Protestant expression of a similar viewpoint. Cf. *The Clergy Review*, 42:171 (March 1957).

the limits which are actually necessary."[1] Dr Glanville Williams
finds this principle "hypocritical", but the stricture seems unjustified.[2] There is a clear moral distinction between injecting a
drug with the express intention of killing the patient, and injecting the same drug in order to ease his pain, in the knowledge that
his expectation of life will thereby be reduced. The distinction is one
generally recognized in the medical profession.[3]

PROPOSED CHANGES IN THE LAW
AND CHRISTIAN ETHICS

Any proposal for compulsory euthanasia would be rejected by
Christians as violating the inherent right to life enjoyed by every
human being, however physically or mentally maimed. A statute
authorizing voluntary euthanasia, even with safeguards, would be
no more acceptable to the Christian conscience. Such a statute
would injure the common good by undermining the respect for
innocent life, a moral idea essential for the maintenance of society's
security.[4] The proposal to provide a legal defence for a doctor who
performed euthanasia would in effect sanction the practice and have
the same effect. This objection would not apply with the same force
to a statute providing a lesser penalty for mercy killing, but such
an enactment might encourage it. A legal definition suggested to
the Royal Commission on Capital Punishment by the Society of
Labour Lawyers was: "If a person who has killed another person
proves that he has killed that person with the compassionate intention of saving him physical or mental suffering, he shall not be
guilty of murder." Motive is notoriously hard to establish in court,
and the Royal Commission rejected the proposal on this ground.[5]

There seems to be no acceptable alternative to the present solution, which leaves the penalty to be fixed by judge or jury, or to be

[1] Address of February 24, 1957, *A.A.S.* 49:129–47, p. 146. Cf. *The Clergy
Review*, 42:173 (March, 1957), article by Dr L. L. McReavy.
[2] Op. cit., pp. 321–2.
[3] See speech of Lord Dawson of Penn. *House of Lords Debates* (5th s.) 103:465–
506 (1936), p. 481, et seq.
[4] It would also create difficulties for Christian judges who could hardly
order euthanasia to be carried out.
[5] H.M.S.O. London Cmd. 8932 of 1953, 790 (10).

modified by executive clemency. In those States where there is no
death penalty, or where it is limited to certain forms of murder, this
approach is obviously facilitated. Within the framework of the
moral principles outlined, it is best to leave discretion to be exercised by the medical profession. This solution is not logically
satisfying, it may on occasion result in inequality of sentences for
indistinguishable cases, and decisions may turn on technical distinctions. These defects are unavoidable, and are preferable to
the abuses to which a system of legalized euthanasia would inevitably lend itself. This conclusion is not confined to Christians.
As Professor Kalven writes: "In the end and with no great conviction
in my conclusion, I would favour leaving things as they are and
trusting for awhile yet to the imperfect but elastic equity in the
administration of the law as written."[1]

[1] *New York University Law Review*, 31:1237 (1956).

Appendices

BIRTH CONTROL LEGISLATION IN AMERICAN STATES

States	No Laws	Sales Prohibited	Allowed to Doctors	Allowed to Pharmacists	Special Licence	Advertisement Prohibited	Exemptions for medical schools, text books, professional journals	Citation
Alabama	x							
Alaska	x							
Arizona						x		Ar. Code (ann.) 1939, 43–302
Arkansas		x	x		x	x	x	St. 1947, 82: 944–54
California						x		Business and Professional Code 1954, 601
Colorado		x	x	x		x	x	Stats. 1953, 40–9–17
Connecticut		x				x		Stats. 1958, 53–32
Delaware		x	x	x		x		Code 1953, 16: 2501–2504
D. of Columbia	x							
Florida	x							
Georgia	x							
Hawaii						x (outside only)		Laws 1955, 155–73

States	No Laws	Sales Prohibited	Allowed to Doctors	Allowed to Pharmacists	Special Licence	Advertisement Prohibited	Exemptions for medical schools, text books, professional journals	Citation
Idaho		X	X		X	X	X	Code 1948, 18-603, 39: 801 to 810
Illinois	X							
Indiana		X	X	X		X	X	Stats. 1956, 10: 2803–10: 2806
Iowa		X	X			X	X	Code 1950, 725: 5, 6, 10
Kansas		X				X	X	Gen. Stats. 1949, 21–1101
Kentucky		X	X		X	X	X	Revised Statutes 1953, 214: 190 to 214: 270
Louisiana						X		Revised Statutes 1950, 14: 88
Maine						X		Revised Statutes 1954, 134: 11
Maryland	X							
Massachusetts		X				X		Annotated Laws 1956, 272: 20 & 21
Michigan						X		Stats. 1938, 28: 229
Minnesota		X	X			X		Stats. 1947, 617: 25
Mississippi		X				X		Code 1942, 2289

States	No Laws	Sales Prohibited	Allowed to Doctors	Allowed to Pharmacists	Special Licence	Advertisement Prohibited	Exemptions for medical schools, text books, professional journals	Citation
Missouri		x	x	x		x	x	Statutes 1953, 563: 300: 280: 290
Montana		x	x	x		x	x	Statutes 1947, 94:3616 to 94:3619
Nebraska		x				x	x	Revised Statutes 1943, 71-1104 to 71-1115
Nevada		x	x			x		Revised Statutes 1956, 202.190.220. 210. 230.
New Hampshire	x							
New Jersey		x[1]				x		Stats. 1952, 2A 170-76
New Mexico	x							
New York		x	x	x		x	x	Consolidated Laws 1944, 106: 1142: 1145
North Carolina	x							
North Dakota	x							
Ohio		x	x	x		x	x	Code 1954, 2905: 34 to 37

[1] Without just cause.

States	No Laws	Sales Prohibited	Allowed to Doctors	Allowed to Pharmacists	Special Licence	Advertisement Prohibited	Exemptions for medical schools, text books, professional journals	Citation
Oklahoma	x							
Oregon		x	x		x	x	x	Revised Statutes 1957, 435·010 to 435.990
Pennsylvania						x	x	Purdon's Statutes 1945, 18–4525
Rhode Island	x							
South Carolina	x							
South Dakota	x							
Tennessee	x							
Texas	x							
Utah	x							
Vermont	x							
Virginia	x							
Washington						x		Rev. Code 1951, 9.68.030
West Virginia	x							
Wisconsin		x[1]	x	x		x		Stats. 1953, 351.235
Wyoming		x	x	x		x	x	Stats. 1945, 9–513–515

[1] Sales to unmarried persons and from slot machines forbidden.

REGULATIONS GOVERNING THE PROVIDING OF SEMINAL FLUID FOR ARTIFICIAL HUMAN INSEMINATION — NEW YORK

(S. 112 of Sanitary Code of New York City, 1947, 1950)

Regulation 1. A person from whom seminal fluid is to be collected for the purpose of artificial human insemination shall have a complete physical examination with particular attention to the genitalia at the time of the taking of such seminal fluid.

Regulation 2. Such person shall have a standard serological test for syphilis and a smear and culture for gonorrhea not less than one week before such seminal fluid is obtained.

Regulation 3. No person suffering from any venereal disease, tuberculosis or infection with brucella organism, shall be used as a donor of seminal fluid for the purpose of artificial insemination.

Regulation 4. No person having any disease or defect known to be transmissible by the genes shall be used as a donor of seminal fluid for the purpose of artificial human insemination.

Regulation 5. Before artificial human insemination is undertaken, both the proposed donor and the proposed recipient shall have their bloods tested with respect to the Rh. factor at a laboratory approved for serology by the Board or Commissioner of Health. If the proposed recipient is negative for the Rh. factor, no semen shall be used for artificial insemination other than from a donor of seminal fluid whose blood is also negative from this factor.

Regulation 6. Where artificial human insemination is performed, the physician performing the same shall keep a record which shall show:

1. The name of the physician.
2. The name and address of the donor.
3. The name and address of the recipient.
4. The results of the physical examination and the results of the serological examination, including the tests for the Rh. factor.
5. The date of the artificial insemination.

Such records shall be regarded as confidential and shall not be open to inspection by the public or by any other person than the Commissioner of Health, an authorized representative of the Department of Health and such other persons as may be authorized by law to inspect such records. The custodian of any such records, the said Commissioner or any other person authorized by law to inspect such records shall not divulge any part of any such records so as to disclose the identity of the persons to whom they relate except as provided by law.

THE MEDICO-LEGAL ASPECTS OF ARTIFICIAL INSEMINATION

Document prepared and issued by the Medical Defence Union for the guidance of medical practitioners

---

This subject really falls into three classes:

(1) Negligence.

(2) Possible proceedings for dissolution of marriage.

(3) Alleged conspiracy.

In all cases, however, a request in writing should be obtained from the husband and the wife for artificial insemination to be carried out stating whether the husband will be the donor or whether semen will be obtained from an alien donor or from a "Bureau or Bank". The husband and wife should be over twenty-one years of age. The practitioner should explain to the husband and wife that a positive result could not be guaranteed. If an alien donor is to be used he should sign consent to being associated with the procedure.

1. NEGLIGENCE. As the act of artificial insemination is a surgical or medical procedure the medical practitioner must, of course, exercise reasonable care and skill not only in the procedure itself but also, in the case of heterologous insemination, in the selection of the donor or of the source, in the case of a bureau or bank, from which the semen is to be obtained. In this respect it is suggested that the medical practitioner should observe the following precautions:

(a) The donor should preferably not be a relative of either spouse.

(b) The mental and physical history, personal and familial; and the health of the donor must be carefully investigated and should include such tests as a Wassermann, a complete blood count, compatible Rh. factor and full general examination to eliminate T.B., diabetes, epilepsy, endocrine dysfunction, psychosis.

(c) The fertility of the donor should be examined.

(d) The donor should be of age and not more than forty years.

(e) The characteristics and race of the donor should be selected having regard to those of the husband.

(f) Before using semen from a "Bureau or Bank" the medical practitioner should be satisfied as to the professional standing of and the methods employed at such "Bureau or Bank".

2. POSSIBLE PROCEEDINGS FOR DISSOLUTION OF MARRIAGE. So far there has been no decision of our Courts to the effect that a wife artificially inseminated by means of an alien donor has been guilty of adultery or that such donor, if a married man, is guilty of adultery by thus supplying semen. However, during the course of his judgment in the House of Lords in the case of *Russell v. Russell*, Lord Finlay (sic. in fact Lord Dunedin) expressed the view "fecundation *ab extra* is adultery" which view, in fact, follows the finding of the Supreme Court of Ontario in 1921. This being so it would seem that the medical practitioner should do what he can to ensure that his patient and the donor by reason of this heterologous insemination are not involved in Divorce Proceedings and if so involved that there is a good defence to a charge of adultery. No one, of course, can prevent such a suit being brought, but the chances of it being brought can be very much reduced and a complete answer provided if it can be established that both spouses fully understood what was being done and that this was, in fact, carried out at their joint request and, in the case of a married donor, if the written consent of his wife were obtained.

3. ALLEGED CONSPIRACY. In a very great number of cases the lawful progeny of married couples on the death of one of their parents stand to inherit either titles, estates or funds, and in default of their being such lawful progeny the titles, estates or funds pass to others. While children born in wedlock are treated prima facie as being legitimate, so far as we can ascertain the Courts have not as yet been called upon to decide the legitimacy of a child born in wedlock who is the product of heterologous insemination. Accordingly, it is possible that a medical practitioner who had carried out such an insemination might be sued jointly with the husband and wife and possibly the donor for conspiracy to defeat the claims of those who would inherit in default of the husband and wife having legal issue. It is difficult to suggest any means which would provide a complete defence, but the position of the medical practitioner would be largely safeguarded were he to obtain from the husband and wife an assurance in writing that the birth of a child by the wife would not defeat the claims of any persons contingently interested in default of their having issue.

It is desirable that this last statement and the request and statement referred to in the first paragraph, should be witnessed by some responsible impartial third person, in whose presence the medical man has explained what is involved and the reasons why the request and the statements are respectively required.

The Council has approved the following documents as suitable for completion (1) by the parties availing themselves of artificial insemination as a form of treatment for sterility or impotence on the part of the male, and (2) by the donor.

(1) To Dr
    of
We (full name of husband) and (full name of wife)   of
        (full address) being desirous of having a child and having been advised that it is impossible to achieve by normal sexual intercourse between us hereby request and authorize you to inseminate artificially (full name of wife) by means of semen supplied by a donor selected by you. We hereby assure you that the birth of such a child will not defeat the claims of any person to any titles, estates, interests or funds.
Dated this   day of   19
Witness to the signature
of Mr and Mrs
Signature of witnesses:
         Address:
         Occupation:

(2) I,   of
hereby consent to supply semen to Dr
for the purpose of artificially inseminating a woman whose name has not been disclosed to me. It has been explained to me that the use of semen supplied by me for this purpose might be held to be adultery and I have accordingly only consented to supply semen on condition that (a) my name be not disclosed and (b) the written consent of the woman and the husband (if any) to the procedure be obtained.
Dated this   day of   19
Witnesses.

AUTHOR'S NOTE. The above forms might bar an adultery suit but the assurance as to property can only be given as to what was known at the time, and a subsequent legacy etc., might well give rise to fraud.

SUMMARY OF RECOMMENDATIONS OF FEVERSHAM COMMITTEE ON ARTIFICIAL INSEMINATION

272. The following is a summary of our recommendations:

A.I.H.

The fact that a live child has been born as a result of artificial insemination of a woman with the seed of her husband should be a bar to proceedings by either spouse for nullity of marriage on the ground of impotence. (paragraph 108)

A.I.D.

(1) Acceptance by a wife of artificial insemination with the seed of a donor without the consent of her husband should be made a new ground for divorce or judicial separation, and in England these circumstances should also enable a husband to take matrimonial proceedings in a magistrates' court. (paragraph 117)

(2) The law should be not amended to permit a decree of nullity of marriage to be obtained on the ground of sterility. (paragraph 139)

(3) The fact that a live child has been born as the result of artificial insemination of a woman with the seed of a donor, to which the parties to the marriage consented, should be a bar to proceedings by either spouse for nullity of marriage on the ground of impotence. (paragraph 156)

(4) The law of Scotland should be amended to give a child born of A.I.D. to which a husband has consented the same rights of maintenance as an adopted child, and in England the child should be entitled to claim that provision for his maintenance be made out of the deceased husband's estate. (paragraph 159)

(5) There should be no amendment of the laws relating to legitimacy or registration of birth. (paragraph 187)

(6) The law should not be amended to enable a wife to take proceedings for divorce on the ground that her husband has donated semen for the purpose of A.I.D. without obtaining her consent. (paragraph 195)

(7) While the practice of A.I.D. is strongly to be discouraged, it should not be declared criminal or be regulated by law. (paragraphs 239 and 262)

STERILIZATIONS REPORTED IN THE U.S.A.

From date of enactment of first sterilization law (Indiana 1907) to January 1, 1958.[1]

State	1957	1956	Total	Grand Total Male	Grand Total Female
Alabama[2]			224	129	95
Arizona		8	30	10	20
California	13	23	19,998	10,132	9,866
Connecticut	2	7	544	46	498
Delaware	8	12	879	451	428
Georgia	268	268	2,758	1,205	1,553
Idaho			33	8	25
Indiana	29	34	2,354	1,157	1,197
Iowa	48	69	1,738	498	1,240
Kansas			3,025	1,763	1,262
Maine	5	1	310	45	265
Michigan	47	27	3,597	958	2,639
Minnesota	12	19	2,325	518	1,807
Mississippi		6	602	154	448
Montana			256	72	184
Nebraska	5	8	857	401	456
New Hampshire	8	8	678	152	526
New York[2]			42	1	41
North Carolina	305	216	4,777	989	3,788
North Dakota	14	14	975	359	616
Oklahoma			556	122	434
Oregon	23	38	2,200	848	1,352
South Carolina	34	43	235	18	217
South Dakota	4	2	783	281	502

[1] Compiled from figures published by the various States.
[2] Not reported. Alabama law inoperative since 1935. New York law declared unconsitutional in 1912. Washington ibid. 1942.

State	1957	1956	Total	Grand Total Male	Female
Utah	12	15	744	340	404
Vermont	1		253	83	170
Virginia	128	87	6,811	2,678	4,133
Washington[1]			685	184	501
West Virginia		3	98	15	83
Wisconsin	7	1	1,779	391	1,408
Totals	973	909	60,166	24,008	36,158

[1] Washington law declared unconstitutional in 1942.

STERILIZATIONS REPORTED IN THE U.S.A.

(Per 100,000 population) (1957)

Based on latest U.S. Dept. of Commerce, Bureau of the Census, Population Estimate.

Georgia	7·09	Minnesota	·36
N. Carolina	6·78	Nebraska	·34
Virginia	3·37	Vermont	·27
N. Dakota	2·17	Wisconsin	·18
Delaware	1·82	California	·09
Iowa	1·71	Connecticut	·09
S. Carolina	1·43	Arizona	o·
New Hampshire	1·4	Idaho	o·
Utah	1·4	Kansas	o·
Oregon	1·3	Mississippi	o·
Indiana	·64	Montana	o·
Michigan	·61	Oklahoma	o·
South Dakota	·57	West Virginia	o·
Maine	·53		

APPENDIX VII

YEARS IN WHICH STERILIZATION STATUTES FIRST PASSED IN THE U.S.A.

Alabama	1919	Montana	1923
Arizona	1929	Nebraska	1915
California	1909	New Hampshire	1917
Connecticut	1909	North Carolina	1919
Delaware	1923	North Dakota	1913
Georgia	1937	Oklahoma	1931
Idaho	1925	Oregon	1917
Indiana	1907	South Carolina	1935
Iowa	1911	South Dakota	1917
Kansas	1913	Utah	1925
Maine	1925	Vermont	1931
Michigan	1913	Virginia	1924
Minnesota	1925	West Virginia	1929
Mississippi	1928	Wisconsin	1913

TYPES OF STATE STERILIZATION STATUTES IN THE U.S.A.

State	Voluntary[1]	Compulsory[2]	Voluntary[3] and Compulsory	Extra[4] Mural	Eugenics[5] Board
Alabama		X			
Arizona		X			
California		X			
Connecticut		X			
Delaware		X		X	
Georgia		X			X
Idaho		X		X	X
Indiana		X			
Iowa		X		X	X
Kansas		X			
Maine			X		
Michigan		X		X	
Minnesota	X				
Mississippi		X			
Montana		X			X
Nebraska		X			
New Hampshire		X			
North Carolina			X	X	X
North Dakota		X			
Oklahoma		X			
Oregon		X		X	X
South Carolina		X			
South Dakota			X	X	
Utah		X		X	
Vermont	X				
Virginia		X			
West Virginia		X			
Wisconsin		X			

[1] Consent of defective person, spouse or guardian required.
[2] Consent of defective person not required.
[3] Law contains provision for either voluntary or compulsory.
[4] Law contains provision for individuals outside of institutions.
[5] Authorization agency for sterilization operation. (Other States: operations passed on by designated State agencies.)

SUMMARY OF UNITED STATES STERILIZATION STATUTES

I. *Alabama*. (Code of Alabama, 1940, Title 45, Sec. 243. (1476).)
Compulsory and mandatory.

Persons covered: Inmates of Partlow State School for Mental Defectives.
Grounds: None stated.
Initiation: Asst. Superintendent of school consults with Superintendent of school.

Authority making
order: Asst. Superintendent and Superintendent of school.

II. *Arizona*. (Arizona Code Annotated 1939, Vol. I, Art 4, Secs. 8–401 through 8–406.) (Laws 1929, Ch. 44, Secs. 1–6.)
Compulsory and permissive.

Persons covered: Any person confined in a State hospital for the insane who is afflicted with an hereditary form of insanity that is recurrent, idiocy, imbecility, feeble mindedness or epilepsy.
Grounds: Hereditary and social.
Initiation: Superintendent of hospital petitions State Board of Medical Examiners.

Authority making
order: State Board of Medical Examiners.
Note: Inmate has right to counsel and to appeal to the courts. "Nothing in this act shall be construed so as to prevent the medical or surgical treatment for sound therapeutic reasons of any person in this State, by a physician or surgeon licensed by this State, which treatment may incidentally involve the nullification or destruction of the reproductive functions."

III. *California*. (Senate Bill No. 730 passed Senate April 12, 1951; passed Assembly May 8, 1951; signed by Governor May 23, 1951.)
Compulsory and permissive.

Persons covered: Any person who has been lawfully committed or admitted to any State hospital or State home and who is afflicted with or suffers from any of the following conditions:

  (a) mental disease, which may have been inherited and is likely to be transmitted to descendants.

  (b) mental deficiency in any of its various grades.

  (c) marked departure from normal mentality.

Grounds: Hereditary for the insane; none are stated for mental deficients.

Initiation: Superintendent of hospital or home gives certification to the Directors of Mental Hygiene.

Authority making order: Director of Mental Hygiene.

Note: Inmate has right of appeal.

IV. *Connecticut.* (General Statutes of Connecticut, Revision of 1949, Vol. II, Secs. 4182–4183.)

Compulsory and mandatory.

Persons covered: Inmates by whom procreation would be inadvisable who are confined in the State Prison, State Hospitals for Mental Illness at Middletown, Newton and Norwich, Mansfield State Training School and Hospital and Southbury Training School.

Grounds: Hereditary or medical. "If ... procreation by any such person would produce children with an inherited tendency to crime, mental illness, feeble mindedness, idiocy or imbecility and there is no probability that the condition of any such person so examined will improve to such an extent as to render procreation by any such person advisable, or if the physical or mental condition of any such person will be substantially improved thereby."

Initiation: The warden, superintendent or doctor in charge of each institution named, reports to a special board of each institution.

Authority making order: The responsible body is a special board at each institution which is composed of two skilled surgeons and the doctor in charge of the institution.

Note: "Section 2684. Penalty for unlawful operation. Except as authorized by section 2683, any person who shall

perform, encourage, assist in or otherwise promote the
performance of either of the operations described in
said section, for the purpose of destroying the power
to procreate in the human species, or any person who
shall knowingly permit either of such operations to
be performed upon such person, unless the same shall
be a medical necessity shall be fined not more than
one thousand dollars or imprisoned in the State
Prison not more than five years, or both."

V. *Delaware*. (Revised Code of Delaware 1953, volume 4. Titles 16–32.)
Compulsory and permissive.

Persons covered: (a) All persons legally confined in any State or county
institution which has charge of insane, feeble
minded or epileptic persons.

(b) any feeble minded, epileptic, chronically or re-
currently insane person confined in any institution within the State, supported in whole or
part by the State or any county thereof, or any
such person at large.

(c) habitual or confined criminals who have been
convicted of at least three felonies by any courts of
this State or of any other State of the United
States.

Grounds: For those in category (a) above, where procreation is
inadvisable; none stated for category (b); for those in
category (c) above, that the criminality is caused by
mental abnormality or mental disease.

Initiation: Board or commission controlling appropriate institution makes application to the State Department of
Public Welfare.

Authority making Special panels appointed by the State Department of
order: Public Welfare.

VI. *Georgia*. (Code of Georgia Annotated, Book 28, Title 99, Ch. 99–13.)
Compulsory and mandatory.

Persons covered: Patients or inmates of any State home or hospital for
mental or physical disease; any State colony or institution for the care of the mentally or physically
defective, deficient, or diseased; any State prison or
penitentiary, correction school or reformatory, detention home or camp.

Grounds: Hereditary.
Initiation: Superintendent, manager or director of the insti-
                    tution in which the patient or inmate is confined sub-
                    mits recommendation to the State Board of Eugenics.
Authority making   State Board of Eugenics, composed of Chairman of
   order: State Board of Control, Director of State Board of
                    Health and Superintendent of Milledgeville State
                    Hospital.
Note: Right of inmate to receive notice and to appeal to
                    courts.

VII. *Idaho*. (Laws of Idaho Title 66, Ch. 8. 66–801 through 66–812. Also
    1955 S. B. No. 82 amending section 39–101.)
Compulsory and mandatory.
Persons covered: All feeble minded, insane, epileptic, habitually crimi-
                    nal, morally degenerate and sexually perverted per-
                    sons who are, or are likely to become a menace to
                    society.
Grounds: Hereditary and social.
Initiation: Superintendents or Warden of appropriate insti-
                    tution report quarterly to the State Board of Health:
                    Eugenics Section.
Authority making
   order: State Board of Health: Eugenics Section.
Note: Right of appeal, etc.

VIII. *Indiana*. (Burns Indiana Statues, Annotated [1950 Replacement]
    Vol. 5, part 2, Title 22, Ch. 16, Secs. 22–1601 through 22–1618.)
Compulsory and permissive.
Persons covered: (a) Any person afflicted with hereditary forms of
                       insanity that are recurrent, epilepsy or incurable
                       primary or secondary types of feeble mindedness,
                       who is an inmate of any hospital or other State or
                       county institution which has the care or custody
                       of insane, feeble minded or epileptic persons.
                   (b) any person afflicted with idiocy, imbecility, or
                       feeble mindedness for whom application for com-
                       mitment to an institution for the feeble minded
                       has been filed in a court of competent jurisdiction.
                   (c) any person afflicted with insanity for whom appli-
                       cation for commitment to an institution for the

insane has been filed in a court of competent jurisdiction.

Grounds: Hereditary for the insane; social for all categories.

Initiation: For (a) the superintendent of the institution in which the patient is confined petitions the Commissioner of Mental Health. For those in (b) and (c) above, certification is made by examining doctors appointed by court.

Authority making order: For (a) the Commissioner of Mental Health. For (b) and (c) the court in which the application for commitment is filed.

Note: Provisions for appeal.

IX. *Iowa*. (Iowa Code Annotated: Vol. 9, Ch. 145.)
Compulsory and mandatory.

Persons covered: All persons living in the State who are feeble minded, insane, syphilitic, habitual criminals, moral degenerates or sexual perverts and who are a menace to society.

Grounds: Hereditary and social.

Initiation: Each member of the State Board of Eugenics, etc., submit names in quarterly reports to the State Board of Eugenics.

Authority making order: State Board of Eugenics.

Note: Provisions for notice and appeal to courts.

X. *Kansas*. (General Statutes, Annotated 135, Ch. 76, Art. 1.)
Compulsory and mandatory.

Persons covered: Any inmate of State Penitentiary, Hutchinson Reformatory, State hospitals for the insane, State Hospital for Epileptics, State Training School or State Industrial School for Girls.

Grounds: Hereditary and medical.

Initiation: Warden or superintendents of appropriate institutions.

Authority making order: The chief medical officer of any institution, the governing board of such institution and the Secretary of the State Board of Health constitute the Board of Examiners which makes the order.

Note: Section 76–155. "Penalty for unlawful operations except as authorized by this act, every person who shall perform, encourage, assist in or otherwise promote

the performance of either of the operations described
in this act, for the purpose of destroying the power to
procreate the human species, unless the same shall be
a medical necessity, shall be fined not less than 100
dollars nor more than 500 dollars, and imprisoned in
the county jail not less than six months nor exceeding
one year."

XI. *Maine*. (Revised Statutes of Maine [1944], Vol. I, Ch. 23.)
Voluntary and compulsory and mandatory.

Persons covered: (a) Any feeble minded person or person afflicted with
mental disease who is at large.

(b) inmates of any State institution which has the care
or custody of feeble minded persons.

Grounds: Hereditary or medical for those at large; hereditary
only for those confined in State institutions as defined
above.

Initiation: (a) For those designated in (a) above, the operation is
recommended, upon consent of the person or his
nearest relative or guardian, by a doctor who may call
council of two doctors to examine patient. For those
designated in (b) above, the recommendation is made in
writing by the medical staff or institution physician
and is accompanied by the sworn statement of the
superintendent.

Authority making Operation voluntary for those at large. For those in
order: institutions as defined above the Commissioner of
Institutional Service is responsible.

Note: Provisions for appeal.

XII. *Michigan*. (Compiled Laws of the State of Michigan 1948, Vol. IV,
Ch. 720.)
Compulsory and mandatory.

Persons covered: (a) Inmates of thirteen named institutions and any
other hospital, training school, farm colony,
prison or public institution maintained in whole
or in part by the State of Michigan.

(b) mentally defective persons at large.

Grounds: Hereditary and social.

Initiation: (a) Superintendent of appropriate institutions.

(b) Petition to probate court by relatives or one of list
of officials.

Authority making Probate Court which appoints first two doctors to
  order: make investigation.
Note: Provisions for hearing and appeal.

XIII. *Minnesota*. (Minnesota Statutes Annotated, Vol. 17, Ch. 256, Secs.
  256.07 through 256.10.)
Voluntary only.
Persons covered: (a) All persons lawfully committed as mentally
                     deficient to the guardianship of the Director of
                     Social Welfare.
                 (b) All persons committed as insane to the custody of
                     the superintendent of a State hospital for the in-
                     sane in which they have been confined for at least
                     six consecutive months.
Grounds: None stated.
Initiation: Director of Public Institutions after consultations.
Authority making
  order: The Director of Public Institutions.

XIV. *Mississippi*. (Mississippi Code 1942 Annotated, Vol. 5, Title 25,
  Ch. 3, Art. 10, Secs. 6957 through 6964.)
Compulsory and permissive.
Persons covered: Patients or inmates of the Mississippi State Insane
                  Hospital, East Mississippi Insane Hospital or Missis-
                  sippi School and Colony for the Feeble minded.
Grounds: Hereditary and social.
Initiation: The superintendent of the institution in which the
                  patient is confined petitions the Board of Trustees or
                  the directors of such institutions.
Authority making The local Board of Trustees or the Directors of the
  order: Institution.
Note: Provisions for appeal.
                  Nothing in this statute shall be construed so as to
                  prevent the medical or surgical treatment for sound
                  therapeutic reasons of any person in this State by
                  a physician or surgeon licensed by this State, which
                  treatment may incidentally involve the nullification
                  or destruction of the reproductive functions.

XV. *Montana*. (Revised Codes of Montana 1947, Vol. 3, Ch. 6, Secs. 38-
  601 through 38-608.)
Compulsory and mandatory.

Persons covered: Idiots, feeble minded, insane or epileptic persons who are inmates of State custodial institutions.

Grounds: Hereditary or medical.

Initiation: Chief physician of inmate's institution submits certificate to the State Board of Eugenics.

Authority making order: The State Board of Eugenics approves certificate by endorsement.

Note: Provision for appeal.

XVI. *Nebraska*. (Revised Statutes of Nebraska 1943, Vol. IV, Ch. 83, Art. 5, Secs. 83–501 through 83–509.)

Compulsory and mandatory.

Persons covered: Feeble minded, insane, habitually criminal, morally degenerate and sexually perverted patients or inmates who are subject to parole or discharge from the Institution for the Feeble minded, hospitals for the insane, Reformatory for Women, Industrial Home, industrial schools and the Penitentiary.

Grounds: Hereditary and social.

Initiation: Superintendents of appropriate institutions to Board of Examiners in quarterly reports.

Authority making order: The Board of Examiners.

Note: Provisions for appeal.

"If it shall appear from the warrant of commitment that any male inmate shall have been convicted for rape, incest, any crime against nature or for violation of section 28–901, then it shall be the duty of the board of examiners, if ordered by the court, to perform or cause to be performed an operation for the castration of such male inmate; Provided, however, if such operation of castration is performed, the inmate shall be eligible to apply for a commutation of sentence within one year after said operation." (Sec. 83–504).

XVII. *New Hampshire*. (Revised Laws of New Hampshire 1943, Vol. I, Title XV, Ch. 160, Secs. 1 through 14.)

Compulsory and permissive.

Persons covered: Inmates of any State or county institution who are afflicted with hereditary forms of insanity that are recurrent, idiocy, imbecility, feeble mindedness or epilepsy.

Grounds: Hereditary and social.

Initiation: Petition of superintendent of institution is presented to Board of County Commissioners or governing body of appropriate institution.

Authority making Either County Commissioners or governing body of
order: appropriate institution.

Note: Provisions for appeal.

"Nothing herein shall be construed so as to prevent medical or surgical treatment for sound therapeutic reasons of any person in this State, whether such treatment involves the nullification or destruction of the reproductive functions or otherwise." (1929, 138: 12)

XVIII. *North Carolina*. (General statutes of 1943, Vol. 2, Ch. 35, Secs. 35-6 through 35-57.)

Voluntary and compulsory and mandatory.

Persons covered: (a) Any mentally diseased, feeble minded or epileptic inmate or patient of any penal or charitable institution which is supported wholly or in part by the State or any subdivision thereof.

(b) any such person at large.

Grounds: Hereditary, social, or medical.

Initiation: The head of the institution or County Superintendent of Public Welfare petitions the Eugenics Board of North Carolina.

Authority making
order: Eugenics Board of North Carolina.

Note: Provisions for hearing and appeal.

"Nothing contained in this article shall be construed so as to prevent the medical or surgical treatment for sound therapeutic reasons of any person in this State by a physician or surgeon licensed in this State, which treatment may incidentally involve the nullification or destruction of the reproductive functions. (1933, c. 224, s. 17).

XIX. *North Dakota*. (North Dakota Revised Code 1943, Vol. 2, Title 23, Ch. 23-08, Secs. 23-0801 through 23-0815.)

Compulsory and mandatory.

Persons covered: Feeble minded, insane, epileptic, habitually criminal, morally degenerate and sexually perverted inmates (who are potential producers of offspring and who, because of the inheritance of inferior or anti-social traits, probably would become social menaces or wards of the State), confined in the State Penitentiary, State Hospital for the Insane, State Training School and the Grafton State School. Criminals covered by the act are those moral degenerates and sexual perverts who are addicted to the practice of sodomy, the crime against nature or other gross, bestial and perverted sexual habits and practices prohibited by statute.

Grounds: Hereditary and medical.

Initiation: Warden, superintendent etc., of named institutions in quarterly reports.

Authority making
  order: Board of Examiners.

Note: Provisions for appeal.

XX. *Oklahoma.* (Oklahoma Statutes 1941, Title 35, Ch. 2, Secs. 141–146.)
Compulsory and permissive.

Persons covered: Male patients under sixty-five and female patients under forty-seven about to be discharged from the Hospital for the Insane at Norman, the Hospital at Supply, Hospital for the Insane at Vinita, Institute for the Feeble minded at Enid, State Penitentiary at McAlester, State Reformatory at Granite, any other penal institution existing or to be created or any other such institution supported in whole or in part from public funds.

Grounds: Hereditary and social.

Initiation: Superintendent or warden petitions State Board of Affairs.

Authority making
  order: State Board of Affairs.

Note: Provisions for service and appeal.

XXI. *Oregon.* (Oregon Compiled Laws Annotated, Vol. 8, Title 127, Ch. 8,
    Secs. 127–801 through 127–811.)
Compulsory and mandatory.

Persons covered: All persons who are feeble minded, insane, epileptic, habitual criminals, incurable syphilitics, moral degenerates or sexual perverts; any person convicted of the crime of rape, incest, sodomy, contributing to the delinquency of a minor by sexual act or act of sexual perversion, the crime against nature or any other crime specified in section 23–910 of the laws; or any person convicted of attempting to commit any of said crimes.

Grounds: Hereditary or social.

Initiation: Quarterly reports to the State Board of Eugenics are made by the Superintendents of the Oregon State Hospital and other named institutions.

Authority making
order: State Board of Eugenics.

Note: Provisions for appeal.

XXII. *South Carolina.* (Code of Laws of South Carolina 1942, Vol. 3, Sec. 5009.)

Compulsory and permissive.

Persons covered. Any inmate of State penal or charitable institutions who is afflicted with any hereditary form of insanity that is recurrent, idiocy, imbecility, feeble mindedness or epilepsy.

Grounds: Hereditary and social.

Initiation: Superintendent of institution petitions the Executive Committee of the State Board of Health.

Authority making
order: Executive Committee of State Board of Health.

Note: Provisions for appeal.

XXIII. *South Dakota.* (South Dakota Code of 1939, Vol. 1, Title 30, Ch. 20.05, Secs. 30.0501, through 30.0514.)

Voluntary and compulsory and mandatory.

Persons covered: A: Any feeble minded person and those feeble minded inmates about to be discharged from the State School and Home for the Feeble minded.

Grounds: That such feeble minded person is of such an age as to be capable of procreation and, by reason of his feeble mindedness, would not be capable of properly performing the duties of parenthood.

Initiation: Any State resident's complaint, asking that order and commitment be made. Filed with Chairman of county's commission for feeble minded.

(Laws of 1943 [Ch. 112 – H.B. 206—approved March 8, 1943])

Persons covered: Any person committed to the Yakton State Hospital and about to be discharged who is afflicted with or suffering from

(a) mental disease which may have been inherited and is liable to be transmitted to descendants,

(b) perversion or marked departure from normal mentality,

(c) disease of a syphilitic nature.

Grounds: That such person is capable of procreation and that procreation would be probable.

Initiation: At least ten days before the operation, the Superintendent of the hospital notified in writing the inmate, etc.

Authority making order: Superintendent of Yankton State Hospital, supported by majority of medical staff.

Note: Provisions for appeal.

XXIV. *Utah*. (Uta Code Annotated 1943, Vol. 5, Title 89, Secs. 89–0–1 through 89–0–12. Supplement, Secs. 89–0–1 through 89–0–8 amended; Secs. 89–0–13 and 89–0–14 added. Amended by L.1945, H.B. 87, Approved February 27, 1945.)

Compulsory and permissive.

Persons covered: Any inmate (whether voluntary or committed) confined in the Utah State Hospital, Utah State Training School, State Industrial School or State Prison; or any person adjudged to be insane, an idiot, an imbecile, feeble minded, epileptic or who is afflicted with habitual degenerate sexual criminal tendencies.

Grounds: Hereditary and social.

Initiation: Superintendent or Warden petitions board of institution.

Authority making order: Board of particular institution to which petition is directed.

Note: Provisions for hearing and appeal. "Except as authorized by this title, every person who performs, encourages, assists in or otherwise promotes the performance of any of the operations described in this title for the purpose of destroying the power to procreate the human species, unless the same shall be a medical necessity, is guilty of a felony."

XXV. *Vermont*. (Vermont Statutes, Revision of 1947, Ch. 425, Secs. 10,
   027 through 10,030.)

Voluntary only.

Persons covered:	Any mentally defective or insane resident of State who is likely to procreate mentally defective or insane persons, if not sterilized.
Grounds:	Hereditary and social.
Initiation:	When such person is confined in a State institution, the Commissioner of Institutions and Corrections is authorized with the consent of the inmate and his natural or legal guardian, to contract for examination and certification under oath by two physicians and surgeons not employed by the State. In all other cases, two physicians and surgeons, legally qualified to practice in the State, make the examination and certification under oath. The consent of the inmate or his legal or natural guardian is required.
Authority making order:	None—no order is made.

XXVI. *Virginia*. (Code of Virginia 1950, Vol. 6, Title 37, Secs. 37-231
   through 37-245. 1950 Cum. Supp. Secs. 37-231 and 37-241.)

Compulsory and permissive.

Persons covered:	Any inmate, afflicted with hereditary forms of mental illness that are recurrent, mental deficiency or epilepsy, who is confined in Western State Hospital, Eastern State Hospital, Southwestern State Hospital, Central State Hospital, Lynchburg State Colony or Petersburg State Colony.
Grounds:	Hereditary and social.
Initiation:	Hospital or colony superintendent petitions State Hospital Board.
Authority making order:	State Hospital Board or member or members thereof designated by such Board.
Note:	Provisions for Appeal. Reservation re therapeutic sterilization. "Nothing in this chapter shall be construed so as to prevent the medical or surgical treatment for sound therapeutic reasons of any person in this State, by a physician or surgeon licensed by this State, which treatment may incidentally involve the

nullification or destruction of the reproductive functions."

XXVII. *West Virginia.* (West Virginia Code of 1949 Annotated, Ch. 16 Art. 10, Secs. 1394–1400.)
Compulsory and permissive.

Persons covered: Any inmate, afflicted with any hereditary form of insanity that is recurrent, idiocy, imbecility, feeble mindedness or epilepsy, who is confined in Weston State Hospital, Huntington State Hospital, Spencer State Hospital, Lakin State Hospital, West Virginia Industrial School for Boys, Industrial Home for Girls, Industrial School for Coloured Boys or Industrial Home for Coloured Girls.

Grounds: Hereditary and social.

Initiation: Superintendent of institution in which patient is confined petitions in writing the State Public Health Council.

Authority making
order: Public Health Council.

Note: Provisions for appeal. Reservation re medical sterilization. "Nothing in this article shall be construed to authorize the operation of castration nor the removal of sound organs from the body, but this provision shall not be construed so as to prevent the medical or surgical treatment for sound therapeutic reasons of any person in this State, by a physician or surgeon licensed by this State, in such a way as may incidentally involve the nullification or destruction of the reproductive functions."

XXVIII. *Wisconsin.* (Wisconsin Statutes 1949, Title VII, Sec. 46.12.)
Compulsory and permissive.

Persons covered: Inmates and patients of institutions having charge of criminal, mentally ill, mentally deficient and epileptic persons.

Grounds: Procreation is inadvisable.

Initiation: Department of Public Welfare submits names to special Board.

Authority making Department of Public Welfare, upon unanimous
order: finding of experts and superintendents.

LAWS OF THE STATES OF THE UNITED STATES PUNISHING HOMOSEXUAL OFFENCES

ALABAMA

Any person who commits an assault on another with intent to . . . commit the crime against nature, shall on conviction, be punished by imprisonment in the penitentiary, for not less than two or more than twenty years. (*Code of Alabama* 1940) (14.38)

Any person who commits a crime against nature, either with mankind or with any beast, shall, on conviction, be imprisoned in the penitentiary for not less than two nor more than ten years. (14.106)

Emission need not be proved, but proof of penetration is necessary. *Tarrant v. State* (12 Ala. App. 172)

ALASKA

Unnatural crimes. That if any person shall commit sodomy, or the crime against nature, or shall have unnatural, carnal copulation by means of the mouth, or otherwise, either with beast or mankind of either sex, such person, upon conviction thereof, shall be punished by imprisonment in the penitentiary not less than one year nor more than ten years. (*Compiled Laws* 1949) (65.9.10)

ARIZONA

Sodomy. Any person who shall commit sodomy, or the crime against nature, with mankind or beast, shall be punished by imprisonment in the State prison not more than five (5) years nor less than one (1) year. Said crime may be committed by the penetration of the mouth or rectum of any human being by the organ of any male person; proof of emission shall not be required, and any sexual penetration, however slight shall be sufficient. (*Annotated Code* 1939) (43.406)

Fellatio and Cunnilingus. Any person who shall wilfully commit any lewd or lascivious act upon or with the body of (or) any part or member thereof, of any male or female person, with the intent of arousing, appealing to or gratifying the lust or passion or sexual desires of either of such persons, in any unnatural manner, shall be guilty of a felony and imprisoned not less than one (1) year nor more than five (5) years. (43.407)

ARKANSAS

Sodomy or Buggery. Every person convicted of sodomy, or buggery, shall be imprisoned in the penitentiary for a period not less than one (1) nor more than twenty-one (21) years. (*Annotated Statutes* 1947) (41.813)

N.B. The original penalty (minimum) was five years in 1947, but this has subsequently been reduced. (Acts 1955 No. 128 para. 1 p. 301)

Proof of actual penetration into the body shall be sufficient to sustain an indictment for the crime against nature. (41.814)

The testimony of the prosecuting witness must be corroborated if that witness were an accomplice, but if witness did not consent, the witness was not an accomplice and testimony need not be corroborated. *Hummel v. State of Arkansas*, 196 S.W. (2d) 594

CALIFORNIA

Crime against nature. Every person who is guilty of the infamous crime against nature, committed with mankind or with any animal, is punishable by imprisonment in the State prison not less than one year. (*Penal Code* 1949) (286)

N.B. In the original code (1949) the words "nor more than ten years" were added to the above, but these were deleted in 1952.

Penetration sufficient to commit the crime. Any sexual penetration, however slight, is sufficient to complete the crime against nature. (287)

Sex perversions. Any person participating in the act of copulating the mouth of one person with the sexual organ of another is punishable by imprisonment in the State prison for not exceeding fifteen years, or by imprisonment in the county jail not to exceed one year. (288a)

The penalty is not less than three years in the State prison if the accused is (a) ten years older than the partner and the partner is under fourteen years of age, (b) if violence or duress has been used.

N.B. These last alternative penalties were added subsequent to the code of 1949.

Anyone convicted of the above acts "or any person who since the said date or at any time hereafter is determined to be a sexual psychopath under the provisions of chapter 4 of part I of division 6 of the Welfare and Institutions Code", is required to register any change of address within ten days, and to be fingerprinted, etc. Non-compliance is a misdemeanour. The law applies to any person convicted irrespective of the State in which the conviction took place. (290)

COLORADO

Crime against nature. The infamous crime against nature or the attempt to commit said crime, either with man or beast, or any unnatural copulation committed, or the attempt to commit any unnatural copulation per anus or per os or in any other way whatsoever shall subject the offender to be imprisoned in the penitentiary for a term of not less than one year and not more than fourteen years.

The solicitation of any unnatural carnal copulation shall subject the offender to confinement in the county jail for not less than thirty days nor more than two years. (*Revised Statutes* 953) (40.2.31)

N.B. Before 1953 the maximum penalty was life imprisonment.

Subject to the provisions of the State constitution, each and every person who may be convicted of the crime of rape, kidnapping, wilful and corrupt perjury or subordination of perjury, arson, burglary, robbery, sodomy or the crime against nature, incest, larceny, forgery, counterfeiting or bigamy, shall be deemed infamous, and shall be therefore incapable of holding any office of honour, trust or profit, of voting at any election, of serving as a juror. (39.10.18).

CONNECTICUT

Bestiality and Sodomy. Any person who has carnal copulation with any beast, or who has carnal knowledge of any man, against the order of nature, unless forced or under fifteen years of age, shall be imprisoned in the State prison for not more than thirty years. (*Revised Statutes* 1949) (8544) 1958 Revision. c.944, sec. 53–216.

DELAWARE

Sodomy; penalty. Whoever shall commit the crime against nature shall be deemed guilty of felony, and shall be fined not exceeding $1,000, and shall be imprisoned not exceeding three years. (*Annotated Code* 1953) (11.831)

FLORIDA

Crime against nature; punishment. Whoever commits the abominable and detestable crime against nature, either with mankind or beast, shall be punished by imprisonment in the State prison not exceeding twenty years. (*Ann. Florida Statutes* 1944) (800.01)

Whoever commits any unnatural or lascivious act with another person shall be punished by fine not exceeding $500, or by imprisonment not exceeding six months. (800.02)

GEORGIA

Sodomy defined. Sodomy is the carnal knowledge and connection against the order of nature, by man with man, or in the same unnatural manner with woman. (*Ann. Code* 1953) (26.5901)

Per anus is not the only way of committing the crime. (17 App. 825) (2)

The punishment of sodomy shall be as follows:

(a) Where committed on a person under the age of sixteen years a sentence to the penitentiary for not less than ten years nor more than thirty years.
(b) Where committed on a person sixteen years or more, by sentence to the penitentiary for not less than one year nor more than ten years.
(c) Where previous conviction or plea of guilty of offence of sodomy is alleged in the indictment and proven on the trial, by sentence to the penitentiary for not less than ten nor more than thirty years. (26.5902)

N.B. This graded system of penalties replaced a penalty at labour for life, unless the jury with the approval of judge recommended that offence should be treated as misdemeanour. (27.2501)

Insertion of the male organ between legs or thighs of another person is not penetration within meaning of the law. *Wharton v. State* 58 App. 439, 198 S.E. 823.

The crime of sodomy, in Georgia, cannot be committed, as defined, between two women; hence a person convicted on an indictment charging her with sodomy, both participants in the act being females, will be discharged on habeas corpus, on the ground that she is being illegally restrained of her liberty, in that the indictment on which she was convicted was null and void. *Thompson v. Aldridge* 187.467 (200 S.E. 799)

HAWAII

Sodomy defined; penalty. Whoever commits sodomy, that is, the crime against nature, either with mankind or any beast, shall be fined not more than $1,000, and imprisoned at hard labor not more than twenty years. (*Laws* 1955) (31:309.34)

Jury may convict on uncorroborated testimony of accomplice. (11 H 571)

Emission need not be shown. (25 H 814, 816)

May be committed per os. (26 H 360)

Disorderly conduct: (g) Frequents or loiters about any public place soliciting men for the purpose of committing a crime against nature or other lewdness. (314.2). Penalty not more than $1,000 or not more than one year imprisonment or both. (314.3)

IDAHO

Crime against nature; punishment. Every person who is guilty of the infamous crime against nature, committed with mankind or with animal, is punishable by imprisonment in the State prison not less than five years. (*Idaho Code* 1948) (18.6605)

State v. Altwater. Included within the meaning of the law are all unnatural copulations committed per os or per anum. (29 Idaho 107)

Any sexual penetration however slight, is sufficient to complete the crime against nature. (18.6606)

Every person who assaults another with intent to commit rape, the infamous crime against nature, mayhem, robbery, or grand larceny, is punishable by imprisonment in the State prison not less than one year nor more than fourteen years. (18.907)

ILLINOIS

Definition; punishment. The infamous crime against nature either with man or beast, shall subject the offender to be punished by imprisonment in the penitentiary for a term of not less than one year and not more than ten years. (*Revised Statutes* 1957) (38.141)

Emission. It shall not be necessary to prove emission to convict any person of the crime against nature. (38.142)

Infamous crimes; disqualification. Every person convicted of the crime of murder, rape . . . sodomy, or other crime against nature . . . shall be deemed infamous, and shall forever thereafter be rendered incapable of holding any office of honour, trust or profit, of voting at any election, or serving as a juror, unless he or she is again restored to such rights by the terms of a pardon for the offence or otherwise according to law. (38.587)

People v. Smith, 258 Ill. 502. The insertion of the tongue does not constitute the crime against nature.

INDIANA

Sodomy. Whoever commits the abominable and detestable crime against nature with mankind or beast; or whoever entices, allures, instigates or aids any person under the age of twenty-one (21) years to commit masturbation or self-pollution shall be deemed guilty of sodomy, and, on conviction shall be fined not less than one hundred dollars ($100) nor more than one thousand dollars ($1,000), to which may be added imprisonment in the State prison not less than two (2) years nor more than fourteen (14) years. (*Indiana Statutes Ann.* 1956) (10.4221)

Glover v. State, 179 Ind. 459. The crime of sodomy includes the offence of copulation by the mouth.

IOWA

Sodomy; definition. Whoever shall have carnal copulation in any opening of the body except sexual parts, with another human being, or shall have carnal copulation with a beast, shall be deemed guilty of sodomy. (*Code* 1950) (705.1)

Any person who shall commit sodomy, shall be imprisoned in the penitentiary for not more than ten years. (705.2)

KANSAS

Crime against nature. Every person who shall be convicted of the detestable and abominable crime against nature, committed with mankind or with beast, shall be punished by confinement and hard labor not exceeding ten years. (*General Statutes* 1949) (21.907)

State v. Hurlbert 118 Kan. 362. Proof of actual lecherous penetration per os sufficient.

KENTUCKY

Sodomy: Buggery. Any person who commits sodomy or buggery, with man or beast, shall be confined in the penitentiary for not less than two nor more than five years. (*Revised Statutes* 1955) (436.050)

LOUISIANA

Crime against nature. Crime against nature is the unnatural carnal copulation by a human being with another of the same or opposite sex or with an animal. Emission is not necessary, and when committed by a human being with another, the use of genital organ of one of the offenders of whatever sex is sufficient to constitute the crime.

   Whoever commits the crime against nature shall be fined not more than $2,000, or imprisoned, with or without hard labour, for not more than five years, or both. (*Revised Statutes* 1950) (14.89)

MAINE

Crime against nature; penalty. Whoever commits the crime against nature, with mankind or with a beast, shall be punished by imprisonment for not less than one year, nor more than ten years. (*Revised Statutes* 1954) (134.3)

MARYLAND

Sodomy. Every person convicted of the crime of sodomy shall be sentenced to the penitentiary for not less than one year nor more than ten years. (*Annotated Code* 1957) (27.553)

Every person who shall be convicted of taking into his or her mouth the sexual organ of any other person or animal, or who shall be convicted of placing his or her sexual organ in the mouth of any other person or animal, or who shall be convicted of committing any other unnatural or perverted sexual practice with any other person or animal, shall be fined not more than one thousand ($1,000) dollars or be imprisoned in a jail or in the House of Correction or in the penitentiary for a period not exceeding ten years, or shall be both fined and imprisoned within the limits above prescribed in the discretion of the court. (27.554)

NOTE. Particular perverted acts need not be specified in the indictment.

MASSACHUSETTS

Sodomy and Buggery. Whoever commits the abominable and detestable crime against nature, either with mankind or with a beast, shall be punished by imprisonment in the State prison for not more than twenty years. (*Ann. Laws* 1956) (272.34)

Unnatural and lascivious acts. Whoever commits any unnatural and lascivious act with another person shall be punished by a fine of not less than $100 nor more than $1,000 or by imprisonment in the State prison for not more than five years, or in jail or the house of correction for not more than two and a half years. (272.35)

Whoever commits any unnatural and lascivious act with a child under the age of sixteen shall be punished by a fine of not less than $100 nor more than $1,000 or by imprisonment in the State prison for not more than five years or in jail or the house of correction for not more than two and one half years, and whoever over the age of twenty-one commits a second or subsequent offence shall be sent to imprisonment in the State prison for a term or not less than five years. (272.35a)

MICHIGAN

Crime against nature or sodomy; punishment. Any person who shall commit the abominable and detestable crime against nature either with mankind or with any animal shall be guilty of a felony, punishable by imprisonment in the State prison not more than fifteen years, or if such person was at the time of the said offence a sexually delinquent person, may be punished by imprisonment in the State prison for an indefinite term, the minimum of which shall be one day and the maximum of which shall be life. (*Michigan Ann. Statutes* 1938 and 1957) (28.335)

Emission need not be proved. In any prosecution for sodomy, it shall not be necessary to prove emission, and any sexual penetration, however slight, shall be deemed sufficient to complete the crime specified in the next preceding section. (28.356)

Any male person over the age of fifteen years who shall debauch and deprave the morals of any boy under fifteen years of age by enticing or soliciting such boy to commit the abominable and detestable crime against nature, either with any man or beast, shall be guilty of a felony punishable by imprisonment in the State prison for not more than five years. (28.572)

MINNESOTA

Sodomy. A person who carnally knows in any manner any animal or bird, or carnally knows any male or female person by the anus or with the mouth, or voluntarily submits to such carnal knowledge; or attempts sexual intercourse with a dead body, is guilty of sodomy, and is punishable with imprisonment in the State prison for not more than twenty years, and any sexual penetration, however slight, shall be sufficient to complete the crime. (*Ann. Statutes* 1947) (617.14)

MISSISSIPPI

Unnatural intercourse. Every person who shall be convicted of the detestable and abominable crime against nature committed with mankind or with a beast, shall be punished by imprisonment in the penitentiary for a term of not more than ten years. (*Annotated Code* 1942) (2413)

State v. Hill, 179 Miss. 732. Cunnilingus by woman is not sodomy.

MISSOURI

The abominable and detestable crime against nature; penalty. Every person who shall be convicted of the detestable and abominable crime against nature, committed with mankind or with beast, with the sexual organs or with the mouth, shall be punished by imprisonment in the penitentiary for not less than two years. (*Ann. Statutes* 1953) (563.230)

MONTANA

Crime against nature. Every person who is guilty of the infamous crime against nature, committed with mankind or with any animal, is punishable by imprisonment in the State prison for not less than five years. (*Revised Code* 1947) (94.4118)

Penetration sufficient to complete the crime. Any sexual penetration, however slight, is sufficient to complete the crime against nature. (94.4119)

No child under the age of sixteen years can be an accomplice to the commission or attempted commission of the infamous crime against nature. (94.4120)

NEBRASKA

Sodomy defined; penalty. Whoever has carnal copulation with a beast, or in any opening of the body except sexual parts with another human being shall be guilty of sodomy and shall be imprisoned in the penitentiary not more than twenty years. (*Revised Statutes* 1943) (28.919)

Sledge v. State, 142 Neb. 350. The crime includes both per os and per anum.

NEVADA

Crime against nature defined. The infamous crime against nature, either with man or beast, shall subject the offender to be punished by imprisonment in the State prison for a term not less than one year and which may extend to life. (*Revised Statutes* 1957) (201.190)

In re Benites, 37 Nev. 145. This section includes all unnatural acts in whatever form or by whatever means perpetrated, and an indictment charging that the accused did unlawfully commit *the infamous crime against nature* with a man, stating the nature of the act was sufficient.

NEW HAMPSHIRE

No specific statute against buggery, sodomy, crime against nature, etc. BUT:
Offences against chastity. 9. Lascivious acts.
Whoever commits any unnatural and lascivious act with another person shall be imprisoned not more than five years or fined not more than $1,000 or both. (*Revised Statutes Ann.* 1955) (579.9)

NEW JERSEY

Sodomy. Sodomy or the infamous crime against nature, committed with man or beast is a high misdemeanour, and shall be punished by a fine of not more than $5,000 or by imprisonment for not more than twenty years or both. (*Statutes Ann.* 1953) (2A: 143.1)

Any person who commits sodomy or the infamous crime against nature with a child under the age of sixteen years, is guilty of a high misdemeanour and shall be punished by imprisonment for not more than thirty years. (2A: 143.2)

NEW MEXICO

Sodomy consists of a person taking into his or her mouth or anus the sexual organ of any person or animal or placing his or her sexual organ in the mouth or anus of any other person or animal. Any penetration however slight is sufficient to complete the crime of sodomy. Both parties may be principals. (*Statutes* 1953 and 1955) (40.7.6)

Any person convicted of the crime of sodomy as defined in section 1 of this Act (40.7.6) shall be imprisoned for not less than one year or fined in any sum not less than $1,000, or both in the discretion of the courts. (40.7.7)

An attempt to commit the above offence is punished by a penalty of not more than ten years imprisonment and a fine of not more than $1,000 dollars. (40.7.8)

NEW YORK

Sodomy (third degree). A person who carnally knows any male or female person by the anus or with the mouth under circumstances not amounting to sodomy in the first degree or sodomy in the second degree is guilty of a misdemeanour. (*Consolidated Laws* 1944 as amended) (690)

NOTE (1) Sodomy in the first degree involves intercourse by the anus or by or with the mouth without the consent of the other person, or when one of the persons is incapable of giving consent by reason of mental or physical weakness or immaturity, or when resistance is forcibly overcome, or when the resistance is prevented by fear of immediate or great bodily harm, or when it is prevented by stupor or weakness produced by an intoxicant, a narcotic or an anaesthetic, or when the other person is in the custody of the law or unconscious. Punished by not more than twenty years imprisonment or an indeterminate sentence.

(2) Sodomy in the second degree involves a relationship between a person of twenty-one or over and a person under the age of eighteen years, under conditions not amounting to first degree sodomy. Punishable by not more than ten years imprisonment.

NORTH CAROLINA

Crime against nature. If any person shall commit the abominable and detestable crime against nature, with mankind or beast, he shall be imprisoned in the State's prison not less than five nor more than sixty years. (*General Statutes* 1953) (14.177)

State v. Fenner, 166 N.C. 247. It includes all unnatural intercourse between male and male.

NORTH DAKOTA

Sodomy defined; punishment. Every person who carnally knows in any manner any animal or bird, or carnally knows any male or female person by the anus or by or with the mouth, or voluntarily submits to such carnal knowledge, or attempts sexual intercourse with a dead body, is guilty of sodomy and shall be punished by imprisonment in the penitentiary for not less than one year nor more than ten years, or in the country jail for not more than one year. Any sexual penetration, however slight, is sufficient to complete the crime. (*Revised Code* of 1943) (12.2207)

OHIO

No person shall have carnal copulation with a beast or in any opening of the body, except sexual parts, with another human being. Whoever violates this section is guilty of sodomy and shall be imprisoned not less than one nor more than twenty years. (*Revised Code* 1954) (2905.44)

OKLAHOMA

Crime against nature. Every person who is guilty of the detestable and abominable crime against nature, committed with mankind or with a beast, is punishable by imprisonment in the penitentiary not exceeding ten years. (*Ann. Statutes* 1937) (21.886)

Any sexual penetration suffices. (21.887)

La Favour v. State, 77 Okl. Cr. 383. Mankind includes male and female.

OREGON

Sodomy (1) Any person who commits sodomy or the crime against nature, or any act or practice of sexual perversity either with mankind or beast, or sustains osculatory relations with the private parts of any person, or permits such relations to be sustained with his private parts, shall be punished upon conviction by imprisonment in the penitentiary for not more than fifteen years.

(2) Proof of actual penetration into the body is sufficient to sustain an indictment for the crime against nature. (*Revised Statutes* 1955) (167.040)

PENNSYLVANIA

Sodomy. Whosoever carnally knows in any manner any animal or bird, or carnally knows any male or female person by the anus or with the mouth, or whoever voluntarily submits to such carnal knowledge, is guilty of sodomy, a felony, and upon conviction thereof, shall be sentenced to pay a fine not exceeding five thousand dollars ($5,000), or to undergo imprisonment, by separate or solitary confinement at labour, not exceeding ten (10) years, or both. (*Ann. Statutes* 1945) (18.4501)

Carnal knowledge shall be deemed complete upon proof of penetration only. (18.4103)

Assault and solicitation to commit sodomy. Whoever, unlawfully and maliciously, assaults another with intent to commit sodomy, or solicits, and incites another to permit and suffer such persons to commit sodomy with him or her, is guilty of a felony, and upon conviction thereof, shall be sentenced to pay a fine not exceeding one thousand dollars ($1,000), or undergo imprisonment, by separate or solitary confinement at labour, not exceeding five (5) years, or both. (18.4502)

RHODE ISLAND

Every person who shall be convicted of the abominable and detestable crime against nature, either with mankind or with any beast, shall be imprisoned not exceeding twenty years nor less than seven years. (*General Laws* 1956) (11.10.1)

Assault with intent to commit, above one to twenty years. (11.5.1)

SOUTH CAROLINA

Buggery. Whoever shall commit the abominable crime of buggery, whether with mankind or with beast, shall, on conviction, be deemed guilty of felony, and shall be imprisoned in the penitentiary for five years, and shall pay a fine of not less than $500, or both, at the discretion of the court. (*Code of Laws* 1952) (16.412)

SOUTH DAKOTA

Crime against nature; penalty; construction. Every person who is guilty of the detestable and abominable crime against nature committed with mankind or with a beast is punishable by imprisonment in the State penitentiary not exceeding ten years.

Any sexual penetration, however slight, is sufficient to complete the crime against nature. (*Code of* 1939) (13.1716)

TENNESSEE

Crimes against nature. Crimes against nature, either with mankind or any beast, are punishable by imprisonment in the penitentiary not less than five nor more than fifteen years. (*Ten. Code* 1955) (39.707)

NOTE. Offenders are also disfranchised. (40.2712)

TEXAS

Sodomy. Whoever has carnal copulation with a beast, or in any opening of the body, except sexual parts, with another human being, or whoever shall use his mouth on the sexual parts of another human being for the purpose of having carnal copulation, or who shall voluntarily permit the use of his own sexual parts in a lewd or lascivious manner by any minor, shall be guilty of sodomy, and upon conviction thereof shall be deemed guilty of a felony, and shall be confined in the penitentiary not less than two (2) nor more than fifteen (15) years. (*Penal Code* 1952) (10.524)

Lewis v. State, 36 Cr. R. 37. Held that woman was included under the term mankind.

UTAH

Every person who assaults another with intent to commit rape, the infamous crime against nature, or mayhem is punishable by imprisonment in the State prison not less than one or more than ten years. (*Penal Code* 1953) (76.7.7)

Every person who is guilty of sodomy or any other detestable and abominable crime against nature, committed with mankind or with any animal with either the sexual organs or the mouth, is punishable by imprisonment in the State prison not less than three years nor more than twenty years. (76.53.22)

State v. Peterson, 81 U. 340. Penetration per os is included in the statute as sodomy.

VERMONT

Lewdness; penalty. A person participating in the act of copulating the mouth of one person with the sexual organ of another shall be imprisoned in the State prison not less than one year nor more than five years. (*Revised Statutes* 1947) (8480)

Lewdness. A person guilty of open and gross lewdness and lascivious behaviour shall be imprisoned not more than five years or fined not more than $300. (8478)

NOTE. If the lewdness occurs with one under sixteen the minimum punishment is one year and the maximum five. (8479)

VIRGINIA

Crime against nature. If any person shall carnally know in any manner any brute animal, or carnally know any male or female person by the anus or by or with the mouth, or voluntarily submit to such a carnal knowledge, he or she shall be guilty of felony and shall be confined in the penitentiary not less than one nor more than three years. (*Code* 1950) (18.98)

WASHINGTON

Every person who carnally knows in any manner any animal or bird; or
who carnally knows any male or female person by the anus or with the
mouth or tongue; or who voluntarily submits to such carnal knowledge;
or who attempts sexual intercourse with a dead body, shall be guilty
of sodomy and shall be punishable as follows: (1) When such an act is
committed upon a child under age of fifteen years by imprisonment in
the State penitentiary for not more than twenty years, (2) In all other
cases by imprisonment in the state penitentiary for not more than ten
years. (*Revised Code* 1957) (9.97.100)

WEST VIRGINIA

Crimes against nature. If any person shall carnally know in any manner
any brute animal, or carnally know any male or female by the anus or by
or with the mouth, or voluntarily submit to such carnal knowledge, he
or she shall be guilty of a felony, and, upon conviction thereof, shall be
confined in the penitentiary not less than one nor more than ten years.
(*Code* 1955) (6068) (61.8.13)

WISCONSIN

Sexual Perversion. Whoever does either of the following may be fined not
more than $500 or imprisoned not more than five years or both: 1. Com-
mits an abnormal act of sexual gratification involving the sex organ of one
person and the mouth or anus of another; or 2. Commits an act of sexual
gratification involving his sex organ and the sex organ, mouth or anus of
an animal. (*Statutes* 1955) (944.17)

WYOMING

Sodomy. Whoever commits the abominable and detestable crime against
nature, by having carnal knowledge of a man or beast; or who being a
male carnally knows any man or woman through the anus, or in any other
manner contrary to nature; and whoever entices, allures, instigates or
aids any person under the age of twenty-one (21) years to commit
masturbation or self-pollution, is guilty of sodomy, and shall be imprisoned in the penitentiary not more than ten years. (*Statutes* 1955)
(9.520)

NOTE ALSO:

DISTRICT OF COLUMBIA

(a) Every person who shall be convicted of taking into his or her mouth or
anus the sexual organ of any other person or animal, or who shall be
convicted of having carnal copulation in an opening of the body except

sexual parts with another person, shall be fined not more than $1,000 or be imprisoned for a period not exceeding ten years. Any person convicted under this section of committing such act with a person under the age of sixteen years shall be fined not more than $1,000 or be imprisoned for a period not exceeding twenty years. And in any indictment for the commission of any of the acts, hereby declared to be offences, it shall not be necessary to set forth the particular unnatural or perverted sexual practice with the commission of which the defendant may be charged, nor to set forth the particular manner in which said unnatural or perverted sexual practice was committed, but it shall be sufficient if the indictment set forth that the defendant committed a certain unnatural and perverted sexual practice with a person or animal, as the case may be: *provided* that the accused on motion, shall be entitled to be furnished with a bill of particulars, setting forth the particular acts which constitute the offence charged.

(b) Any penetration, however slight, is sufficient to complete the crime specified in this section. Proof of emission shall not be necessary. (*Code* 1951) (22.3502)

LAWS OF THE UNITED KINGDOM PUNISHING HOMOSEXUAL OFFENCES

1. *THE SEXUAL OFFENCES ACT*, 1956. (4 and 5 Eliz. 2, c. 69.)

(a) *Buggery*.

(1) It is a felony for a person to commit buggery with another person or with an animal.

(2) Section thirty-nine of this Act (which relates to the competence as a witness of the wife or husband of the accused) does not apply in the case of this section, except on a charge of an offence with a person under the age of seventeen.

(3) For the purpose of the last foregoing subsection a. person shall be presumed, unless the contrary is proved, to have been under the age of seventeen at the time of the offence charged if he is stated in the charge or indictment, and appears to the court, to have been so. (*Section* 12)

R v. Tate, 1908. 2 K.B. 680: *R v. Hartley*, 1941. 1. K.B. 5.

The jury must be warned against accepting the uncorroborated evidence of an accomplice, and failure to do so will lead to the setting aside of the verdict.

(b) *Indecency between men*.

It is an offence for a man to commit an act of gross indecency with another man, whether in public or private, or to be a party to the commission by a man of an act of gross indecency with another man, or to procure the commission by a man of an act of gross indecency with another man. (*Section* 13)

(c) *Indecent assault on a man*.

(1) It is an offence for a person to make an indecent assault on a man.

(2) A boy under the age of sixteen cannot in law give any consent which would prevent an act being an assault for the purpose of this section.

(3) A man who is a defective cannot in law give any consent which would prevent an act being an assault for the purposes of this section, but a person is only to be treated as guilty of an indecent assault on a defective

by reason of that incapacity to consent, if that person knew or had reason to suspect him to be a defective.

(4) Section thirty-nine of the Act (which relates to the competence as a witness of the wife or husband of the accused) does not apply in the case of this section, except on a charge of indecent assault on a boy under the age of seventeen.

(5) For the purposes of the last foregoing subsection a person shall be presumed, unless the contrary is proved, to have been under the age of seventeen at the time of the offence charged if he is stated in the charge or indictment, and appears to the court, to have been so. (*Section* 15)

(d) *Assault with intent to commit buggery.*
(1) It is an offence for a person to assault another person with intent to commit buggery.

(2) Section thirty-nine of this Act (which relates to the competence as a witness of the wife or husband of the accused) does not apply in the case of this section, except on a charge of assault on a person under the age of seventeen.

(3) Do. as in case c. 5. above. (*Section* 16)

(e) *Solicitation by men.*
It is an offence for a man persistently to solicit or importune in a public place for immoral purposes. (*Section* 32)

(f) *Power of arrest in cases of trading in prostitution, or of soliciting by men.*
Anyone may arrest without a warrant a person found committing an offence under section thirty, thirty-one or thirty-two of this Act. (*Section* 41)

(g) *Meaning of "sexual intercourse".*
Where, on the trial of any offence under this Act, it is necessary to prove sexual intercourse (whether natural or unnatural), it shall not be necessary to prove the completion of the intercourse by the emission of seed, but the intercourse shall be deemed complete upon proof of penetration only. (*Section* 44)

(h) *Penalties.* Laid down in second schedule to the Act.   Maximum.

3. (a)	Buggery (section 12)	. .	Life imprisonment.
3. (b)	Attempted Buggery	. .	Ten years imprisonment.
16. (a)	Indecency between men	.	Two years imprisonment.

16. (b) Attempt to procure comm. of act
        of gross indecency by a man with
        another man   .   .   .   Two years imprisonment.

18.   Indecent assault on a man.
    (1) On indictment   .   .   Ten years imprisonment.
    (2) Summarily (s.19 of Mag. Courts
        Act).   .   .   .   .   Six months or £100 fine
                                               or both.

19.   Assault with intent to commit
        buggery   .   .   .   .   Ten years imprisonment.

32.   Solicitation by a man
    (1) On indictment   .   .   Two years imprisonment.
    (2) Summarily   .   .   .   Six months.

NOTE. Offences against by-laws may be punished by £5 fine in magistrates courts.

Where victim of indecent assault is under sixteen, with consent of the accused and the Director of Public Prosecutions if conducting the case, it may be tried in a magistrate's court.

2. SCOTLAND

Special provisions for punishing solicitation by men apply. Every male person soliciting in a public place persistently for immoral purpose may on conviction before a court of summary jurisdiction be imprisoned for a term not exceeding six months with hard labour. (The Immoral Traffic [Scotland] Act 1902. S. 1[1] [b]. The Criminal Law Amendment Act 1912 S. 7[2])

Conviction on indictment for above offence . . . imprisonment with or without hard labour for not more than two years.

Conviction for offence on indictment for second time . . . in addition to prison sentence may be privately whipped. (The Criminal Law Amendment Act. S. 7[5])

NOTE. A fine not exceeding £25 may be substituted for imprisonment. (Summary Jurisdiction [Scotland] Act 1908, section 43)

THE LAW OF EUROPEAN COUNTRIES CONCERNING HOMOSEXUAL OFFENCES

I. BELGIUM

Homosexual acts are not punishable as such, but only if there are circumstances of indecent assault, relations with minors, abuse of authority, violation of public decency, etc. (*Penal Code* 1867)

(a) "Any indecent assault committed without violence or threat against or with the assistance of a child of either sex, before the latter has completed the sixteenth year of age, is punishable with penal servitude." (Art. 372, Belgium Criminal Code)

(b) Punishment varies. If the victim is under sixteen the penalty is fifteen years imprisonment, and consent is no defence. In cases of other assaults if the victim is under twenty-one but over sixteen, the penalty is ten years. For other indecent assaults the penalty is five years.

II. DENMARK

Homosexual acts *per se* ceased to be crimes in 1930. They are only punishable if they involve minors, dependants, affronts to public decency, etc.

(a) Indecency with members of the same sex under the age of fifteen is punishable by six years imprisonment. Such acts with persons under eighteen are punishable with four years imprisonment. Under twenty-one such acts may still be punishable if it is through abuse of superior age, with three years imprisonment. (See articles 225 and 220 of Criminal Code)

(b) "Anyone who violates decency or gives public scandal by lewd behaviour is punishable with imprisonment up to four years or under extenuating circumstances with *haevte* (mild imprisonment from two days to two years) or fine." (Article 232)

(c) Soliciting even without expectation of gain is forbidden by police regulations.

(d) Special provisions apply to sexual acts where both parties are minors.

III. FRANCE

Homosexual acts between consenting adults are not offences unless they involve abuse of authority, fraud, public indecency, or soliciting. They are not mentioned in the Code Napoleon (1810) still in force in France.

(a) "Any attempted or completed indecent assault committed without violence against a child of either sex of the age of less than fifteen years is punishable by penal servitude." (Art. 331)

(b) Attempted or completed indecent assault accompanied by violence on members of either sex is punished without distinction by penal servitude. (Art. 332)

(c) "Anyone who commits a public outrage to decency is punishable with imprisonment from three months to two years, and by a fine from 2,000 francs to 24,000 francs." (Art. 330)

(d) Soliciting is a punishable offence without distinguishing between the sexes of those soliciting and those being solicited. (Law of April 13, 1946. Dalloz. o. 177)

(e) "Whosoever commits an indecent or unnatural act with an individual of his own sex under the age of twenty-one shall be punishable by imprisonment from six months to three years and by a fine from 2,000 to 500,000 francs." (Art. 331 II). (*Note*. No such provision existed in the *Code Napoleon*, and article 331 II is a modification of February 8, 1945, of an original law of August 6, 1942, enacted by the Vichy Government.)

(f) Special provisions apply to sexual acts where both parties are minors. If they are under eighteen the law is mitigated. A minor is not punishable for homosexual acts committed with an adult.

IV. GERMANY

All homosexual acts between males are punishable but the law does not punish such acts between females.

"A male person who commits, or submits to, an act of indecency with another person, is punishable with imprisonment (up to a maximum of five years). In the case of a participant who at the time of the offence was under the age of twenty-one years, the Court may abstain from inflicting punishment if his offence was only very slight." (Article 175 of Criminal Code, introduced in 1935 and confirmed by third criminal law amendment act of August 1953. Homosexual acts between males were also punishable under the criminal code of 1871)

(a) Certain cases of gross indecency are punished with ten years imprisonment (penal servitude).

i. acts of indecency accompanied by violence.

ii. acts of indecency committed by abuse of authority or dependence.

iii. seduction of one under twenty-one by one over twenty-one.

iv. professional prostitution or solicitation. (Art. 175 a)

(b) Indecent acts committed with person below the age of fourteen of either sex is punishable with imprisonment for not less than six months up to penal servitude for ten years. (Article 176 [3])

V. GREECE

Homosexual acts between consenting adults are not punishable unless they involve abuse of authority, seduction, public indecency, etc.

VI. ITALY

Homosexual acts between consenting adults are not offences unless they violate public decency.

(a) "Whoever commits acts of indecency with or in the presence of a person below the age of sixteen is punishable with imprisonment between six months and three years." (Art. 530, I, Italian Penal Code)

(b) "Anyone who commits in a public place, or in a place which is open or exposed to the public, acts of obscenity shall be punished with imprisonment from three months to three years." (Article 527)

VII. NETHERLANDS

Homosexual acts between consenting adults in private are not offences.

(a) Acts of indecency with persons of either sex under sixteen years of age are punishable by up to six years imprisonment. (Article 247)

(b) Public indecency even if unintentionally in presence of third person "shall be punished with imprisonment of up to two years or by fine up to a maximum of 300 guilders". (Article 239)

(c) "Any adult who commits an indecent act with a minor of his own sex of whom he knew or ought to know that he is under the age of twenty-one years is punishable with imprisonment up to a maximum of four years." (Article 248 bis. Enacted in 1911)

N.B. Acts between persons both of whom are between sixteen and twenty-one and which take place in private are not punishable.

Boys under twenty-one are not punishable in connection with homosexual acts committed with adults.

VIII. NORWAY

The Norwegian Criminal Code provides: "Indecent intercourse between male persons, or aiding and abetting therein, shall be punishable with imprisonment for no more than one year." However, it adds "An offender shall be prosecuted only if this is considered necessary in the public interest." (Article 213)

For many years no prosecution has occurred where both parties were over twenty-one years of age. Recommended to be changed so that law confined to minors. (Norwegian Penal Code Commission)

(a) Indecent *intercourse* with child under fourteen is punished by imprisonment for between three and fifteen years: for child between fourteen and sixteen, punishment from six months to five years. (Arts. 195 and 196)
Indecent *acts* with child under sixteen are punishable with imprisonment from six months to three years: under fourteen or within authority or care of offender, six months to three years. (Art. 212 II)
Indecent intercourse with one under eighteen within charge of offender is punishable by imprisonment of up to one year. (Art. 197)

(b) "Whosoever by word, gesture, or improper conduct in a public place, or by any means likely to cause disturbance of the peace, unmistakeably invites or entices to indecent behaviour, shall be punishable by imprisonment up to three months. Imprisonment up to six months can be given for a repeated offence. A fine may be imposed in case of extenuating circumstances." (Art. 378)

IX. SPAIN

Homosexual acts in themselves are not criminal offences. Minors are protected by the ordinary legislation applying to all types of sexual offenders. The laws relating to rogues and vagabonds provide for *measures of security* for criminals whom the courts have declared to be "dangerous and anti-social", and persons who habitually indulge in homosexual behaviour may be imprisoned under these provisions.

X. SWEDEN

Homosexual acts between consenting parties over eighteen are not punishable unless they affront public decency, etc.

(a) Indecency with children (male) below the age of fifteen is punished with imprisonment for not more than two years or penal servitude for not more than four. (18.10.1)

(b) Abuse of authority for homosexual purposes is punishable. (18.10.a.) Acts of public indecency are punishable by fine or imprisonment for not more than two years.

(c) Adults are punishable "for acts of sexual indecency with a person of the same sex under the age of fifteen with penal servitude for a maximum of four years or with imprisonment . . . for acts of sexual indecency with a person of their own sex between the ages of fifteen and eighteen with imprisonment up to two years." (Chap. 18, art. 10)

(d) Any person over the age of eighteen years who has sexual relations with a person of the same sex over the age of eighteen years but under the age of twenty-one years by taking advantage of the other person's inexperience or dependence shall be punished (by penal servitude up to a maximum of two years or by imprisonment). (18.10 III)

(e) Homosexual acts between minors are subject to special provisions.

XI. SWITZERLAND

Homosexual acts between consenting adults in private are not punishable.

(a) Carnal knowledge of children below age of sixteen is punishable with penal servitude. (Art. 191 I) Abuse of authority for homosexual purposes is also punishable. (Art. 194 II)

(b) "Anyone who commits in public an act contrary to decency shall be punishable with imprisonment or fine." (Art. 203)
"Anyone who publicly and with indecent intent importunes a person who has given him no reason for such acts shall upon complaint be punishable by arrest or fine." (Art. 205)

(c) "Whosoever persuades a young person of the same sex over the age of sixteen years to commit or submit to an act of indecency shall be liable to imprisonment." (Art. 194) (Young person, fourteen to twenty)

(d) Offences between minors are dealt with more leniently.

XII. AUSTRIA

As in Germany all forms of "indecency against nature" are punishable. The penalty is five years penal servitude. First offenders may be placed on probation and the sentence reduced from three to six months.

PROPOSALS OF THE AMERICAN LAW INSTITUTE ON HOMOSEXUAL OFFENCES

SODOMY AND RELATED OFFENCES. s.207.5

1. *Deviate sexual intercourse by force or its equivalent.*

A person who causes another to carry out or submit to any act of deviate sexual intercourse commits a felony of the second degree if:

(a) The victim is compelled to participate by force or violence or out of fear that death or serious physical injury or extreme pain is about to be inflicted on him or a member of his family, or by threat to commit any felony of the first degree; or

(b) For the purpose of preventing the victim from resisting, the actor administers or employs without the victim's knowledge or consent, drugs, intoxicants or other substances or force resulting in a major deficiency of ordinary power to make judgments or control behaviour; or

(c) the victim is unconscious or physically powerless to resist; or

(d) the victim is less than ten years old (whether or not the actor is aware of that).

2. *Gross Imposition.*

A person who causes another to carry out or submit to an act of deviate sexual intercourse in situations not covered by s. (1) commits a felony of the third degree if:

(a) The victim is compelled to participate by any intimidation (which would prevent resistance by a person of ordinary resolution, reasonably calculated to prevent resistance); or

(b) The actor knows that the victim's submission is due to substantially complete incapacity to appraise or control his own behaviour, but this paragraph shall not apply where a victim over eighteen years of age loses that capacity as a result of voluntary use of drugs (or intoxicants) in the company of the actor; or

(c) The victim submits because he is unaware that a sexual act is being committed upon him; or

(d) The victim is less than eighteen years old and the actor is at least five years older than the victim, but it shall be a defence under this paragraph if the actor proves that the victim had previously engaged promiscuously in deviate sexual intercourse.

3. *Minors, Wards and Persons in Custody.*
A person who causes another to carry out or submit to an act of deviate sexual intercourse in situations not covered by s. (1) and (2) commits a misdemeanour if:

(a) The victim is less than twenty-one years old and the actor is charged with his care, treatment, protection or education; or

(b) The victim is in custody of law or detained in hospital, school, or other institution and the actor is associated in any capacity with his custody or control or with the institution or authority having such custody or control.

4. *Consensual Sodomy: Public Solicitation.*
A person who engages in an act of deviate sexual intercourse or who in any public place solicits another with whom he had no previous acquaintance to engage in deviate sexual intercourse commits a misdemeanour.

5. *Prompt Complaint: Corroboration.*
Subsection 5 of s. 207.4 shall apply to offences under subsections (1), (2) and (3) of this section.

NOTE: The subsection reads: No prosecution may be instituted or maintained under this section unless the offence was brought to the notice of public authority by complaint or otherwise within six months after its occurrence or, where the victim was less than sixteen years old or otherwise incompetent to make complaint, within six months after a competent person specially interested in the victim, e.g. a parent or guardian, learns of the offence. No person shall be convicted of an offence under this section upon the uncorroborated testimony of the alleged victim.

6. *Definition.*
Deviate sexual intercourse means penetration by the male sex organ into any opening of the body of a human being or animal, other than carnal knowledge within s. 207.4, and any sexual penetration of the vulva or anus of a female or by an animal.

MODEL PENAL CODE, APRIL 1955, DRAFT 4. pp. 91–3

NOTE: Classification of Offences.

Under s.1.05 of the Code, a felony is any offence which carries a penalty of more than one year; a misdemeanour an offence with a penalty of three months to a year; a petty misdemeanour an offence carrying a penalty of up to three months.

s.6.06 provides that the penalty for a felony of the first degree shall be one year to twenty years with a maximum of life imprisonment; for a felony of the second degree one year or three years with a maximum of ten years; for a felony of the third degree a minimum of not less than one year nor more than two years and a maximum of five years.

PROPOSED BILL TO LEGALIZE EUTHANASIA

published by the Euthanasia Society of America

An Act to amend the public health law, and the penal law, in relation to voluntary euthanasia.

The people of the State of New York, represented in Senate and Assembly, do enact as follows:

SECTION ONE

Chapter forty-nine of the laws of 1909, entitled An Act in relation to the public health, constituting chapter forty-five of the consolidated laws, is hereby amended by adding thereto a new article, to be article fifteen, to read as follows:

Article 15. Voluntary Euthanasia
Section 300. Definitions.
       301. Who may receive euthanasia.
       302. Jurisdiction of courts.
       303. Application to courts.
       304. Investigation and report of committee appointed by court.
       305. Administration of euthanasia.
       306. Immunity from criminal or civil liability.

Sec. 300. Definitions. As used in this article:
"Euthanasia" means the termination of human life by painless means for the purpose of ending severe physical suffering.
"Patient" means the person desiring to receive euthanasia.
"Physician" means any person licensed to practise medicine in the State of New York.

Sec. 301. Who may receive euthanasia. Any person of sound mind over twenty-one years of age who is suffering from severe physical pain caused by a disease for which no remedy affording lasting relief or recovery is at the time known to medical science may have euthanasia administered.

The desire to anticipate death by euthanasia under these conditions shall not be deemed to indicate mental impairment.

Sec. 302. *Jurisdiction of courts.* Any justice of the Supreme Court of the judicial district, in which the patient resides or may be, or any judge of a county court of any county in which the patient resides or may be, to whom a petition for euthanasia is presented, shall have jurisdiction of and shall grant euthanasia upon the conditions and in conformity with the provisions of this article.

Sec. 303. *Application to court.* A petition for euthanasia must be in writing signed by the patient in the presence of two witnesses who must add their signatures and the post-office addresses of their domicile. Such petition must be made in substantially the following form:

To the...Court
I...........................residing at.....................
hereby declare as follows: I am .... years of age and am suffering severe physical pain caused, as I am advised by my physician, by a disease for which no remedy affording lasting relief or recovery is at this time known to medical science.

I am desirous of anticipating death by euthanasia and hereby petition for permission to receive euthanasia.

The names and addresses of the following persons are as follows or, if unknown to me, I so state:

Father ....
Mother ....
Spouse..................................
Children ....
Uncles ....
Aunts...................................
    Signed...................................
In the presence of
.... residing at ....
.... residing at ....
Date.......................

Such petition must be accompanied by a certificate signed by the patient's attending physician in substantially the following form:

To the.....................................Court

I......................... of...............................
do hereby certify as follows:

I have attended the patient,...................................
since.......................................

It is my opinion and belief that the patient is suffering severe physical pain caused by a disease for which no remedy affording lasting relief or recovery is at the present time known to medical science.

The disease from which the patient is suffering is known as..........
....

I am satisfied that the patient understands the nature and purpose of the petition in support of which this certificate is issued and that such disease comes within the provisions of section 301 of article fifteen of the Public Health Law.

Signature.....................................
Date...................... Medical Qualifications..............

If, for any reason, the patient is unable to write, he may execute the petition by making his mark which shall be authenticated in the manner provided by law.

Sec. 304. *Investigation and report of committee appointed by court.* The judge or justice to whom a petition for euthanasia has been presented shall appoint a committee of three competent persons, who are not opposed to euthanasia as herein provided, of whom at least two must be physicians and members of a county or district medical society, who shall forthwith examine the patient and such other persons as they deem advisable or as the court may direct and, within five days after their appointment, shall report to the court whether or not the patient understands the nature and purpose of the petition and comes within the provisions of section 301 of this article. The court must either grant or deny the petition within three days of its receipt.

The said committee shall serve without compensation.

If the said committee shall report in the affirmative the court shall grant the petition unless there is reason to believe that the report is erroneous or untrue, in which case the court shall state in writing the reason for denying the petition.

If the petition shall be denied an appeal may be taken to the appellate division of the supreme court, and/or to the Court of Appeals.

Sec. 305. *Administration of euthanasia.* When the petition has been granted as herein provided, euthanasia shall be administered in the presence of the committee, or any two members thereof, appointed according to section 304 of this article, by a person chosen by the patient or by said committee, or any two members thereof, with the patient's consent; but no person shall be obliged to administer or to receive euthanasia against his will.

Sec. 306. Immunity from criminal or civil liability. A person to whom euthanasia has been administered under the conditions of this act shall not be deemed to have died a violent or unnatural death nor shall any physician or person who has administered or assisted in the administration thereof be deemed to have committed any offence criminal or civil, or be liable to any person whatever for damages or otherwise.

SECTION TWO

The penal law is hereby amended by adding thereto a new section, to be section 1056, to read as follows:

Sec. 1056. Application of article to euthanasia. Death resulting from euthanasia administered pursuant to and in accordance with the provisions of article fifteen of the public health law shall not constitute a crime or be punishable under any provisions of this act.

SECTION THREE

This act shall take effect immediately.

SELECT BIBLIOGRAPHY

Chapter 1

ACTON, Lord, *Essays on Freedom and Power*, New York, 1955.

AQUINAS, Thomas, *Summa Theolobica—Treatise on Law*, I-II, q.XC–CVIII.

ALLEN, C., *Legal Duties*, Oxford 1931.

AMES, J. B., "Law and Morals", *Harvard Law Review*, 22: 97 (1908).

ANON., "Law or Sin", Leading Article in *The Times*, March 19, 1959.

ARISTOTLE, *Politics* (translated Ernest Barker), Oxford 1950.

AUGUSTINE, *The City of God*, London 1950.

AUSTIN, J., *The Province of Jurisprudence Determined and the Uses of the Study of Jurisprudence*, London 1954.

BARKER, E., *Essays on Government*, Oxford 1951.

——*Traditions of Civility*, Cambridge 1948.

BARTH, K., "The Christian Community and the Civil Community", in *Against the Stream*, London 1954.

——*Church and State*, London 1959.

BENNETT, John C., *Christians and the State*, New York 1958.

BERNS, Walter, *Freedom, Virtue and the First Amendment*, Louisiana 1957.

BERTKE, S., *The Possibility of Invincible Ignorance of the Natural Law*, Washinton, D.C. 1941.

BLANSHARD, Paul, *American Freedom and Catholic Power*, Boston 1949.

BOUYER, Louis, *The Spirit and Forms of Protestantism*, London 1956.

BROWN, Brendan F., "The Natural Law Basis of Juridical Institutions in the Anglo-American Legal System", *Catholic University of America Law Review*, 4: 81–94 (1954).

BRINTON, Crane, *A History of Western Morals*, New York 1959.

BRUNNER, Emil, *The Divine Imperative*, Westminster, Maryland 1943.

BURCKHARDT, Jacob, *Force and Freedom*, New York 1943.

CAHILL, W. F. "One Phase of the New Debate on the Iniquitous Law", *The Catholic Lawyer*, 5: 119 (Spring 1959).

——"Some General Criteria of Morality", *The Catholic Lawyer*, 4: 41 (Winter 1958).

CALVIN, John, Institutes of the Christian Religion, (2 vols) London 1935.

COGLEY, John, (ed.), *Religion in America*, New York 1958.

COHEN, J., ROBSON, R. A. H., and BATES, A., "Ascertaining the Moral Sense of the Community", *Journal of Legal Education*, 8: 137 (1955).

COMMAGER, Henry, Steele, *Majority Rule and Minority Rights*, London 1943.

CONNERY, John R., "Religious Pluralism and Public Morality", America, February 21 1959.

CORWIN, Edward S., *The "Higher Law" Background of American Constitutional Law*, Cornell 1957.

DAWSON, Christopher, *Religion and the Modern State*, London 1956.

D'ENTRÈVES, A. P., *Natural Law*, London 1952.

DUFF, Edward, *The Social Thought of the World Council of Churches*, New York 1956.

DEVLIN, Patrick, *The Enforcement of Morals*, London 1959.

EDWARDS, Quentin, *What is Unlawful?*, London 1959.

EHLER, S. Z., and MORRALL, J. B., *Church and State through the Centuries*, London 1954.

FAGAN, Edward T., "Natural Law", *The Catholic Lawyer*, 2: 324 (October 1956).

FORD, John and KELLY, Gerald, *Contemporary Moral Theology*, Westminster, Maryland 1958.

FRIEDMANN, W., *Law in a Changing Society*, London 1959.

FLETCHER, Joseph, *Morals and Medicine*, Princeton 1954.

FULLER, Lon L., "Positivism and Fidelity to Law—A Reply to Professor Hart", *Harvard Law Review*, 71: 630–672 (February 1958).

GILBY, Thomas, *Between Community and Society*, London 1953.

——*Principality and Polity*, London 1958.

——"The Crimination of Sin", Blackfriars, 41: 53–61 (March 1960).

GOBLE, G. W., "The Dilemma of the Natural Law", *The Catholic Lawyer* 2: 226 (July 1956).

GOODHART, A. L., *English Law and the Moral Law*, London 1953.

HALL, Jerome, *General Principles of the Criminal Law*, Indiana 1947.

HARDING, Arthur, A., (ed.), *Religion, Morality and Law*, Dallas Texas 1956.

HART, H. L. A., "Immorality and Treason", *The Listener*, 62: 162–3, July 30, 1959.

——"Positivism and the Separation of Law and Morals", *Harvard Law Review*, 71: 593–629 (February 1958).

HAWKINS, D. J. B., *Man and Morals*, London 1960.

INGE, W. R., *Christian Ethics and Moral Problems*, London 1930.

KEGLEY, C. W., and BRETALL, R. W., *Reinhold Niebuhr. His Religious, Social and Political Thought*, New York 1956.

KELSEN, Hans, "The Pure Theory of Law", *The Law Quarterly Review* 50: 474 (1934) and 51: 517 (1935).

KENEALY, William J., "Whose Natural Law?", *The Catholic Lawyer* 1: 259 (October 1955).

KENNY, Terence, *The Political Thought of John Henry Newman*, London 1957.

LAMB, George, (trans.), *Tolerance and the Catholic*, New York 1955.

LANGMEAD CASSERLEY, J. V., *Morals and Man in the Social Sciences*, London 1951.

LECLER, Joseph, *The Two Sovereignties*, London 1952.

LEO XIII, "Immortale Dei" (1885) in *The Pope and the People*, London 1932.

———"Libertas Praestantissimum" (1888) in *The Pope and the People*, London 1932.

LIPPMANN, Walter, *Essays in the Public Philosophy*, Boston 1955.

MARITAIN, Jacques, *Freedom in the Modern World*, London 1935.

———*Man and the State*, London 1954.

———*The Person and the Common Good*, New York 1947.

MURRAY, John Courtney, Collection of articles by, *Catholic Mind*, 57: No. 1143 (May–June 1959).

———"For the Freedom and Transcendence of the Church" *The American Ecclesiastical Review*, 126: 28.

———"Freedom, Responsibility and the Law", *The Catholic Lawyer*, 2: 214 (July 1956).

———"Governmental Repression of Heresy", Proceedings of the Catholic Theological Society of America, Washington, D.C. 1949, pp. 26–98.

———"On the Structure of the Church-State Problem", in *The Catholic Church in World Affairs*, ed. Waldemar Gurian and M. A. Fitzsimons, Notre Dame, Indiana 1954.

———"The Making of a Pluralist Society—a Catholic View", *Religious Education*, 53: 521 (November-December 1958).

———"The Problem of the Religion of the State", *The American Ecclesiastical Review*, 124: 327 (1951).

———Other articles by Fr Murray have appeared in *Theological Studies*. Note especially: 9: 491 (1948), 10: 177 (1949), and 12: 155 1951).)

———*We Hold These Truths*, New York 1960.

NIEBUHR, H. Richard, "Theology, Not Queen but Servant", *Journal of Religion*, 35: 1–5 (1955).

NIEBUHR, Reinhold, *Does the State and Nation belong to God or the Devil?*, London 1937.

———*Love and Law in Protestantism and Catholicism*, London 1954.

———*The Nature and Destiny of Man*, Volume I, London 1941.

———Volume II, London 1943.

OLIVECRONA, Karl, (ed.), *Inquiries into the Nature of Law and Morals*, Stockholm 1953.

O'SULLIVAN, Richard, Christian Philosophy in the Common Law, (*Aquinas Papers No. 6*), Oxford 1947.

———"Natural Law and the Common Law", *Transactions of the Grotius Society*, 31: 117–38 (1945).

———*The Inheritance of the Common Law*, London 1950.

———*What is a Christian Country?*, London 1945.

OTTAVIANI, Alfredo, Cardinal, "Church and State: Some Present Problems in the light of the teaching of Pius XII", *The American Ecclesiastical Review* 128: 321 (1953).

PETRAZYCKI, Leon, *Law and Morality*, Cambridge 1955.

PIUS XII, Address to the Fifth National Convention of the Union of Italian Catholic Jurists, December 9, 1953, *The Pope Speaks*, Maryland 1: 64.

———Address to First International Congress on Histopathology of the Nervous System, September 14, 1952, *The Catholic Mind* 51: 305.

———Address to Seventh International Congress of Catholic Doctors, September 11, 1956, *The Catholic Lawyer* 3: 242 (July 1957).

———"Humani Generis", encyclical, August 12, 1950, *Acta Apostolicae Sedis*, 42: 561–78 (1950).

POLLOCK, Frederick, *A First Book of Jurisprudence*, London 1923.

POUND, Roscoe, "Fifty Years of Jurisprudence", *Harvard Law Review*, 51: 777–812 (1938).

———*Law and Morals*, Oxford 1926.

RACKHAM, H., *Aristotle's Ethics for English Readers*, Oxford 1944.

RADCLIFFE, Lord, *The Problem of Power*, London 1958.

RAMSEY, Paul, (ed.), *Faith and Ethics*. The Theology of H. Richard Niebuhr, New York 1955.

Report of the Committee on Homosexual Offences and Prostitution, (Wolfenden Report), H.M.S.O. Cmd. 247, London 1957.

ROMMEN, H., *The State in Catholic Thought*, St Louis 1945.

RUSSELL, Ralph, "English and American Democracy and the Papacy", *The Downside Review*, 72: 30–49 (Winter 1953–4).

SCHWARZ, L. B., "Ascertaining the Moral Sense of the Community", *Journal of Legal Education*, 8: 319 (1956).

Symposium on Law and Christianity, *Oklahoma Law Review*, 12: 45–146 (February 1959).

Symposium on Law and Christianity, *Vanderbilt Law Review*, 10: 879–968 (August 1957).

Symposium: Religion and the Free Society (*The Fund for the Republic*). New York 1958.

Symposium: The Churches and the Public (*The Fund for the Republic*). Santa Barbara, California, 1960.

Symposium: "What Should be the Relation of Morals to Law? A Round Table", *Journal of Public Law*, 1: 259–322 (1952).

TILLICH, Paul, *Love, Power and Justice*, Oxford 1954.

TODD, John M., (ed.), *The Springs of Morality*, New York 1956.

TROELTSCH, E., *Social Teaching of the Christian Churches*, New York 1949.

VANN, Gerald, "What is Natural?", *Commonweal* 59: 274–6 (December 1953).

VISSER 'T HOOFT, W. A., and OLDHAM, J. H., *The Church and its Function in Society*, London 1937.

WEIGEL, G., "The Church and the Democratic State", *Theology Digest*, 1: 169–75 (Autumn 1953).

WILLIAMS, Glanville, *The Sanctity of Life and the Criminal Law*, New York 1957.

WOLIN, Sheldon, S., "Politics and Religion: Luther's Simplistic Imperative", *The American Political Science Review*, 56: 24–42 (1950).

WOLLHEIM, Richard, "Crime, Sin and Mr Justice Devlin", *Encounter*, 13: 34–40 (November 1959).

Chapter 2

BAILEY, D. S., *The Mystery of Love and Marriage*, London 1952.

BEST, WINFIELD and JAFFEE, F. S., *Simple Methods of Contraception*, New York 1958.

BONNAR, A., *The Catholic Doctor*, 6th ed., New York 1952.

CARNEY, F. W., *The Purposes of Christian Marriage*, Washington 1950.

COGLEY, J., "Controversy in Connecticut" *Commonweal*, 67: 657 (March 28, 1958).

"Contraceptives and the Law", *University of Chicago Law Review*, 6: 260–9 (February 1939).

COUGHLAN, Robert, "Birth Control Challenge", *Life International*, 28: 69 (February 29, 1960).

DAVIS, H., *Contraception: Its Moral Aspect and Implications*, London 1933.

DE GUCHTENEERE, R., *Judgment on Birth Control*, New York 1931.

DE LESTAPIS, S., *La Limitation des Naissances*, Paris 1959.

DENNETT, M. W., *Birth Control Laws*, New York 1926.

DOMS, H., *The Meaning of Marriage*, New York 1939.

Ethical and Religious Directives for Catholic Hospitals, St Louis 1955.

EVERSLEY, D. E. C., *Social Theories of Fertility and the Malthusian Debate*, Oxford 1959.

FAGLEY, R. M., "Population and International Development", *Advance*, May 23, 1958.

———*The Population Explosion and Christian Responsibility*, New York 1960.

FINN, J. "Controversy in New York", *Commonweal*, September 12, 1958

FINNEY, P. and O'BRIEN, P., *Moral Problems in Hospital Practice*, St Louis 1956.

FLETCHER, J., *Morals and Medicine*, Princeton 1954.

FORD, J. C., "Contraception", *Theological Studies*, 5: 506–10 (December 1944).

FREEDMAN, R. F., WHELPTON, Pascal, K., and CAMPBELL, A. A. "Family Planning in the U.S." *Scientific American* 200: 50, (April 1959).

Ibid: *Family Planning, Sterility and Population Growth*, New York 1958.

GIBBONS, W. J., *The Catholic Value System in Relation to Human Fertility*, Princeton 1949.

———"Fertility Control in the light of some recent Catholic statements", *Eugenics Quarterly*, 3: 7 (March 1956).

GILBY, Thomas, "First and Seconds in Sex", *Blackfriars*, 41: 272–83 (July–August 1960).

GOOD, F. L., and KELLY, O. F., *Marriage, Morals and Medical Ethics*, Dublin 1952.

GRIESE, N. O., *The Morality of Periodic Continence*, Washington 1942.

HILL, R., STYCOS, J. Mayone, and BACK, K., *The Family and Population Control*, Chapel Hill 1959.

HIMES, N. E., *Medical History of Contraception*, Baltimore 1936.

———*The Truth about Birth Control*, New York 1931.

JAMES, E. O., *Marriage and Society*, London 1952.

"Judicial Regulation of Birth Control under Obscenity Laws", *Yale Law Journal*, 50: 682–9 (February 1941).

KALVEN, H., "A Special Corner of Civil Liberties", *New York University Law Review* 31: 1223–1229 (1956).

KELLY, G., "Catholic Teaching on Contraception and Sterilization", *Linacre Quarterly*, 21: 72–79, 110–118 (August–November 1954).

———"Official Statement on Rhythm", *Linacre Quarterly*, 19: 39 (1952).

———*Medico-Moral Problems*, St Louis 1956.

LAMBETH CONFERENCE 1958, THE, London 1958.

LAMBETH CONFERENCES 1867–1930, THE, London 1948.

LATZ, L., *The Rhythm of Sterility and Fertility in Women*, Chicago 1944.

L. F. jr., "Constitutional Law, Police Power, Birth Control and Contraceptives", *George Washington Law Review*, 7: 255-7 (December 1938).

LORIMER, F., BOURGEOIS-PICHAT, J. and KIRK, D., "Inquiry concerning some ethical principles relating to human reproduction", *Cross-Currents*, 8: 24-42 (Winter 1958).

MAHONEY, E. J., " 'The Perverted Faculty' Argument against Birth Prevention", *The Ecclesiastical Review*, 79: 133-145 (August 1928).

MALTHUS, T., *An Essay on the Principle of Population*, London 1798.

MCAULIFFE, M. F., *Catholic Moral Teaching on the Nature and Object of Conjugal Love*, Washington D.C. 1954.

MCCORMACK, A., *Overpopulation. Is Birth Control the Answer?*, London 1959.

———*People, Space, Food*, London 1960.

———*Pius XII and Overpopulation*, London 1960.

MEDAWAR, P. B., *The Future of Man: The Reith Lectures 1959*, London 1960.

MEIER, R. L., *Modern Science and the Human Fertility Problem*, London 1959.

MILES, D. D., "The Constitutionality of Anti-Birth Control Legislation", *Wyoming Law Journal*, 7: 138-42 (1952-3).

MOORE, E. R., *The Case against Birth Control*, New York 1931.

MURPHY, E. F., "St Thomas and Birth Control", *The American Ecclesiastical Review*, 66: 497 (April 1922).

NEVETT, A., *The Population Dilemma*, London 1959.

NIEBUHR, R., *The Nature and Destiny of Man*, New York 1949.

O'GALLAGHAN, D., Fertility Control by Homonal Medication, *The Irish Theological Quarterly* 27: 1-15 (January 1960).

PIUS XI. *Casti Connubii—On Christian Marriage*, New York 1931.

PIUS XII. Address to Catholic Midwives 1951, *Acta Apostolicae Sedis*, 43: 835-54.

———Address to Catholic Delegates World Population Congress, September 9, 1954. *The Catholic Mind*, 53: 256.

———Address to National Congress of Family Front, November 26, 1951, *Acta Apostolicae Sedis*, 43: 855-860.

———Address to Seventh International Haematological Congress, 1958, *Acta Apostolicae Sedis*, 50: 734-5.

———*Summi Pontificatus*, October 20, 1939, *Acta Apostolicae Sedis*, 21: 426.

PLACE, F. (ed. N. E. Himes), *Illustrations and Proofs of the Principle of Population*, London 1930.

Population Policy in Great Britain, London P.E.P. 1948.

RUSSELL, J. *World Population and World Food Supplies*, London 1955.

——"Christian Theology and the Population Problem", *The Month*, 19: 197 (April 1958).

Report on Responsible Parenthood and the Population Problem (Oxford Conference, April 1959), *The Ecumenical Review*, 12: 85–92 (October 1959).

Report of the Royal Commission on Population, *Cmd.* 7695. London 1949.

SANGER, M., *Autobiography*, New York 1938.

——*My Fight for Birth Control*, New York 1931.

SCHWITALLA, A. M., "Contraception", *Catholic Encyclopaedia Supplement II*, Vol. XVIII, New York 1954.

"Some Legal Aspects of the Birth Control Problem", *Harvard Law Review*, 45: 723–9, (February 1932).

STAMP, L. Dudley, *Our Developing World*, London 1960.

STONE, A. and PILPEL, H. F., "The Social and Legal Status of Contraception", *North Carolina Law Review*, 22: 212–25 (April 1944).

STOPES, M., *Contraception: Its Theory, History and Practice*, London 1934.

——*Roman Catholic Methods of Birth Control*, London 1933.

SULLOWAY, A. H., *Birth Control and Catholic Doctrine*, Boston 1959.

SUTHERLAND, H., *Control of Life*, London 1951.

——*Laws of Life*, London 1935.

Symposium on Morals, Medicine and the Law, *New York University Law Review*, 31: 1157–1245 (1956).

Symposium on Emigration, *The Catholic Lawyer*, 4: 103–151 (Spring 1958).

TESSON, E., "L'Eglise et la régulation des naissances" *Etudes* 291: 375–385 (December 1956).

The Family in Contemporary Society, London 1958.

"The Use of Drugs for Contraception", *The Guardian*, March 22, 1960.

THOMAS, J. L., *Marriage and Rhythm*, London 1957.

TIETZE, C., POLIAKOFF, S. R. and ROCK, J., "The Clinical Effectiveness of the Rhythm Method of Contraception", *Journal of Fertility and Sterility*, 2: 444 (1951).

TROWBRIDGE, C. P., "Catholicism Fights Birth Control", *New Republic*, January 22, 1945.

UNDERWOOD, K., *Protestant and Catholic*, Boston 1957.

World Population and Resources, London P.E.P. 1955.

UNITED NATIONS PUBLICATIONS

ST/SOA Series A. Population Studies, Reports on Interrelationships between population growth and economic and social changes.

Especially:

No. 17. *Determinants and Consequences of Population Trends* (1954).

No. 28. *The Future Growth of World Population* (1958).

Report of Population Commission 1957 (UNESCO).

Background Facts on World Population and Population Trends 1957 (UNESCO).

The Demographic Year Books, 1956, 1957, 1958, 1959.

Proceedings of the World Population Conference 1954.

WARNER, H. C., "Theological Issues of Contraception", *Theology*, 57: 8–14 (January 1954).

WHITE, V., "The Ethics of Contraception", *Clergy Review*, 7: 365 (1934).

WILLIAMS, Glanville, *The Sanctity of Life and the Criminal Law*, New York 1957.

WOODSIDE, M., *Sterilization in North Carolina*, Chapel Hill 1950.

ZEEGERS, J. L., "The Meaning of the Population Problem of the World", *Cross Currents*, 8: 22 (Winter 1958).

ZIMMERMAN, A. F., *Overpopulation*, Washington D.C. 1947.

———*Overpopulation*, The *"Catholic Viewpoint"*, London 1959.

Chapter 3

Artificial Human Insemination. The Report of a Commission appointed by His Grace the Archbishop of Canterbury, London 1948.

Artificial Human Insemination. The Report of a Conference held under the auspices of the Public Morality Council, London 1947.

Artificial Insemination by Donor: Two Contributions to a Christian Judgment, London 1960.

BARTHOLOMEW, G. W., "Legal Implications of Artificial Insemination", *Modern Law Review*, 21: 236 (May 1958).

BARTON, M., WALKER, K. and WIESNER, B. P., "Artificial Insemination", *British Medical Journal*, I: 40, (January 13, 1945).

BONNAR, A., "A.I.D. and A.I.H.", *The Tablet*, 211: 163 (February 15, 1958).

BOSC, J., "La fécondation artificielle", *Reforme Hebdomodaire Protestant Français*, 4: No. 171 (June 26, 1948).

CONNELL, F. J., "Artificial Insemination", *The American Ecclesiastical Review*, 112: 141 (1945).

Contributed. "The Secret Lords of Birth", *Justice of the Peace and Local Government Review*, 122: 183 (March 22, 1958).

CLIFFORD, J. J., "Sterility Tests and their Morality", *The Ecclesiastical Review*, 58: 364 (1942).

DAVIS, Henry, *Artificial Human Fecundation*, New York 1951.

——*Moral and Pastoral Theology*, Vol. II, London 1949.

DEHAUT, F., *De la fécondation artificielle dans l'espèce humaine comme moyen de remedier à certaines causes de sterilité chez l'homme et chez la femme*, Paris 1865.

FAIRFIELD, Letitia, "The Perils of A.I.D.", *The Tablet*, 211: 78 (January 25, 1958).

FLETCHER, Joseph, *Morals and Medicine*, Princeton 1947.

FLOOD, Peter, (ed.), *New Problems in Medical Ethics*, Vol. II, Maryland 1952.

FOLSOME, C. E., "The Status of Artificial Insemination", *American Journal of Obstetrics and Gynaecology*, 45: 917 (1943).

FORBES, R., "The Medico-Legal Aspects of Artificial Insemination", *Medico-Legal and Criminal Review*, 12: 138-152 (1944).

GITTINGER, D. W., "Artificial Insemination: Its Place in Washington Law", *Washington Law Review*, 32: 280 (1957).

GLOVER, William K., *Artificial Insemination among Human Beings*, Washington D.C. 1948.

HAHLO, H. R., "Some Legal Aspects of Human Artificial Insemination", *South African Law Journal*, 74: 167 (May 1957).

HANLEY, T. R., "The Natural Law on Marriage", *The Ecclesiastical Review*, 108: 195-208, 298-309.

HEALY, Edwin F., *Medical Ethics*, Chicago 1956.

HOLLOWAY, A. D., "Artificial Insemination: An Examination of the Legal Aspects", *American Bar Association Journal*, 43: 1089 (December 1957).

HOYT, M., "Artificial Insemination—Legal Status of Child", *Wisconsin Law Review*, 1950: 136-147 (January 1950).

HUBBARD, H. A., "A Reply to Dean Tallin", *Canadian Bar Review*, 34: 425 (1956).

HUXLEY, Julian, *The Uniqueness of Man*, London 1941.

KELLY, Gerald, "Artificial Insemination: Theological and Natural Law Aspects", *University of Detroit Law Journal*, 33: 135 (1955-6).

——"Directives on Artificial Insemination", *Linacre Quarterly*, 22: 90 (August 1955).

——*Medico-Moral Problems*, St. Louis 1956.

——"The Morality of Artificial Fecundation", *American Ecclesiastical Review*, 101: 107 (1939).

——"Moral Aspects of Artificial Insemination", *Linacre Quarterly*, 14: 19-24 (1947).

KELLY, Gerald, "Notes on Moral Theology", *Theological Studies*, 7: 106–9 (1947).

———"Teaching of Pius XII on Artificial Insemination", *Linacre Quarterly*, 23: 5–17, (February 1956).

KOERNER, Alfred, "Medico-Legal Considerations in Artificial Insemination", *Louisiana Law Review*, 8: 484–503 (May 1948).

The Lambeth Conference, Encyclical and Reports, London 1958.

LA ROCHELLE, S. A. and FINK, C. T., *A Handbook of Medical Ethics*, Maryland 1957.

Law Society's Memorandum on Artificial Insemination to the Feversham Committee, June 1959 (Law Society's Annual Report 1959–60 at pp. 50–8).

LEVINSON, Samuel A., *Symposium on medicolegal Problems*. Philadelphia, 1948.

LEVISOHN, A. A., "Dilemma in Parenthood: Socio-Legal Aspects of Human Artificial Insemination", *Chicago-Kent Law Review*, 36: 1 (April 1959).

LOGATTO, Anthony F., "Artificial Insemination. I. Legal Aspects", *The Catholic Lawyer*, *I*: 172 (July 1955).

———"Artificial Insemination. II. Ethical and Sociological Aspects", *The Catholic Lawyer*, *I:* 267 (October 1955).

MACARTHY, J., "The Morality of Artificial Fecundation", *The Irish Ecclesiastical Record*, 74: 328–333 (1946).

MACFADDEN, C. J., *Medical Ethics for Nurses*, Philadelphia 1946.

MAHONEY, E. J., "Artificial Fecundation", *The Clergy Review*, 23: 564 (December 1943) and 25: 268 (January 1945).

PETZ, Jerome A., "Artificial Insemination—Legal Aspects", *University of Detroit Law Journal*, 34: 404 (1956–7).

PIUS XI, *Casti Connubii. Encyclical on Christian Marriage*, Rome 1930.

PIUS XII, "Address to Fourth Convention of Catholic Doctors in Rome", *Acta Apostolicae Sedis*, 41: 557 (September 1949).

———"Address on Moral Problems of Married Life", *Acta Apostolicae Sedis*, 43: 850 (October 1951).

———"Address to Second World Congress on Fertility and Sterility", *The Pope Speaks, III*: 191 (May 1956), *Acta Apostolicae Sedis*, 48: 468.

PLOSCOWE, M., *Sex and the Law*, New York 1951.

———"Your Test Tube Baby may be illegitimate", *Law Guild Review*, 8: 496–500 (November–December 1948).

PUXON, Margaret, "Without Father Bred", *Solicitor's Journal* 102: 95, (February 8, 1958).

Report of the Departmental Committee on Human Artificial Insemination, London H.M.S.O. Cmd. 1105 of 1960.

Report of Sub-Committee of Michigan State Bar Committee on Domestic Relations Law, *University of Detroit Law Journal* 34: 473 (April 28, 1956).

RICE, C. E., "A.I.D.—An Heir of Controversy", *Notre Dame Lawyer*, 34: 510-529 (August 1959).

RICHARDSON, I. L. M., "Artificial Insemination", *Australian Law Journal*, 30: 125 (July 1956).

ROHLEDER, H., *Test Tube Babies*, New York 1934.

Royal Commission on Marriage and Divorce, London, Cmd. 9678 of 1956.

RUSSELL, Bertrand, *Marriage and Morals*, London 1929.

SCHELLEN, A. M. C. M., *Artificial Insemination in the Human*, London 1957.

SEYMOUR, F. I. and KOERNER, A., "Artificial Insemination; present status in the United States as shown by recent survey", *Journal of the American Medical Association*, 116: 2747-2749 (June 21, 1941).

"The Socio-Legal Problems of Artificial Insemination", *Indiana Law Journal*, 28: 620-40 (Summer 1953).

Symposium on Artificial Insemination, *Syracuse Law Review*, 7: 96 (Fall 1955).

Symposium on Morals, Medicine and the Law, *New York University Law Review*, 31: 1157-1245 (1956).

TALLIN, G. P. R., "Artificial Insemination", *Canadian Bar Review*, 34: 1 (January 1956).

WILLIAMS, Glanville, *The Sanctity of Life and the Criminal Law*, New York 1957.

WILLINK, Henry, "Legal Aspects of Artificial Insemination", *The Practitioner*, 158: 349.

Chapter 4

ADAMS, Theodore W., "Thoughts on the Control of Postpartum Sterilization; Presidential Address", *Western Journal of Surgery*, 62: 101 (1954).

BONNAR, A., *The Catholic Doctor*, New York 1950.

BOULWARE, T. M., HOWE, C. D. and SIMPSON, S. T., "A Discussion of Postpartum Sterilization", *American Journal of Obstetrics and Gynaecology*, 68: 1124 (1954).

DONNELLY, Richard C., "Liability of Physicians for Sterilization in Virginia", *Virginia Medical Monthly*, 78: 25 (January 1951).

GEST, John B., "Eugenic Sterilization: Justice Holmes v. Natural Law", *Temple Bar Quarterly*, 23: 306 (1950).

HATTON, Robert E., "Is Compulsory Sterilization the Long Sought Solution for the Problem of our Mental Incompetents?", *Kentucky Law Journal*, 23: 517 (1934).

HEALY, E., *Medical Ethics*, Chicago 1956.

HINTON, J. P. and CALCUTT, J. F., *Sterilization: A Christian Approach*, London 1935.

HUGHES, James E., "Eugenic Sterilization in the United States", *Public Health Reports* (1940) Supp. No. 162.

Human Sterilization: Some Principles of Christian Ethics (Church of England Moral Welfare Council), London 1951.

KELLY, Gerald, *Medico-Moral Problems*, St Louis 1956.

Lambeth Conference 1958, The, *The Encyclical Letter from the Bishops, together with the Resolutions and Reports*, London 1958.

LANDMAN, J. H., *Human Sterilization*, New York 1932.

LEHANE, J. B., *The Morality of American Civil Legislation Concerning Eugenical Sterilization*, Washington 1944.

MILLER, Justin and DEAN, Gordon, "Liability of Physicians for Sterilization Operations", *American Bar Association Journal*, 16: 158 (1930).

MONTAGU, M. F., "The Biologist looks at Crime", *Annals of the American Academy of Political and Social Science*, 217: 46 (1941).

MYERSON, Abraham, "Certain Medical and Legal Phases of Eugenic Sterilization", *Yale Law Journal*, 52: 618 (1943).

———"Certain Medical and Legal Phases of Eugenic Sterilization", *Annals on Internal Medicine*, 18: 580 (1943).

———"Sterilization", *Atlantic Monthly*, 186: 52 (1940, II, 5).

———"Summary of the Report of the American Neurological Association Committee for the Investigation of Sterilization", *American Journal of Medical Jurisprudence* 1: 253 (1938).

O'BRIEN, J. P., *The Right of the State to make Disease an Impediment to Marriage*, Washington 1952.

O'HARA, James B. and SANKS, T. Howland, "Eugenic Sterilization", *Georgia Law Journal*, 45: 20 (1956).

PEARSE, Harry A. and OTT, Harold A., "Hospital Control of Sterilization and Therapeutic Abortion", *American Journal of Obstetrics and Gynaecology*, 60: 285 (1950).

PEARSE, Harry A. and TRISLER, J. David, "Administrative Aspects of Sexual Sterilization", *Western Journal of Surgery*, 63: 545 (1955).

PIUS XI, *On Christian Marriage*, New York 1931.

Report of Departmental Committee on Sterilization, "The Brock Report", 1934 Cmd. 4485.

Report of American Neurological Association on Sterilization (1936).

Report of the Family in Contemporary Society (Church of England), London 1958.

Symposium on Morals, Medicine and the Law, *New York Law Review*, 31: 1157 (1956).

SCHIFFER, Robert R., "Constitutionality of Sterilization Statutes", *Marquette Law Review*, 27: 99 (1943).

SMITH, Hubert Winston, "Antecedent Grounds of Liability in the Practice of Surgery", *Rocky Mountain Law Review*, 14: 233 at 276–84 (1942).

WILLIAMS, Glanville, *The Sanctity of Life and the Criminal Law*, New York 1957.

WOODSIDE, Moya, *Sterilization in North Carolina*, Chapel Hill 1950.

PUBLICATION OF HUMAN BETTERMENT ASSOCIATIONS OF AMERICA

1. *Legal Bibliography on Sterilization*. Compiled by Samuel Highleyman under the supervision of Richard C. Donnelly, New York 1957.
2. *Sterilizations reported in the United States*, New York 1958.
3. *Suggested Sterilization Bill*.

Chapter 5

AMERICAN LAW INSTITUTE, *Model Penal Code Draft* 4, New York 1955.

ANOMALY, *The Invert and His Social Adjustment*, Baltimore 1948.

AUGUSTINE, ST, *The City of God* (2 Volumes), London 1950.

——*The Confessions*, London 1949.

BAILEY, D. S., *Homosexuality and the Western Christian Tradition*, London 1955.

BARTON, G. A., "Sodomy" in *Encyclopaedia of Religion and Ethics*, XI: 672, New York 1921.

BENSING, R. C., Comparative Study of American Sex Statutes, *Journal of Criminal Law*, 42: 57–72 (May–June 1951).

BERGLER, E. and KNOGER, W. S., *Kinsey's Myth of Female Sexuality*, New York 1954.

BLACKSTONE, W., *Commentaries of the Laws of England*, Oxford 1765–9.

BOWMAN, K. M. and ENGLE, B., "A Psychiatric Evaluation of the Laws of Homosexuality", *Temple Law Quarterly Review*, 29: 273 (Spring 1956).

Ibid., "The Problem of Homosexuality", *Journal of Social Hygiene*, 39: 2–16. (January 1953).

BOWMAN, K. M., *Review of Sex Legislation and Control of Sex Offenders in U.S.A.* (Cal. Sex. Dev. Research 22, Vol. 20, No. 1, March 1954).

BONNAR, A., *The Catholic Doctor*, New York 1941.

BUCKLEY, M. J., *Morality and the Homosexual*, London 1960.

CARPENTER, E., *The Intermediate Sex*, London 1908.

CHESSER, E. *Live and Let Live*, London 1958.

COHEN, E. S., "Administration of the Criminal Sexual Psychopath Statute in Indiana, *Indiana Law Journal*, 32: 450 (Summer 1957).

COKE, E., *Institutes*, London 1817.

CONNERY, R., *A Theologian Looks at the Wolfenden Report*, America, 98: 485-6 (January 25, 1958).

CORY, D. W., *The Homosexual in America*, New York 1956.

"Crime and Sin: Reflections on some Wolfenden Proposals", *Law Times*, 224: 283 (November 29, 1957).

DAVIES, K., *Factors in the Sex Life of 2,200 Women*, New York 1929.

DAVIS, H., *Moral and Pastoral Theology* (Vol. II), New York 1935.

EAST, W. N., "Sexual Offenders—A British View", *Yale Law Journal*, 55: 527-57. (April 1946).

EDDY, J. P., "Law and Homosexuality", *Criminal Law Review*, January 22, 1956.

ELLIS, H., *Studies in the Psychology of Sex* Vol. II, *Sexual Inversion*, Philadelphia 1915.

FAHR, S. M., "Iowa's New Sexual Psychopath Law", *Indiana Law Review*, 41: 523 (Summer 1956).

FINGER, F. W., "Sex Beliefs and Practices among Male College Students", *Journal Abnormal and Social Psychology*, 42: 57-67.

FORD, C. S. and BEACH, F. A., *Patterns of Sexual Behaviour*, New York 1951.

"Homosexual Offences", *Scots Law Times*, 84-5 (August 9, 1949).

KARPMAN, B., "Considerations bearing on the problems of sexual offences", *Journal American Institute of Criminal Law*, 43: 13-28 (May-June 1952).

Ibid., "Sex Life in Prison", *Journal American Institute of Criminal Law*, 38: 475-86 (January-February 1948).

KINSEY, A. C., *Sexual Behaviour in the Human Female*, London 1953.

Ibid., *Sexual Behaviour in the Human Male*, London 1948.

GLUECK, B. C. Jnr, "Evaluation of the Homosexual Offender", *Minnesota Law Review*, 41: 187 (January 1957).

GUTTMACHER, M. and WEIHOFEN, H., "Sex Offences", *Journal American Institute of Criminal Law*, 43: 153-75 (July-August 1953).

Ibid., "Sexual Psychopath: A Symposium", *Journal American Institute of Criminal Law*, 43: 592-62 (January-February 1953).

HACKER, F. J. and FRYM, M., "Sexual Psychopath Act in Practice: A Critical Discussion", *California Law Review*, 43: 766 (December 1955).

HAMMELMANN, H. A., "Committee on Homosexual Offences and Prostitution", *Modern Law Review*, 21: 68 (January 1958).

HARVEY, J. F., "Homosexuality as a Pastoral Problem", *Theological Studies*, 16: 97 (March 1955).

HEALY, Edwin F., *Medical Ethics*, Chicago 1956.

HIRSCHFELD, M., *Sexual Anomalies and Perversions*, London 1944.

HYDE, H. M., *The Trials of Oscar Wilde*, London 1943.

LEWIS, C. S., "The Humanitarian Theory of Punishment", *Res Judicatae*, 6: 244 (1953).

LICHT, H., *Sexual Life in Ancient Greece*, London 1949.

McDOUGALL, W., *An Introduction to Social Psychology*, London 1916.

MAY, G., "Experiments in Legal Control of Sex Expression", *Yale Law Journal*, 39: 219–44 (December 1929).

PERKINS, R. M., *Criminal Law*, Brooklyn 1957.

PLOSCOWE, M., *Sex and the Law*, New York 1951.

POLLOCK, F. and MAITLAND, F. W., *The History of the English Law before the time of Edward I*, Cambridge 1898.

PUXON, M., "Not as other Men", *Solicitors' Journal*, 101: 735 (September 28, 1957).

RADZINOWICZ, L., *Sexual Offences—a report of the Cambridge Department of Criminal Science*, Cambridge 1957.

RAVENSCROFT, D. R., "Examination of the Nebraska Statute providing for Commitment and Treatment of Sexual Psychopaths", *Nebraska Law Review*, 29: 506–15 (March 1950).

REES, J. T. and USILL, H. V., *They Stand Apart*, New York 1955.

REPORTS, "California Sexual Deviation Research, January 1953.

——"Final Report on California Sexual Deviation Research", March 1954.

——"Employment of Homosexuals and other Sex Perverts in Government" (Res. 280, 81st Cong., 2nd s., Doc. 241, December 15, 1950).

——"Committee on Homosexual Offences and Prostitution", London 1957, H.M.S.O. Cmd. 247 (*Wolfenden Report*).

——"New Jersey Commission on Sexual Offenders", 1950.

——"Royal Commission on the Law relating to Mental Illness and Mental Deficiency" (1954–7 H.M.S.O. 1957, Cmd. 169).

——"Roman Catholic Advisory Committee on Prostitution and Homosexual Offences and the Existing Law" (*Dublin Review*. 230: 60–5, Summer 1956).

——"Sexual Offenders and Social Punishment" (Published for

the Church of England Moral Welfare Council 1956, Ed. D. S. Bailey).

SCHWARZ, L. B., "Review of Sexual Behaviour in the Human Male" by A. C. Kinsey, *University of Pennsylvania Law Review*, 96: 914–917 (1948).

"Sex and the Law", *Solicitor's Journal*, 74: 717–18 (November 1, 1930).

SMITH, C. E., "Homosexual Federal Offender: a study of 100 cases", *Journal American Institute of Criminal Law*, 44: 582–91 (January–February 1954).

SUTHERLAND, E. H., "Sexual Psychopath Laws", *Journal American Institute of Criminal Law*, 40: 543–54 (January–February 1950).

"Symposium on the Homosexual and the Law", *The New Statesman and Nation*, June 25, 1960.

TAPPAN, P., "Sex Offender Laws and their Administration", *Fed. Probation.* 14: 32–7 (September 1950).

Ibid., "The Sexual Psychopath: A Civic Social Responsibility", *Journal of Social Hygiene*, 35: 354–368 (November 1949).

THOMAS AQUINAS ST, *Summa Theologica* II: II, New York 1912–1932.

WESTERMARCK, E., *Christianity and Morals*, New York 1939.

———*The Origin and Development of the Moral Ideas*, London 1917.

WESTWOOD, G. (Pseud.), *A Minority*, London 1960.

"Wolfenden Report", *Criminal Law Review*, 665 (October 1957).

"Wolfenden Report", *Justice of the Peace*, 121: 607 (September 21, 1957).

Ibid., 121: 623 (September 28, 1957).

"Wolfenden Report", *Law Times*, 224: 182 (October 4, 1957).

Chapter 6

ALPERT, H., "Suicides and Homicides", *American Sociological Review*, 15: 673 (1950).

AQUINAS, Thomas, *Summa Theologica, II–II.* q. 64.

BAGLEY, A. B., "Is Suicide a Crime in Massachusetts?", *Boston University Law Review*, 13: 5300–4 (1933).

BERGLER, E., "Suicide: psychoanalytic and medicolegal aspects", *Louisiana Law Review*, 8: 504–33 (May 1948).

BLACKSTONE, *Commentaries*, Volume IV, Oxford 1775.

CAMUS, A., *The Myth of Sisyphus*, London 1955.

CAVAN, R. S., *Suicide*, Chicago 1926.

COKE, *Institutes*, Volume III, London 1797.

"Criminal Liability of participants in suicide", *Maryland Law Review* 5: 324–331 (April 1941).

CRIPPS, *Church and Clergy*, London 1937.

"Direct and Indirect Suicide", *Irish Ecclesiastical Record*, 82: 340–3, (November 1954).

DONNE, John, *Biathanatos*, London 1644.

DUBLIN, L. I., and BUNZEL, B., *To Be or Not To Be*, New York 1933.

DURKHEIM, E., *Suicide*, London 1952.

EAST, W. Norwood, *Medical Aspects of Crime*, London 1936.

FARBEROW, N. L., "Personality Patterns of Suicidal Mental Hospital Patients", *Genetic Psychology Monographs*, 42: 3–79 (1950).

FEDDEN, H. R., *Suicide*, London 1938.

FRENAY, A. D., *The Suicide Problem in the U.S.A.*, Boston 1927.

FREUD, S., "Mourning and Melancholia", Collected Papers, IV, London 1925.

GURNHILL, J., *The Morals of Suicide* London 1900.

HALE, *Pleas of the Crown*, London 1678.

HARRINGTON, J. A. and CROSS, K. W., "Cases of Attempted Suicide admitted to a General Hospital", *British Medical Journal*, September 19, 1959, p. 463.

HENSON, H. H., *Suicide*, Oxford 1897.

HOFFMAN, L., *Suicide Problems*, Newark N.J. 1927.

HOOK, Sidney, "The Ethics of Suicide", *International Journal of Ethics*, 37: 173 (1927).

HUME, David, *Essay on Suicide*, London 1789.

JAMES, William, *Is Life Worth Living?*, Philadelphia 1896.

"Judicial Interpretation of Suicide," *University of Pennsylvania Law Review*, 105: 391 (January 1957).

LANDSBERG, P. L., *The Experience of Death: The Moral Problem of Suicide*, London 1953.

MACDONALD, J. H. A., *On the Criminal Law of Scotland*, 5th edition, Edinburgh 1948.

MANNHEIM, H., *Criminal Justice and Social Reconstruction*, London 1946.

MENNINGER, Karl, *Man Against Himself*, London 1938.

MIKELL, William, E., "Is Suicide Murder?", *Columbia Law Review*, 3: 379 (January 1903).

MOORE, Charles, *A Full Inquiry into the Subject of Suicide*, London 1790.

MORSELLI, Henry, *Suicide*, New York 1882.

MORTIMER, R. C., *Christian Ethics*, London 1950.

O'SULLIVAN, Richard, "The Ethics of Suicide", *The Catholic Lawyer*, 2: 147 (April 1956).

PERKINS, R. M., *Criminal Law*, Brooklyn 1957.

PLATO, *The Law*, Book IX, London 1934.

RADZINOWICZ, L., *History of the English Criminal Law*, Volume I, London 1948.

ROBERTS, H., *Euthanasia and Other Aspects of Life and Death*, London 1936.

REPORT of Committee on Coroners, Cmd. 5070 of 1935, London.

REPORT of a Committee appointed by the Archbishop of Canterbury, "Ought Suicide to be a Crime?", London 1959.

REPORT of a Committee of magistrates and doctors set up by the British Medical Association in June 1946. Summary British Medical Journal Supplement, May 17, 1947, p. 103.

REPORT by a Joint Committee of the British Medical Association and the Magistrates Association. "The Law and Practice in relation to Attempted Suicide in England and Wales", London 1958.

REPORT of the Criminal Code Commissioners, Cmd. 2345, London 1879.

REPORT of the Royal Commission on Capital Punishment, Cmd. 8932 of 1953, London.

REPORT (Second) of Criminal Law Revision Committee (Suicide), Cmd. 1187 of 1960.

ROOK, Sir Alan, "Student Suicides", British Medical Journal, March 7, 1959, p. 599.

SAINSBURY, P., "Social Aspects of Suicide in London", Howard Journal, 9: 202, (1956).

——Suicide in London: An Ecological Study, London 1955.

"Self Sacrifice and Suicide", The Clergy Review, 40: 170–4 (March 1955), 40: 534–37 (September 1955).

SHNEIDMAN, E. S., and FARBEROW, N. L., (edited), Clues to Suicide, New York 1957.

STENGEL, E. and COOK, N., Attempted Suicide: Social Significance and Effects, London 1958.

——"Recent Research into Suicide and Attempted Suicide", Journal of Forensic Medicine, 1: 252 (1953–4).

STENGEL, E., "The Reactions of Society to Attempted Suicide", Howard Journal, 9: 199 (1956).

STEPHEN, F., History of the Criminal Law, Volume III, London 1883.

"Suicide", The Encyclopaedia of Religion amd Ethics, Volume XII, 21–40, Edinburgh 1921.

VANDER HEEREN, A., "Suicide", Catholic Encyclopaedia, Volume 14, New York 1912.

"Suicide-Criminal Aspects", Villanova Law Review, 1: 316 (May 1956).

"Suicide in Iowa Criminal Law", Minnesota Law Review, 18: 745–7 (May 1934).

"Suicidio", Enciclopedia Cattolica, Volume XI, 1490–4, Vatican 1953.

VON ANDICS, M., Suicide and the Meaning of Life, London 1947.

WEISS, J. M. A., "Suicide: An Epidemiological Analysis", The Psychiatric Quarterly, 28: 225 (April 1954).

WESTCOTT, Wynn, *Suicide*, London 1885.

WESTERMARCK, E., *The Origin and Development of the Moral Ideas*, Volume II, London 1906.

——*Christianity and Morals*, London 1939.

WILLIAMS, Glanville (edited), *The Reform of the Law*, London 1951.

——*The Sanctity of Life and the Criminal Law*, New York 1957.

WOLFROM, R., "Criminal Aspects of Suicide", *Dickinson Law Review*, 39: 42–56 (October 1934).

WOODSIDE, Moya, "Attempted Suicides arriving at a General Hospital", *British Medical Journal*, August 16, 1958, p. 411.

ZILBOORG, Gregory, "Suicides among Civilized and Primitive Races", *American Journal of Psychiatry*, 92: 1347 (1935–6).

Chapter 7

BANKS, A. L., "Euthanasia", *Bulletin of the New York Academy of Medicine*, 26: 297 (1950).

BONNAR, A., *The Catholic Doctor*, New York 1950.

BULLETINS OF THE EUTHANASIA SOCIETY OF AMERICA

EUTHANASIA, *Linacre Quarterly*, 14 (April 1947) (Whole issue deals with topic).

FLETCHER, J., *Morals and Medicine*, Princeton 1954.

HORDERN, M., "Reflections on Euthanasia", *Christianity and Crisis*, 10: 45–6 (1950).

KAMISAR, Y., "Some non-religious views against proposed 'mercy-killing' legislation", *Minnesota Law Review*, 42: 16 (May 1958).

KELLY, G., *Medico-Moral Problems*, St Louis 1956.

——"The Duty of Using Artificial Means of Preserving Life", *Theological Studies*, 11: 203–20 (1950).

——"The Duty to Preserve Life", *Theological Studies*, 12: 550 (1951).

KOESSLER, M., "Euthanasia in the Hadamar Sanatorium and International Law", *Journal of Criminal Law* (Chicago) 43: 735–55 (March–April 1953).

MAHONEY, E. J., "The Holy See on Euthanasia", *The Clergy Review*, 35: 41–2, (January 1951).

MANNHEIM, H., *Criminal Justice and Social Reconstruction*, London 1946.

MARTIN, T. O., "Euthanasia and Modern Morality", *Jurist*, 10: 437–64 (October 1950).

MATTHEWS, W. R., *Voluntary Euthanasia—The Ethical Aspect*, London 1950.

McReavy, L. L., "Use of Medicinal Drugs to Shorten Life", *The Clergy Review*, 42: 173 (March 1957).

Millard, C. K., "The Case for Euthanasia", *The Fortnightly Review*, 136: 701 (1931).

O'Donovan, W. J., "Euthanasia", Blackfriars, 32: 24–30 (January 1951).

Parliamentary Debates, House of Lords (5th Series) 103: 465–506 (1936), 169: 551–576 (1950).

Pius XII. Address of May 25, 1948 to Italian Congress of Medical Men. *L'Osservatore Romano*, May 23, 1948.

———Address of February 24, 1957 on religious and moral aspects of pain prevention. *A.A.S.* 49: 129–147.

———Address of November 24, 1957 to International Audience of Physicians. *New York Times*, November 25, 1957. *A.A.S.* 49: 1027–1033.

———Address of September 9 to "Collegio Internationali Neuro-Psycho-Pharmacologico", *L'Osservatore Romano*, September 13, 1958. *A.A.S.* 50: 687–700.

Potter, C. F., "The Case for Euthanasia", *Reader's Scope*, May 1947.

Roberts, H., *Euthanasia and Other Aspects of Life and Death*, London 1936.

Rose, H. H., "Euthanasia", *Encyclopaedia of Religion and Ethics*, Vol. V: 598–601, Edinburgh 1921.

Silving, H., "Euthanasia: A Study in Comparative Criminal Law", *University of Pennsylvania Law Review* 103: 350 (December 1954).

Sperry, W., *The Ethical Basis of Medical Practice*, New York 1950.

Stephen, H., "Murder from the Best of Motives", *Law Quarterly Review*, 5: 188 (1889).

Sullivan, J. V., *Catholic Teaching on the Morality of Euthanasia*, Washington D.C. 1949.

Symposium on Morals, Medicine and the Law, *New York University Law Review*, 31: 1157–1245 (1956).

Tesson, E., "Le Meutre par Pitié", *Etudes*, 271: 351–60 (December 1951).

"Use of Drugs to Prolong Life", *The Clergy Review*, 42: 171 (March 1957).

Walsh, J. J., "Life is Sacred", *The Forum*, 94: 333 (1935).

Walter, F., *Die Euthanasie und die Heiligkeit des Lebens*. Munich 1935.

Wechsler, H. and Michael, J., "A Rationale of the Law of Homicide", *Columbia Law Review*, 37: 701 (1937).

Williams, Glanville, "Mercy Killing Legislation—A Reply", *Minnesota Law Review*, 43: 1 (November 1958).

———*The Sanctity of Life and the Criminal Law*, New York 1957.

APPENDIX XVI

TABLE OF CASES

forbidden by Holy Office, 186; the State and, 187; Christian view of State practice, 187–8, 191–2; Christian view of voluntary practice, 189–91, 193–4; in Catholic hospitals, 194–5; Catholic doctors and, 195–6; Catholic judges and, 196–7; Liberal Christian view, 197; Moslem view, 197; Judaism and, 197

Stoics, suicide extolled by, 247

Stone, Dr Abraham, 115, 153

Stone, Dr Hannah, 61

Stopes, Dr Marie, 54, 61, 118

Suicide, a social problem, 232; rates in various countries, 232; history of English law on, 233–6; condemned by canon law, 233; civil penalties, 234–5; treated as felony, 234–5; present position, 236–9; punishment of attempts at, 236, 237; insurance companies and, 236; position of accessories, 237–8; participants in pacts, 237–8; coroners' verdicts and Anglican burial service, 239; felo de se verdict, 239; police policy towards attempts at, 239–40; effect of recent legislation, 240; prison sentences, 240–1; U.S. States and, 241–3; U.S. position on abetting, 243–6; view of Ancient Greeks, 246–7; in Roman law, 247; Roman writers and, 247; Stoic view, 247; Augustine formulates Christian doctrine, 248–9; Church law, 249; Aquinas elaborates Christian doctrine, 249–50; general Christian condemnation, 250–1; rationalist views, 251–2; causes and theories of, 252–6; theory of attempts at, 256; irrelevance of criminal law, 256; medical opinion favours change in law, 256–7; proposed change in law for attempts at, 257–9; proposed change in law

for abetting, 259–60; measures to prevent, 261

Suicides Anonymous, 261

Swammerdam, Johan, 117

Sweden, depression clinic in Stockholm, 261

Switzerland, law on abetting suicide, 259

TERTULLIAN, condemnation of homosexuality, 205

Texas, innocence of suicides, 241; no penalty for abetting, 243

Theodosian Code, and homosexuality, 205

Tietze, Dr C., 92

Truelove, Edward, 53n, 54n

UNITED NATIONS, and world population, 105–6; and contraception, 114

United States, birth rate, 97n; and birth control devices for aid-receiving nations, 98; population growth, 106; suicide rate, 232

VALENTINIAN, EMPEROR, and sodomists, 205

Vasectomy, 160, 161; effects of, 177–8

Vermeersch, Fr., 124

Vermont, no laws against sodomy, 198

Voltaire, and suicide, 251

Voluntary Euthanasia Legalization Society, 265–6

WARNER, CANON, 74, 76

Wesley, John, 233

Westermarck, E., 211

Westminster, Archbishop of, on homosexuality and the law, 224–5

Wheatley, Lord, definition of adultery, 130–3

Williams, Dr Glanville, 46, 133, 151, 162, 163, 175, 189, 252, 267–8, 274, 277